CHANGE AND CONTINUITY
IN THE 2012 ELECTIONS

To our wives:

Janet, Cindy, Angelle, and Barb

CHANGE AND CONTINUITY IN THE 2012 ELECTIONS

Paul R. Abramson
Michigan State University

John H. Aldrich
Duke University

Brad T. Gomez
Florida State University

David W. Rohde
Duke University

 |

Los Angeles | London | New Delhi
Singapore | Washington DC

Los Angeles | London | New Delhi
Singapore | Washington DC

FOR INFORMATION:

CQ Press

An Imprint of SAGE Publications, Inc.

2455 Teller Road

Thousand Oaks, California 91320

E-mail: order@sagepub.com

SAGE Publications Ltd.

1 Oliver's Yard

55 City Road

London EC1Y 1SP

United Kingdom

SAGE Publications India Pvt. Ltd.

B 1/I 1 Mohan Cooperative Industrial Area

Mathura Road, New Delhi 110 044

India

SAGE Publications Asia-Pacific Pte. Ltd.

3 Church Street

#10-04 Samsung Hub

Singapore 049483

Acquisitions Editor: Charisse Kiino

Editorial Assistant: Davia Grant

Production Editor: Laura Barrett

Copy Editor: Sarah J. Duffy

Typesetter: C&M Digitals (P) Ltd.

Proofreader: Kris Bergstad

Indexer: Teddy Diggs

Cover Designer: Janet Kiesel

Marketing Manager: Amy Whitaker

Printed in the United States of America

Library of Congress Cataloging-in-Publication Data

Abramson, Paul R.

Change and continuity in the 2012 elections / Paul R. Abramson, Michigan State University, John H. Aldrich, Duke University, Brad T. Gomez, Florida State University, David W. Rohde, Duke University.

pages cm

Includes bibliographical references and index.

ISBN 978-1-4522-4045-9 (pbk. : alk. paper)

1. Presidents—United States—Election—2012. 2. United States. Congress—Elections, 2012. 3. Voting—United States. 4. Elections—United States. 5. United States—Politics and government—2009-
I. Title.

JK5262012 .A37 2015

324.973'0932—dc23   2013048916

This book is printed on acid-free paper.

MIX

Paper from
responsible sources

FSC® C014174

www.fsc.org

14 15 16 17 18 10 9 8 7 6 5 4 3 2 1

Contents

Tables and Figures

Tables

About the Authors

The authors, from left to right: Abramson,
Aldrich, Gomez, and Rohde.

Paul R. Abramson is professor of political science at Michigan State University. He is coauthor of *Value Change in Global Perspective* (1995) and author of *Politics in the Bible* (2012), *Political Attitudes in America* (1983), *The Political Socialization of Black Americans* (1977), and *Generational Change in American Politics* (1975). Along with John H. Aldrich and David W. Rohde, he is coauthor of sixteen additional books in the Change and Continuity series, all of which were published by CQ Press.

John H. Aldrich is Pfizer-Pratt University Professor of Political Science at Duke University. He is author of *Why Parties: A Second Look* (2011), *Why Parties* (1995), and *Before the Convention* (1980) and coeditor of *Positive Changes in Political Science* (2007). He is past president of both the Southern Political Science Association and the Midwest Political Science Association. In 2001 he was elected a fellow of the American Academy of Arts and Sciences. He is currently president of the American Political Science Association.

Brad T. Gomez is associate professor of political science at Florida State University. His research interests focus on voting behavior and public opinion, with a particular interest in how citizens attribute responsibility for sociopolitical events. His published work appears in the *American Political Science Review*, *American Journal of Political Science*, *Journal of Politics*, and other journals and edited volumes.

David W. Rohde is Ernestine Friedl Professor of Political Science and director of the Political Institutions and Public Choice Program at Duke University. He is coeditor of *Why Not Parties?* (2008) and *Home Style and Washington Work* (1989), author of *Parties and Leaders in the Postreform House* (1991), and coauthor of *Supreme Court Decision Making* (1976).

Preface

On November 6, 2012, Democrat Barack Obama was reelected president of the United States. Obama's narrow popular vote majority victory over the Republican nominee, former Massachusetts Governor Mitt Romney, marked the first time that Democrats have won back-to-back majorities in presidential elections since Franklin D. Roosevelt in 1944. The Democrats gained two Senate seats in 2012, allowing the party to retain its majority status in the upper chamber. The Democrats also gained eight seats in the House of Representatives, but the Republicans maintained a sizeable majority and thus control of that body.

In the short term, the continuance of divided partisan control of government limits the prospects for significant policy changes during Obama's second term. Yet some view the 2012 election as a consolidation of a long-term Democratic majority, one that could forge public policy at the national level for decades to come. Democrats have now won the popular vote in five of the last six presidential elections. The party currently draws support from a coalition of the highly educated, women, African Americans, and Latinos. The latter two groups are expected to increase as a share of the U.S. population over the next twenty years, and electoral participation among both groups has increased steadily in recent years. Yet any talk of a long-term electoral advantage for the Democrats presupposes that current voters will maintain their loyalties to the two political parties and that group allegiances will be stable over time. The past shows that this can be a tenuous assumption.

Is America in the midst of an electoral transformation? What were the sources of Obama's victory in 2012, and how do they differ from Democratic coalitions of the past? Does his victory signal a long-term negative trajectory for Republicans' chances in presidential elections? And are these electoral forces at play in presidential elections similar to those that structure congressional elections? These are the sorts of questions that we seek to answer here.

OUR ANALYSIS

In our study of the 2012 elections, we rely on a wide variety of evidence. Because the bulk of our analysis focuses on individuals' voting decisions, we rely extensively on survey evidence—four surveys in particular. In studying voter turnout, we employ the Current Population Survey (CPS) conducted by the U.S. Census Bureau. The CPS provides information on the registration and voting of over 133,000 individuals from over 80,000 households. In examining voting patterns, we rely heavily on a survey of over 26,000 voters interviewed as they exited the voting polls and conducted by Edison Research for a consortium of news organizations, commonly referred to as the "pool poll." In studying the party loyalties of the American electorate, we also analyze the General Social Surveys (GSS) conducted by the National Opinion Research Center at the University of Chicago, which measured party identification twenty-seven times between 1972 and 2008, usually relying on about 1,500 respondents.

Our main source of survey data is the 2012 American National Election Studies (ANES) survey based on 2,054 face-to-face interviews conducted before the 2012 election and 1,929 interviews conducted after the election, using the version of the data released for analysis on June 10, 2013. This 2012 ANES is part of an ongoing series funded mainly by the National Science Foundation. These surveys, carried out originally by a team of scholars at the University of Michigan, began with a small study of the 1948 election; the first major study was in 1952. The ANES investigative team has studied every subsequent presidential election, as well as all thirteen midterm elections from 1954 to 2002. The 2012 ANES was conducted jointly by Stanford University and the University of Michigan. In the course of our book, we use data from all twenty-nine surveys conducted between 1948 and 2012.

The ANES data are available to scholars throughout the world. Although we are not responsible for the data collection, we are responsible for our analyses. The scholars and staff at the ANES are responsible for neither our analyses nor our interpretation of these data. Similarly, the organizers and researchers of the CPS, GSS, and national pool poll bear no responsibility for our analyses or interpretation.

ACKNOWLEDGMENTS

Many people assisted us with this study. We are deeply appreciative of the hard work put forth by our research assistants, Mark Dudley and Joshua Lerner at Duke University and Megan Wiggins at Florida State University. Mark assisted with the data analysis for Chapters 1, 2, 6, 7, 8, and 9; Josh assisted with Chapter 9; and Megan assisted with the data analysis for Chapters 3, 4, 5, and 10.

We would also like to thank Lee J. Abramson, who assisted us with the calculation of the issue preferences of the electorate found in Chapter 6.

In our study of turnout, we were greatly assisted by Michael P. McDonald of George Mason University, who for several years has provided a valuable resource to scholars of the voter turnout. McDonald's website, the United States Elections Project (http://elections.gmu.edu), provides users with detailed national and state-level estimates of voter turnout based on both voting-age and voting-eligible population estimates.

Several years ago, Russell J. Dalton of the University of California at Irvine and Robert W. Jackman late of the University of California at Davis helped us locate information about cross-national estimates of voter turnout. Abraham Diskin of the Hebrew University of Jerusalem helped us locate turnout data for Israel and provided us with updated data for this volume. William Claggett at Florida State University, a long-time reader of the Change and Continuity series, offered several suggestions during the development of this latest volume. Corwin D. Smidt at Michigan State University exposed us to several recent studies on religion and politics.

We are grateful for support from the Department of Political Science at Michigan State University, the Department of Political Science at Duke University, the Political Institutions and Public Choice Program at Duke University, and the Department of Political Science at Florida State University.

At CQ Press we are grateful to Charisse Kiino for encouragement and Davia Grant for help in the early editorial stages. We are especially grateful to them for finding reviewers who had assigned our book in the past, thereby allowing us to receive input from instructors and, indirectly, from students. The reviewers were Robert Shapiro, Columbia University; Jack Citrin, University of California, Berkeley; Costas Panagopoulos, Fordham University; Thomas Marshall, The University of Texas at Arlington; Brad Lockerbie, East Carolina University; and Wayne Steger, DePaul University. We are grateful to Laura Barrett, our production editor, and Amy Whitaker and Andrew Lee for their efforts in marketing our book. Sarah Duffy did an excellent job of copyediting the manuscript.

This book continues a series of sixteen books that we began with a study of the 1980 elections. In many places we refer to our earlier books, all of which were published by CQ Press. Some of this material is available online through the CQ Voting and Elections Collection, which can be accessed through many academic and public libraries.

Like our earlier books, this one was a collective enterprise in which we divided the labor. Yet, for the first time, membership in the collective has changed. With Paul Abramson's retirement from the writing and data analysis, Brad Gomez was invited to join the authorship team. Gomez had primary responsibility for the Introduction and Chapters 3, 4, and 5; John Aldrich for Chapters 1, 6, 7, and 8; and David Rohde for Chapters 2, 9, and 10. Aldrich and Rohde worked jointly on Chapter 11. Abramson commented on all eleven chapters.

We appreciate feedback from our readers. Please contact us if you disagree with our interpretations, find factual errors, or want further clarification about our methods or our conclusions.

Paul R. Abramson
Michigan State University
abramson@msu.edu

John H. Aldrich
Duke University
aldrich@duke.edu

Brad T. Gomez
Florida State University
bgomez@fsu.edu

David W. Rohde
Duke University
rohde@duke.edu

Introduction

Presidential elections in the United States are partly ritual, a reaffirmation of our democratic values. But they are far more than rituals. The presidency confers a great deal of power, and those powers have expanded during most of the twentieth century and into the twenty-first century. It is precisely because of these immense powers that presidential elections have at times played a major role in determining public policy, and in some cases altered the course of American history.

The 1860 election, which brought Abraham Lincoln and the Republicans to power and ousted a divided Democratic Party, focused on whether slavery should be extended to the western territories. After Lincoln's election, eleven southern states attempted to secede from the Union, the Civil War broke out, and, ultimately, the U.S. government abolished slavery completely. Thus an anti-slavery plurality—Lincoln received only 40 percent of the popular vote—set in motion a chain of events that freed some four million black Americans.

In the 1896 election, Republican William McKinley defeated the Democrat and Populist William Jennings Bryan, thereby beating back the challenge of western and agricultural interests to the prevailing financial and industrial power of the East. Although Bryan mounted a strong campaign, winning 47 percent of the popular vote to McKinley's 51 percent, the election set a clear course for a policy of high tariffs and the continuation of the gold standard for American money.

Lyndon B. Johnson's 1964 landslide over Republican Barry M. Goldwater provided the clearest set of policy alternatives of any election in the twentieth century.[1] Goldwater offered "a choice, not an echo," advocating far more conservative social and economic policies than Johnson. When Johnson received 61 percent of the popular vote to Goldwater's 38 percent, he saw his victory as a mandate for his Great Society programs, the most far-reaching social legislation since World War II. The election also seemed to offer a clear choice between escalating American involvement in Vietnam and restraint. But America's involvement in Vietnam expanded after Johnson's election, leading to growing opposition to Johnson within the Democratic Party, and four years later he did not seek reelection.

Only the future can determine the ultimate importance of the 2012 election. Some scholars argue that American elections have become less important with time, and there is some truth to their arguments.[2] Yet elections do offer important choices on public policy, choices that may affect the course of governance—even if only in the short term.

Despite the continued, decade-long presence of American combat forces in Afghanistan, the 2012 presidential election focused mainly on domestic policy issues. Incumbent President Barack Obama was elected four years earlier in the midst of the most serious economic crisis since the Great Depression. Within a month of his inauguration, Obama signed a $787 billion economic stimulus bill aimed at offsetting the deepening worldwide recession. His administration also chose to use government funds to purchase a 60 percent equity stake in the automobile giant General Motors, allowing the company to reorganize under Chapter 11 bankruptcy while keeping it operational (and its over 123,000 North American employees working).[3] The Obama administration also provided an additional $6 billion loan to Chrysler so the company could be removed from bankruptcy and sold to the Italian automaker Fiat. For his part, the Republican nominee for president in 2012, former Massachusetts Governor Mitt Romney, argued that Obama's economic programs had done more to stifle economic growth than stimulate it. Growth had been exceedingly slow during Obama's first term, and unemployment, which had reached 10 percent in the fall of 2009, remained over 8 percent for most the campaign season. Romney espoused cuts in government spending, reduced taxes for all income levels, and cuts in the corporate tax rate—traditional Republican economic positions—to spur the economy and stimulate job growth.

Health care reform was another domestic issue that divided the candidates. The central legislative achievement of Obama's first term was the passage of the Affordable Care Act of 2010, commonly known as "Obamacare." The legislation marks the most significant change to the nation's health care system since the creation of Medicare and Medicaid during the 1960s. It mandates that all individuals who are not currently insured or already covered under government insurance programs buy a private health insurance policy or pay a penalty (a "tax" according the U.S. Supreme Court). To lower the costs of policies, Obamacare promotes the creation of state-level health insurance exchanges to foster competition between insurance providers and grants subsidies to low-income individuals and families to offset costs. Romney labeled Obama's health care reforms a federal take-over of health insurance and pledged to repeal most of it if elected. Romney's opposition to Obamacare struck some as a bit contrived, however, since the Affordable Care Act was modeled on a 2006 Massachusetts health insurance reform that Governor Romney signed into law. In fact, the Massachusetts reform was informally known as "Romneycare." Yet Romney argued that the president's plan overstepped federal authority and imposed a one-size-fits-all approach on the states. Romney sought to give states latitude in crafting their own health care reform plans, while encouraging both a shift to high-deductible private policies and a more widespread adoption of individual health savings accounts. Romney's plan would have provided taxpayers with deductions on their federal taxes for most of their out-of-pocket health care expenses.

Like most presidential elections featuring the sitting president on the ballot, the 2012 election was cast as a referendum on the policies and performance of the incumbent. This should have advantaged Romney. No incumbent president in the post–World War II period had been reelected with unemployment as high as Obama experienced in his fourth year in office. And the president's health care reform law has never met with public approval; since its passage, a clear plurality of Americans has said they oppose the law.[4] Nevertheless, on November 6, 2012, Barack Obama was reelected president of the United States, defeating Mitt Romney 51.1 percent to 47.2 percent.

The 2012 election would seem to be the product of electoral continuity. Not only was the incumbent president reelected, but the House of Representatives remained under the control of the Republicans and the Senate stayed in the hands of the Democrats. The divided partisan control of government—a norm in modern politics—limits the prospects for significant policy changes during President Obama's second term. Indeed, at the time of our writing, interparty conflict (and a small degree of intraparty conflict among Republicans) and gridlock best characterize politics since the 2012 election. House Republicans have voted more than forty times to repeal or delay all or part of Obamacare—a purely symbolic effort given the Democrats' control of the Senate and White House.[5] And in September 2013, House Republicans forced a sixteen-day government shutdown and threatened default on U.S. debt in an effort to defund Obamacare, an effort that proved fruitless.[6] The prospects for major policy changes during the remainder of Obama's second term, with the possible exception of immigration reform, seem bleak unless the Democrats can gain control of the House during the 2014 midterm election—an unlikely event since midterms rarely benefit the president's party.

Some argue, however, that the 2012 election was emblematic of a new political era, one in which demographic trends, specifically a growing professional class and an increase in America's nonwhite population, are creating an "emerging Democratic majority."[7] The Democrats now routinely lose among white voters from nearly every demographic subgroup. Yet the party has won the popular vote in five of the last six presidential elections, beginning with Bill Clinton's victory in 1992.

Is America in the midst of an electoral transformation? What were the sources of Obama's victory in 2012, and how do they differ from Democratic coalitions of the past? Does his victory signal a long-term negative trajectory for Republicans' chances in presidential elections? And are these electoral forces similar to those that structure congressional elections? These are the sorts of questions that we seek to answer here.

This book continues a series of sixteen books that we began with a study of the 1980 elections. Our focus has always been both contemporary and historical. Thus, we offer an extensive examination of the 2012 presidential and congressional campaigns and present a detailed analysis of individual-level voting behavior, examining those factors that lead citizens to vote as well as those that affect how they vote. We also aim to place the 2012 elections in proper historical and analytical contexts.

CHANGE AND CONTINUITY

Elections are at once both judgments on the issues of the day and the product of long-term changes in the relationship between the political parties and voters. Democrats' aspirations for an emerging electoral majority following their 2012 presidential victory are not unfounded. If one is to believe the projections of the U.S. Census Bureau, many of the social groups that have supported Democrats in recent elections, particularly Latinos, are growing as a percentage of the overall U.S. population. And turnout among these groups is also increasing. In fact, the 2012 election marked the first time in U.S. history that the turnout rate among African American voters exceeded that for white voters. Yet any talk of a long-term electoral advantage for the Democrats presupposes that current voters will maintain their allegiances to the two political parties and that group loyalties will be stable over time. The past shows that this can be a tenuous assumption.

It is not uncommon for winning parties to make hyperbolic claims about the "historic" nature of their victories or to assert that their win is a sign of impending electoral dominance. Indeed, in 2008, Democrats were exuberant over Obama's sizeable victory over John McCain and were even more pronounced in their claims of a bright Democratic future. Some observers saw the election as restoring Democrats to their status as the majority party, which they had enjoyed between 1932 and 1968. Lanny J. Davis, a former special counsel to President Clinton, wrote following the 2008 election: "Tuesday's substantial victory by Barack Obama, together with Democratic gains in the Senate and House, appear to have accomplished a fundamental political realignment. The election is likely to create a new governing majority coalition that could dominate American politics for a generation or more."[8] Two years later, the Democrats lost sixty-three seats and their majority status in the House of Representatives—the largest seat change since 1946—and six seats in the Senate, where they maintained a slim majority.[9]

In 2004, following incumbent president George W. Bush's victory over Democratic nominee John Kerry, scholars speculated about a pro-Republican realignment. Indeed, speculation about Republican dominance can be traced back to the late 1960s, when Kevin P. Phillips, in his widely read book *The Emerging Republican Majority,* argued that the Republicans could become the majority party, mainly by winning support in the South.[10] Between 1969, when his book was published, and 1984, the Republicans won three of the four presidential elections, winning by massive landslides in 1972, when Richard M. Nixon triumphed over George S. McGovern, and in 1984, when Ronald Reagan defeated Walter F. Mondale. In 1985, Reagan himself proclaimed that a Republican realignment was at hand. "The other side would like to believe that our victory last November was due to something other than our philosophy," he asserted. "I just hope that they keep believing that. Realignment is real."[11] Democratic victories in the 1992 and 1996 presidential elections called into question the claims of a pro-Republican realignment.

Obviously, not all elections are transformative. So how is electoral change—not simply the ebbs and flows from election to election, but changes in the fundamental factors that link parties and voters—to be understood?

For generations of political scientists, theories of electoral change have centered on the concept of political realignment.[12] Political scientists define *realignment* in different ways, but they are all influenced by V. O. Key Jr., who developed a theory of "critical elections" in which "new and durable electoral groupings are formed."[13] Elections like that in 1860 in which Lincoln's victory brought the Republicans to power, in 1896 in which McKinley's victory solidified Republican dominance, and in 1932 in which the Democrats came to power under Franklin D. Roosevelt are obvious candidates for such a label.

But later Key argued that partisan shifts could also take place over a series of elections—a pattern he called "secular realignment." During these periods, "shifts in the partisan balance of power" occur.[14] In this view, the realignment that first brought the Republicans to power might have begun in 1856, when the Republicans displaced the Whigs as the major competitor to the Democrats, and might have been consolidated by Lincoln's reelection in 1864 and Ulysses S. Grant's election in 1868. The realignment that consolidated Republican dominance in the late nineteenth century may well have begun in 1892, when Democrat Grover Cleveland won the election but the Populist Party, headed by James D. Weaver, attracted 8.5 percent of the popular vote, winning four states and electoral votes in two others. In 1896, the Populists supported William Jennings Bryan and were co-opted by the Democrats, but the electorate shifted to the Republican Party. The pro-Republican realignment might have been consolidated by McKinley's win over Bryan in 1900 and by Theodore Roosevelt's victory in 1904.

Though the term *New Deal* was not coined until Franklin Roosevelt's campaign of 1932, the New Deal realignment may have begun with Herbert C. Hoover's triumph over Democrat Al Smith, the first Roman Catholic to be nominated by a major political party. Although badly defeated, Smith carried two New England states, Massachusetts and Rhode Island, which later became the most Democratic states in the nation.[15] As Key points out, the beginnings of a shift toward the Democrats was detectable in Smith's defeat.[16] However, the "New Deal coalition" was not created by the 1932 election but after it, and it was consolidated by Roosevelt's 1936 landslide over Alfred M. Landon and his 1940 defeat of Wendell Willkie. The New Deal coalition structured the distribution of party support within the electorate during the earliest decades of the post–World War II period, and its decline and eventual replacement are important to understanding the changes and continuities of modern electoral politics.

Past partisan realignments in the United States have had five basic characteristics. First, realignments have traditionally involved changes in the regional bases of party support. Consider, for instance, the decline of the Whig Party and rise of the Republicans. Between 1836 and 1852, the Whigs drew at least some of their electoral support from the South.[17] The last Whig candidate to be elected, Zachary Taylor in 1848, won sixty-six of his electoral votes from the fifteen slave states. In his 1860 victory, Lincoln did not win a single electoral vote from the fifteen slave states. Regionalism may be less important to future electoral changes, however. Today, television and other media have weakened regionalism in the United States, and politics is much more nationalized. Two-party competition has diffused throughout the country, and the issues on which the parties compete tend to be more national in scope.[18]

Second, past party realignments have involved changes in the social bases of party support. Even during a period when one party is becoming dominant, some social groups may be moving to the losing party. During the 1930s, for example, Roosevelt gained the support of industrial workers, but at the same time he lost support among business owners and professionals.

Third, past realignments have been characterized by the mobilization of new groups into the electorate. Indeed, the mobilization of new voters into the electorate can result in significant electoral volatility.[19] Between Calvin Coolidge's Republican landslide in 1924 and Roosevelt's third-term victory in 1940, turnout among the voting-age population rose from 44 percent to 59 percent. Although some long-term forces were pushing turnout upward, the sharp increase between 1924 and 1928 and again between 1932 and 1936 resulted at least in part from the mobilization of new social groups into the electorate. Ethnic groups that were predominantly Catholic were mobilized to support Al Smith in 1928, and industrial workers were mobilized to support Franklin Roosevelt in 1936.

Fourth, past realignments have occurred when new issues have divided the electorate. In the 1850s, the Republican Party reformulated the controversy over slavery to form a winning coalition. By opposing the expansion of slavery into the territories, the Republicans contributed to divisions within the Democratic Party. Of course, no issue since slavery has divided America as deeply, and subsequent realignments have never brought a new political party to power. But those realignments have always been based on the division of the electorate over new issues.

Lastly, most political scientists argue that partisan realignments occur when voters change not just their voting patterns but also the way they think about the political parties, thus creating an erosion of partisan loyalties. For example, in 1932, during the Great Depression, many voters who thought of themselves as Republicans voted against Hoover. Later, many of these voters returned to the

Republican side, but others began to think of themselves as Democrats. Likewise, in 1936 some voters who thought of themselves as Democrats disliked FDR's policies and voted against him. Some of these defectors may have returned to the Democratic fold in subsequent elections, but others began to think of themselves as Republicans.

Not all scholars believe that the concept of realignment is useful. In 1991, Byron E. Shafer edited a volume in which several chapters questioned its utility.[20] More recently, David R. Mayhew published a monograph critiquing scholarship on realignment, and his book received widespread critical acclaim.[21] Mayhew cites fifteen claims made by scholars of realignment and then tests these claims. He argues that many of these claims do not stand up to empirical scrutiny, questions the classification of several elections as "realigning," and suggests that the concept of realignment should be abandoned.

While we agree with some of the claims made by Mayhew, we see no reason to abandon the concept completely. Some electoral changes may correspond to the critical election-realignment dynamic—a long period of stability in the party system is altered by a rapid and dramatic change, which leads to a new, long-term partisan equilibrium. Using biological evolution as a theoretical analogue, Edward G. Carmines and James A. Stimson argue that partisan realignments of this type are similar in form to the evolutionary dynamic known as cataclysmic adaptation.[22] But the authors note that biological examples of the cataclysmic adaptation dynamic are extraordinarily rare and suggest that critical election realignments are likely to be rare also.

Carmines and Stimson articulate two additional evolutionary models of partisan change. They argue that Key's secular realignment dynamic is consistent with the model of Darwinian gradualism. In this view, electoral change does not result from a critical moment, but instead is "slow, gradual, [and] incremental."[23] As noted in Key's original work, the secular realignment dynamic "operate[s] inexorably, and almost imperceptibly, election after election, to form new party alignments and to build new party groups."[24]

The third model of partisan change espoused by Carmines and Stimson is consistent with the punctuated equilibrium model of evolution.[25] In this dynamic process,

> the system moves from a fairly stationary steady state to a fairly dramatic rapid change; the change is manifested by a "critical moment" in the time series—a point where change is large enough to be visible and, perhaps the origin of a dynamic process. Significantly, however, the change—the dynamic growth—does not end with the critical moment; instead it continues over an extended period, albeit at [a] much slower pace.[26]

In our view, the punctuated equilibrium model best captures the dynamic nature of electoral change in the United States since the 1960s.

The 1960s were a critical moment in American politics. The events of the decade were the catalysts for fundamental changes in the rules that govern political parties and the partisan sentiments that would govern voters for years to come.[27] Of particular interest is the transformative power of the issue of race. By 1960, the national Democratic Party's sponsorship of civil rights for African Americans had created a schism between the more liberal elements of the party and white southern Democrats. But it had also allowed the party to chip away at black voters' allegiance to the Republican Party, "the party of Lincoln." The partisan loyalties of African Americans had been shaped by the Civil War, and black loyalties to the Republican Party—where and when allowed to vote—lasted through the 1932 election. By 1960, a majority of African Americans identified with the Democratic Party, but there was still a substantial minority of Republican identifiers. Between 1960 and 1964, however, African American loyalties moved sharply toward the Democrats. The civil rights demonstrations of the early 1960s and the eventual passage of the 1964 Civil Rights Act solidified the position of the Democratic Party as the party of civil rights. By late 1964, over 70 percent of African Americans identified as Democrats, a level of loyalty that persists today. The change in partisanship among blacks and the subsequent mobilization of black voters following the passage of the 1965 Voting Rights Act provided the rapid, critical moment that disrupted the stable equilibrium created by the New Deal Coalition. And, as the punctuated equilibrium dynamic suggests, the electorate continued to change in a direction set forth by the critical era of the 1960s, but it did so at a slower rate and it continues to have ramifications for politics today.

The political events of the 1960s also had an effect on white partisanship, but the change was neither immediate nor decisive. From the mid-1960s to the mid-1970s, there was a substantial erosion in party loyalties among whites. The proportion of the white electorate who considered themselves "independent" increased noticeably. By 1978, nearly 40 percent of whites said they were either pure independents or independents who "leaned" toward one of the two parties, nearly double that found in the late 1950s and early 1960s.[28] These changes led some scholars to use the term *dealignment* to characterize American politics during the period.[29] The term was first used by Ronald Inglehart and Avram Hochstein in 1972.[30] A dealignment is a condition in which old voting patterns break down without being replaced by newer ones. Yet beginning in the 1980s, the proportion of whites claiming to be pure independents declined, as whites nationally began to lean toward the Republican Party. In the once "solid Democratic South," whites have become decidedly Republican.

Despite these changes, the Republicans have never emerged as the majority party among the electorate. Democrats, however, saw a growth in political loyalties between 2004 and 2012, and they have once again emerged as the majority party, albeit a small majority. Democrats' electoral gains have largely been the product of the critical events of the 1960s, which established them as the party of civil rights. As America's nonwhite population has increased—more than half of the growth in the U.S. population between 2000 and 2010 was due to an increase in the nonwhite population—and Democrats have been the beneficiaries. For instance, roughly two out of every three Hispanic voters in the United States identify with Democratic Party, and 45 percent of Hispanic voters say that Democrats have more concern for them, compared to only 12 percent who say that Republicans do.[31] America's racial and ethnic minorities continue to view the Democrats' adherence to the civil rights agenda of the 1960s as providing them with a natural political home, and America's whites are increasingly more likely to side with the Republicans. In our view, the 2012 elections do not represent a fundamental change in America's electoral politics. Instead, the 2012 elections continue to reflect electoral alignments set in motion by a critical era that occurred nearly a half century ago.

VOTERS AND THE ACT OF VOTING

Voting is an individual act. Indeed, the national decision made on (or before) November 6, 2012, was the product of more than 221 million individual decisions.[32] Two questions faced Americans eighteen years and older: whether to vote and, if they did, how to cast their ballots. These decisions, of course, are not made in isolation. Voters' decisions are influenced by the social, economic, and information contexts in which they live; they are influenced by the political attitudes that they have acquired throughout their lifetime; and they are influenced by the voting decisions they have made in the past.[33] Voters' decisions are also constrained by America's electoral rules and two-party system—these are the primary sources of continuity in our political system.

How voters make up their minds is one of the most thoroughly studied subjects in political science—and one of the most controversial.[34] Voting decisions can be studied from at least three theoretical perspectives.[35] The first approach is *sociological* in character and views voters primarily as members of social groups. Voters belong to primary groups of family members and peers, secondary groups such as private clubs, trade unions, voluntary associations, and broader reference groups such as social classes and religious and ethnic groups. Understanding the political behavior of these groups is central to understanding voters, according to Paul F. Lazarsfeld, Bernard R. Berelson, and their colleagues. Social characteristics determine political preferences.[36] This perspective is still popular, although more so among sociologists than political scientists.[37]

A second approach places greater emphasis on the *psychological* (or more aptly, attitudinal) variables that affect voting. The "socio-psychological model" of voting behavior was developed by Angus Campbell, Philip E. Converse, Warren E. Miller, and Donald E. Stokes, scholars at the University of Michigan Survey Research Center, in their classic book *The American Voter*.[38] The Michigan scholars focused on attitudes most likely to have the greatest effect on the vote just before the moment of decision, particularly attitudes toward the candidates, the parties, and the issues. An individual's party identification emerged as the most important social-psychological variable that influences voting behavior. The Michigan approach is the most prevalent among political scientists, and party identification continues to be emphasized as one of the most influential factors affecting individual vote choice, although many de-emphasize its psychological underpinnings.[39]

A third approach draws heavily from the work of economists. According to this perspective, citizens weigh the costs of voting against the expected benefits when deciding whether to vote. And when deciding for whom to vote, they calculate which candidate favors policies closest to their own policy preferences. Citizens are thus viewed as rational actors who attempt to maximize their expected utility. Anthony Downs and William H. Riker helped to found this *rational choice* approach.[40] The writings of Riker, Peter C. Ordeshook, John A. Ferejohn, and Morris P. Fiorina are excellent examples of this point of view.[41]

Taken separately, none of these approaches adequately explains voting behavior; taken together, the approaches are largely complementary.[42] Therefore, we have chosen an eclectic approach that draws on insights from each viewpoint. Where appropriate, we employ sociological variables, but we also employ social-psychological variables such as party identification and feelings of political efficacy. The rational choice approach guides our study of the way issues influence voting behavior.

SURVEY RESEARCH SAMPLING

Because of our interest in individual-level voting behavior, our book relies heavily on surveys of the American electorate. It draws on a massive exit poll conducted by Edison Research for the National Election Pool, a consortium of six news organizations, as well as surveys conducted in people's homes by the U.S. Census Bureau and telephone polls conducted by the Pew Research Center. But our main data source for 2012 is a face-to-face survey of 2,054 U.S. citizens conducted in their homes as part of the American National Election Studies (ANES) Time Series Survey.[43] Originally conducted by the Survey Research Center (SRC) and Center for Political Studies (CPS) at the University of Michigan, the ANES surveys have been conducted using national samples in every presidential election since 1948 and in every midterm election between 1954 and 2002.[44] The 2012 ANES was conducted jointly by Stanford University and the University of Michigan, with funding by the National Science Foundation.[45] Since 1952, the ANES surveys have measured party identification and feelings of political effectiveness. The CPS, founded in 1970, has developed valuable questions for measuring issue preferences. The ANES surveys are the best and most comprehensive for studying the issue preferences and party loyalties of the American electorate.[46]

Readers may question our reliance on the ANES surveys of 2,054 people when some 221 million Americans are eligible to vote. Would we have similar results if all adults eligible to vote had been surveyed?[47] The ANES uses a procedure called multistage probability sampling to select the particular individuals to be interviewed. This procedure ensures that the final sample is likely to represent the entire population of U.S. citizens of voting age, except for Americans living on military bases, in institutions, or abroad.[48]

Because of the probability procedures used to conduct the ANES surveys, we are able to estimate the likelihood that the results represent the entire population of noninstitutionalized citizens living in the United States. Although the 2012 ANES survey sampled only about 1 in every 108,000 voting-eligible Americans, the representativeness of a sample depends far more on the size of the sample than the size of the population being studied, provided the sample is drawn properly. With samples of this size, we can be fairly confident (to a level of .95) that the results we get will fall within three percentage points of that obtained if the entire population had been surveyed.[49] For example, when we find that 54 percent of respondents approved of the job Barack Obama was doing as president, we can be reasonably confident that between 51 percent (54 – 3) and 57 percent (54 + 3) approved of his performance. The actual results could be less than 51 percent or more than 57 percent. But a confidence level of .95 means that the odds are nineteen to one that the entire electorate falls within this range. The range of confidence becomes somewhat larger when we look at subgroups of the electorate. For example, with subsets of about five hundred (and the results in the 50 percent range) the confidence error rises to plus or minus six percentage points. Because the likelihood of sampling error grows as our subsamples become smaller, we often supplement our analysis with reports of other surveys.

Somewhat more complicated procedures are needed to determine whether the difference between two groups is likely to reflect the relationship found if the entire population were surveyed. The probability that such differences reflect real differences in the population is largely a function of the size of the groups being compared.[50] Generally speaking, when we compare the results of the 2012 sample with an earlier ANES survey, a difference of four percentage points is sufficient to be reasonably confident that the difference is real. For example, in 2008 during the final year of the George W. Bush presidency and during the onset of the "Great Recession," only 2 percent of respondents said that the economy had improved in the last year; in 2012, 28 percent did. Because this difference is greater than four percentage points, we can be reasonably confident that the electorate was more likely to think the national economy was improving in 2012 than they were to think it was improving back in 2008.

When we compare subgroups of the electorate sampled in 2012 (or compare those subgroups with subgroups sampled in earlier years), a larger percentage is usually necessary to conclude that differences are meaningful. For example, 53 percent of men and 55 percent of women approved of Obama's performance as president. Even though 930 men and 1,001 women answered this question, a two-point difference is too small to safely conclude that this gender difference was real. Generally speaking, in comparisons of men and women a difference of five percentage points is needed.[51] By contrast, 42 percent of whites approved of

Obama's performance as president, whereas 94 percent of blacks did. Granted, 1,356 whites were interviewed, but only 237 blacks.[52] In general, a difference of nine percentage points is needed to conclude that differences between whites and blacks are meaningful.

This discussion represents only a ballpark guide to judging whether reported results are likely to represent the total population. Better estimates can be obtained using the formulas presented in many statistics textbooks. To make such calculations or even a rough estimate of the chances of error, the reader must know the size of the groups being compared. For that reason, we always report in our tables and figures either the number of cases on which our percentages are based or the information needed to approximate the number of cases.

PLAN OF THE BOOK

We begin by following the chronology of the campaign itself. Chapter 1 examines the battle for the Republican Party presidential nomination. Eight major Republican candidates campaigned for the chance to square off against Obama in the general election. As is typical when an incumbent president stands for reelection, President Obama faced no opposition for the Democratic Party nomination. In Chapter 1, we discuss the regularities in the nomination process that explain why some candidates run while others do not. We then examine the rules governing the nomination contests, and we also assess the importance of campaign finance. The dynamics of multicandidate contests and the concept of momentum used by John H. Aldrich to discuss nomination contests in the 1970s are covered in Chapter 1 as well.

Chapter 2 moves to the general election campaign. Because of the rules set forth by the U.S. Constitution for winning presidential elections, candidates must think about how to win enough states to gain a majority (270) of the electoral vote (538 since 1964). We examine the Electoral College strategies adopted by the campaigns. There were three presidential debates and one vice presidential debate, and we discuss their impact. Last, we turn to the end game of the campaign, the battle over turnout. It was widely argued that the Democrats' innovative "ground game" allowed them to win these get-out-the-vote efforts; we evaluate this claim.

Chapter 3 turns to the actual election results, relying largely on the official election statistics. Our look at the electoral vote is followed by a discussion of the election rules, noting that the U.S. plurality vote system supports "Duverger's law." We examine the pattern of results during the seventeen postwar elections as well as those in all forty-six elections between 1832 and 2012. We then analyze the state-by-state results, paying particular attention to regional shifts in the elections between 1980 and 2012. We focus special attention on electoral change in the postwar South, because this region has been the scene of the most dramatic changes in postwar U.S. politics. Finally, we study the results of the last five presidential elections to assess the electoral vote balance.

Chapter 4 analyzes the most important decision of all: whether to vote. We examine the dynamics of electoral participation in U.S. politics, particularly changes in turnout during the postwar period. Although turnout grew fairly consistently between 1920 (the year women were enfranchised throughout the United States) and 1960, it fell in 1964 and in each of the next four elections. We show that the decline in turnout during this period coincides with steep declines in partisan attachment and political efficacy in the electorate. As partisan attachments have increased in recent decades, turnout has risen, but it remains lower than its 1960 high. Turnout is low in the United States compared with other advanced democracies, but it is not equally low among all social groups. In Chapter 4, we examine social differences in turnout in detail, using both the 2012 ANES survey and the Current Population Survey conducted by the U.S. Census Bureau.

In Chapter 5, we examine how social forces influence the vote. The ANES surveys enable us to analyze the vote for Obama and Romney by race, gender, region, age, education, income, union membership, and religion. The impact of these social factors has changed considerably in the postwar period as the New Deal coalition broke down and new partisan alignments emerged after the critical era of the 1960s. We show that minorities—specifically blacks and Latinos—are now central to the modern Democratic coalition.

Chapter 6 examines attitudes toward both the candidates and the issues. We begin by examining voters' feelings toward the candidates (using "feeling thermometers") before turning our attention to their appraisals of the candidates' personal traits. We then attempt to assess the extent to which voters based their votes on issue preferences. We conclude that voters' issue concerns were particularly important in determining their vote choices in 2012.

We then turn to how presidential performance influences voting decisions—this is particularly important when an incumbent is on the ballot. Existing research suggests that many voters decide how to vote on the basis of "retrospective evaluations" of the incumbents. In other words, voters decide mainly on the basis of what the candidates have done in office, not what they promise to do if elected. In Chapter 7, we show that retrospective evaluations, particularly those related to the performance of the economy, were a powerful reason for Obama's victory. Interestingly, while voters appeared to be disenchanted with the status of the war in Afghanistan, they did not appear to hold President Obama responsible.

In Chapter 8, we explore the impact of party loyalties on voting using the ANES data. Since the 1980s, there was a substantial shift in whites' partisan loyalties—particularly in the South—toward the Republican Party. The clear advantage Democrats once held among whites dissipated. While the 2008 election that initially brought Obama to office saw a resurgence in whites' Democratic identification, that advantage proved temporary as whites' party loyalties reverted to near parity in 2012. We examine partisanship among whites and blacks separately, tracking change from 1952 to 2012. This analysis reveals that the patterns of change among whites and blacks have been markedly different. We also compare Latino partisanship in recent elections. Finally, we take a close look at the role of party loyalties in shaping issue preferences, retrospective evaluations, and voting preferences. We find that the relationship between party identification and the vote was very strong in 2000, 2004, 2008, and 2012.

In Chapters 9 and 10 we are reminded that Election Day 2012 featured many elections. In addition to the presidential election, there were twelve gubernatorial elections, elections for thousands of state and local offices, as well as thirty-three elections for the U.S. Senate and elections for all 435 seats in the U.S. House of Representatives.[53] We focus our analysis on the 2012 House and Senate elections, which are by far the most consequential for national public policy.

Chapter 9 examines the pattern of congressional outcomes for 2012 and brings to light those factors that affect competition in congressional elections. We review the pattern of incumbent success in House and Senate races between 1954, the first Democratic victory in their forty-year winning streak, and 2012. The proportion of House incumbents reelected in 2012 was below the thirty-election average, while the success rate for Senate incumbents was above the average for that chamber. We examine the interplay of national and regional factors in structuring congressional election outcomes. And, of course, we give particular attention to the critical factors of candidate recruitment, reapportionment and redistricting, and campaign finance. Finally, we speculate on the future of congressional elections and party polarization in Congress in 2014 and beyond.

Chapter 10 explores how voters make congressional voting decisions. Using the same ANES surveys we employed to study presidential voting, we examine how social factors, issues, partisan loyalties, incumbency, and retrospective evaluations of congressional and presidential performance influence voters' choices for the House and Senate. We also try to determine the existence and extent of presidential "coattails," that is, whether Democrats were more likely to be elected to Congress because of Obama's presidential victory.

Finally, in Chapter 11, we attempt to place the 2012 elections in the proper historical context. Though we examine changes and continuities in American elections over the course of the nation's history, the great advantage of our analysis is its use of high-quality surveys of the electorate over the last sixty years. This wealth of data provides extraordinary insights regarding the political preferences of the American people, how those preferences have varied with time, and how they relate to voting behavior. Thus, we explore the long-term changes and continuities in the politics of American national elections.

Chapter 1

The Nomination Struggle

The Republican Party's presidential nomination campaign was especially interesting, even if a bit chaotic, with the sudden rise and equally rapid decline of a seemingly endless sequence of candidacies. Through it all, former Governor Mitt Romney (MA) persevered with the backing of a minority of Republicans in the electorate, a minority that became, first, a plurality of the Republican electorate and, then, a majority of the delegates selected to attend the Republican National Convention.[1] After a roller coaster opening for nearly everyone else in the race, Romney gradually increased his popular following among Republicans in the electorate, going from about 25 percent support at the end of 2011, into the lead for good in late February, and then to be the first choice for nomination of about 40 percent of Republican identifiers in April. All the while, first one candidate, then another, burst onto the scene, winning this primary or that caucus, springing up in the polls, only to fall back just as suddenly.

While there were a number of unique aspects to this contest, the major story was actually one of continuity with multicandidate nomination contests since 1972. The result is that there are lessons to be learned about the nature of presidential nominations revealed in 2012 as there have been in prior campaigns. Of course, President Obama's renomination illustrates one regularity about the nomination system that went into place in 1972: incumbents are extraordinarily unlikely to lose. In his case, like others before, that is because the incumbent has no serious opposition at all. But even in those rare cases when there is serious contestation, they are likely to win, just as they have always have won renomination under the current system.[2] But Romney's victory in a party with no incumbent seeking nomination illustrated a number of regularities to be discovered in these more interesting and competitive contests.

Reforms in the late 1960s and early 1970s had brought about a new form of nomination campaign, one that required public campaigning for resources and votes. The "new nomination system of 1972," as we call it, has shaped many aspects of all contests from 1972 onward, and we examine the similarities that have endured over its forty-year existence. Each contest, of course, differs from all others because of the electoral context at the time (e.g., the state of the economy or of war and peace) and because the contenders themselves are different. And in the new nomination system, the rules change to some degree every four years as well. The changes in rules, and the strategies that candidates adopt in light of those rules, combine with the context and contenders to make each campaign unique.

In 2012, two changes in rules (or their application) had major consequences for the conduct of the campaign on the Republican side (of course, rules have little effect on an uncontested race such as Obama's renomination!). One set of rule changes occurs every four years and consistently alters the contours without, however, fundamentally changing the strategy of campaigning for nomination. These are the dates on which the various state delegation selection events are held. The major consequence had been, through 2008, what is known as *front-loading*. State legislatures (which determine the dates of primaries) and state parties (which determine the dates of caucuses) had increasingly tried to hold their primaries or caucuses as early in the year as possible. This front-loading became one of the most important forces shaping campaign strategy from 1996, when front-loading first became significant, to 2008. Front-loading reversed direction in 2012, and that again changed the strategies that the candidates followed and the special features of the Republican contest that year. Learning from the experiences of their predecessors, in 2012 the candidates carefully designed their strategies around the no-longer-quite-so-front-loaded campaign. This confluence of circumstances accounts for many of the most striking aspects of this campaign—its early beginning and its early end, albeit a less early end than in more front-loaded campaigns. This confluence also helps us understand why Romney was able to prevail over a large set of opponents, many of whom were more popular, at least briefly, among potential primary voters.

The second major change is in the nature of funding of presidential (and congressional) campaigns in general and in the presidential nomination campaigns in particular. Between 1976 and 2008 candidates turned to the federal government for provision of matching funds, thereby effectively doubling small contributions. And this feature played a major role in determining who serious candidates were and in helping shape who won.[3] After changes in the last decade, and in the growing competitive costs for conducting a campaign, virtually no serious candidate would accept federal funds—and the limitations that acceptance of them impose. Instead, candidates and various campaign-related organizations gather ever-increasing war chests on their own, with campaign spending thereby being all but unrestricted as well. Interestingly, it appears that the candidates have adjusted to these new funding realities without dramatically altering the nature of dynamics of campaigning and voting. That is to say, many of the regularities that we observed under the older funding regime continue today under the new funding regime.

In this chapter, we examine some of the regularities of the campaigns since 1972 to see how they helped shape the 2012 nomination contest. Next, we turn to the first step of the nomination process: the decisions of politicians to become—or not to become—presidential candidates. Then we examine some of the rules of the nomination system they face. Finally, we consider how the candidates ran and why Romney won.

WHO RAN

A first important regularity of the nomination campaign is that when incumbents seek renomination, only a very few candidates will contest them, and perhaps no one will at all. In 1972, although President Richard M. Nixon did face two potentially credible challengers to his renomination, they were so ineffective that he was essentially uncontested. Ronald Reagan in 1984, Bill Clinton in 1996, George W. Bush in 2004, and Barack Obama in 2012 were actually unopposed. This was the case, in large part, because even a moderately successful president is virtually undefeatable for renomination. Conversely, Gerald R. Ford in 1976, Jimmy Carter in 1980, and George H. W. Bush in 1992 faced one, or at most two, credible challengers. Although Bush defeated his challenger, Pat Buchanan, rather easily, Ford and Carter had great difficulty defeating their opponents, Reagan and Democratic senator Edward M. Kennedy of Massachusetts, respectively. Those two campaigns, while demonstrating that incumbents are not assured of victory, nevertheless demonstrate the power of presidential incumbency because both incumbents were in fact victorious despite facing the strongest imaginable challengers and despite being relatively weak incumbents.

The second major regularity in the nomination system concerns the other set of contests, those in which the party has no incumbent seeking renomination. In such cases, a relatively large number of candidates run for the nomination. Eight major candidates sought the Republican Party's nomination in 2012. Several more had declared but dropped out of the race before January 1, 2012. There have been eleven such campaigns since 1980, and the number of major candidates that were in the race as the year began varied remarkably little: seven in 1980 (R), eight in 1984 (D), eight (D) and six (R) in 1988, eight in 1992 (D), eight in 1996 (R), six in 2000 (R), nine in 2004 (D), and eight in both parties' contests in 2008, to go along with the eight-candidate Republican contest in 2012. The major exception to this regularity is that only Vice President Al Gore and former New Jersey senator Bill Bradley sought the Democratic nomination of 2000, even though many others seriously considered doing so.

The eight candidates whose campaigns were still active on January 1, 2012, were Rep. Michele Bachmann (MN), former Rep. Newt Gingrich (GA), former Gov. and Ambassador Jon Huntsman (UT), Rep. Ron Paul (TX), Gov. Rick Perry (TX), former Gov. Buddy Roemer (LA), former Gov. Mitt Romney (MA), and former Sen. Rick Santorum (PA). Businessman Herman Cain (GA) and former Gov. Tim Pawlenty (MN) had declared—and suspended—their candidacies in 2011. And there were a good number of others who were touted as strong candidates, only to choose not run in 2012. Many, for example, thought that such candidates as Gov. Chris Christie (NJ) or Gov. Mitch Daniels (IN) would be the strongest candidates.

We have so far illustrated two regularities: few or no candidates will challenge incumbents, but many candidates will seek the nomination when no incumbent is running. A third regularity is that among the candidates who are politicians, most hold, or have recently held, high political office. This regularity follows from "ambition theory," developed originally by Joseph A. Schlesinger to explain how personal ambition and the pattern and prestige of various elected offices lead candidates to emerge from those political offices that have the strongest electoral bases.[4] This base for the presidential candidates includes the offices of vice president, senator, governor, and, of course, the presidency itself. Note that Bachmann and Paul were the only sitting members of the U.S. House to run for the presidential nomination. House members do not have as strong an electoral base from which to run for the presidency and may have to forgo a safe House seat to do so. As a result, few run and fewer still are strong contenders.

Most candidates in 2012, as in all earlier campaigns under the new nomination system, emerged from one of the strong electoral bases. Table 1-1 presents the data for 2012 and for all campaigns from 1972 to 2012 combined. Over two-thirds of the presidential candidates had already served as president, vice president, senator, or governor; another one in eight was a member of the U.S. House. Note, however, that, unlike in many other years, in 2012 only one senator entered the race, while three candidates were current or former members of the U.S. House. Many of the presidents in the early years of the nation were chosen from the outgoing president's cabinet (especially the sitting secretary of state) and other high-level presidential appointees, but the cabinet is no longer a serious source of presidential candidates.[5] Although mayors rarely run for president, the mayor of New York City is particularly prominent in the media, and Mayor Rudy Giuliani's unique role in the aftermath of the September 11, 2001, attacks on the United States gave him great national visibility for his 2008 race. But note how rare his case is.

A fourth regularity, also consistent with ambition theory, is that of the many who run in nomination contests without incumbents, only a few put their current office at risk to do so. Among the Republicans in 2012, only the two current House members and Gov. Perry were in office (and he was not up for reelection in 2012), while five others were former officeholders.

TABLE 1-1   Current or Most Recent Office Held by Declared Candidates for President: Two Major Parties, 1972–2012

Office held	Percentage of all candidates who held that office	Number 1972–2012	Number 2012
President	6	8	1
Vice president	3	4	0
U.S. senator	37	48	1
U.S. representative	14	18	3
Governor	22	29	5
U.S. cabinet	3	4	0
Other	7	9	1
None	8	11	1
Total	100	131	12

Source: 1972–1992: *Congressional Quarterly's Guide to U.S. Elections,* 4th ed. (Washington, D.C.: CQ Press, 2001), 522–525, 562; 1996: Paul R. Abramson, John H. Aldrich, and David W. Rohde, *Change and Continuity in the 1996 and 1998 Elections* (Washington, D.C.: CQ Press, 1999), 13; 2000: *CQ Weekly,* January 1, 2000, 22; 2004: *CQ Weekly,* Fall 2003 Supplement, Vol. 61, Issue 48. The 2008 results were compiled by the authors. 2012: "Republican Presidential Candidates," *New York Times,* http://elections.nytimes.com/2012/primaries/candidates.

THE RULES OF THE NOMINATION SYSTEM

The method that the two major parties use for nominating presidential candidates is unique and amazingly complicated. To add to the complication, the various formal rules, laws, and procedures for the nomination are changed, sometimes in large ways and invariably in numerous small ways, every four years. Beyond the formal rules lie informal standards and expectations, often set by the news media or the candidates themselves, that help shape each campaign. As variable as the rules are, however, the nomination system of 1972 has one pair of overriding characteristics that define it as a system: first, even though the formal nomination is made by vote of delegates at the national party conventions, since 1972 the major-party presidential nominees have effectively been selected in public and by the public; second, as a result all serious candidates have pursued the nomination by seeking the support of the public through the various communication media.

The complexity of the nomination contests is a consequence of four major factors. The first of these, federalism, or the state as the unit of selection for national nominees, is at least 180 years old. The second factor, the rules on the selection (and perhaps instruction) of delegates to the convention, and the third factor, the rules on financing the campaign, are the oft-revised products of the reform period. The fourth factor is the way in which candidates react to these rules and to their opponents, and grows out of the keen competition for a highly valued goal. The first three factors are described in more detail in the sections that follow, while the last informs the discussion throughout the rest of the chapter.

Federalism or State-Based Delegate Selection

National conventions to select presidential nominees were first held for the 1832 election, and for every nomination since then the votes of delegates attending the conventions have determined the nominees. Delegates have always been allocated at the state level; whatever other particulars may apply, each state selects its parties' delegates through procedures adopted by state party organizations if they choose to use caucuses and conventions, by state law if primary elections are employed, or both. Votes at the convention are cast by state delegation, and in general the state is the basic unit of the nomination process.[6] Thus there are really fifty separate delegate selection contests in each party.[7] There is no national primary, nor is there serious contemplation of one.

The fact that there are more than fifty separate contests in each party creates numerous layers of complexity, two of which are especially consequential. First, each state is free to choose delegates using any method consistent with the general rules of the national party. Many states choose to select delegates via a primary election, which is a state-run election like any other, except that each primary selects delegates for only one party's convention. The Democratic Party requires that its primaries be open only to registered Democrats. States not holding primaries use a combination of caucuses and conventions, which are designed and run by each political party and not by the state government. Caucuses are simply local meetings of party members. Those attending the caucuses report their preferences for the presidential nomination and choose delegates from their midst to attend higher-level conventions such as at the county, congressional district, state, and eventually the national levels.

The second major consequence of federalism is that the states are free (within bounds described below) to choose when to hold their primaries or caucuses. These events are thus spread out over time, although both parties now set a time period—the delegate selection "window"—during which primaries and caucuses can be held. The specific provisions for the GOP in 2012 are a window that "opened" March 6:

> In an effort to decrease the large cluster of contests at the beginning of the primary and caucus calendar, the phenomenon known as front-loading, the Republican Party adopted these two important changes to national party rules for the 2012 primary process:
>
> - Delegate selection events could not be held before the first Tuesday in March, with exceptions for Iowa, Nevada, New Hampshire, and South Carolina, which could hold their events on or after February

1 (regardless, Iowa, New Hampshire, and South Carolina scheduled January events for 2012); and

- A related change required states that held contests before April 1 to allocate delegates on a proportional basis, although it did not impose a specific proportional system. Many state parties used winner-take-all in the past, but the new rule required that delegates be awarded to presidential candidates in proportion to their primary vote totals, in some fashion.[8]

New Hampshire has held the first primary in the nation since the state began to hold primaries in 1920, and state law requires that New Hampshire's primary be held before any other state holds its. A more recent tradition, dating from 1976, is that Iowa holds the first caucuses before the New Hampshire primary, but this "tradition" has been challenged by other states, which have tried from time to time to schedule even earlier caucuses. In 2012, as in 2008, some states continued to push their starting dates earlier and earlier. As a result, Iowa held its caucus on January 3, making the last two campaigns by far the two earliest starts to delegate selection. South Carolina and Nevada were granted exceptional timing by the Democratic national party to hold their primaries early in 2008, with that exception continuing into 2012 (and essentially agreed to by the Republican Party). South Carolina chose to hold its primary on January 21, 2012. Therefore, New Hampshire was again forced to hold its primary very early in 2012, to maintain its "first in the nation" status, this time holding it on January 10.

Two large states decided to hold their primaries early in 2008—Michigan on January 15 and Florida on January 29—thereby defying their national parties. The result was conflict over whether the delegates would be given votes or "punished" for intentionally violating party rules. A compromise was eventually reached on the Democratic side. On the Republican side in both 2008 and 2012, Wyoming, Michigan, and Florida saw their delegate totals cut in half because they held their primary or caucus before the Republicans' window opened.

All this shows why there is pressure toward front-loading and how that pressure was overcome and even reversed for 2012. In Figure 1-1, we compare the cumulative total of delegates awarded by week of the campaigns in 1976, 2008, and 2012. In 1976, 60 percent of the delegates were selected by the seventeenth week of the campaign. In 2008, front-loading had moved the 60 percent mark to the fifth week, but in 2012 that percentage reverted back toward the 1976 timing. While the 50 percent mark was reached five weeks earlier in 2012 than in 1976, there was a clear reversal from what had been a continuing push to move toward the front. The main reason for this change was the move of the California primary, and other early June primaries, from 1976 first up toward the beginning and then, between 2008 and 2012, back to June again. These large states meant that there were many delegates up for grabs later in 2012 than in 2008.

FIGURE 1-1   Front-loading in Republican Nomination Campaigns, 1976, 2008, and 2012 Compared

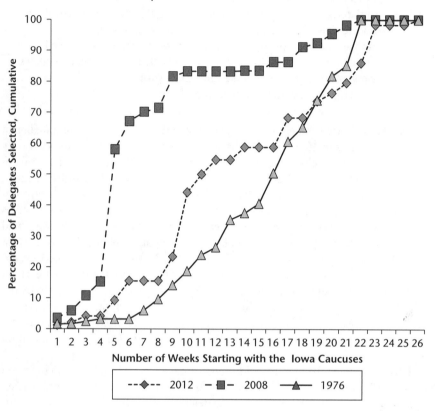

Source: Compiled by authors.

The Nomination System of 1972: Delegate Selection

Through 1968, presidential nominations were won by appeals to the party leadership. To be sure, public support and even primary election victories could be important in a candidate's campaign, but their importance stemmed from the credibility they would give to the candidacy in the eyes of party leaders. The 1968 Democratic nomination, like so many events that year, was especially tumultuous.[9] The result was that the Democratic Party undertook a series of reforms, led by the McGovern-Fraser Commission and adopted by the party convention in 1972. The reforms were sufficiently radical in changing delegate selection procedures that they, in effect, created a new nomination system. Although it was much less aggressive in reforming its delegate selection procedures, the Republican Party did so to a certain degree. However, the most consequential results of the Democratic reforms, for our purposes—the proliferation of presidential primaries and the media's treatment of some (notably the Iowa) caucuses as essentially primary-like—spilled over to the Republican side as well.

In 1968 Democratic senators Eugene J. McCarthy of Minnesota and Robert F. Kennedy of New York ran very public, highly visible, primary-oriented campaigns in opposition to the policies of President Lyndon B. Johnson, especially the conduct of the war in Vietnam. Before the second primary, held in Wisconsin, Johnson surprisingly announced, "I shall not seek and I will not accept the nomination of my party for another term as your President."[10] Vice President Hubert H. Humphrey took Johnson's place in representing the establishment and the policies of the Democratic Party. Humphrey, however, waged no public campaign; he won the nomination without entering a single primary, thereby splitting an already deeply divided party.[11] Would Humphrey have won the nomination had Robert Kennedy not been assassinated the night he defeated McCarthy in California, effectively eliminating McCarthy as a serious contender? No one will ever know. Democrats did know, however, that the chaos and violence that accompanied Humphrey's nomination clearly indicated that the nomination process should be opened to more diverse candidacies and that public participation should be more open and more effective in determining the outcome.

The two most significant consequences of the reforms were the public's greater impact on each state's delegate selection proceedings (many delegates would now be bound to vote for the candidate for whom they were chosen) and the proliferation of presidential primaries.[12] Caucus-convention procedures became timelier, were better publicized, and, in short, were more primary-like. Today in most elections, including in 2012, the media treat Iowa's caucuses as critical events, and the coverage of them is similar to the coverage of primaries— how many "votes" were "cast" for each candidate, for example.

At the state level, many party officials concluded that the easiest way to conform to the new Democratic rules in 1972 was to hold a primary election. Thus the number of states (including the District of Columbia) holding Democratic primaries increased from fifteen in 1968 to twenty-one in 1972 to twenty-seven in 1976, and the number of Republican primaries increased comparably. By 1988 thirty-six states were holding Republican primaries, and thirty-four were holding Democratic ones. In 2000 forty-three states were conducting Republican primaries, and Democratic primaries were being held in forty states. In 2012 there were thirty-nine primaries on the Republican side. Thus it is fair to say that the parties' new nomination systems have become largely based on primaries or more primary-like conventions.

The only major exception to this conclusion is that about one in five delegates to the Democratic National Convention is chosen because he or she is an elected officeholder or a Democratic Party official. Supporters of this reform of party rules (first used in 1984) wanted to ensure that the Democratic leadership would have a formal role to play at the conventions of the party. These "superdelegates" may have played a decisive role in the 1984 nomination of Walter F. Mondale and again in 2008 when Obama, like Mondale, had a majority of the non-superdelegates, but not a majority of all delegates. Each candidate needed only a relatively small number of additional superdelegates to commit to vote for him to win the nomination. They both received those commitments the day after the regular delegate selection process ended, and, with that, they were assured the nomination.[13]

The delegate selection process has, as noted, become considerably more front-loaded, which changed nomination politics.[14] The rationale for front-loading was clear enough: the last time California's (actual or near) end-of-season primary had an effect on the nomination process was in the 1964 Republican and the 1972 Democratic nomination contests. Once candidates, the media, and other actors realized, and reacted to, the implications of the reformed nomination system, the action shifted to the earliest events of the season, and nomination contests, especially those involving multiple candidates, were effectively completed well before the end of the primary season. More and more state parties and legislatures (including California's) realized the advantages of front-loading, bringing more attention from the media, more expenditures of time and money by the candidates, and more influence to their states if they held primaries sooner rather than later. By 2008, however, other factors started to affect state decisions. First, the rewards for early primaries were concentrated in a relatively small number of the very earliest primaries. And, as we noted above, the national parties regulated which ones could go when, and threatened to penalize states that violated the national party decisions. Indeed, Michigan and Florida were actually penalized in 2008 and 2012. In addition, the very early presidential primaries forced states to make an increasingly difficult choice. If they held their presidential primaries early in the year, they had to decide whether to hold the primary elections for all other offices at the same time, which was proving quite a bit earlier than made sense for candidates for local, state, and even national congressional posts, or to pay the costs of two primaries, one for the president and one for all other offices. Since states like California, for example, which were not able to reap the major benefits of being among the very earliest of events, received lesser benefits of being early, they chose to return to late in the season.

If the rationale for front-loading was clear by 1996, when it first became controversial, the consequences were not. Some argued that long-shot candidates could be propelled to the front of the pack by gathering momentum in Iowa and New Hampshire and could, before the well-known candidates could react, lock up the nomination early. The alternative argument was that increasing front-loading helps those who begin the campaign with the advantages associated with being a front-runner, such as name recognition, support from state and local party or related organizations, and, most of all, money.

Indeed, as the primary season became more front-loaded, the well-known, well-established, and well-financed candidates increasingly dominated the primaries. Sen. George S. McGovern of South Dakota and Gov. Jimmy Carter of Georgia won the Democratic nominations in 1972 and 1976, even though they began as little-known and ill-financed contenders. George H. W. Bush, successful in the 1980 Iowa Republican caucuses, climbed from being, in his words, "an asterisk in the polls" (where the asterisk is commonly used to indicate less than 1 percent support) to become Reagan's major contender and eventual vice presidential choice. And Colorado senator Gary Hart nearly defeated former vice president Mondale in 1984. In 1988 the two strongest candidates at the start of the Republican race, George H. W. Bush and Bob Dole, contested vigorously, with Bush winning. Gov. Michael S. Dukakis of Massachusetts, the best-financed and best-organized Democrat, won the nomination surprisingly easily. Clinton's victory in 1992 appeared, then, to be the culmination of the trend toward an insuperable advantage for the strongest and best-financed candidates. Clinton was able to withstand scandal and defeat in the early going and eventually cruise to victory.

The campaign of former Democratic senator Paul Tsongas of Massachusetts in 1992 illustrates one important reason for Clinton's victory. Tsongas defeated the field in New Hampshire, and, as usual, the victory and the media attention it drew opened doors to fund-raising possibilities unavailable to him even days earlier. Yet Tsongas faced the dilemma of whether to take time out of daily campaigning for the public's votes so that he could spend time on fund-raising or to continue campaigning in the upcoming primaries. If he campaigned in those primaries, he would not have the opportunity to raise and direct the funds he needed to be an effective competitor. Front-loading had simply squeezed too much into too short a post–New Hampshire time frame for a candidate to be able to capitalize on early victories as, say, Carter had done in winning the nomination and election in 1976. The events of 1996 supported the alternative argument—that increased front-loading benefits the front-runner—even though it took nearly all of Dole's resources to achieve his early victory that year.[15]

This lesson was not lost on the candidates for 2000, especially George W. Bush. In particular, he began his quest in 1999 (or earlier!) as a reasonably well-regarded governor, but one not particularly well known to the public outside of Texas (although, of course, sharing his father's name made him instantly recognizable). He was at that point only one of several plausible contenders, but he worked hard to receive early endorsements from party leaders and raised a great deal of money well ahead of his competition. When others sought to match Bush's early successes in this "invisible primary," they found that he had sewn up a great deal of support. Many, in fact, withdrew before the first vote was cast, suddenly realizing just how Bush's actions had lengthened the odds against them. Bush was therefore able to win the nomination at the very opening of the primary season. Incumbent vice president Al Gore, on the other side, also benefited from the same dynamics of the invisible primary, although in the more classical role of one who began the nomination season as the odds-on favorite and therefore the one most able to shut the door on his opposition well before it was time for most voters to cast their ballots.[16]

The pre-primary period on the Republican side in 2008 was quite variable, with first McCain, then Giuliani, then Romney surging to the front. McCain's campaign was considered all but dead in the water by that point, but it gathered strength again before 2007 ended. There was, then, no strong front-runner in the GOP; the campaign was wide open. It was not so wide open, however, that pundits imagined former Arkansas Governor Mike Huckabee had a chance, and so his victory in the Iowa caucuses was a genuine surprise (at least from the perspective of, say, October 2007). On the Democratic side, Hillary Clinton was a clear front-runner. In retrospect, it was also clear that Obama had developed an impressive organization both by mobilizing support across the nation and by fund-raising, especially through adroit use of the Internet. Thus once his organizational strength became publicly visible, it was no surprise that he and Clinton easily defeated their rivals.

The 2012 contest had some similarities to 2008, with Romney moving from his also-ran slot to replace McCain as the candidate who early on seemed strong, lost steam, and then resurged back to victory. One effect of the decline in front-loading was that Romney, even though ahead, was not able to completely shut the door on his opposition until much later in the season. Simply too few delegates were selected early in 2008. This extended length of time had several effects, as we detail below, including permitting relative long-shot candidacies such as Santorum's to emerge rather later in the season than usual and giving all candidates longer to raise funds, and thus maintain candidacies longer. Perhaps even more costly, it also permitted Romney's opponents to run negative campaigns against him, quite possibly hurting his ability to shape his own image and providing fodder for attacks in the general election campaign.

The Nomination System of 1972: Campaign Finance

Campaign finance is the second aspect of the reform of the presidential nomination process. In this case, changes in law (and regulation in light of the law) and in the technology for raising money in nomination contests have made the financial context widely different from one campaign to the next. The 2012 campaign was no exception. As the first run under a new regulatory environment in light of the Supreme Court case popularly known as *Citizens United*, candidates tried a large variety of new or modified strategies for campaign financing in response.[17]

Our story begins, however, with the Federal Election Campaign Act of 1971, and especially the 1974 and 1976 amendments to the act. The Watergate scandal during the Nixon administration included revelations of substantial abuse in raising and spending money in the 1972 presidential election (facts discovered in part in implementing the 1971 act). The resulting regulations limited contributions by individuals and groups, virtually ending the power of individual "fat cats" and requiring presidential candidates to raise money in a broad-based campaign. The federal government would match small donations for the nomination, and candidates who accepted matching funds would be bound by limits on what they could spend.

These provisions, created by the Federal Election Commission to monitor campaign financing and regulate campaign practices, altered the way nomination campaigns were funded. Still, just as candidates learned over time how to contest most effectively under the new delegate selection process, they also learned how to campaign under the new financial regulations. Perhaps most important, presidential candidates learned—though it is not as true for them as for congressional candidates—that "early money is like yeast, because it helps to raise the dough."[18] They also correctly believed that a great deal of money was necessary to compete effectively.

The costs of running presidential nomination campaigns, indeed campaigns for all major offices, have escalated dramatically since 1972. But a special chain of strategic reactions has spurred the cost of campaigning for the presidential nomination. The *Citizens United* case seems to have reached a culmination of an increasingly unregulated environment.

When many states complied with the McGovern-Fraser Commission reforms by adopting primaries, media coverage grew, enhancing the effects of momentum, increasing the value of early victories, and raising the costs of early defeat. As we described earlier, these reactions, in turn, led states to create the front-loaded season that candidates faced up to 2008. All of these factors created not only a demand for more money, but also a demand for that money to be raised early, ahead of the primary season. Indeed, media and other observers used the amount of early money raised as a marker of just how strong a candidate's campaign was likely to be, as they assessed the opening rounds of the contests. As noted above, Bush's strong, early fund-raising in 2000 (or actually 1999) forced contenders to begin serious fund-raising even earlier.

By 2008, however, very few candidates were accepting federal matching funds, because doing so would bind them to spending limits in individual states and over the campaign as a whole. Among Republicans, only McCain accepted these funds; among Democrats, Biden, Dodd, Edwards, and Gravel accepted such funding. By 2012, only one candidate, Buddy Roemer, applied for federal funding, and his candidacy was considered sufficiently hopeless that many debates did not even bother to include him among the contestants.

Much money is being raised. Through May 2008, the fund-raising totals for the three major contenders were $296 million for Obama, $238 million for Clinton, and $122 million for McCain.[19] By the same point in 2012, Romney reported raising $121 million, with Paul having raised $40 million, Gingrich $24 million, and Santorum $22 million.

The 2008 campaign also marked the dramatic expansion in the use of the Internet to raise money, following on the efforts of Democrat Howard Dean, the former governor of Vermont, in 2004 (and, to an extent, McCain in 2000). Ron Paul, for example, raised more than $6 million on a single day, December 6, 2007, through the Internet, a strategy he built on in 2012. But Obama's success served as the model for future campaigns, such as the $55 million he raised in February 2008 at a critical moment for the campaign.[20] Indeed, not only did Obama's organizational ability lead to all but the ending of federal funding of presidential nominations, but the carryover to the fall signaled its demise in general election campaigns as well (see Chapter 2). Finally, Internet fund-raising solved the "Tsongas dilemma" described earlier, because the Obama team could raise money on the Internet without the candidate having to leave the campaign trail.

The *Citizens United* decision in 2010 changed the landscape dramatically. In the narrow, it overturned the 2002 Bipartisan Campaign Reform Act and held that corporations and unions could spend unlimited money in support of political objectives and could enjoy First Amendment free speech rights, just as individuals could. These organizations, however, continued to be banned from directly contributing to candidates and parties. This case and especially a subsequent one decided by a U.S. Court of Appeals in light of this case, spurred the development of what are known as *super PACs*, which are political action committees that can now accept unlimited contributions from individuals, corporations, and unions and spend as much as they like, so long as it is not in explicit support of a candidate or party's election campaign or coordinated with their campaign organization.[21] According to data from the Center for Responsive Politics, expenditures on behalf of the three major nomination contenders were quite large. About $14 million was spent in behalf of Romney, $19 million for Gingrich, and $21 million for Santorum. Note that the expenditures in behalf of the last two approximate the amount of money their campaigns raised themselves (see above).[22] These organizations altered the terms of the campaign in that their expenditures had to be independent of the candidates and their (and their party's) organizations. It is therefore not necessarily the case that the candidate and, in the fall, the party will retain total control over the campaign and its messages.

Another consequence of these changes is that what were once dubbed "fat cats" are once again permitted. The 2012 exemplar is Sheldon Adelson, a casino magnate and a strong supporter of Israel. He contributed $5 million to the Winning Our Future super PAC in support of Newt Gingrich before the South Carolina primary. The PAC ran an advertising campaign, effectively against Romney's candidacy, presumably helping create the surprising Gingrich victory there. Adelson and his wife contributed another $5 million immediately thereafter, in preparation for the Florida primary, which this time turned out less well for Gingrich, effectively ending his candidacy. The common interpretation was that Adelson's support, and it alone, made possible the late portion of Gingrich's campaign. Without it he might not have been able to compete in South Carolina.

And it is only the post–*Citizens United* environment that permits one individual to have made such an apparently discernible difference.[23] A side note is that the ad campaign in South Carolina featured attacks on Romney's work for Bain Capital, a line of attack that Democrats picked up from the Gingrich attack ads.

With all these changes, the candidates remain convinced that raising money early is, if not actually necessary, at least extremely helpful. In 2012 all candidates raised at least half their funds before 2011 ended except Romney (he raised 46 percent by then) and Santorum (who had raised under 10 percent by then).[24] While Santorum's case demonstrates that significant sums can be raised during the campaign itself, just as Obama had shown four years earlier, his campaign suffered from lagging receipts compared to his competitors. Therefore, early is most helpful and perhaps even necessary.

THE DYNAMICS OF MULTICANDIDATE CAMPAIGNS

The most significant feature, from the candidates' perspectives, of the nomination process is its dynamic character. This system was designed to empower the general public, giving it opportunities to participate more fully in the selection of delegates to the national party conventions, and often even instructing them on how to vote. The early state delegate selection contests in Iowa and New Hampshire allowed largely unknown candidates to work a small state or two using the "retail" politics of door-to-door campaigning to achieve a surprising success that would attract media attention and then money, volunteers, and greater popular support. In practice, this was exactly the route Jimmy Carter followed in 1976.

John H. Aldrich developed this account of momentum in campaigns, using the 1976 campaigns to illustrate its effect. He first showed that there is no stable balance to this process.[25] In practical terms, he predicted that one candidate will increasingly absorb all the money, media attention, and public support, and thereby defeat all opponents before the convention. He further showed that the tendency for this process to focus rapidly on a single winner increases the *more* candidates there are. This finding was just the opposite of the original theories in this area and, indeed, what at the time seemed obvious: the greater the number of candidates, the longer it would take to reach victory. But common sense was not a helpful guide in this case.

There is one exception to this pure momentum result: the possibility of an unstable but sustainable balance with two candidates locked in a nearly precise tie. Early campaigns offered two illustrations compatible with two candidates in (unstable) equipoise, the 1976 Republican and 1980 Democratic contests.[26] In both cases, a relatively moderate but unpopular incumbent was challenged by a popular contender who represented the ideological (and thus relatively more extreme) heart of his party. In both cases, the campaigns lasted for a considerable period in this nearly even balance. And in both cases, the incumbents eventually moved ahead, sufficiently so that they achieved a majority of committed delegates by the end of the primary season. There is a second route to a long-lasting two-candidate campaign, a route that has now also appeared twice. In both the 1984 and 2008 Democratic contests, the campaigns began with a large number of candidates. Each featured a strong, well-financed, well-known, well-organized candidate who, it turned out, was challenged strongly by a heretofore little known (to the public) candidate who offered a new direction for the party. The multicandidate contest quickly shrank to just two viable candidates.

It is not a coincidence that the latter two cases were on the Democratic side. In that party, there is a large bloc of uncommitted party leaders, the superdelegates, to woo late in the campaign. With the ending of front-loading (at least for 2012) the conditions become ripe for an extended, close contest between two equally plausible candidates lasting well into the spring before one or the other is able to secure a firm hold on a majority of actual delegates. In the more usual case of momentum yielding one leader who emerges to win, front-loading strengthens the rapidity of the dynamics of momentum. This dynamic fits every other campaign in which no incumbent president is seeking renomination—until 2012.

In Figure 1-2, we report the length of all campaigns without a presidential incumbent running—that is, the number of weeks between the New Hampshire primary and the end of the campaign.[27] The standard until 1988 was that the campaign lasted until the end of the primary season. But beginning with 1988 on the Republican side, and extending with no exceptions until 2008's Democratic contest, all subsequent campaigns ended shortly after the New Hampshire primary. The change in delegate selection rules undid front-loading and means that the 2012 campaign lasted as long as any other ever has. One consequence of this is tying even an all-but-inevitable winner like Romney in 2012 to continued campaigning for Republican votes—and continued vulnerability to attack from one's own partisan side—much longer than before. While Romney had momentum and while no other candidate could realistically imagine winning nomination, it all goes back to rule one—the nominee is the candidate who wins a majority of votes cast by delegates at the national convention. In earlier years, momentum and winning a majority of delegates meshed smoothly, as front-loading meant that a momentum-induced victor could secure that majority early on. In 2012's campaign, it simply took weeks and months longer before a sufficient number of delegates was actually selected to translate momentum into nomination.

How Romney Won

It was by no means inevitable that Romney would win the 2012 Republican presidential nomination, even though he started with significant assets. He was better known than his competitors and among the leading contenders in poll standings as 2012 opened. He was experienced in politics in general and in campaigning in particular, and he had run a credible, although not terribly

FIGURE 1-2   Length of Multicandidate Campaigns, 1976–2012

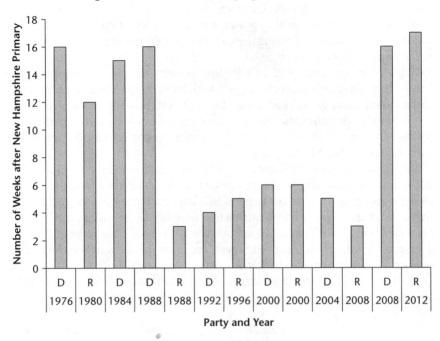

Party and Year

Source: Compiled by authors.

successful, campaign in 2008.[28] He had put together a strong campaign and financial organization, and he had long been in the field campaigning. This put him in a position a bit like Hillary Rodham Clinton's in 2008. He was the strongest contender with a lead on most of the field, but not a runaway sure thing. Indeed, he had several liabilities. The most important one was the ability to convince the conservative wing of the Republican Party that he was one of them. Part of this was policy. Perhaps the most prominent example of his inability to convince strongly conservative Republicans that he was really one of them was health care. As Governor of Massachusetts, he had successfully fought for a statewide, government-run health insurance plan that was the model for the Obama-supported health care law (the Affordable Care Act) that proved so controversial among the Republican right. His Mormon faith at least moderated enthusiasm among conservative Christian Republicans. As a result, many hesitated to endorse his candidacy, searching to see if a better alternative came along. While, as we discussed earlier, some of the potentially strongest alternatives chose not to run at all, there were a considerable number who hoped to become that alternative.

In many respects, it seemed that the Republican Party gave virtually each claimant for the conservative vote a chance—and then quickly rejected them, one after the other. Bachmann broke through first, with a victory in the closely watched and hotly contested Iowa "straw poll" on August 13, 2011. That brought her attention, but perhaps because it was so early or perhaps because it is a contrived event, it had little lasting power, and her inability to follow up that slim victory with any serious showing thereafter (including in the real Iowa event) led her to end her campaign early.

Cain's moment came next. In part because of a simply described tax plan ("9-9-9" standing for 9 percent rate each for a business tax, for a flat income tax, and for a federal sales tax) and in part because of victory in a Florida straw poll on September 24, 2011, he too got a moment of heightened attention and popular support. That ended in late 2011 as charges of sexual harassment and misconduct dogged his campaign.

Rick Perry entered the campaign "late" (officially entering on August 13, 2011). He showed an ability to raise money quickly, however (raising $17 million by the end of September according to FEC data), and he used it to attract attention through a series of advertisements that were primarily positive claims about his policy stances and his record as governor. Those high moments ended with a series of blunders and negative impressions left in the seemingly endless series of televised debates among the Republican candidates. In a debate in November 2011, for example, he could not remember the names of all three government agencies he promised to eliminate. A fifth-place finish in New Hampshire effectively ended his chances for real.

This left a three-person race. To be sure, Paul was a fourth candidate who continued his candidacy late into the season (formally suspending his campaign on May 14, 2012).[29] But the race was effectively down to Romney, Gingrich, and Santorum. Figure 1-3 gives one sort of overview of the race. There we report the results of Gallup polls that asked Republican respondents who they would support for the presidential nomination, at polls conducted over the course of the campaign. While the graph begins in December 2011, so many contenders were effectively eliminated by the end of January that we follow the paths of only these four. Note, among other things, that Paul held steady at about 10 percent to 12 percent support, while there was much more dynamism for the fortunes of the other three. Tables 1-2 and 1-3 provide the more formal accounting, reporting the actual primary vote (or caucus participation) for each candidate at all Republican events over the course of 2012.

After Perry's rapid fall, Gingrich's turn came next. As former Speaker of the House and architect of the Republican majority in the 1994 congressional elections, he had much to commend him. It also left baggage (resignation as Speaker in light of romantic entanglements, among other concerns). In December 2011, he was leading in the Gallup poll (see Figure 1-2). That lead quickly evaporated over a series of concerns about his insider political status and then about his personal style and even his personality. His poll standings fell to 17 percent (tied with Santorum) right before the Iowa caucuses, leaving him seven points behind Romney, and he finished in fourth place in Iowa. Such a result would doom many candidacies, but with the newfound money (noted above) and his experience, he

FIGURE 1-3 Popular Support for Major Republican Candidates for Presidential Nomination, 2012

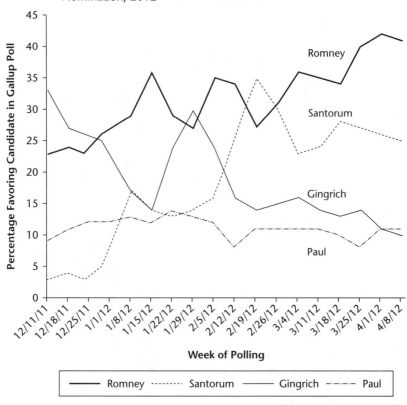

Week of Polling

Source: Compiled by authors.

was able to focus his efforts on the South Carolina primary, a place more congenial to him and less so to Romney. He used the opportunity to launch a series of tough attacks, particularly concerning Romney's role at Bain Capital. These led (or so it was generally interpreted in the media) to a decisive victory there (see Table 1-3). Under continuing pressure from leading Republicans nationally, however, what began as a lead in Florida, the next primary, changed to a slide, along with a rise in support for the remaining conservative contender, Santorum. It was also a state more congenial than South Carolina to Romney. Romney won that primary (46 percent), leaving Gingrich's campaign in disarray (with 32 percent) and leading to its eventual demise.

This left Santorum. He started early but seemed to be able to garner no serious attention or consideration, in part because his organizations (both campaign and financial) were weak and ineffective. With little national name recognition at the outset and weak organizations, his poll standings lagged.

TABLE 1-2 Results of Republican Caucuses, 2012 (percent)

State		Date	Romney	Santorum	Gingrich	Paul	Perry	Huntsman	Bachmann	Other
Iowa	Caucus	1/3/2012	24.51	24.54	13.29	21.41	10.33	0.61	4.97	0.33
Nevada	Caucus	2/4/2012	50.01	9.94	21.10	18.74	0.00	0.00	0.00	0.21
Colorado	Caucus	2/7/2012	34.85	40.31	12.79	11.75	0.00	0.00	0.00	0.30
Minnesota	Caucus	2/7/2012	16.85	44.95	10.76	27.15	0.00	0.00	0.00	0.29
Washington	Caucus	3/3/2012	37.65	23.81	10.28	24.81	0.00	0.00	0.00	3.44
Alaska	Caucus	3/6/2012	32.23	30.11	13.29	24.13	0.00	0.00	0.00	0.24
Idaho	Caucus	3/6/2012	61.59	18.17	2.10	18.10	0.00	0.00	0.00	0.04
North Dakota	Caucus	3/6/2012	23.71	39.74	8.48	28.07	0.00	0.00	0.00	0.00
Kansas	Caucus	3/10/2012	20.93	51.21	14.40	12.60	0.00	0.00	0.00	0.85
Hawaii	Caucus	3/13/2012	44.47	25.31	10.91	19.31	0.00	0.00	0.00	0.00

Source: Adapted from "Dave Leip's Atlas of U.S. Presidential Elections," http://www.uselectionatlas.org. Compiled by authors.

Note: Maine and Wyoming held caucuses, beginning on February 4 and February 11, respectively, for which no results are reported. Guam, Northern Mariana Islands, and the Virgin Islands had caucuses on March 10, and American Samoa had caucuses on March 13; these results are not reported.

TABLE 1-3   Results of Republican Primaries, 2012 (percent)

State	Date		Romney	Santorum	Gingrich	Paul	Perry	Huntsman	Bachmann	Other
New Hampshire	Primary	1/10/2012	39.28	9.43	9.43	22.89	0.71	16.89	0.00	1.38
South Carolina	Primary	1/21/2012	27.85	16.97	40.42	12.98	0.42	0.00	0.00	1.36
Florida	Primary	1/31/2012	46.40	13.35	31.93	7.02	0.41	0.37	0.00	0.52
Missouri	Primary	2/7/2012	25.30	55.20	0.00	12.20	1.00	0.40	0.70	5.20
Arizona	Primary	2/28/2012	46.87	27.05	16.02	8.61	0.40	0.00	0.00	1.04
Michigan	Primary	2/28/2012	41.10	37.87	6.53	11.63	0.00	0.00	0.00	2.88
Georgia	Primary	3/6/2012	25.91	19.55	47.19	6.56	0.00	0.00	0.00	0.79
Massachusetts	Primary	3/6/2012	72.05	12.06	4.60	9.53	0.27	0.61	0.00	0.89
Ohio	Primary	3/6/2012	37.96	36.95	9.33	14.60	0.62	0.53	0.00	0.00
Oklahoma	Primary	3/6/2012	28.05	33.80	27.48	9.63	0.45	0.26	0.33	0.00
Tennessee	Primary	3/6/2012	28.06	37.11	23.96	9.04	0.35	0.00	0.34	1.13
Vermont	Primary	3/6/2012	39.45	23.61	8.13	25.29	0.89	1.97	0.00	0.64
Virginia	Primary	3/6/2012	59.54	0.00	0.00	40.46	0.00	0.00	0.00	0.00
Alabama	Primary	3/13/2012	28.99	34.50	29.30	4.98	0.30	0.17	0.27	1.49
Mississippi	Primary	3/13/2012	30.66	32.73	31.15	4.40	0.46	0.00	0.33	0.27
Illinois	Primary	3/20/2012	46.69	35.01	7.98	9.32	0.60	0.00	0.00	0.40
Louisiana	Primary	3/24/2012	26.69	48.99	15.91	6.15	0.51	0.00	0.33	1.41
District of Columbia	Primary	4/3/2012	70.08	0.00	10.93	12.17	0.00	6.82	0.00	0.00
Maryland	Primary	4/3/2012	49.26	28.72	10.96	9.50	0.45	0.60	0.00	0.51
Wisconsin	Primary	4/3/2012	44.03	36.83	5.84	11.15	0.00	0.65	0.77	0.74
Connecticut	Primary	4/24/2012	67.43	6.83	10.30	13.48	0.00	0.00	0.00	1.96
Delaware	Primary	4/24/2012	56.46	5.91	27.08	10.55	0.00	0.00	0.00	0.00
New York	Primary	4/24/2012	62.72	10.02	12.65	14.61	0.00	0.00	0.00	0.00
Pennsylvania	Primary	4/24/2012	57.70	18.36	10.41	13.08	0.00	0.00	0.00	0.44
Rhode Island	Primary	4/24/2012	63.02	5.66	6.04	23.85	0.00	0.00	0.00	1.42

(Continued)

TABLE 1-3 (Continued)

State		Date	Romney	Santorum	Gingrich	Paul	Perry	Huntsman	Bachmann	Other
Indiana	Primary	5/8/2012	64.61	13.43	15.50	6.47	0.00	0.00	0.00	0.00
North Carolina	Primary	5/8/2012	65.62	10.39	7.64	11.12	0.00	0.00	0.00	0.00
West Virginia	Primary	5/8/2012	69.56	12.09	6.29	11.04	0.00	0.00	0.00	1.01
Nebraska	Primary	5/15/2012	70.46	13.85	5.16	9.92	0.00	0.00	0.00	0.61
Oregon	Primary	5/15/2012	70.91	9.39	5.37	12.78	0.00	0.00	0.00	1.55
Arkansas	Primary	5/22/2012	68.39	13.33	4.89	13.39	0.00	0.00	0.00	0.00
Kentucky	Primary	5/22/2012	66.77	8.87	5.95	12.53	0.00	0.00	0.00	5.88
Texas	Primary	5/29/2012	69.09	7.97	4.71	12.02	0.00	0.60	0.83	4.78
California	Primary	6/5/2012	79.07	5.28	3.72	10.29	0.00	0.00	0.00	1.63
Montana	Primary	6/5/2012	68.43	8.93	4.35	14.40	0.00	0.00	0.00	3.88
New Jersey	Primary	6/5/2012	81.05	5.22	3.11	10.35	0.00	0.00	0.00	0.28
New Mexico	Primary	6/5/2012	73.17	10.56	5.88	10.39	0.00	0.00	0.00	0.00
South Dakota	Primary	6/5/2012	66.23	11.43	3.91	13.02	0.00	0.00	0.00	5.42
Utah	Primary	6/26/2012	93.05	1.48	0.47	4.75	0.00	0.00	0.00	0.24

Source: Adapted from "Dave Leip's Atlas of U.S. Presidential Elections," http://www.uselectionatlas.org. Compiled by authors.

Note: Missouri held both a primary (on February 7) and a caucus (which ran March 15–24). The results from the primary are adapted from the Missouri Secretary of State's Office, www.sos.mo.gov. No results from the March caucus have been released (as caucus-goers cast votes for delegates rather than in preference of any candidates) and, as such, are not reported. Puerto Rico held a primary on March 18 for which no results are reported.

He did something similar to what Jimmy Carter did on the Democratic side in 1976 (and then many others followed), which was to focus his efforts on Iowa almost to the exclusion of every other aspect of the campaign. And like Carter, Santorum emerged as a contender, doing so only in the very last week or so before the caucuses. Initial counts had him a close second to Romney there, which later turned out to be a very narrow victory (a 34 "vote" edge). His rise in the polls thereafter first caught him up to a second-place tie with Gingrich until South Carolina, and then, with Gingrich's fall and the end of all but Paul's contestation of Romney, a rise into strong second place and, briefly, even first place among Republicans. He quickly fell back after Romney won Florida, but remained solidly in second place among Republican partisans. He was unable to capitalize on his emergence in part because he was not organized to campaign in many states, and thus his needed "knockout victories" over Romney never materialized. Facing a primary in his home state of Pennsylvania, where polls showed he had a good chance of losing, and with his three-year-old daughter, who suffers from a rare genetic disorder, having a relapse, Santorum ended his campaign.

Why was Romney able to withstand such a barrage of contenders? Three reasons stand out. That Romney was unable to convince the right wing of the party that he supported their views was not all negative. The right wing was concerned precisely because he was virtually uncontested in securing the support of the rest of the Republican Party, the more moderate conservatives.[30] Thus, he had a solid base that none of the conservative contenders could touch (a base that could be augmented by plausible claims that, as the more moderate alternative, he alone stood the best chance to defeat Obama). Second, for reasons detailed above, all the conservative alternatives had flaws that kept them from being the one of their group to have lasting power as *the* conservative choice. Perhaps Santorum finally achieved that status, if for no other reason than no one else was left. But that came so late that Romney's final major advantage took over. His experience, early start, and strong campaign organization permitted him to build campaign organizations in virtually every state. No other candidate even came close to matching his ability to seek delegates everywhere in the country. With the exception of the Minnesota caucuses, in no other state did he poll under 20 percent support, and he rarely dipped under 40 percent of the primary vote outside the South, and then only barely. Even there he held at least a quarter of the vote and handily won the biggest delegate catch there, Florida. As a result, his march toward 50 percent of the delegates was inexorable.

The Republican National Convention

That Romney's victory was inexorable did not mean it was rapid. As we discussed earlier (and see Figure 1-2), the reversal of front-loading, combined with a candidate that a major part of the party was slow to endorse, meant that the campaign lasted into June. Even as competitors backed away, Romney was unable to turn his full attention away from the nomination and toward the general election campaign. Of course, he was able to begin to prepare for the fall, and especially for the national party convention, which essentially is the transition to the general election campaign, even if unable to give it his undivided attention.

Conventions no longer have a decision-making role in choosing a presidential nominee. The public effectively chooses that nominee. It is true that the delegates play little role as long as a candidate wins a majority of delegates before the convention, as they have in all contests since 1972, and thus it is possible they may have a genuine decision to make some day. But as we described above, there is good reason to think that this eventuality is unlikely in the foreseeable future. As such, the convention can be seen more as the opening of the general election campaign than as the decision point of the nomination campaign.

All three major decisions made at the convention have become general election events. The platform is worked out in advance of the convention to reduce the chances of controversy at the convention itself and to ensure it reflects the views that the nominee wants to run on in the fall. The selection of the vice presidential running mate has long been the choice of the presidential nominee, and it is seen as the first major presidential-like decision by the soon-to-be-nominee, who all but invariably makes that decision in public deliberations well before the convention. In this case, Romney chose Rep. Paul Ryan (WI) to unite the party behind a young conservative known for policymaking, especially budget-related policies. The rest of the national convention is the stage on which the party and its nominees present themselves to the nation. Their acceptance speeches provide the now-formal nominees with the opportunity to speak at length to the entire nation alone on the stage.

In 2012, the Republicans held their convention late in August in Tampa, Florida. It may be remembered as the convention affected by Hurricane Isaac (which fortunately only sideswiped Tampa) and which led to the cancellation of the first day's events after a ten-minute opening session. However, its timing had other effects that may have been more consequential to the Romney campaign.

Presidents running for reelection may value a convention late in the summer, as a direct beginning of them moving on to the campaign trail in the fall. After all, the president gets to run for reelection in the best way possible and can do so for a full four years—that way is by being the president. The challenger cannot contest in that way. Indeed, presidential candidates remain constrained to separate nomination and general election campaign funds, so the money that Romney raised to win the nomination was not available for running against Obama, and, of course, he had to keep raising and spending nomination campaign funds until he actually had the nomination in hand. But the more important effect was almost certainly that Romney remained a candidate, while Obama remained an active president, and it was not really until the fall campaign formally began—at the conventions themselves—that Romney was able to be on equal footing with Obama, simply as their parties' nominees for president.

Chapter 2

The General Election Campaign

Once they have been nominated, candidates choose their general election campaign strategies based on their perceptions of what the electorate wants, the relative strengths and weaknesses of their opponents and themselves, and their chances of winning. A candidate who is convinced that he has a dependable lead may choose strategies very different from those used by a candidate who believes he is seriously behind. A candidate who believes that an opponent has significant weaknesses is more likely to run an aggressive, attacking campaign than one who does not perceive such weaknesses.

After the 2012 conventions, the race was close. Most observers, and both candidates' organizations, believed that either President Barack Obama or Mitt Romney could win and that the campaign could really make a difference. Chapters 4 through 8 of this book will consider in detail the impact of particular factors (including issues and evaluations of Obama's job performance) on the voters' decisions. This chapter will provide an overview of the campaign— an account of its course and a description of the context within which strategic decisions were made.

THE STRATEGIC CONTEXT AND CANDIDATES' CHOICES

One aspect of the strategic context that candidates must consider is the track record of the parties in recent presidential elections. In presidential races the past is certainly not entirely prologue, but it is relevant. From this perspective, the picture was slightly more encouraging for the Democrats than for the Republicans. From 1952 through 2008 there had been fifteen presidential elections, and the Republicans had won nine of them. On the other hand, the Democrats had won three of the last five races since 1996, and in 2000 they secured a narrow popular-vote margin despite falling short in the electoral vote.

The nature of the American system for electing presidents requires that we examine the state-by-state pattern of results. U.S. voters do not directly vote for president or vice president. Rather, they vote for a slate of electors pledged to support a presidential and a vice presidential candidate. Moreover, in every state except Maine and Nebraska, the entire slate of electors that receives the most popular votes is selected. In no state is a majority of the vote required. Since the 1972 election, Maine has used a system in which the plurality-vote winner for the whole state wins two electoral votes. In addition, the plurality-vote winner in each of Maine's two House districts receives that district's single electoral vote. Beginning in 1992, Nebraska allocated its five electoral votes in a similar manner: the statewide plurality-vote winner gained two votes, and each of the state's three congressional districts awarded one vote on a plurality basis.[1]

If larger states used the district plan employed by Maine and Nebraska, the dynamics of the campaign would be different. For example, candidates might target specific congressional districts and would probably campaign in all large states, regardless of how well they were doing in the statewide polls. But given the winner-take-all rules employed in forty-eight states and the District of Columbia, candidates cannot safely ignore the pattern of past state results. A state-by-state analysis of the five presidential elections from 1992 through 2008 suggests that the Democrats had reason to be hopeful about the effort to win the 270 electoral votes required for victory in 2012.

As Figure 2-1 reveals, eighteen states plus the District of Columbia voted Democratic in all five of these elections. Only thirteen states were equally loyal to the GOP. (See Chapter 4 on long-term voting patterns.) These consistently loyal states provided a prospective balance of 242 electoral votes for the Democrats to only 102 for the Republicans. Less problematic for the GOP candidates were the next groups of states. Six states voted Republican in every election but one, with a total of 69 electoral votes. Balancing these were only three states with 15 electoral votes that supported the Democrats in four of the five contests. Thus, if each of these states' political leanings were categorized solely on the basis of the last five elections, one might expect that 257 electoral votes were likely to go to the Democrats in 2012, while only 171 were as likely to go to the Republicans, placing Obama 86 votes ahead of Romney and only 13 votes short of the number required to win.

If this past pattern persisted during the 2012 election, the GOP ticket would have been at a serious disadvantage. But, of course, things were not that simple, and many factors made Republican chances considerably better than they looked based on these numbers. Most obviously, they had *won* two of the three previous elections, and the loss in 2008 occurred in the context of the worst economic downturn since the Great Depression, for which many blamed President Bush and his party. Moreover, the economic recovery was modest and many potential voters were unhappy with the president's performance generally and his stewardship of the economy in particular.

FIGURE 2-1   States That Voted Democratic in at Least Four out of Five Elections, 1992–2008, with Number of Electoral Votes

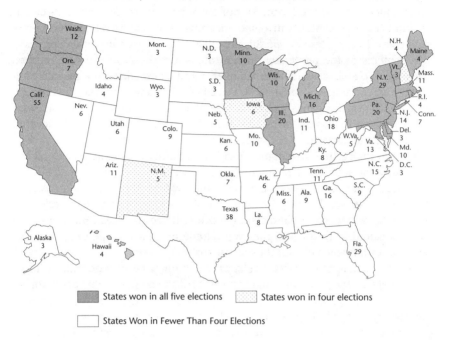

Source: Compiled by authors.

Thus, in the view of most observers, either party could win, and both campaign organizations saw virtually the same set of states determining the outcome. These would be the "battleground" states, where both campaign organizations would concentrate the lion's share of their time, money, and effort. Indeed, even before the beginning of 2012 the two parties had already focused their attention on a set of twelve or thirteen states, and most of the other states would be largely ignored until election day.[2] The larger states in this group— particularly Florida, Michigan, Ohio, and Pennsylvania—would be the main focus of their efforts. Many of the non-battleground states, on the other hand— even large ones like California, New York, and Texas—would see little evidence that a presidential campaign was in progress. A state perspective focused on the electoral college would dominate the strategy of the 2012 campaign.[3]

POLITICAL CONTEXT, OVERALL STRATEGY, AND OPENING MOVES

The strategic choices of candidates and parties are shaped by the particular context of the election. One feature of that context is whether an incumbent is running.

Incumbent races are different from contests without incumbents. They tend to unfold in a regular pattern, and the first stage of the pattern centers on the public's attitudes toward the current occupant of the White House. As we will discuss in detail in Chapter 7, elections involving incumbents tend to be referenda on presidential performance. From 1956 through 2000 (a time when we have dependable measurements of the public's evaluation of the president's performance), there were nine elections in which an incumbent president could stand for reelection. (In three other elections—1960, 1988, and 2000—the incumbent was constitutionally ineligible to run again.) In five of those elections, the president had approval ratings above 50 percent during the spring before the vote—that is, before the general election campaign, and even well before the selection of the opposing nominee by his party's convention. In all five instances, the incumbent won comfortably. On the other hand, the incumbent's approval was below 50 percent in four cases. In all of those instances, he either withdrew from the race or lost.[4] A tenth incumbent race was 2004, when President George W. Bush sought reelection. Between the beginning of March and the end of July of that year, Bush's approval rating measured by the Gallup poll ranged between 46 and 53 percent.[5] The outcome was a narrow victory for the incumbent.

These data suggest that Obama's approval rating was an important indicator of his prospects for reelection, and in early 2012 the news was decidedly mixed. Using the same window of March 1–July 31 used for Bush, the approval ratings from twenty-one polls by five major polling agencies ranged from 41 percent to 52 percent, with an average of 48 percent.[6] Thus the president's standing was right on the historical borderline between victory and defeat, confirming the prospects for a real contest that either major party could potentially win. This moved the race into the second stage of the pattern of incumbent races, in which the public evaluates the opposing candidate and makes a judgment on whether he is a plausible alternative to the incumbent. In years when the incumbent's approval is quite high (e.g., 1956, 1964), the electorate doesn't seriously consider the challenger and the race is effectively over before it begins. Clearly 2012 was not to be one of those cases, and Mitt Romney would have the opportunity to make his case for election.[7]

The Obama campaign's strategic planning started long before 2012. In fact, it began just days after the 2008 victory. A few dozen aides gathered in Chicago to conduct an extensive invesigation of the 2008 effort, producing a 538-page report that shaped preparation for the reelection bid.[8] The staff focused on rallying and turning out Obama supporters on election day. We will consider those efforts later in this chapter. They also planned strategy for countering the Republicans' campaign. Once it was clear that Romney would be the opponent, James Messina (the Obama campaign's manager) proposed an unconventional approach. At a strategy meeting in May 2012, he advocated that the campaign launch an extensive negative ad campaign against Romney. This idea was contrary to accepted practice, which was to start slowly and to emphasize positive messages at the outset. Moreover, since all campaigns have limited resources, this tactic carried considerable risk. Witnesses at the meeting claimed that Messsina said: "If it doesn't work, we're not going to have enough money to go have a second theory in the fall."[9]

The president endorsed the plan, and the ad campaign was launched. The negative blitz focused on Romney's business record and personal finances. It put Romney on the defensive, forcing his campaign to counter the Democrats' charges instead of being able to focus on weaknesses in Obama's record. Moreover, because of the demands of his nomination contest, the Romney campaign would be short on money until the GOP convention confirmed his nomination, permitting him to use general-election funds. Republican super PACs, which could spend independently, partially compensated for Romney's money squeeze, but their ads were mostly anti-Obama rather than pro-Romney. The Romney efforts were also helped by a $20 million dollar loan to the campaign secured by a finance aide and some close advisors to the candidate. However, the ad purchases that these funds permitted were limited compared to those of the opponent.[10] Romney also had to contend with other advantages that accrue to an incumbent. Obama's campaign ran ads at the end of April questioning Romney's likely performance in a national security crisis and attacking him for sending jobs overseas. Then on May 2, the anniversary of the death of Osama bin Laden, the president was in Kabul, Afghanisan, reminding people of his responsibilities as commander-in-chief.[11]

Recognizing that the economic environment would set the stage for a difficult reelection race, the Obama forces also focused on shaping the electorate through registration and turnout efforts, just as they had in 2008. It was with regard to this aspect of the campaign that the views of Obama's and Romney's campaign advisors differed most. The president and his people believed that they could repeat their advantage of 2008 and produce a group of voters in which Democrats outnumbered both Republicans and independents, and in which minoritiy voters (especially blacks and Latinos) were robustly represented. Republican planners, on the other hand, anticipated that because of the slow economic recovery and public dissatisfaction with other aspects of Obama's performance, the electorate would more resemble that of 2010. They thought that turnout by minorities and younger citizens would disproportionately decline compared to 2008 and that pro-GOP segments like older voters would make up a larger portion of the votes cast.

Given the expectations for a close contest, there was, as we mentioned above, a strong focus on the battleground states during the Democrats' planning. If the president could carry all of the states that John Kerry had in his losing race in 2004, they would provide 246 electoral votes (down from Kerry's 251 due to reapportionment after the 2010 census). Due to the size of this potential bloc of votes, Obama had a number of posssible paths to get to the necessary 270.[12] The simplest was Florida. Its 29 votes would provide more than the necessary margin. He had carried it 51 to 48 percent in 2008 and had devoted a good deal of attention to it in the past four years. A second strategy, also oriented toward the South, would be to carry both Virginia and North Carolina, with 28 combined votes. These, too, Obama had won the last time, but his margin in North Carolina was only 0.3 percent, so this course seemed difficult. Also challenging was the Midwestern plan that sought both Ohio and Iowa, adding 24 votes for a total of exactly 270, because the president had been behind in Ohio polls for much of the previous year. Finally there was the Western scenario. In this one Iowa would be combined with Colorado, Nevada, and New Mexico. These states totaled 26 votes and were another set the Democrats had carried in 2008. Of course, the Obama campaign did not have to choose among these plans; they could all be pursued simultaneously. The point was that any one of them, or even partial achievement of two or more, would be enough to win.

For the Romney camp the plan was more general. The Republican candidate and his advisors wanted to make the election a referendum on Obama and his performance. With unemployment hovering above 8 percent of the workforce, the president's approval rating at about 50 percent, and a majority of the public telling pollsters that the country was on the wrong track, the GOP believed that the best course was to criticize the president resolutely for his failures and to paint Romney, with his extensive business experience, as the man who could do better. This plan was basically designed to block Obama's paths to success and potentially to carve off one or more of the former Kerry states (such as Michigan, Minnesota, Pennsylvania, or Wisconisn) that seemed like they might potentially be vulnerable.

FROM THE CONVENTIONS TO THE DEBATES

The Conventions and September Events

The two months before election day were bracketed by two hurricanes, Isaac and Sandy. The former struck the Gulf area in late August, forcing postponement or cancellation of the events planned for the first day of the Republican convention in Tampa, Florida. The convention produced a very conservative platform that proposed reshaping Medicare so that those who were covered would receive a fixed amount of money each year to buy their own coverage, and contending that "the unborn child has a fundamental individual right to life that cannot be infringed."[13] It also said, "We will create humane procedures to encourage illegal aliens to return home voluntarily, while enforcing the law against those who overstay their visas," and it opposed gay marriage and restrictions on guns.[14]

Romney's acceptance speech mixed attacks on the persident's record with positive elements of his own biography. Regarding Obama he said: "You know that there's something wrong with the kind of job he's done as president when the best feeling you had was the day you voted for him." And Romney contended: "This president can tell us it was someone else's fault. This president can tell us that the next four years he'll get it right. But this president cannot tell us that you are better off today than when he took office."[15] Romney particularly sought to appeal to female voters, recalling that his mother had run for the Senate because she thought that women should have as much say as men in the nation's decisions.

The Democrats met in Charlotte, North Carolina, the following week. Their platform reflected the ideological polarization between the parties. It endorsed gay marriage for the first time and reaffirmed support for abortion rights. The Democrats opposed attempts to "privatize or voucherize" Medicare and called climate change legislation (which the Republicans opposed) a top priority.[16] The high point of the Democrats' gathering turned out not to be Obama's acceptance speech, but rather a speech by former President Bill Clinton the night before that delighted the crowd in the hall and received positive reactions from television viewers. Clinton took on the arguments the GOP had made at their convention, arguing that the "Republican argument against the president's re-election was pretty simple: We left him a total mess, he hasn't finished cleaning it up yet, so fire him and put us back in."[17] He offered a point-by-point defense of the president's record, including a detailed argument for "Obamacare," that was extensively laced with statistics, yet the audience responded enthusiastically. He criticized the Republicans for misrepresenting the president's record and for their ideological rigidity, saying: "They think government is always the enemy, they're always right, and compromise is weakness."[18] The Nielsen Company reported that an estimated 25.1 million people watched Clinton's speech, even though it was scheduled opposite a professional football game, which drew 25 percent fewer people during the speech.[19]

The following night President Obama accepted the nomination for a second term. He defended his record and said that he was not offering a path forward that was "quick or easy," but he painted the choice as fundamentally about the role of government. He said: "This is what the election comes down to. Over and over, we've been told by our opponents that bigger tax cuts and fewer regulations are the only way, that since government can't do everything, it should do almost nothing."[20] Obama expressed pride in what had been accomplished and strong hope for the country's future, and he asked for the votes of those who shared his vision.

It is often the case that nominating conventions provide a boost in the polls to the candidate of the party holding them. After all, the party and its candidate receive a lot of attention and they largely control what is seen and heard. In 2012, with the conventions so close together, it is difficult to be sure of the effects, but data from the Gallup daily tracking poll appear to show essentially no gain for the GOP, followed by a small (but transitory) gain for Obama.[21] The contest remained close with seven weeks left. Then on September 17, a story broke that seized the public's attention. *Mother Jones* magazine released a video recorded earlier in the year at a meeting between Romney and a group of donors. In it Romney said that 47 percent of the people would vote for Obama "no matter what." These were people

> who are dependent on government, who believe they are victims, who believe the government has a responsibility to care for them. . . . These are

people who pay no income tax. . . . And so my job is not to worry about those people. I'll never convince them that they should take personal responsibility and care for their lives.[22]

Not surprisingly, the video and the reports on it produced strong public reactions and attacks from Democrats. Obama's campaign manager, Jim Messina, said: "It's hard to serve as president for all Americans when you've disdainfully written off half the nation."[23] Romney spokespersons sought to avoid direct comments on the videos, trying to defend the candidate's record more generally. But the campaign staff knew they were in trouble, and the polls began to reflect that.

"We had struggled pretty dramatically in September," said Neil Newhouse, Mr. Romney's pollster. "The 47 percent remark came out, and that was on top of the bounce that Obama got from his convention, so needless to say September was not our best month. It showed in the data. It was grim."[24]

The shifts in the polls over the two weeks following the release of the video launched a controversy that would continue until election day: charges (mainly from conservatives) that the polls were inaccurate because they were "skewed." The disagreement stemmed from different opinions about the expected nature of the electorate, as we mentioned above. Polling organizations weight their interviews based on predictions about the demographic mix of the electorate that will vote. The Republicans claimed that the public polls rested on the incorrect assumption that the 2012 electorate would be similar to that of 2008. "I don't think [the polls] reflect the composition of what 2012 is going to look like," said Neil Newhouse.[25] Newhouse claimed that in 2012 "you have a more enthused and energetic Republican electorate. . . . So instead of a 7 [percentage point advantage for Democrats], I expect something smaller than that."[26]

The Debates

Regardless of the precise standings of the candidates, Romney's campaign staff thought they were in trouble in September, and the main chance they saw for turning things around was the upcoming first presidential debate on October 3. And in that context, they did see hope. Romney's senior strategists argued that Obama would underestimate their candidate and fail to prepare adequately. Moreover, the Democrats' negative campaign would lead the public to approach the debate with low expectations for Romney that he could exceed.[27] The GOP candidate devoted a lot of time and effort to debate preparation. Practice sessions were conducted with Senator Rob Portman of Ohio playing the role of the president. The final practice was conducted with Romney in full makeup in a room that replicated the hall where the real session would take place. The Sunday before the event, a group of top advisors gathered in Boston to reassure the candidate, and former president George W. Bush phoned to offer encouragement.[28]

Obama's advisors saw the same potential problems for their candidate that the GOP advisors had. Ronald Klain, a strategist who had assisted Democrats in debate preparation for two decades, warned Obama that incumbent presidents almost always lose the first debate. Moreover, Romney had gone through twenty debates over the previous year, while the president was out of practice. But Obama was unconvinced, and when he went to a Nevada resort for a few days of reparation he ducked out one day for a visit to Hoover Dam.[29]

In the actual event, it quickly became apparent that the expectations of both parties' strategists were correct. Romney was relaxed and confident, projecting a moderate image. Obama, on the other hand, was hesitant and halting in his statements. Romney took positions that were more moderate than those he had taken in the primaries and in previous weeks during the campaign. He stated that he did not support tax cuts for the wealthy even though he previously said that his tax plan would cut taxes for everyone, "including the top 1 percent." And when asked if there was too much government regulation, he responded: "regulation is essential."[30] The president failed to effectively challenge Romney for being inconsistent. This may, in part, have been due to advice he had received from advisors to avoid confrontational exchanges with his opponent because they might alienate voters and damage their good opinion of the president.[31] Those people undoubtedly regretted that advice on debate night. The audience for the debate was substantial. The Nielsen ratings indicated that 67.2 million people had seen it on television, the largest audience for a first debate since 1980, and there were additional viewers on the Internet.[32] And their view of the outcome was unequivocal: in a CNN/ORC International poll, Romney was seen as the winner by 42 points, 67 to 25 percent.[33]

Next in the debate sequence was the vice presidential debate on October 11. Not surprisingly, it received less attention than the presidential events. Romney's running mate, Rep. Paul Ryan of Wisconsin, sought to defend the GOP nominee and to soften his image with personal stories, but Vice President Joe Biden frequently interrupted with disagreements and comments, including attacks on Ryan's proposal to alter the Medicare program that he had included in the House Republicans' budget proposal. Biden also mocked Ryan for attacking and opposing Obama's economic stimulus proposal and then seeking funds for his constituents under that plan.[34]

Five days later, the second presidential debate took place. This time Obama did not hold back from the attack: the exchanges were sharp, and the tensions between the candidates were apparent. The president began with an attack that his campaign had been using widely in the industrial Midwestern states, attacking Romney for his opposition to the administration's bailout of the major auto companies in 2009. Then during his closing statement, the president criticized his opponent for his remarks about "the 47 percent." Obama said: "When he said behind closed doors that 47 percent of the country considers themselves victims who refuse personal responsibility—think about who he was talking about."[35] Throughout the debate Romney attacked Obama's record of performance, mentioning multiple times the number of people who were unemployed. In the aftermath, the public's view of the results were much closer than after the first debate, with respondents to a CNN/ORC International poll choosing Obama as the winner by 46 to 39 percent.[36]

The final debate, on October 22, was supposed to focus on foreign policy, but the discussion frequently veered off to domestic issues, including the economy, the auto bailout, and Romney's tax plan. Romney attacked the administration for being weak and ineffective, especially in the Middle East. He criticized the president for reducing the number of ships in the Navy to the lowest level in a century. Obama admitted that the country had fewer ships, but he went on: "Well, Governor, we also have fewer horses and bayonets, because the nature of our military's changed. We have these things called aircraft carriers where planes land on them. We have these ships that go underwater, nuclear submarines."[37] The president also attacked his opponent for having foreign policy and other views rooted in the past. He said: "you seem to want to import the foreign policy of the 1980s, just like the social policies of the 1950s, and the economic policies of the 1920s."[38] After the debate, polls gave the edge to Obama. A CNN poll picked him as the winner with 48 percent to Romney's 40 percent, while a CBS poll of undecided voters had 53 percent saying Obama was the winner, with 23 percent for Romney, and 24 percent saying it was a tie.[39]

The consensus among political scientists is that presidential debates usually do not have a significant impact on a race.[40] The most prominent explanation is that by the time the debates occur, the vast majority of voters have made up their minds and are thus unlikely to have their position reversed by the event. There are, however, a few exceptions where some analysts perceive a greater impact. These include 1960 (Kennedy vs. Nixon), 1976 (Ford vs. Carter), and 1984 (Reagan vs. Mondale). Robert Erikson and Christopher Wlezien took a systematic look at the ten presidential elections with debates (1960 and 1976–2008), comparing the poll standings of candidates before and after the debates. They found that, with one exception, the pre-debate polls were closely matched by the post-debate polls. The exception was 1976, when Carter was already in decline before the debates and the decline persisted. They conclude that debates do not have as great an impact as the conventions (the effect of which they find to be substantial), but that they may have as much or more of an effect than other campaign events.[41] It appears, however, that 2012 may be another exception. Data from Real Clear Politics (which averages results for all major polls over a time interval) shows that on October 3, the day of the first debate, Obama had a 3.1 percentage point lead in the poll averages, while on October 23 (the last debate's date), Romney led by 0.9 points.[42] That was a four-point swing in favor of Romney, and it left the race in doubt with just two weeks to go.

THE END GAME AND THE STRUGGLE OVER TURNOUT

The Final Two Weeks

On October 24, two days after the final debate, Obama launched a tour of a set of eight swing states over two days. Appearing in Denver, Colorado, he attacked

Romney for changing positions so often that voters could not trust him, saying that Romney hoped that the public would come down with "Romnesia" and forget.[43] Other stops on the tour included California (appearing on *The Tonight Show with Jay Leno*), Florida, Virginia, and Ohio. Obama's Ohio efforts focused persistently on his auto bailout plan (which had provided federal funds to prevent General Motors and Chrysler from going bankrupt), and the GOP campaign was worried. The recovery of the auto industry had helped Ohio outperform the national economy, and this helped propel the president to a solid position in polls of the state. So the Republicans sought to counter the president's appeal on the issue. A few days after Obama's visit, the Romney forces debuted a commercial that indicated that "Chrysler, a bailout recipient, is going to begin producing Jeeps in China, leaving the misleading impression that the move would come at the expense of jobs here."[44] The ad provoked a lot of negative reactions. Chrysler called the suggestions that they were moving jobs to China "fantasies," and news media in the state and nationally characterized the ad as misleading. The Democrats countered with their own ad claiming that Romney's assertions were false and reminding voters that the Republican candidate had opposed Obama's bailout plan.[45]

While this dispute was playing out in the Midwest, in the East a diffferent drama was occurring. A storm had been moving up the East Coast, and on Monday, October 29, Hurricane Sandy came ashore at New Jersey and New York. It would be the most damaging storm of the year. The destruction was enormous, closing area airports due to flooding and knocking out power in southern Manhattan and forcing the cancellation of the New York Marathon. Much of the New Jersey coast was devastated. The president immediately promised a strong federal response, cancelling campaign activities. The following day he spoke to victims at a Red Cross office. On Wednesday, Obama toured hard-hit areas with New Jersey's Republican Governor Chris Christie. (Christie had been the keynote speaker at the Republican convention, where he extensively attacked the president and his administration.)

This crisis gave the president the opportunity to be seen dealing with a pressing public problem without being overtly political. It was no surprise that this would yield political benfits in public opinion. What was surprising was the reinforcement of this effect from a most unusual source: Governor Christie. He was effusive in his praise of the president, saying on Fox News that "I have to give the president great credit."[46] He went on to say that Obama's response had been "outstanding" and that "he deserves my praise, and he will get it no matter what the calendar says." When asked if Romney might be invited to tour the state as well, Christie responded: "I have no idea, nor am I in the least concerned or interested. I've a job to do here in New Jersey that's much bigger than presidential politics, and I could (not) care less about any of that stuff."[47] Obama returned the favor, telling people in an emergency shelter: "I want you to know that your governor is working overtime to make sure that as soon as possible that everything can get back to normal," and later praised Christie's "extraordinary leadership."[48]

Obama's and Romney's campaigning were interrupted by the hurricane crisis, but others continued in their stead. Chief among these for the Democrats was Bill Clinton. The former president began working on Obama's behalf shortly after the party's convention. For example, he appeared in Florida on September 11, reprising many details of his convention speech. There he said: "The test is not whether you think everything is hunky-dory; if that were the test, the president would vote against himself. The test is whether he's taking us in the right direction, and the answer to that is yes."[49] But after the October decline, he offered to step up his efforts. The day after the last debate Clinton met with Jim Messina and offered to campaign for the president every one of the last ten days of the campaign. Then, after viewing his proposed schedule, he called Messina and said: "I can do more than this."[50]

At the close of the campaign, the economic news remained mixed. On the Friday before election day, the Labor Department announced that 171,000 seasonally adjusted jobs were added in October, about the average since July and double the rate in the spring. The unemployment rate increased slightly from 7.8 percent to 7.9 percent, mainly because more Americans were looking for work.[51]

Mobilizing the Vote

In 2008, the Democrats' voter identification and mobilization efforts had been very successful.[52] But in 2012 they took a big leap forward in terms of technology and effort. When Jim Messina took on the job of campaign manager, he said:"We are going to measure every single thing in this campaign."[53] Messina "hired an analytics department five times the size that of the 2008 campaign."[54] These analysts believed that the product of their efforts—their data—was the principal advantage Obama had over his opponent, and they guarded it diligently. The operation was even separated to a degree from the rest of the Chicago headquarters, in a windowless room within the office.

Despite the success of 2008, one problem the campaign had was too many databases. Fund-raising lists were separate from get-out-the-vote lists. So over the eighteen months beginning in early 2009, "the campaign started over, creating a single massive system that could merge the information collected from pollsters, fundraisers, field workers, and consumer databases as well as social media and mobile contacts with the main Democratic voter files in the swing states."[55] This enormous compilation permitted the camaign to do more than just isolate individuals who might support the president. It made it possible to predict who was likely to donate online or by mail. They could also model who might volunteer. They experimented with different messages for different groups of people, and then tracked the results and used them to make future larger appeals more efficient.

Since Obama had no primary contest, the main use for the database early on was to raise money, with more success than many thought possible. The core device was the use of dozens of targeted email appeals each day. The staff "discovered that people who signed up for the campaign's Quick Donate program, which allowed repeat giving online via text message without having to re-enter credit-card information, gave about four times as much as other donors. So the program was expanded and incentivized."[56] The Obama operation was often able to get initial small donors to give again, and to increase the amount when they did. The campaign eventually amassed a total of 812,858 donors, 69 percent of whom began with a donation of $200 or less. Romney's campaign, on the other hand, had only about half as many donors (393,603), a smaller percentage of whom started with donations under $200.[57] The Democrats were also better able to induce repeat donations: the average number of itemized contributions per donor to Obama in 2012 was 5.01 (up from 3.75 four years earlier), while the average for Romney was 2.26.

The fund-raising data, however, show that "not all dollars are created equal." The Romney campaign "raised as much as Obama's once you count joint fundraising committee and party money [about $1 billion for each party]—and more if you count allied Super Pacs. But the fundraising did little to mobilize." Moreover, because a larger share of Obama's funds went directly to his campaign committee, they were worth more. "Political parties cannot take advantage of advertising price discounts (lowest unit rate costs) that are available only to candidates."

In the last month, Obama's massive trove of data was refocused on the turnout effort. The campaign amassed polling data on 29,000 people in Ohio alone.[58] This sample permitted more detailed analysis on demographic groups than had usually been possible in campaigns. The polling and voter-contact data were also used to run electoral simulations nightly to estimate the chances of carrying individual states. The results were used to allocate resources. The data also permitted "the first-ever attempt at using Facebook on a mass scale to replicate the door-knocking efforts of field organizers." Persons connected with the Obama efforts were encouraged to download a phone app. Near the end of the campaign, those people

> were sent messages with pictures of their friends in swing states. They
> were told to click on a button to automatically urge those targeted voters
> to take certain actions, such as registering to vote, voting early or getting
> to the polls. The campaign found that roughly 1 in 5 people contacted by
> a Facebook pal acted on the request.[59]

The Romney campaign, too, sought to build its get-out-the-vote effort, also trying to employ social media. The campaign's digital director, Zac Moffatt, said: "We have digital staff in every target state, with regional digital directors for every part of the country." And while they trailed Obama in Facebook "likes," 8.6 million to 30.6 million, they asserted that a higher proportion of their followers discussed the presidential contest (30 percent to 10 percent).[60] These efforts were supplemented by the work and independent spending of conservative super PACs. For example, Americans for Prosperity, funded by the Koch brothers, a pair of billionaire businessmen, said in late October that it had "more than 100 paid field workers nationwide and about 5,000 volunteers to go door to door. The group plans to spend $130 million this year on all activities, up from $14 million four years ago."[61]

One aspect of the turnout efforts was a focus on demographic groups, and in this connection the greatest focus was on Latinos. Obama had won about two-thirds of this group's votes in 2008, and the Republicans recognized they had to increase their appeal to Latino voters, who in 2012 constituted about 10.4 percent of the voting-age population of the United States. One part of their strategy was to emphasize the slow economic recovery and focus on social issues because poll data indicated that Latinos were more conservative on those matters than most Democratic voters. The GOP's task was complicated by the conservative stands on immigration of Romney and his opponents during the primary season. Romney tried to moderate his position in the general election, but with limited success. The Democrats also focused strongly on the Latino vote, and their advantage was reinforced when in late June Obama adopted a policy of blocking the deportation of many young illegal immigrants who had been brought to the United States as children. A *Wall Street Journal*/NBC poll showed that the proportion of Latinos nationally who said they had "very positive" views of Obama jumped ten percentage points (to 41 percent) over the previous month, and among this group Obama led Romney 66 to 26 percent.[62]

Another aspect of the get-out-the-vote efforts involved litigation. As in the 2008 race, Republicans in many states sought to block efforts to make registration easier and to increase voter identification requirements. They also tried to restrict early voting. Many of these efforts were met by lawsuits from Democrats and others concerned about voting rights. The restrictions often did not fare very well with the courts. Lawrence Norden of the Brennan Center for Justice at New York University Law School said: "Every voter restriction challenged this year has been either enjoined, blocked, or weakened." This included blocked or delayed voter ID laws in Pennsylvania, South Carolina, Texas, and Wisconsin.[63] In addition, an Ohio attempt to cut short early voting was voided by the federal courts. Anticipating a possible photo finish in the race, both parties had marshaled lawyers around the coutry for challenges to vote counts, but the clear result on election day made those plans moot.

The Final Days

As we noted above, on October 23 the Real Clear Politics average of polls showed Romney with a 0.9 percentage point lead. Over the next week the poll average remained at that level, but on October 31 (two days after Hurricane Sandy hit), a spate of new polls showed another shift: the race was tied. Then over the next few days Obama began to open up a small lead, and on election day he led by a margin of 0.7 points in the poll average. It was hardly a safe cushion, and the outcome remained in doubt, but it was an improvement. It left both candidates feeling that victory was withing reach, and the campaigns launched a massive final effort for the last couple of days.

On the Sunday and Monday before election day, the four candidates for president and vice president combined for fourteen stops in eight states each day. On Sunday, Romney made the last of at least fourteen trips to Iowa during the general election. In Des Moines, he asked 4,000 attendees at a rally to reach out to friends who were undecided. His speech continued his frequent argument that Obama had failed to bring the change that he had promised. He said: "You can't measure change in speeches. You measure change in achievements."[64]

Romney had originally planned to end his campaigning Monday night in New Hampshire, where he had a vacation home and where he had announced his candidacy in June 2011. However, with the race so tight he and his staff decided to add two more stops, in Cleveland and Pittsburgh on Tuesday.[65] Various journalists drew different conclusions from these last-minute additions. To some, the visit to Pennsylvania was evidence that the campaign really thought that Romney was going to win because they were expending effort in a state the GOP had not carried in over twenty years.[66] (Pennsylvania polls had shown the race tightening over previous days.) Others, however, saw the choice as a long-shot effort in light of the president's improved position nationally.[67]

Obama's last efforts were as vigorous as Romney's, but they carried with them more nostalgia because this would be his final campaign. In the waning months of the campaign he frequently made reference to "lasts" ("the last debate prep practice," "the last debate"). The crowds were often smaller than they had been four years earlier, "but they are enthusiastic, and he draws energy from them."[68] On Sunday he made another stop in New Hampsire, accompanied by Bill Clinton, where the former president again attacked Romney for frequent switches in his position on the auto bailout.[69] Obama ended the campaign in Des Moines, Iowa, at 10 p.m. after ealier visits to Madison, Wisconsin, and Columbus, Ohio. He made reference to the Iowa caucuses in 2008, and his victory in them that had launched his susccessful effort to secure his party's nomination. There he said: "I've come back to Iowa one more time to ask for your vote. To ask for you to help us finish what we started, because this is where our movement for change began. Right here."[70]

DID THE CAMPAIGN MAKE A DIFFERENCE?

It is appropriate to ask whether the general election campaign made any difference, and the answer depends on the yardstick used to measure the campaign's effects. Did it determine the winner? Did it affect the choices of a substantial number of voters? Did it put issues and candidates' positions clearly before the voters? Would a better campaign by one of the candidates have yielded a different result? Did the campaign produce events that will have a lasting impact on American politics? We cannot provide firm answers to all of these questions, but we can shed light on some of them.

Regarding the outcome and voters' decisions, it seems quite clear that the campaign did indeed have an effect.[71] As noted above, the relative standing of the candidates ebbed and flowed from the conventions to November, and these changes seemed to be linked in part to events in the campaign. The Democrats' convention seemed to give them a boost denied to their opponents, but Obama's lackluster performance in the first debate appeared to reverse the trend. Then, after falling a bit behind, the president seemed to benefit from public reactions to his efforts in response to Hurricane Sandy. Nine percent of respondents to the exit polls indicated that they had made up their minds either on election day or "in the last few days," and Obama won this group by about six points. While we may not be certain of the import of various events during the months after both candidates' nominations, or the precise magnitude of their impact, it seems fair to conclude that either of the major candidates could have won if the voting had taken place at a different date during the period.

Another point is the mere fact of the president's success despite the vastly different political landscape compared to four years earlier. In 2008 the playing field was clearly tilted in favor of the Democrats, with Bush being so unpopular and (relatedly) the economy being so deep in recession. Seventy-five percent of respondents in the exit polls thought the country was on the wrong track. In 2012, on the other hand, the Democrats' previous advantages had significantly dissipated. A majority (52 percent) said in the exit polls that the country was on the wrong track, and 77 percent said that the state of the economy was either not so good or poor. Yet Obama's campaign was able to persuade many voters that most of the responsibility for this state of affairs did not belong to the president. When asked who was more to blame for the current economic problems, 53 percent of respondents said George W. Bush, while only 38 percent named Obama. Finally, the exit polls buttressed the view that Obama's hurricane response helped his cause. Exit-poll results showed that 64 percent said that it was at least a minor factor in their vote, and that group chose Obama 62 percent to 36 percent over Romney. Indeed, 15 percent said it was the most important factor, and among them the president won 73 percent to 26 percent.

Perhaps the best evidence of the campaign's impact relates to turnout. As we said, the Republicans believed that their candidate would win because the electorate in 2012 would be significantly less favorable to the Democrats than the electorate of 2008 had been, while the Democrats were convinced that they could maintain the character of the electorate. Indeed, the GOP conviction remained through the counting on election night. For example, when Fox News concluded at 11:13 p.m. on election night that Obama had won the state of Ohio and the presidency, Karl Rove (Bush's former political advisor and the leader of a major GOP super PAC) confronted and contradicted the network's team of voting analysts on the air.[72] Rove had heard contradictory news from within the Romney operation and was convinced there was a problem. But as it turned out, he was wrong about Ohio and the national electorate. Comparing the 2012 and 2008 exit polls, the proportion claiming to be Democrats was only 1 percent smaller (38 vs. 37 percent), and the proportions of independents and Republicans were the same (29 and 32 percent, respectively). Demographically, the proportion of blacks and Asians was the same as in 2008 (13 and 3 percent, respectively), and the proprtion of Latinos was 1 percent higher (10 vs. 9 percent). Moreover, within that latter group, support for Obama increased from 67 percent to 71 percent. Later analysis by the U.S. Census Bureau indicated that turnout among African Americans exceeded that among whites for the first time on record, 66.2 percent to 64.1 percent.[73] Finally, the proportion of young voters (18–29 years old) also increased a bit, from 18 percent to 19 percent, although their support for the president declined from 66 percent to 60 percent.

The success of the Democrats' mobilization effort is indicated by the turnout data compiled for 2008 and 2012 by Michael McDonald of George Mason University.[74] McDonald and his colleagues show that nationally the overall turnout rate among the eligible population declined by 3.4 points, from 61.6 percent to 58.2 percent. However, the decline was not equal across the states. In particular, the decline was smaller, on average, in the batttleground states. Table 2-1 lists the thirteen battleground states and their turnout in the two elections. The average decline in those states was only 2.1 percent. Those results combined with Obama's success in winning twelve of the thirteen most contested states suggest that the Democrats' turnout operation played a significant role in the president's reelection.

TABLE 2-1 Change in Turnout among the Voting-Eligible Population in Battleground States and Nationally, 2008–2012

	Turnout 2012	Turnout 2008	Change 2008–2012
National	61.6	58.2	−3.4
Colorado	71.0	70.3	−0.7
Florida	66.1	63.5	−2.6
Iowa	69.4	69.9	+0.5
Michigan	69.2	64.7	−4.5
Minnesota	77.8	75.7	−3.1
Nevada	57.0	57.1	+0.1
New Hampshire	71.7	70.1	−1.6
New Mexico	60.9	54.7	−6.2
North Carolina	65.5	64.6	−0.9
Ohio	66.9	64.6	−3.3
Pennsylvania	63.6	59.4	−4.2
Virginia	67.0	66.4	−0.6
Wisconsin	72.4	72.5	+0.1
Average change for thirteen battleground states			−2.1

Source: http://elections.gmu.edu. Compiled by authors.

Finally there is the question of whether a better campaign by a candidate, specifically by Romney, would have led to a different result. Many observers have expressed the view that either a better candidate than Romney, or a better campaign by him, could have carried the race.[75] On the first claim, it is not clear what alternative candidate would have been successful, or whether such a candidate could have won the GOP nomination. Regarding the quality of the campaign, however, the views of the critics seem more plausible. One factor was Romney's decision to seek the nomination by running to the right of his opponents by taking extreme positions on immigration and social issues (e.g., promising to eliminate Planned Parenthood and reverse *Roe v. Wade*, among others). That decision "made the distance he had to travel to get back to the middle just too great," and he waited too long (until the first debate) to make the effort.[76] He was unable to convince enough voters that the moderate persona he portrayed in the final six weeks was genuine.

Of course, as we have indicated, the Obama attacks on Romney were very well planned and effective, and there was nothing he could do to prevent that. But there were other mistakes that played into his opponent's plans and undermined efforts to counter them. Obama sought to portray Romney as a rich "fat cat" who was different from ordinary people and who would be unconcerned with their problems as president, and this approach appeared to work. In the exit polls, 53 percent of respondents said that Romney's policies would generally favor the rich, while 44 percent said Obama's policies would favor the middle class. Certainly the worst gaffe on this score was the remark about the "47 percent," but it wasn't the only one. Romney also refused to make public more than two years of his tax returns (permitting the Democrats to claim he had something to hide) and he resisted supplying details on what deductions he would eliminate in his tax reform plan. These and other similar moves made it difficult for the Romney campaign to make a sufficiently convincing case for replacing the incumbent, despite the public's doubts about Obama. We cannot re-run the campaign to demonstrate that alternative strategies by Romney would have succeeded, but there seems to be a good deal of evidence that a better effort could have been made.

Chapter 3

The Election Results

In the waning days of the campaign, it was clear that the election was likely to be close. The average (mean) of nine national public opinion polls conducted during the final week of the campaign showed Barack Obama with 48.8 percent of the vote and Mitt Romney with 48.1 percent, a virtual dead heat.[1] Indeed, these polls were almost evenly split in their predictions: four predicted an Obama victory (by an average of two points), two predicted a Romney win (by an average of one point), and three reported ties. A series of academic models were similarly split in their predictions, further testifying to the closeness of the race.[2] In October 2012, James E. Campbell published the results of thirteen statistical forecasts for the presidential election.[3] The median prediction from these models gave Obama a slight edge with 50.6 percent of the two-party vote, but the models—like the final week's polls—varied in their predictions. Five of the models forecasted an Obama win, five predicted Romney's election, and three were toss-ups. To be sure, "toss-up" was likely the best appraisal of how the election might play out.

Both campaigns began election day, November 6, optimistic about their chances. Romney started his day at his home in Belmont, Massachusetts. After conducting several radio interviews, the candidate reportedly cleaned out the family refrigerator and took out the trash before donning his suit to join his wife, Ann, in casting their ballots at their local polling station.[4] President Obama did not vote on election day. The president—like an estimated 31.6 percent of Americans—voted early.[5] He had flown to Illinois on October 25 and cast his ballot at the Martin Luther King Community Center, the early voting center in the Obama family's Kenwood neighborhood of Chicago.[6] (Obama is the first presidential candidate in history to make use of early voting; his wife, First Lady Michelle Obama, voted by mail.) Without having to go to the polls and no other scheduled campaign events, Obama found time for one of his election day traditions, a pick-up basketball game with friends. The president did not view the game casually, however; the president invited Chicago Bulls Hall of Famer Scottie Pippin to play on his team. Obama's team won by twenty points; it was the only victory that the president was able to guarantee that day.[7]

As election night passed, reality began to settle in at Mitt Romney's election night party at the Boston Convention Center. The candidate and his closest advisors had been confident that a close race would turn their way and that Romney would be elected the nation's forty-fifth president. Though some national polls in the closing days of the campaign had been trending slightly in favor of President Obama, the Romney campaign was confident that these polls were biased in the president's direction.[8] In their estimation, the composition of the 2012 electorate would not look like the one that elected the president in 2008, when typically underrepresented groups turned out in historic numbers. They were wrong. By 10:45 p.m., "several of Mr. Romney's staff members were assembling in the back of a half-filled ballroom, mumbling about the staggering margins by which they had lost states they had expected to be close."[9] At 11:20 p.m., the television networks called the election for Obama. Romney conceded ninety minutes later.[10]

In the final tally, Obama won 51.1 percent of the popular vote, marking the first time since Franklin D. Roosevelt's victory in 1944 that a Democrat has won a majority of the popular vote in two consecutive elections.[11] Romney won 47.2 percent. Independent and third-party candidates won a negligible share of the vote: 1.7 percent, with Libertarian Gary Johnson garnering 0.99 percent. Obama's victory was much narrower than his election in 2008, when he won 52.9 percent of the popular vote to John McCain's 45.7 percent. In fact, Obama's popular-vote margin in 2012 (3.9 percentage points) was the third smallest popular-vote win for an incumbent in American history.[12] Even so, given that nine of the twenty-seven incumbents who ran for reelection were defeated, reelection is a significant achievement.

Table 3-1 presents the official 2012 election results by state and includes those for Maine's two congressional districts and Nebraska's three districts.[13] Obama won roughly 65.9 million votes, down from his record high of 69.5 million votes in 2008. Indeed, compared to 2008, Obama's vote share decreased in all but seven states. In those seven, the average increase in vote share was slightly less than 1 percentage point. In the states in which Obama lost vote share, he did so by an average decline of 2.7 percentage points.

Perhaps the most striking feature of the 2012 results, however, is its similarity to that of 2008. As Figure 3-1 shows, the Electoral College map for Obama's 2012 victory is nearly identical to his first election, with only two states—Indiana and North Carolina (and Nebraska's 2nd Congressional District)—switching to the Republican side of the ledger. Obama carried twenty-six of the fifty states, as well as the District of Columbia, for a total of 332 electoral votes, easily exceeding the 270 electoral votes currently needed for election.[14] Romney won the remaining twenty-four states, but these victories afforded him only 206 electoral votes. Interestingly, Romney and his running mate, Rep. Paul Ryan, both failed to carry their home states. Romney lost Massachusetts by a whopping twenty-three percentage points, and he failed to win his birth state, Michigan, a state in which his father had once

TABLE 3-1 Presidential Election Results by State, 2012

State	Total vote	Obama (Dem.)	Romney (Rep.)	Other	Two-Party Differential		Total vote (%) Rep.	Dem.
Alabama	2,074,338	795,696	1,255,925	22,717	460,229	R	60.5	38.4
Alaska	300,495	122,640	164,676	13,179	42,036	R	54.8	40.8
Arizona	2,299,254	2,299,254	1,025,232	40,368	208,422	R	53.7	44.6
Arkansas	1,069,468	394,409	647,744	27,315	253,335	R	60.6	36.9
California	13,038,547	7,854,285	4,839,958	344,304	3,014,327	D	37.1	60.2
Colorado	2,569,520	1,323,101	1,185,243	61,176	137,858	D	46.1	51.5
Connecticut	1,558,960	905,083	634,892	18,985	270,191	D	40.7	58.1
Delaware	413,921	242,584	165,484	5,853	77,100	D	40.0	58.6
Florida	8,474,179	4,237,756	4,163,447	72,976	74,309	D	49.1	50.0
Georgia	3,900,050	1,773,827	2,078,688	47,535	304,861	R	53.3	45.5
Hawaii	434,697	306,658	121,015	7,024	185,643	D	27.8	70.5
Idaho	652,274	212,787	420,911	18,576	208,124	R	64.5	32.6
Illinois	5,242,014	3,019,512	2,135,216	87,286	884,296	D	40.7	57.6
Indiana	2,624,534	1,152,887	1,420,543	51,104	267,656	R	54.1	43.9
Iowa	1,582,180	822,544	730,617	29,019	91,927	D	46.2	52.0
Kansas	1,159,971	440,726	692,634	26,611	251,908	R	59.7	38.0
Kentucky	1,797,212	679,370	1,087,190	30,652	407,820	R	60.5	37.8
Louisiana	1,994,065	809,141	1,152,262	32,662	343,121	R	57.8	40.6
Maine[a]	713,180	401,306	292,276	19,598	109,030	D	41.0	56.3
Maryland	2,707,327	1,677,844	971,869	57,614	705,975	D	35.9	62.0
Massachusetts	3,167,767	1,921,290	1,188,314	58,163	732,976	D	37.5	60.7
Michigan	4,730,961	2,564,569	2,115,256	51,136	449,313	D	44.7	54.2
Minnesota	2,936,561	1,546,167	1,320,225	70,169	225,942	D	45.0	52.7

(Continued)

TABLE 3-1 (Continued)

State	Total vote	Obama (Dem.)	Romney (Rep.)	Other	Two-Party Differential		Total vote (%) Rep.	Total vote (%) Dem.
Mississippi	1,285,584	562,949	710,746	11,889	147,797	R	55.3	43.8
Missouri	2,757,323	1,223,796	1,482,440	51,087	258,644	R	53.8	44.4
Montana	484,048	201,839	267,928	14,281	66,089	R	55.4	41.7
Nebraska[b]	794,379	302,081	475,064	17,234	172,983	R	59.8	38.0
Nevada	1,014,918	531,373	463,567	19,978	67,806	D	45.7	52.4
New Hampshire	710,972	369,561	329,918	11,493	39,643	D	46.4	52.0
New Jersey	3,638,499	2,122,786	1,478,088	37,625	644,698	D	40.6	58.3
New Mexico	783,758	415,335	335,788	32,635	79,547	D	42.8	53.0
New York	7,061,925	4,471,871	2,485,432	104,622	1,986,439	D	35.2	63.3
North Carolina	4,505,372	2,178,391	2,270,395	56,586	92,004	R	50.4	48.4
North Dakota	322,932	124,966	188,320	9,646	63,354	R	58.3	38.7
Ohio	5,580,822	2,827,621	2,661,407	91,794	166,214	D	47.7	50.7
Oklahoma	1,334,872	443,547	891,325	0	447,778	R	66.8	33.2
Oregon	1,789,270	970,488	754,175	64,607	216,313	D	42.1	54.2
Pennsylvania	5,753,670	2,990,274	2,680,434	83,378	309,840	D	46.6	52.0
Rhode Island	446,049	279,677	157,204	8,752	122,473	D	35.3	62.8
South Carolina	1,964,118	865,941	1,071,645	26,532	205,704	R	54.6	44.1
South Dakota	363,815	145,039	210,610	8,166	65,571	R	57.9	39.9
Tennessee	2,458,577	960,709	1,432,330	35,538	501,621	R	59.5	39.1
Texas	7,993,851	3,308,124	4,569,843	115,884	1,261,719	R	57.2	41.4
Utah	1,017,440	251,813	740,600	25,027	488,787	R	72.8	24.7
Vermont	299,290	199,239	92,698	7,353	106,541	D	31.0	66.6

TABLE 3-1 (Continued)

State	Total vote	Obama (Dem.)	Romney (Rep.)	Other	Two-Party Differential		Total vote (%) Rep.	Total vote (%) Dem.
Virginia	3,854,490	1,971,820	1,822,522	60,148	149,298	D	47.3	51.2
Washington	3,125,516	1,755,396	1,290,670	79,450	464,726	D	41.3	56.2
West Virginia	670,438	238,269	417,655	14,514	179,386	R	62.3	35.5
Wisconsin	3,071,434	1,620,985	1,410,966	39,483	210,019	D	45.9	52.8
Wyoming	249,061	69,286	170,962	8,813	101,676	R	68.6	27.8
District of Columbia	293,764	267,070	21,381	5,313	245,689	D	7.3	90.9
United States	129,067,662	65,899,660	60,932,152	2,235,850	4,967,508	D	47.2	51.1

Source: Federal Election Commission, "Official 2012 Presidential General Election Results," January 17, 2013, http://www.fec.gov/pubrec/fe2012/2012presgeresults.pdf. Based on reports of the secretaries of state of the fifty states and the District of Columbia.

[a] In Maine, the statewide plurality vote winner gained two votes, and each of the state's two congressional districts was awarded one vote on a plurality basis:

Maine	731,163	295,273	421,923	13,967	126,650	D	40.4	57.7
1st District	374,419	223,035	142,937	8,447	80,098	D	38.2	59.6
2nd District	336,226	177,998	149,215	9,013	28,783	D	44.4	52.9

[b] In Nebraska, the statewide plurality vote winner gained two votes, and each of the state's three congressional districts was awarded one vote on a plurality basis:

Nebraska	801,281	452,969	333,319	14,983	119,660	R	56.5	41.6
1st District	264,712	108,082	152,021	4,609	43,939	R	57.4	40.8
2nd District	266,727	121,889	140,976	3,862	19,087	R	52.9	45.7
3rd District	259,223	72,110	182,067	5,046	109,957	R	70.2	27.8

[c] For Oklahoma, no results for other candidates were reported.

Source: Compiled by the authors.

served as governor, by nine-and-a-half points. In Ryan's home state of Wisconsin, Obama not only won statewide by nearly seven percentage points, he also won more votes than the Republican ticket in Ryan's congressional district. This marks the first time since 1972 that a major party's nominees for president and vice president have both failed to carry their home states. In the end, this made little difference; winning Massachusetts, Michigan, and Wisconsin would have added only thirty-seven votes to Romney's electoral tally, still not enough to defeat Obama.[15] It would be misleading, however, to construe Obama's victory merely as a function of Republican failures. Obama won nearly every battleground state in 2012, including Colorado, Florida, Iowa, Nevada, New Hampshire, Ohio, Pennsylvania, Virginia, and Wisconsin, while Romney claimed only North Carolina.[16] Indeed, Obama victories in Colorado, Florida, Nevada, Ohio, and Virginia are all the more remarkable when one considers that Republican George W. Bush carried each of these in the 2000 and 2004 presidential elections. No serious critic could challenge the legitimacy of Obama's victory.

FIGURE 3-1   Electoral Votes by State, 2012

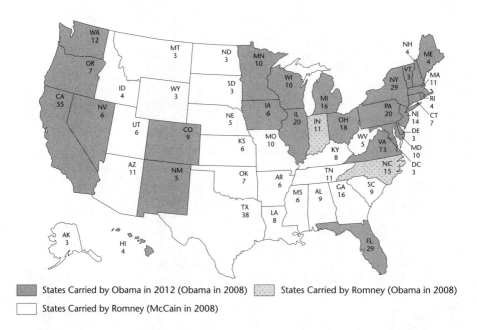

Source: Federal Election Commission, "Official 2012 Presidential General Election Results," January 17, 2013, http://www.fec.gov/pubrec/fe2012/2012presgeresults.pdf. Based on reports of the secretaries of state of the fifty states and the District of Columbia.

Note: Barack Obama won 332 electoral votes, Mitt Romney 206. We classify Nebraska as being carried by McCain in 2008. McCain actually won the statewide race as well as two of Nebraska's three congressional districts, winning four of Nebraska's five electors.

THE ELECTION RULES

Rules matter. And this is certainly the case in U.S. presidential elections.[17] Electoral rules, specifically those pertaining to the Electoral College, structure the nature of party competition and voter behavior, they influence the strategic actions of candidates (as we saw in both Chapters 1 and 2), and they sometimes dictate who wins and who loses.[18] In 2012, Barack Obama won a majority of both the popular and electoral vote, and one might argue that he would have won under most election rules. But the rules governing U.S. presidential elections do not guarantee that the candidate who receives the most votes wins. Indeed, on four occasions in American history—the elections of John Quincy Adams in 1824, Rutherford B. Hayes in 1876, Benjamin Harrison in 1888, and George W. Bush in 2000—the plurality winner of the popular vote failed to achieve a majority in the Electoral College and lost the presidency.[19]

As we saw in Chapter 2, voters do not vote directly for president. Rather, they vote for a slate of electors pledged to support certain presidential and vice presidential candidates. In every state except Maine and Nebraska, the slate that receives the most popular votes (a plurality) is awarded all of the state's electoral votes. In no state is a majority required to win. In 2012, however, both Obama and Romney won majorities in each of the states in which they were victorious. In 2008, Obama won a majority in all but two of the twenty-eight states he carried (Indiana and North Carolina). Neither of these two elections featured a prominent independent or third-party candidate, and this largely determines whether the plurality winner in a state will obtain a majority of the votes. In 2012, only 1.7 percent of the national popular vote went to candidates outside of the two main parties; the independent/third-party vote share in 2008 was 1.4 percent. The 1992 presidential election, however, featured a strong independent candidate; H. Ross Perot appeared on the ballot in all fifty states and won 18.9 percent of the popular vote nationally. The winner of that election, Bill Clinton, garnered only 43.0 percent of the popular vote nationally while carrying thirty-two states and the District of Columbia. Clinton won a majority of votes only in the District of Columbia (84.6 percent) and in his home state of Arkansas (53.2 percent).

The plurality rule, winner-take-all system usually transforms a plurality of the popular vote into a majority of the electoral vote.[20] And it takes a majority of the electoral vote (currently 270 votes) to produce a winner. If no candidate wins a majority of the electoral vote, the House of Representatives, voting by state delegations, chooses among the three candidates with the highest number of electoral votes. Yet the House has not chosen a winner since 1825. So why does the plurality rule, winner-take-all system typically produce a majority winner? The answer lies in the tendency for plurality rule voting systems to yield a two-party system.

The U.S. plurality vote system is a confirmation of Duverger's law, a proposition advanced by French jurist and political scientist Maurice Duverger in the 1950s.[21] According to Duverger, "the simple-majority single-ballot system favours the two-party system."[22] Indeed, Duverger argued that "the American procedure corresponds to the usual machinery of the simple-majority single-ballot system. The absence of a second ballot and of further polls, particularly in the presidential election, constitutes in fact one of the historical reasons for the emergence and the maintenance of the two-party system."[23]

According to Duverger, this principle applies for two reasons. First, a plurality vote system produces a "mechanical factor": third parties may earn a large number of votes nationally but fail to gain a plurality of the votes in many electoral units. Scholars agree that this effect is important, except in countries where smaller parties have a geographic base. Second, some voters who prefer a candidate or party they think cannot win will cast their votes for their first choice between the major-party candidates, which Duverger labels the "psychological factor." This behavior is called "sophisticated" or "strategic" voting, and in Britain is referred to as "tactical" voting. William H. Riker defines strategic voting as "voting contrary to one's immediate tastes in order to obtain an advantage in the long run."[24] Whether strategic voting occurs to any significant extent is controversial, yet evidence suggests that substantial numbers of voters who preferred a third-party or independent candidate in the 1968, 1980, 1992, 1996, and 2000 elections wound up voting for one of the major-party candidates instead of voting their "sincere" preferences.[25] A small amount of strategic voting probably occurred in 2004 as well, with some voters who preferred Nader to both Bush and Kerry voting for the major-party candidates.[26] Because the 2012 American National Election Study did not measure "feelings" toward independent or third-party candidates, it is impossible to estimate how many voters preferred them to Obama and Romney, but it seems very unlikely that strategic voting affected the general election result.[27]

The plurality rule system thus places a heavy burden on third-party or independent candidates. Even a relatively successful third-party candidate typically receives a far smaller share of the electoral vote than of the popular vote.[28] Here it is useful to review the fates of the four most successful third-party and independent candidacies (in popular vote results) since World War II: George C. Wallace won 13.5 percent of the popular vote in 1968, John B. Anderson won 6.6 percent in 1980, and H. Ross Perot won 18.9 percent in 1992 and 8.4 percent in 1996. In 1980 and 1992, Anderson and Perot, respectively, had some modest regional support. Both fared better in New England than elsewhere, and both fared worst in the South.[29] Perot also did well in the mountain states.[30] He even came in second in two states in 1992: Maine, where he came in ahead of George H. W. Bush, and Utah, where he came in ahead of Clinton.[31] In 1996, Perot fared somewhat better in New England, but regional differences were small. Wallace, by contrast, had a regional base in the South. Even though he won a smaller share of the popular vote than Perot in 1992, Wallace came in first in five states (winning a majority in Alabama and Mississippi) and gaining forty-six electoral votes (including one from a faithless elector from North Carolina).[32] But even Wallace won only 8.5 percent of the electoral vote, less than his popular vote share.[33]

While the rules had no immediate effect on the 2012 election per se, they did help create the conditions that led to major-party dominance. Choosing the president by presidential electors is a central part of these rules, and a strong case can be made for eliminating the Electoral College.[34] Some critics, such as presidential scholar George C. Edwards III, argue in favor of direct election of the president. Direct election would force candidates to campaign nationally and would promote equality by making every vote in every state count. Moreover, direct election would eliminate questions of fairness that arise when popular-vote winners do not win the presidency. The main obstacle to adopting a direct election system is that it requires a constitutional amendment, which is unlikely because gaining approval of three-fourths of the states would be difficult in a system that overrepresents the smaller states.[35]

An alternative reform would retain the Electoral College, but would eliminate its importance by establishing a compact among states that would guarantee that electors would vote for the national popular-vote winner regardless of the outcome within their own state. This compact would come into effect only after it is enacted by states collectively possessing a majority of the electoral votes. As of July 2013, nine states and the District of Columbia with a total of 136 electoral votes (roughly 50 percent of the 270 electoral votes needed) had agreed to the National Popular Vote Interstate Compact.[36] Because an interstate compact requires congressional approval, there would still be an additional hurdle, but only a majority of both chambers is required to approve an interstate compact, not the two-thirds supermajority to initiate a constitutional amendment.

As described earlier, Maine and Nebraska both have district systems for choosing electors, and widespread state-level adoption of this method is often put forward as a way of reforming the Electoral College. The district system does away with the winner-take-all rule for assigning electors and makes it possible for candidates to split a state's electoral vote. However, this method does not guarantee that electors will be divided in proportion to candidates' popular-vote shares.[37] Indeed, because partisan majorities in state legislatures typically gerrymander congressional district lines to make the districts uncompetitive and unbalanced in their favor, the adoption of the district method would likely bias Electoral College outcomes.[38] A study by *The Cook Political Report* shows that had there been a uniform application of the district method in 2012, Mitt Romney would have been elected.[39] Romney won more congressional districts than Obama (226 of 435), while carrying twenty-four states for a total of 274 electoral votes. Obama would have received 264 electoral votes based on 209 congressional district wins, twenty-six state popular-vote wins, and the District of Columbia. Obviously, this result is inconsistent with the national popular vote, though it could be argued that the 49.1 percent of the electoral vote that Obama would have received under the district system is less biased than the 61.7 percent of the electoral vote he received in reality.[40] Widespread adoption of the district system is unlikely, however, since most states do not want to diminish their potential influence by making it likely that their electoral votes will be split.

THE PATTERN OF RESULTS

The 2012 election can be placed in perspective by comparing it with previous presidential elections. Three conclusions emerge. First, the election highlights the competitive nature of postwar elections in the United States, which exhibit a relatively even balance between the two major parties. Second, despite consecutive wins for the Democrats, postwar elections continue to display a pattern of volatility. Third, Obama's reelection provides further evidence of an incumbent advantage in presidential elections.

The competitive balance between the two major parties over the postwar period is rather remarkable. In the seventeen elections held since World War II, the Republicans have been victorious in nine, while the Democrats have won eight. The Republicans have been slightly more successful in establishing electoral majorities, winning a majority of the popular vote in seven of these elections (1952, 1956, 1972, 1980, 1984, 1988, and 2004). The Democrats have won a popular-vote majority only four times, including both of Obama's victories (1964, 1976, 2008, and 2012). The average (mean) level of popular support shows the competitive balance: the Republicans have won 48.8 percent of the popular vote, and the Democrats have won 46.9 percent. This division of popular support also demonstrates the dominance of the two major parties in presidential elections. During the postwar period, third-party and independent candidates have garnered only an average of 4.3 percent of the popular vote.

Examining electoral history is like looking at clouds: if you look hard enough, you'll find something that looks like a pattern. Yet with a few important historical exceptions, electoral history is best described as volatile. This is especially true in the postwar period, where competitive balance would appear to place a party's chances at winning the presidency at 50-50.[41] Table 3-2 presents presidential election results since 1832, the first election in which political parties used national nominating conventions to select their candidates. From 1832 to 1948 there are four instances in which the same party won three elections or more in a row. Scholars often associate these episodes with partisan realignments. Walter Dean Burnham, for instance, identifies the elections of 1860, 1896, and 1932 as realigning elections during this period.[42] From 1948 to 2008, despite the election of five two-term presidents, the same party has won three elections in a row only once (the Republicans in 1980, 1984, and 1988).

The postwar period is an era of sustained electoral volatility. From 1952 to 1984, neither party was able to win more than two elections in a row. The Republicans won in 1952 and again in 1956, the Democrats won in 1960 and 1964, and the Republicans won in 1968 and 1972. In all three sets of wins, the second win was by a larger margin than the first. Volatility increased in 1980, when the Democrats, who had won the White House in 1976, failed to hold it. The 1980 and 1984 elections reverted to the pattern of back-to-back party wins when Ronald Reagan was reelected in a landslide.[43] Then in 1988, George H. W. Bush's election gave the Republicans three elections in a row, breaking the pattern of

TABLE 3-2   Presidential Election Results, 1832–2012

Election	Winning candidate	Party of winning candidate	Success of incumbent political party
1832	Andrew Jackson	Democrat	Won
1836	Martin Van Buren	Democrat	Won
1840	William H. Harrison	Whig	Lost
1844	James K. Polk	Democrat	Lost[a]
1848	Zachary Taylor	Whig	Lost
1852	Franklin Pierce	Democrat	Lost
1856	James Buchanan	Democrat	Won
1860	Abraham Lincoln	Republican	Lost
1864	Abraham Lincoln	Republican	Won
1868	Ulysses S. Grant	Republican	Won[b]
1872	Ulysses S. Grant	Republican	Won
1876	Rutherford B. Hayes	Republican	Won
1880	James A. Garfield	Republican	Won
1884	Grover Cleveland	Democrat	Lost
1888	Benjamin Harrison	Republican	Lost
1892	Grover Cleveland	Democrat	Lost
1896	William McKinley	Republican	Lost
1900	William McKinley	Republican	Won
1904	Theodore Roosevelt	Republican	Won
1908	William H. Taft	Republican	Won
1912	Woodrow Wilson	Democrat	Lost
1916	Woodrow Wilson	Democrat	Won
1920	Warren G. Harding	Republican	Lost
1924	Calvin Coolidge	Republican	Won
1928	Herbert C. Hoover	Republican	Won
1932	Franklin D. Roosevelt	Democrat	Lost
1936	Franklin D. Roosevelt	Democrat	Won
1940	Franklin D. Roosevelt	Democrat	Won
1944	Franklin D. Roosevelt	Democrat	Won
1948	Harry S. Truman	Democrat	Won
1952	Dwight D. Eisenhower	Republican	Lost
1956	Dwight D. Eisenhower	Republican	Won
1960	John F. Kennedy	Democrat	Lost
1964	Lyndon B. Johnson	Democrat	Won
1968	Richard M. Nixon	Republican	Lost
1972	Richard M. Nixon	Republican	Won
1976	Jimmy Carter	Democrat	Lost
1980	Ronald Reagan	Republican	Lost
1984	Ronald Reagan	Republican	Won

(Continued)

TABLE 3-2 (Continued)

Election	Winning candidate	Party of winning candidate	Success of incumbent political party
1988	George H. W. Bush	Republican	Won
1992	Bill Clinton	Democrat	Lost
1996	Bill Clinton	Democrat	Won
2000	George W. Bush	Republican	Lost
2004	George W. Bush	Republican	Won
2008	Barack Obama	Democrat	Lost
2012	Barack Obama	Democrat	Won

Source: Presidential Elections, 1789–2008 (Washington, D.C.: CQ Press, 2009).

[a] Whigs are classified as the incumbent party because they won the 1840 election. In fact, their presidential candidate, William Henry Harrison, died a month after taking office and his vice president, John Tyler, was expelled from the party in 1841.

[b] Republicans are classified as the incumbent party because they won the 1864 election. (Technically, Lincoln had been elected on a Union ticket.) In fact, after Lincoln's assassination in 1865, Andrew Johnson, a war Democrat, became president.

postwar volatility. But the Republicans could not sustain their control of the presidency. The Democrats recaptured the White House with Bill Clinton's victory in 1992. Clinton was reelected in 1996, and he did so by capturing a larger popular-vote margin than in his first election. George W. Bush's defeat of Al Gore in 2000 continued the postwar volatility, and Bush, who finished second in the popular vote in 2000, improved his vote share in 2004. Obama's victories in 2008 and 2012 undoubtedly give some Democrats hope that a period of Democratic Party dominance is emerging. Yet Obama's reelection was achieved with a smaller popular-vote margin than his first (unlike all other reelected incumbents during the postwar period) and did not carry with it the legislative majorities generated in 2008.[44] If the Democrats are to retain control of the presidency in 2016 and thus win three elections in a row, they will accomplish something that has been done only once in the past sixty years.

The electoral volatility of the postwar period is not without precedent. In fact, two periods in the nineteenth century were more volatile. From 1840 to 1852, the incumbent party lost four consecutive elections—a period of volatility between the Democrats and the Whigs. This occurred again from 1884 to 1896, when the Republicans and the Democrats alternated elections. Both of these periods, however, were followed by party realignments. In 1854, just two years after the decisive defeat of the Whigs, the Republicans were founded, and by the 1856 election their candidate, John C. Fremont, came in second behind James Buchanan, the Democratic winner.[45] By 1860 the Republicans had captured the presidency and the Whigs were extinct.[46] Although many Whigs, including

Abraham Lincoln himself, became Republicans, the Republican Party was not just the Whig Party renamed. The Republicans had transformed the political agenda by capitalizing on opposition to slavery in the territories.[47]

The 1896 contest, the last of four incumbent party losses, is usually considered a critical election because it solidified Republican dominance.[48] Although the Republicans had won five of the seven elections since the end of the Civil War, after Ulysses S. Grant's reelection in 1872 all their victories had been by narrow margins. In 1896 the Republicans emerged as the clearly dominant party, gaining a solid hold in Connecticut, Indiana, New Jersey, and New York, states that they had frequently lost between 1876 and 1892. After William McKinley's defeat of William Jennings Bryan in 1896, the Republicans established a firmer base in the Midwest, New England, and the Mid-Atlantic states. They lost the presidency only in 1912, when the GOP was split, and in 1916, when Woodrow Wilson ran for reelection.[49]

The Great Depression ended Republican dominance. The emergence of the Democrats as the majority party was not preceded by a series of incumbent losses. The Democratic coalition, forged in the 1930s, relied heavily on the emerging working class and the mobilization of new groups into the electorate.

As the emergence of the New Deal coalition demonstrates, a period of electoral volatility is not a necessary condition for a partisan realignment. Nor perhaps is it a sufficient condition. In 1985 Reagan himself proclaimed that realignment had occurred. Political scientists were skeptical about that claim, mainly because the Democrats continued to dominate the U.S. House of Representatives. George H. W. Bush's election in 1988 suggested that Republican dominance might have arrived, but Clinton's 1992 victory called this thesis into question, and his 1996 victory cast further doubts on the idea that a realignment had occurred. After the 2000 election, the Republicans held control of the House, the Senate, and the presidency for the first time since 1953, although they temporarily lost control of the Senate between June 1991 and January 1993.[50] But the closeness of the election called into question any claim of Republican dominance. The Democrats regained the presidency—by a comfortable margin— with Obama's victory in 2008, and they also won relatively large majorities in both houses of Congress, only to lose control of the House and a sizeable portion of their advantage in the Senate in the 2010 midterm elections. The election of 2012 gave Obama and the Democrats another four years in the White House, but Congress remains under divided party control. No party currently dominates American politics. Volatility persists.

One clear pattern that does emerge when one examines presidential elections across history is that incumbent candidates appear to have an advantage. Between 1792 and 2012, in-office parties held the White House about two-thirds of the time when they ran the incumbent president, but only won half the time when they did not run an incumbent.[51] Obama's victory in 2012 makes him the third straight incumbent president to win reelection. In fact, seven of ten postwar incumbent presidents seeking reelection have won, with Ford losing in

1976, Carter in 1980, and Bush senior in 1992. The 1976 and 1980 elections are the only successive elections in the twentieth century in which two incumbent presidents in a row lost. The only other elections in which incumbent presidents were defeated in two straight elections were in 1888, when Benjamin Harrison defeated Grover Cleveland, and in 1892, when Cleveland defeated Harrison. In Chapter 7, we examine voters' evaluations of presidential performance and how it relates to voting.

STATE-BY-STATE RESULTS

The modern electoral map is a conglomeration of Republican "red states" and Democratic "blue states." Yet this color pairing has no real historical meaning and, in fact, has become convention only in recent years.[52] In 1976, for instance, election-night news coverage on NBC classified Republican (Ford) wins in blue and Democratic (Carter) victories in red. ABC News featured an electoral map that colored Democratic states in blue and Republican states in yellow.

While the colors on the electoral map may be meaningless, the political geography of presidential elections most certainly is not. Because states deliver the electoral votes necessary to win the presidency, the presidential election is effectively fifty-one separate contests, one for each state and one for the District of Columbia. With the exception of Maine and Nebraska, the candidate who wins the most votes in a state wins all of the state's electors. Regardless of how a state decides to allocate its electors, the number of electors is the sum of its senators (two), plus the number of its representatives in the U.S. House.[53] Since 1964, there have been 538 electors and a majority, 270, is required to win. In 2012, the distribution of electoral votes ranged from a low of 3 in Alaska, Delaware, Montana, North Dakota, South Dakota, Vermont, Wyoming, and the District of Columbia, to a high of 55 in California.

Because each state, regardless of population, has two electoral votes for its senators, the smaller states are overrepresented in the Electoral College and the larger states are underrepresented. The twenty least-populated states and the District of Columbia were home to roughly 10.5 percent of the U.S. population according to the 2010 census, but these states had 16.5 percent of the electoral votes. The nine most-populated states, which had 52.2 percent of the population, had only 44.8 percent of the electoral vote.

Even though smaller states are overrepresented in the Electoral College, presidential campaigns tend to focus their resources on larger states unless pre-election polls indicate that a state is unwinnable. Consider the two most populous states, California and Texas. California's fifty-five electoral votes represent one-fifth of the votes needed to win the Electoral College. Texas has thirty-eight electoral votes, one-seventh of the votes necessary to win. Clearly, both are vital for building an Electoral College victory. Yet pre-election polls suggested landslide wins for Obama in California and Romney in Texas, and neither campaign spent significant time or money in either state. During the general election campaign, Romney made one public appearance in California, while Obama did not visit Texas at all.[54] Florida and Ohio, on the other hand, were both competitive large states (twenty-nine and eighteen electoral votes, respectively), and both candidates visited the two states more than any other. Obama made eighteen public appearances in Florida and nineteen campaign stops in Ohio. Romney, who spent more time on the campaign stump overall, made twenty-three public appearances in Florida and thirty in Ohio.[55] Obama won both states by small popular-vote margins.[56]

States are the building blocks of winning presidential coalitions, but state-by-state results can be overemphasized and may sometimes be misleading for three reasons. First, while much attention is given to battleground states, the nature of broadcast and social media coverage means that candidates must run national campaigns. Candidates can make appeals to specific states and regions, but those messages are likely to be reported across geographic boundaries. Thus, while battleground contests and regional bases of support may color a campaign's message and strategy, most campaigns seek to form a broad-based coalition throughout the nation. Indeed, given that forty-four of the forty-seven elections between 1828 and 2012 have resulted in the candidate with the largest number of popular votes also winning a majority of the electoral votes, it would appear that successful campaigns have always been national rather than regional in scope.

Second, comparing state-level election results over time can be misleading and may even conceal change. To illustrate this point, we compare the results of two close Democratic victories—John Kennedy's defeat of Richard Nixon in 1960 and Jimmy Carter's defeat of Gerald Ford in 1976—that have many similarities. In both 1960 and 1976, the Republicans did very well in the West, and both Kennedy and Carter needed southern support to win. Kennedy carried six of the eleven states of the old Confederacy—Arkansas, Georgia, Louisiana, North Carolina, South Carolina, and Texas—and gained five of Alabama's 11 electoral votes, for a total of 81 electoral votes. Carter carried ten of the eleven southern states (all but Virginia) for a total of 118 electoral votes.

The demographic basis of Carter's support was quite different from Kennedy's, however. In 1960, only 29 percent of African Americans in the South were registered to vote, compared with 61 percent of whites. According to our analysis of the American National Election Studies, only about one in fifteen of the Kennedy voters in the South was black. In 1976, 63 percent of African Americans in the South were registered to vote, compared with 68 percent of whites.[57] We estimate that about one in three southerners who voted for Carter was black. A simple state-by-state comparison would conceal this massive change in the social composition of the Democratic presidential coalition.

Third, state-by-state comparisons do not tell us why a presidential candidate received support. Of course, such comparisons can lead to interesting speculation, especially when the dominant issues are related to regional differences. Following the 2012 election, for example, some observers speculated that Obama's victory in Ohio resulted in part from his support of a government-funded bailout of the nearly bankrupt auto industry in 2009, a program which Mitt Romney opposed.[58] Ohio trails only Michigan in automobile manufacturing, and it may be tempting to believe that this issue was pressing on the minds of residents of the Buckeye State. But an inference such as this—based solely on who won the state—may be fallacious and lead to mischaracterizations of the electorate.[59] State-level election results should not be used to infer voters' preferences; for this, we must examine individual-level survey responses—as we do in later chapters.

With these qualifications in mind, we now turn to the state-by-state results. Figure 3-2 shows Obama's margin of victory over Romney in all states. As we noted earlier, Obama's victory in 2012 is remarkably similar to his win in 2008. A continuing base of strength for Obama was the Northeast, sweeping all nine states in the region (by an average popular-vote margin of 19.5 points), just as he did four years earlier.[60] In fact, the Democrats have dominated the Northeast in presidential elections since Clinton's election in 1992. The only northeastern state to cast its electoral votes for a Republican since that time was New Hampshire in 2000, giving George W. Bush four electors.[61] But the region is proving to be a precarious base of electoral support for the Democrats. While comparison of vote shares across the last six elections suggests that the region has not waned in

FIGURE 3-2   Obama's Margin of Victory over Romney, 2012

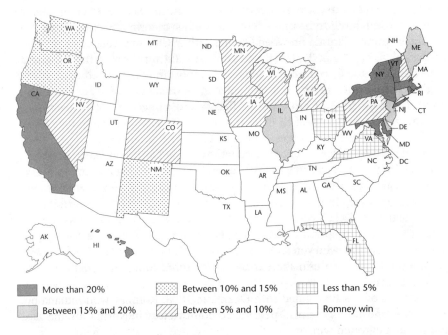

Source: Federal Election Commission, "Official 2012 Presidential General Election Results," January 17, 2013, http://www.fec.gov/pubrec/fe2012/2012presgeresults.pdf. Based on reports of the secretaries of state of the fifty states and the District of Columbia.

its support of the Democratic Party, the region is declining in population and thus carries less weight in the Electoral College. In 1992, the region offered 106 electoral votes. In 2012, that number was only 96, and by one estimate—based on U.S. Census population projections—by the 2024 election, the Northeast's share of electoral votes will decline further to 91.[62] Whether the region continues to vote consistently for the Democratic Party remains to be seen.

Obama's coalition was not restricted to one region. Outside of the Northeast, Obama carried eight other states, as well as the District of Columbia, by ten percentage points or more, including the electorally rich states of California and Illinois. The president's sizeable victories in Oregon and Washington continue his party's dominance in those states, which have voted Democratic in each of the last seven presidential elections. Obama also won comfortable victories in Nevada and Colorado, as he did four years prior. This is notable because between 1964 and 2008 Nevada had voted Democratic only twice (for Clinton in 1992 and 1996), and Colorado had voted Democratic only once (1992). In the South, Obama was able to recapture Florida and Virginia, two of the three southern states he carried in 2008 (North Carolina being the third). This allowed him to capture 42 of the South's 160 electoral votes. Until Obama's victory there in 2008, Virginia had not voted Democratic since Johnson's 1964 landslide, although the state had been inching toward the Democratic column because of the suburban growth from Washington, D.C. Florida, on the other hand, has long been among the battleground states of presidential politics.[63] In the last six elections, each party has won Florida three times, with the average margin of victory being 2.9 percentage points. Florida provided Obama with 29 electoral votes.

Obama's largest electoral prize came from California and its 55 votes. California has now voted for the Democratic candidate in each of the last six presidential elections. Between 1952 and 1988, the state voted for the GOP presidential candidate in nine of the ten elections. But in those elections, California did not differ much from the country as a whole: its average level of Republican support was the same as that of the nation as a whole. One reason for this political change is the state's growing Latino population, which increased from 19 percent in 1980 to 38 percent in 2012. According to Mark Baldassare, based on exit polls in 1990 only 4 percent of California voters were Latino; by 2000, 14 percent were.[64] In 2012, exit polls indicated that Latinos accounted for 22 percent of the California electorate. Of those voters, 72 percent voted for Obama and only 27 percent for Romney.[65]

Mitt Romney's victories in Indiana and North Carolina brought two reliable Republican states back into the party's win column. Since the 1980 election, these two states have voted for the Democratic nominee in a presidential election only once—both sided with Obama in 2008. Romney won Indiana by 10.2 percentage points, but his 2 percentage-point victory in North Carolina was his only battleground win.

The remaining states captured by Romney in 2012 are the core of the Republican electoral coalition. These twenty-two states, which Romney won by an amazing average margin of 20.9 percentage points, all voted Republican in each of the last four presidential elections. Thirteen of these states (Alabama, Alaska, Idaho, Kansas, Mississippi, Nebraska, North Dakota, Oklahoma, South Carolina, South Dakota, Texas, Utah, and Wyoming) have voted Republican in every election dating back to 1980. The problem for Romney (and Republicans generally) is that the twenty-two solidly Republican states he won resulted in only 180 electoral votes. Texas, with its 38 electoral votes, is the largest state in this coalition, followed by Georgia with 16 electoral votes, but five of these states have only 3 electoral votes each. To make the point clearer, consider the subset of thirteen states that have voted Republican since 1980. These thirteen states cumulatively represent 102 electoral votes. This is not much of an advantage when we recall that Democratic-leaning California alone has 55 votes.

The region that offered Romney his greatest electoral reward was the South. Of Romney's electoral votes, 106 were from the South, just over half of his total. In the last half century, the South has been transformed into the base of the Republican Party, and this is the most dramatic change in postwar American politics. Obama clearly benefited by cutting into this base, for he would have been reduced to only 290 electoral votes without Florida and Virginia. However, in all four of the most recent Democratic victories (1992, 1996, 2008, and 2012), the Democratic candidate could have been elected with no southern support. George W. Bush, on the other hand, could not have been elected or reelected without southern electoral votes.

Republican strength in the South and Democratic advantage in the Northeast does not mean that sectionalism has beset the country. Indeed, regional differences in presidential voting have declined in the postwar period and are currently low by historical standards. This can be demonstrated by statistical analysis. Joseph A. Schlesinger has analyzed state-by-state variation in presidential elections from 1832 through 1988, and we have updated his analyses through 2012.[66] Schlesinger measures the extent to which party competition in presidential elections is divided along geographic lines by calculating the standard deviation in the percentage of Democratic vote among the states.[67] The state-by-state variation was 10.29 in 2012, slightly higher than the 9.54 deviation for 2008. This suggests that states were slightly more divided in their support for Obama in 2012, but this deviation is still below the state-by-state deviation of 11.96 in the 1964 contest between Johnson and Goldwater, which was the highest deviation of any postwar election. Schlesinger's analysis clearly reveals the relatively low level of state-by-state variation in the postwar elections.[68] According to his analysis (as updated), all fifteen of the presidential elections from 1888 to 1944 displayed more state-by-state variation than any of the seventeen postwar elections. To a large extent, the decline in state-by-state variation has been a result of the transformation of the South and the demise of local party machines, which has allowed partisan cleavages to become more consistent across states and allowed party competition to increase across the country.[69]

ELECTORAL CHANGE IN THE POSTWAR SOUTH

The South is a growing region that has undergone dramatic political change. Even though five of the eleven southern states have lost congressional representation since World War II, Florida and Texas have made spectacular gains. In the 1944 and 1948 elections, Florida had only 8 electoral votes, but in the 2012 election it had 29. In 1944 and 1948, Texas had 23 electoral votes; in 2012 it had 38. Since the end of World War II, the South's electoral vote total has grown from 127 to 160. The South gained 7 electoral votes following the 2010 census and projections suggest that it may gain an extra 4 by 2024.[70]

The political transformation of the South was a complex process, but the major reason for the change was simple. As V. O. Key Jr. brilliantly demonstrated in *Southern Politics in State and Nation* in 1949, the main factor in southern politics is race. "In its grand outlines the politics of the South revolves around the position of the Negro. . . . Whatever phase of the southern political process one seeks to understand, sooner or later the trail of inquiry leads to the Negro."[71] And it was the national Democratic Party's sponsorship of African American civil rights that shattered the party's dominance in the South.[72]

Between the end of Reconstruction in 1877 and the end of World War II, the South was functionally a one-party system. Unified in its support of racial segregation and in its opposition to Republican social and economic policies, the South was a Democratic stronghold—the "Solid South." Indeed, in fifteen of the seventeen elections from 1880 to 1944, all eleven southern states voted Democratic. Between 1896 (the first election after many southern states adopted the "white primary") and 1944, the average Democratic Party vote share in presidential elections was 71.6 percent.[73] The only major defections were in 1928, when the Democrats ran Alfred E. Smith, a Roman Catholic. As a result, the Republican candidate, Herbert Hoover, won five southern states. Even then, six of the most solid southern states voted for Smith, even though all but Louisiana were overwhelmingly Protestant.

After Reconstruction ended in 1877, many southern blacks were prevented from voting, and in the late nineteenth and early twentieth centuries several southern states changed their voting laws to further disfranchise blacks. The Republicans effectively ceded those states to the Democrats. Although the Republicans garnered black support in the North, they did not attempt to enforce the Fifteenth Amendment, which bans restrictions on voting on the basis of "race, color, or previous condition of servitude."

In 1932, a majority of African Americans in the North remained loyal to the Republicans, although by 1936 Franklin D. Roosevelt had won the support of northern blacks. But Roosevelt made no effort to win the support of southern blacks, most of whom remained disfranchised. Even as late as 1940, about 70 percent of the nation's blacks lived in the states of the old Confederacy. Roosevelt carried all eleven of these states in each of his four victories. His 1944 reelection, however, was the last contest in which Democrats carried all eleven southern states.

World War I led to massive migration of African Americans from the agrarian South and into the industrial North, where—given the absence of laws restricting their suffrage—many would enjoy the franchise for the first time. The influx of African Americans alarmed some Democratic politicians in the North, who would likely see their electoral prospects decline unless they were able to siphon a share of African American voters, who were loyal to the party of Lincoln. In 1932, African American voters in most major cities in the North voted for Herbert Hoover by a roughly two-to-one margin.[74] To appeal to African American voters, many northern Democrats encouraged their party to adopt a supportive position toward civil rights. By 1948, President Harry Truman was making explicit appeals to blacks through his Fair Employment Practices Commission, and in July 1948 he issued an executive order ending segregation in the armed services.[75] These policies led to defections from the "Dixiecrats" and cost Truman four southern states in the 1948 election; he still won the seven remaining southern states by an average margin of 26.2 points. In 1952 and 1956, the Democratic candidate, Adlai E. Stevenson, de-emphasized appeals to blacks, although his opponent, Dwight Eisenhower, still made inroads in the South. In 1960, Kennedy also played down appeals to African Americans, and southern electoral votes were crucial to his win over Nixon.[76] Kennedy also strengthened his campaign in the South by choosing a Texan, Lyndon Johnson, as his running mate. Clearly, Johnson helped Kennedy win Texas, which he carried by only two percentage points.

If Johnson as running mate aided the Democrats in the South, Johnson as president played a different role. His explicit appeals to African Americans, including leading the Civil Rights Act into law in 1964, helped end Democratic dominance in the South. Barry Goldwater, the Republican candidate, had voted against the Civil Rights Act as a member of the Senate, creating a sharp difference between the two candidates. Goldwater carried all five states in the Deep South.[77] The only other state he won was his native Arizona. In 1968 Hubert Humphrey, who had long championed black equality, carried only one southern state, Texas, which he won with only 41 percent of the vote. He was probably aided by George Wallace's third-party candidacy, because Wallace, a segregationist, won 19 percent of the Texas vote. Wallace carried Alabama, Arkansas, Georgia, Louisiana, and Mississippi, while Nixon carried the remaining five southern states. Nixon won every southern state in 1972, and his margin of victory was greater in the South than in the rest of the nation. Although Carter won ten of the eleven southern states in 1976 (all but Virginia), he carried a minority of the vote among white southerners.

In 1980, Reagan won every southern state except Georgia, Carter's home state. In his 1984 reelection victory, Reagan carried all the southern states, and his margin of victory in the South was greater than his margin outside it. In 1988, George H. W. Bush was victorious in all eleven southern states, and the South was his strongest region. Four years later, in 1992, Clinton, a native of Arkansas, made some inroads in the South and somewhat greater inroads in 1996. All the same, the South was the only predominantly Republican region in 1992, and in 1996 Bob Dole won a majority of the electoral vote only in the South and mountain states. In 2000, the South was the only region in which Bush carried every state, and over half of his electoral votes came from that region. Bush again carried every southern state in 2004, along with all of the states in the Mountain West. As was the case four years earlier, more than half of his electoral votes came from the states of the old Confederacy. Despite slippage in 2008 and 2012, Republicans have won every southern state in five of the eleven elections (1972, 1984, 1988, 2000, and 2004) between 1972 and 2012.

Although the transformation of the South is clearly the most dramatic change in postwar American politics, the 2012 election underscores that the Republicans do not hold the same level of dominance in the region that the Democrats once enjoyed. The average Republican vote share in the South between 1972 and 2012 was 54.2 points—much smaller than the 71.6 vote share that we reported earlier for the Democrats from 1896 to 1944. Florida is highly competitive. Clinton won the Sunshine State in 1996, and in 2000 Bush carried the disputed contest by a negligible margin. And Obama narrowly won Florida in both 2008 and 2012. Obama captured North Carolina by a 0.3 percentage-point margin in 2008, but lost it by a slim 2-point margin in 2012. Although Virginia had not voted Democratic since 1964, the growth of the Washington, D.C., suburbs in Northern Virginia has made the state more competitive. Even in Georgia, the Democratic vote in Atlanta and its close-in suburbs can make the state competitive. Clinton carried Georgia in 1992, and McCain won by only 5.2 percentage points in 2008. Republicans have an advantage in the South, to be sure, but Democrats are competitive in a few southern states, thus allowing the South to keep its place of prominence in modern presidential politics.

Some scholars predict that the South will play a part in the next major transformation in American politics, one they argue could make the Electoral College less competitive. John Judis and Ruy Teixeira contend that shifting demographics, specifically a growing professional class and an increase in America's nonwhite population, are setting the stage for an "emerging Democratic majority."[78] Central to this argument is that, in the next two decades, the proportion of Latinos in the electorate is likely to double.[79] Latino growth in the South, where African Americans already compose a large share of the electorate, could greatly benefit the Democrats. Three southern states— Arkansas, North Carolina, and South Carolina—were among the top five states in Hispanic population growth between 2000 and 2010.[80] And Texas (19 percent) and Florida (8 percent) already have the second and third largest Hispanic populations, respectively. It is assumed by Judis and Teixeira that further growth in the Latino population could make Texas a Democratic-leaning state and Florida a safe Democratic state within four election cycles, giving Democrats, who already hold advantages in the electorally rich states of California and New York, an easy path to victory in the Electoral College.[81]

We have heard predictions of impending electoral realignment before, and, as in the past, we encourage caution when evaluating these claims.[82] As noted earlier, after his reelection in 1984, Ronald Reagan proclaimed that his victory represented a Republican realignment. Indeed, some scholars went so far as to argue that the Republicans held an electoral vote "lock."[83] But the Democrats won two consecutive elections in the 1990s. The scenario outlined by Judis and Teixeira offers reason for optimism for the Democrats and pessimism for the Republicans. Yet there are two major assumptions undergirding this scenario that complicate things for the Democrats. First, it should not be assumed that Latino voting participation will increase proportionately with Latino population growth; it has not thus far. As noted in a Pew Hispanic Center report, "Hispanics comprise[d] 17% of the total U.S. population but just 10% of all voters [in 2012]."[84] Hispanics were 23 percent of Florida's population, but only 17 percent of voters on election day. In Texas, Hispanics were 38 percent of the population, but only 22 percent of the electorate.[85] For Democrats to make real substantial gains in the near future, voter participation among Latinos—particularly those in Texas—must grow at a faster rate to become commensurate with the group's share of the population. Second, it should not be assumed that Latinos will continue to support Democrats at the same levels. The Latino vote is not monolithic and has changed somewhat over time (we will have more to say about Hispanic political preferences in Chapter 8). For instance, Cuban Americans in Florida, many of whom fled their homeland to escape Fidel Castro's dictatorship, have long been a reliable voting bloc for Republicans. But recent evidence shows that second- and third-generation Cuban Americans are more liberal and more likely to vote Democratic than the elder generation.[86] This is good news for Democrats, of course, but it also serves to remind both parties that old loyalties are not easily maintained and that voters respond to changing issues and interests, not simply on the basis of ethnicity. Indeed, in the days immediately following the 2012 election, some Republican leaders were already reconsidering their party's position on immigration reform in order to sway Latino voters in the future.[87] However this battle for Latino votes plays out, it appears the South will be the focus of both parties' attention for many elections to come.

THE ELECTORAL VOTE BALANCE

Elections often conclude with the winning party making hyperbolic claims of electoral mandates and partisan realignments. However, as we have seen, comparing presidential elections results over time suggests that party competition for the presidency is high in the postwar period. Today's presidential elections are national in scope, and the Electoral College provides no significant barrier to either political party. Moreover, Andrew Gelman, Jonathan N. Katz, and Gary King present compelling evidence that since the 1950s partisan biases created by the Electoral College are negligible.[88]

Short-term factors, however, do suggest that Democrats are currently advantaged. Since 1988, the Democrats have won four of six elections. But the recent past is not always a guide to the future. Consider the fact that in the six elections between 1968 and 1988, the Republicans held the advantage, winning five of the six and several by significant margins.[89] Republican strength in the 1980s was soon replaced by Democratic victories in the 1990s. Yet because competition for the presidency has always rested on some assessment of a candidate's relative strength in each of the states, recent election results often guide how parties develop future electoral strategies.[90] In Figure 3-3, we illustrate how the states have voted in each of the last five elections.

When Figure 3-3 is compared to a similar figure based on the results between 1988 and 2004, there is a clear shift in the electoral vote balance toward the Democrats. Fifteen states have voted Republican in each of the past five elections. However, these states tally only 121 electoral votes. Texas, with 38 electoral votes, is the only large state among the fifteen, and six of these states have the minimum of 3 votes. Nine other states have voted Republican in four of the five elections, accounting for 85 electoral votes. Two of these, Indiana and North

FIGURE 3-3   Results of the 1996, 2000, 2004, 2008, and 2012 Presidential Elections

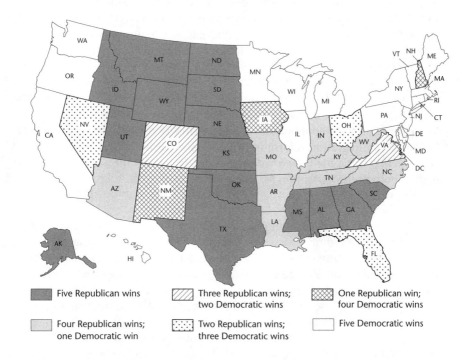

Source: Compiled by authors.

Carolina, voted for Obama in 2008. The remaining seven have not voted Democratic since Clinton's reelection in 1996, meaning that Republican victories there in 2016 will place them in the five-straight Republican wins category. The Republicans have won Colorado and Virginia (22 electoral votes combined) in three of the last five elections, but both voted for Obama in 2008 and 2012, suggesting a possible trend toward the Democratic side of the ledger. In total, these twenty-six "Republican states" represent 228 electoral votes, 42 votes shy of the 270 needed to win the Electoral College.

This leaves Democrats with twenty-four states and the District of Columbia, which total 310 electoral votes, comfortably exceeding the majority needed. Of these, nineteen states and the District of Columbia have voted Democratic in five straight elections. This group alone represents 242 electoral votes, twice as many as all those on the Republican side. Three states—Iowa, New Hampshire, and New Mexico (15 votes collectively)—have voted Democratic in four of the five elections, and three states—Florida, Nevada, and Ohio (53 votes in sum)— on three of the last five occasions.

If we were solely to use these five elections as the basis for determining battleground states for 2016, it would be a narrow field of play. Only five states fall into one of the "three-out-of-five" categories: Colorado, Florida, Nevada, Ohio, and Virginia (Obama swept these states in both 2008 and 2012). In this hypothetical, the Democratic candidate in 2016 would have to win only Ohio *or* Florida to win the Electoral College. If the Democrat were to win only Virginia, it would create an Electoral College tie. But for the Republican to win, he or she would have to sweep the four largest states at minimum.

Undoubtedly, this scenario presents a challenge for the GOP. But this is not the first time in recent history that the Electoral College map has appeared so uninviting for one of the parties and generally uncompetitive. Figure 3-4 illustrates changes over time in the electoral balance of the Electoral College. Similar to Figure 3-3, we calculated how each of the states voted in the prior five elections, but did so for each election from 1988 to 2012.[91] We then categorized states that voted for the same party in three of the five previous elections as highly competitive. States that voted for the same party in four of the five elections were labeled sometimes competitive, and those that voted for the same party in each of the five were labeled uncompetitive.[92]

The figure shows that the number of uncompetitive states has nearly doubled since the 2000 election. Thirty-four of the fifty states currently appear to be uncompetitive, having voted for one of the two parties consistently over each of the last five elections. This rise coincides with a decline in the number of highly competitive states, which as noted earlier is now down to five. This alone would suggest a lack of electoral competition. But perhaps the clearest message conveyed by the figure is that the current electoral vote balance is likely subject to change—indeed, perhaps rapid change. The competitive balance in 1988 is closest to what we see today. Following that election, only eight states were considered highly competitive, and twenty-six were uncompetitive. Yet the challenge

FIGURE 3-4   Competitive Balance in the Electoral College, 2008–2012

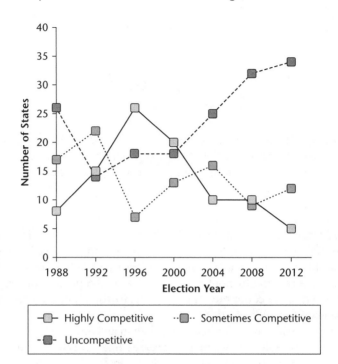

Source: Compiled by authors.

confronting Democrats following the 1988 elections was arguably more daunt-ing than that confronting Republicans today. While there are thirty-four uncom-petitive states following the 2012 elections, eighteen are Democratic and fifteen are Republican states. In 1988, however, twenty-five of the twenty-six uncom-petitive states were Republican states. Based on the electoral vote balance alone, no one could have reasonably predicted Democratic victories in 1992 and 1996.

To assess the future prospects of the major parties, we must go beyond analyz-ing official election statistics. While these statistics are useful for understanding competitive outcomes and future party strategies, they tell us little about why Americans vote the way they do, or whether they vote at all. To understand how social coalitions have changed over time, as well as the issue preferences of the electorate, we must turn to surveys. They reveal how Obama was able to win reelection despite the public's somewhat negative assessments of both the economy and his presidency. Furthermore, to determine the extent to which Americans really are polarized along party lines, we must study surveys to examine the way in which the basic party loyalties of the American electorate have changed during the postwar period. Thus, in the next five chapters, our study turns to survey data to examine the prospects for continuity and change in American electoral politics.

Chapter 4

Who Voted?

Over 129 million Americans cast ballots in the 2012 presidential election—the second highest total in U.S. history. Yet this number is less impressive when one considers that some 93 million Americans who were eligible to vote did not.[1] Overall, the turnout rate in 2012 was 53.6 percent of the population (58.2 percent if we count only those eligible to vote), a three-percentage-point decline from the 2008 election.

Turnout is lower in the United States than in any other Western industrialized democracy. In Table 4-1, we present average turnout rates during the postwar period for twenty-five democracies, including the United States.[2] Obviously, there is much variation in turnout among these countries. And while it is not our goal to provide a full accounting of these differences, several points are worth noting.[3] Australia and Belgium, which have the highest turnout rates shown in Table 4-1, are among several democracies with laws that enforce some form of compulsory voting. Though the penalties for not voting are relatively mild, compulsory voting obviously increases turnout.[4] A country's electoral system has also been shown to affect rates of voter turnout. In countries that use some form of proportional representation (PR) system, political parties have an incentive to mobilize the electorate broadly, since every vote contributes to a party's proportional share. In plurality rule, winner-take-all systems, such as the United States and Britain, many electoral units are not competitive and get-out-the-vote efforts are likely to be of little value.[5] Differences among party systems may also encourage the lower social classes to vote in some societies and do little to encourage them to vote in others.

No matter whether one is examining turnout in legislative or presidential elections, the United States clearly lags behind other industrialized democracies in voter participation.[6] To be fair, U.S. congressional elections, especially midterm elections, are not comparable to parliamentary elections in these other democracies. In the United States, the head of government is elected separately from the legislature. The president, for instance, remains in office regardless of

TABLE 4-1   Voter Turnout in National Elections, 1945–2013 (percent)

Country	National parliamentary	Presidential
Australia (26)	95.0	
Belgium (21)	92.3	
Luxembourg (14)	90.0	
Austria (20)	89.8	(12) 86.2
Malta (17)	89.3	
Iceland (20)	88.4	(6) 81.1
Italy (18)	88.1	
New Zealand (23)	87.9	
Denmark (25)	86.2	
Sweden (20)	85.4	
Netherlands (21)	85.2	
Germany (17)	83.7	
Norway (17)	80.0	
Greece (18)	77.8	
Israel (19)	77.3	
Finland (19)	74.4	(11) 73.5
United Kingdom (18)	73.9	
Spain (11)	73.6	
France (18)	72.9	(9) 81.9
Portugal (14)	72.5	(8) 65.5
Ireland (18)	72.1	(7) 56.9
Canada (22)	71.6	
Japan (25)	69.6	
Switzerland (17)	55.0	
United States (34)	45.1	(17) 55.5

Source: All countries except the United States: mean level of turnout computed from results in International Voter Turnout Database, http://www.idea.int/vt/view_data.cfm. U.S. turnout results, 1946–2010: U.S. Census Bureau, *Statistical Abstract of the United States, 2012* (Washington, D.C.: Government Printing Office, 2012), Table 397, 244, http://www.census.gov/compendia/statab. U.S. results for 2012 calculated by authors; total votes cast in U.S. House elections obtained from Clerk of the House of Representatives, "Statistics of the Presidential and Congressional Election of November 6, 2012"; voting-age population estimates obtained from Michael P. McDonald, "2012 General Election Turnout Rates," http://elections.gmu.edu/Turnout_2012G.html.

Note: For all countries except the United States, turnout is computed by dividing the number of votes cast by the number of people registered to vote. For the United States, turnout is computed by dividing the number of votes cast for the U.S. House of Representatives (or for president) by the voting-age population. Numbers in parentheses are the number of parliamentary or presidential elections. For all countries with bicameral legislatures, we report turnout for the lower house.

the outcomes of the congressional midterms. In parliamentary systems, the head of government is dependent upon the performance of his or her legislative party in parliamentary elections. Even in a semipresidential system such as

president may be forced to replace his prime minister and cabinet
of a National Assembly election. Yet even when the president is on
turnout for U.S. House elections during the seventeen presidential
elections since World War II was only 51.4 percent, which is substantially lower
than that of any democracy except for Switzerland. Indeed, turnout for U.S.
presidential elections ranks well below voting rates in Austria, Finland, France,
Iceland, and Portugal. Voter participation in U.S. presidential elections is
roughly equivalent to presidential turnout in Ireland, where the presidency is
essentially a ceremonial position.

In comparative perspective, the low turnout rate of the United States can be
explained in part by institutional differences. But this does little to explain the
tremendous amount of individual-level variation in voter turnout that occurs
within the United States. If roughly 58 percent of Americans participate in
presidential elections, that means 42 percent *do not*. Thus, before discovering
how people voted in the 2012 election, we must answer a more basic question:
who voted? The answer to this question is also partly institutional because federal and state laws in the United States—both historically and still today—often
serve to inhibit (and sometimes facilitate) individuals' ability to vote. Political
parties also play a role in affecting individuals' turnout decisions since parties'
electoral strategies help to define which voters are mobilized. And, of course,
personal characteristics, such as an individual's socioeconomic status, political
predispositions, and feelings of efficacy, contribute to his or her decision to go to
the polls. Using survey data from the 2012 American National Election Study,
we will consider how each of these factors affected who voted in the most recent
presidential election. Before doing so, however, it is important to place the study
of turnout in a broader historical context.[7]

VOTER TURNOUT, 1789-1916

As noted by the historian Alexander Keyssar, "[a]t its birth, the United States was
not a democratic nation—far from it. The very word democracy had pejorative
overtones, summoning up images of disorder, government by the unfit, even mob
rule."[8] Between 1789 and 1828, popular elections were rare in the United States.
The Constitution did not require the Electoral College to be selected by popular
vote, so many state legislatures simply appointed their presidential electors.
Indeed, as late as the election of 1824, six of the twenty-four states appointed their
slate of electors. Since U.S. senators were also appointed by state legislatures, voting in national elections was essentially limited to casting ballots for members of
the House of Representatives.[9] Even then, voter participation was strictly limited.
Race exclusions and property requirements, combined with the lack of female
suffrage, effectively narrowed the eligible electorate during this period to white
male landowners.[10] As a result of this limited electoral competition and restricted
suffrage, voter turnout rates during this period are the lowest in American history.

The presidential election of 1828 is the first election in which the vast majority of states chose their presidential electors by popular vote, thus making it the first for which meaningful measures of voter turnout can be calculated.[11] Historical records can be used to determine how many people voted in presidential elections, but constructing a measure of the turnout rate requires us to choose an appropriate denominator. Turnout in presidential elections is typically determined by dividing the total number of votes cast for president by the voting-age population.[12] But given limited voting rights, should the turnout denominator be all people who are old enough to vote? Or should it include only those who were eligible to vote? The answer will greatly affect our estimates of turnout in presidential elections through 1916 since voting rights differed significantly among the states during this time. Women, for instance, were eligible to vote in a handful of states before the ratification of the Nineteenth Amendment in 1920.[13] Clearly, women should be included in the turnout denominator in states where they had the right to vote, but including them in the states where they could not vote would grossly deflate our estimates of turnout.

In Figure 4-1, we present two sets of estimates of turnout in presidential elections from 1828 through 1916. The alternative estimates reflect difference in the choice of denominator used to measure the turnout rate. The first set was compiled by Charles E. Johnson Jr., who calculated turnout by dividing the number of votes cast for president by the voting-age population. The second set is based on calculations by Walter Dean Burnham, who measures turnout by dividing the total number of votes cast for president by the number of Americans eligible to vote (the voting-eligible population). Burnham excludes African Americans before the Civil War, and from 1870 on he excludes aliens where they were not allowed to vote, basing his estimates on what he calls the "politically eligible" population. But the main difference between Burnham's estimates and Johnson's estimates is that Burnham excludes women from the turnout denominator in states where they could not vote.

Most political scientists would consider Burnham's calculations more meaningful than Johnson's. But whichever set of estimates one employs, the pattern of change is very similar. One clearly sees the effect of the advent of mass political parties and reemergence of two-party competition on voter participation. There is a large increase in turnout after 1836, when both the Democrats and Whigs began to employ popular appeals to mobilize the electorate. Turnout jumped markedly in 1840, the "Log Cabin and Hard Cider" campaign in which William Henry Harrison, the hero of the Battle of Tippecanoe (1811), defeated the incumbent Democrat, Martin Van Buren. Turnout waned somewhat after 1840, only to increase by roughly ten percentage points in 1856 after the Republican Party, founded in 1854, polarized the nation by taking a clear stand against slavery in the territories. In Abraham Lincoln's election in 1860, four out of five eligible white men went to the polls.

Turnout vacillated during the Civil War and Reconstruction era. The presidential election of 1864, held just weeks after General Sherman's Union troops

FIGURE 4-1   Voter Turnout in Presidential Elections, 1828–1916

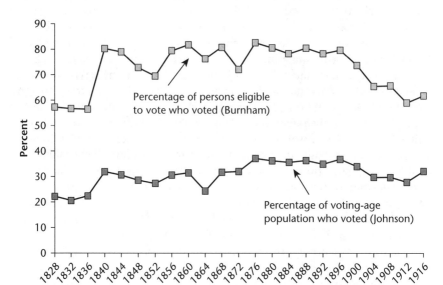

Sources: Estimates of turnout among the voting-age population based on Charles E. Johnson Jr., *Nonvoting Americans,* series P-23, no. 2, U.S. Department of the Census (Washington, D.C.: Government Printing Office, 1980), 2; estimates of turnout among the population eligible to vote based on calculations by Walter Dean Burnham, "The Turnout Problem," in *Elections American Style,* ed. A. James Reichley (Washington, D.C.: Brookings Institution, 1987), 113–114.

Note: Johnson's estimate for 1864 is based on the entire U.S. adult population. Burnham's estimate for that year excludes the eleven Confederate states that did not take part in the election.

seized Atlanta, saw a decline in turnout. Voter participation increased in 1868, but the turnout rate declined sharply in the 1872 election, the first to take place after African Americans were granted suffrage by the ratification of the Fifteenth Amendment.[14] Voter participation peaked in the 1876 contest between Republican Rutherford B. Hayes and Democrat Samuel J. Tilden. Though Tilden won a majority of the popular vote, he did not win an electoral majority, and twenty electoral votes were disputed. To end the ensuing controversy, an informal compromise was made where the Democrats conceded the presidency to the Republican, Hayes, and the Republicans agreed to end Reconstruction.

Once the protection of federal troops was lost, many African Americans were prevented from voting. Although some southern blacks could still vote in 1880, their overall turnout dropped sharply, which reduced southern turnout as a whole. Between 1880 and 1896, national turnout levels were relatively static, but turnout began a long decline in 1900, an election that featured a rematch of the candidates from 1896, Republican incumbent William McKinley and William Jennings Bryan (Democrat and Populist). By the late nineteenth century, African

Americans were denied the franchise throughout the South, and poor whites often found it difficult to vote as well.[15] Throughout the country, registration requirements, which were in part designed to reduce fraud, were introduced. Because individuals were responsible for placing their names on the registration rolls before the election, the procedure created an obstacle that reduced electoral participation.[16]

Introducing the secret ballot also reduced turnout. Before this innovation, most voting in U.S. elections was public. Because the political parties printed their own ballots, which differed in size and color, any observer could see how a person voted. The "Australian ballot"—as the secret ballot is often called—was first used statewide in Massachusetts in 1888.[17] By the 1896 election, nine in ten states had followed Massachusetts's lead.[18] Although the secret ballot was designed to reduce fraud, it also reduced turnout.[19] When voting was public, men could sell their votes, but candidates were less willing to pay for a vote if they could not see it delivered. Ballot stuffing was also more difficult when the state printed and distributed the ballots. Moreover, the Australian ballot also proved to be an obstacle to participation for many illiterate voters, though this was remedied in some states by expressly permitting illiterate voters to seek assistance.[20]

As Figure 4-1 shows, turnout trailed off rapidly in the early twentieth century. By the time the three-way contest was held in 1912 between Democrat Woodrow Wilson, Republican William Howard Taft, and Theodore Roosevelt, a Progressive, only three in five politically eligible Americans were going to the polls. In 1916, turnout rose slightly, but just over three-fifths of eligible Americans voted, and only one-third of the total adult population went to the polls.

VOTER TURNOUT, 1920–2012

With the extension of suffrage to all women by constitutional amendment in 1920, the rules that governed eligibility for voting became much more uniform among the states. This makes it easier to calculate turnout from 1920 onward, and we provide estimates based on both the voting-age and voting-eligible populations. As suffrage becomes more universal these two populations grow in similarity (and the large gap between the measures that is evident in Figure 4-1 dissipates). Indeed, these alternative measures of voter turnout produce fairly similar estimates, although differences have increased since 1972. In the modern period, we prefer focusing on turnout among the voting-age population for two reasons. First, it is difficult to estimate the size of the eligible population. Walter Dean Burnham and coauthors Michael P. McDonald and Samuel L. Popkin have made excellent efforts to provide these estimates.[21] Even so, Burnham's estimates of turnout differ from McDonald and Popkin's, with the latter reporting somewhat higher levels of turnout in all five elections between 1984 and 2000. One difficulty in determining the eligible population is estimating the number of ineligible felons.[22] Incarceration rates, which have grown markedly during the last four decades, are frequently revised, and the number of permanently disfranchised is nearly impossible to measure satisfactorily.[23] According to McDonald, in 2012 over 1.6 million prisoners were ineligible to vote, as were 1.3 million on probation and over 600,000 on parole.[24]

Second, excluding noneligible adults from the turnout denominator may yield misleading estimates, especially when U.S. turnout is compared with turnout levels in other democracies. For example, about one in ten voting-age Americans cannot vote, whereas in Britain only about one in fifty is disfranchised. In the United States, about one in seven black males cannot vote because of a felony conviction. As Thomas E. Patterson writes in a critique of McDonald and Popkin, "To ignore such differences, some analysts say, is to ignore official attempts to control the size and composition of the electorate."[25]

In Table 4-2, we show the percentage of the voting-age population who voted for the Democratic, Republican, and minor-party and independent candidates ("other candidates") between 1920 and 2012. The table also shows the percentage that did not vote, as well as the overall size of the voting-age population.

Barack Obama won a majority of the popular vote in 2012, but that does not mean that his supporters composed a majority of the voting-age population. As Table 4-2 shows, it is more likely for a majority of American adults to stay away from the polls on election day than support any one candidate. In all the elections between 1920 and 2012, except 1964, the percentage that did not vote easily exceeded the share cast for the winning candidates. In 2012, only 27.4 percent of American adults could be counted as an Obama voter (25.2 percent of the adult population cast ballots for Romney). In both absolute and proportional terms, fewer Americans voted for Obama in 2012 than in 2008. The proportion of Americans who supported Obama in 2012 was slightly below the average for all winning presidential candidates before 2008 (29.2 percent).

In Figure 4-2, we show the percentage of the voting-age population that voted for president in each of these twenty-three elections, as well as the percentage of the politically eligible population between 1920 and 1944 and the voting-eligible population between 1948 and 2012.[26] The extent to which these trend lines diverge depends on the percentage of the voting-age population that is eligible to vote. In eras when most were eligible, such as between 1940 and 1980, it makes very little difference which turnout denominator one employs. But today there is a much larger noncitizen population, and incarceration rates are high. Back in 1960, when turnout peaked, only 2.2 percent of voting-age Americans were not citizens; as of 2008, 8.6 percent were not. In 1960, only 0.4 percent of Americans were ineligible to vote because of their felony status; in 2008, 1.6 percent were ineligible. Thus as Figure 4-2 shows, in 1960 there was very little difference between turnout among the voting-age population and turnout among the voting-eligible population. In the 2012 election, 129,067,662 votes were cast for president. Because the voting-age population was 240,926,957,

TABLE 4-2 Percentage of Adults Who Voted for Each of the Major-Party Candidates, 1920–2012

Election year	Democratic candidate		Republican candidate		Other candidates	Did not vote	Total	Voting-age population
1920	James M. Cox	14.8	Warren G. Harding	26.2	2.4	56.6	100	61,639,000
1924	John W. Davis	12.7	Calvin Coolidge	23.7	7.5	56.1	100	66,229,000
1928	Alfred E. Smith	21.1	Herbert C. Hoover	30.1	0.6	48.2	100	71,100,000
1932	Franklin D. Roosevelt	30.1	Herbert C. Hoover	20.8	1.5	47.5	100	75,768,000
1936	Franklin D. Roosevelt	34.6	Alfred M. Landon	20.8	1.5	43.1	100	80,174,000
1940	Franklin D. Roosevelt	32.2	Wendell Willkie	26.4	0.3	41.1	100	84,728,000
1944	Franklin D. Roosevelt	29.9	Thomas E. Dewey	25.7	0.4	44.0	100	85,654,000
1948	Harry S. Truman	25.3	Thomas E. Dewey	23.0	2.7	48.9	100	95,573,000
1952	Adlai E. Stevenson	27.3	Dwight D. Eisenhower	34.0	0.3	38.4	100	99,929,000
1956	Adlai E. Stevenson	24.9	Dwight D. Eisenhower	34.1	0.4	40.7	100	104,515,000
1960	John F. Kennedy	31.2	Richard M. Nixon	31.1	0.5	37.2	100	109,672,000
1964	Lyndon B. Johnson	37.8	Barry M. Goldwater	23.8	0.3	38.1	100	114,090,000
1968	Hubert H. Humphrey	26.0	Richard M. Nixon	26.4	8.4	39.1	100	120,285,000
1972	George S. McGovern	20.7	Richard M. Nixon	33.5	1.0	44.8	100	140,777,000
1976	Jimmy Carter	26.8	Gerald R. Ford	25.7	1.0	46.5	100	152,308,000
1980	Jimmy Carter	21.6	Ronald Reagan	26.8	4.3	47.2	100	163,945,000
1984	Walter F. Mondale	21.6	Ronald Reagan	31.3	0.4	46.7	100	173,995,000
1988	Michael S. Dukakis	23.0	George H. W. Bush	26.9	0.5	49.7	100	181,956,000
1992	Bill Clinton	23.7	George H. W. Bush	20.6	10.8	44.9	100	189,493,000
1996	Bill Clinton	24.1	Bob Dole	19.9	4.9	51.1	100	196,789,000
2000	Al Gore	24.8	George W. Bush	24.5	1.9	48.8	100	205,813,000
2004	John F. Kerry	26.7	George W. Bush	28.1	0.6	44.6	100	220,804,000
2008	Barack Obama	30.0	John McCain	26.0	0.8	43.2	100	230,917,000
2012	Barack Obama	27.4	Mitt Romney	25.2	0.9	46.5	100	240,926,957

Sources: Voting-age population, 1920–1928: U.S. Census Bureau, Statistical Abstract of the United States, 1972, 92nd ed. (Washington, D.C.: Government Printing Office, 1972), Table 597, 373; voting-age population, 1932–2000: U.S. Census Bureau, Statistical Abstract of the United States, 2004–2005, 124th ed. (Washington, D.C.: Government Printing Office, 2004), Table 409, 257; voting-age population, 2004–2012: Michael P. McDonald's United States Election Project, http://elections.gmu.edu/voter_turnout.htm; number of votes cast for each presidential candidate and the total number of votes cast for president: Federal Election Commission, "Official 2012 Presidential General Election Results," January 17, 2013, http://www.fec.gov/pubrec/fe2012/2012presgeresults.pdf.

Note: The names of the winning candidates are italicized.

FIGURE 4-2 Percentage of Voting-Age Population and of the Politically Eligible and the Voting-Eligible Population Voting for President, 1920–2012

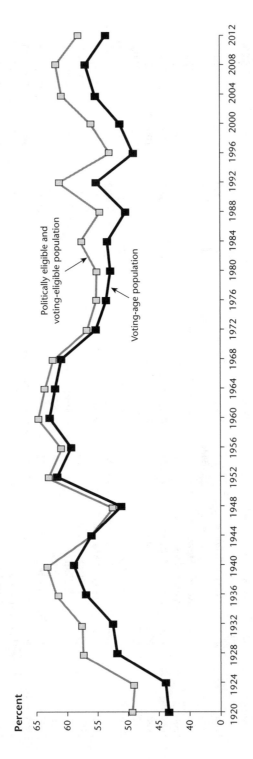

Sources: Voting-age population, see Table 4-3 in this volume; politically eligible population, 1920–1944: Walter Dean Burnham, "The Turnout Problem," in *Elections American Style,* ed. A. James Reichley (Washington, D.C.: Brookings Institution, 1987), 113–114; voting-eligible population, 1948–2000: Michael P. McDonald and Samuel L. Popkin, "The Myth of the Vanishing Voter," *American Political Science Review* 95 (December 2001): 966; 2000–2012: Michael P. McDonald's United States Election Project, http://elections.gmu.edu/voter_turnout.htm.

turnout among this population was 53.6 percent. But according to McDonald, the population eligible to vote was only 221,925,820. Using this total as our denominator, turnout is 58.2 percent. If we use McDonald's measure to calculate turnout in all seventeen postwar presidential elections, turnout would rise from 55.5 percent to 58.2 percent. However, U.S. turnout would still be lower than turnout in parliamentary elections in any country except Switzerland and lower than in presidential elections in any country except Ireland.

Turnout among the voting-age population generally rose between 1920 and 1960. Two exceptions were the elections of 1944 and 1948, when turnout decreased markedly due to social dislocations during and after World War II. Campaign-specific conditions sometimes account for increases in turnout in certain elections. In 1928, for instance, the jump in turnout can be attributed to the candidacy of Alfred Smith, the first Catholic candidate to receive a major-party nomination. The increase in 1936 partly reflects Franklin Roosevelt's efforts to mobilize the lower social classes, especially the industrial working class. The extremely close contest between Republican Vice President Richard Nixon and the second Catholic candidate, Democrat John F. Kennedy, partly accounts for the high turnout in 1960, when it rose to 62.8 percent of the voting-age population and was slightly higher among the politically eligible population.[27] The presidential election of 1960 produced the highest level of turnout among voting-age adults in American history. Yet the turnout percentage for the politically eligible population in 1960 was far below the typical levels found between 1840 and 1900. Moreover, the U.S. turnout in 1960 was still well below the average level of turnout in most advanced democracies (see Table 4-1).

Although short-term forces drove turnout upward in specific elections, long-term forces also contributed to the increase in turnout during this period. For example, women who came of age before the Nineteenth Amendment often failed to exercise their right to vote, but women who came of age after 1920 had higher levels of turnout and gradually replaced older women in the electorate.[28] Because all states restricted voting to citizens, immigrants enlarged the voting-age population, but could not increase the number of voters until they became citizens. After 1921, however, as a result of restrictive immigration laws, the percentage of the population that was foreign-born declined. Moreover, levels of education rose throughout the twentieth century, a change that acts as an upward force on turnout. Americans who have attained higher levels of education are much more likely to vote than those with lower levels of education.

From 1960 to 1988 turnout declined in the United States. Turnout among the voting-age population was roughly nine points higher in 1960 than it was in 2012. The decline in turnout during this period occurred even though there were several institutional changes that should have increased turnout. Between 1960 and the century's end, the country underwent changes that tended to increase turnout. After passage of the Voting Rights Act of 1965, turnout rose dramatically among African Americans in the South, and their turnout spurred voting among southern whites. Less restrictive registration laws introduced over the last three decades also have made it easier to vote. The National Voter Registration Act, better known as the "motor voter" law, went into effect in January 1995, and it may have added nine million additional registrants to the rolls.[29]

One recent institutional innovation that has altered the way many voters cast their ballots is the adoption of early voting in many states.[30] Early voting makes going to the polls more convenient by allowing voters to cast ballots on one or more days before election day.[31] Texas was among the first states to use early voting in 1988. Since then, the number of states adopting early voting laws has increased in every election period. In 2012, thirty-two states and the District of Columbia had laws allowing in-person early voting.[32] The remaining states offer some form of absentee voting, and two states, Oregon and Washington, conducted voting strictly by mail.[33] We analyzed the 2012 Current Population Survey (CPS) conducted by the U.S. Census Bureau to determine the extent to which voters made use of these convenience-voting mechanisms in 2012.[34] Figure 4-3 shows that early voting varies greatly among the states. Nationally, 31.8 percent of Americans reported voting early. The two states with vote-by-mail reported rates of early voting over 90 percent, while at the low end, thirteen states (all of which have absentee voting only) reported rates of less than 10 percent.

And yet despite all of the institutional changes related to voting since the 1960s, turnout has not increased. Except for a small increase in turnout in 1984, turnout among the voting-age population clearly declined between 1960 and 1988, falling most between 1968 and 1972.[35] Turnout then rose almost five points in 1992, perhaps as a result of Ross Perot's third-party candidacy.[36] But in 1996 turnout fell some six percentage points, reaching only 48.9 percent. In 2000, 2004, and 2008 turnout rose. Both George W. Bush elections were expected to be close going into election day, and this may have stimulated voter participation. In 2008, Barack Obama's historic campaign as the nation's first African American nominee from a major party excited many minority and young voters. Though few people expected that election to be close, the Obama campaign ran an inventive ground game, incorporating many Internet-based technological advances in their attempt to get out the vote. Although some observers expected a large increase in turnout in 2008, it rose only 1.4 percentage points.

VOTER TURNOUT AMONG SOCIAL GROUPS

In 2012, turnout declined. But the aggregate numbers mask many interesting nuances in the composition of the electorate. For instance, according to the U.S. Census Bureau, for the first time in American history, blacks voted at a higher rate than whites. Interestingly, increased levels of participation among African Americans do not appear to be an aberration associated with Obama's candidacy. According to Census figures, black turnout rose by an average of 3.3 percent in each election since 1996 (white turnout declined in both 2008 and 2012).

FIGURE 4-3 Percentage of Voters Who Voted Early by State

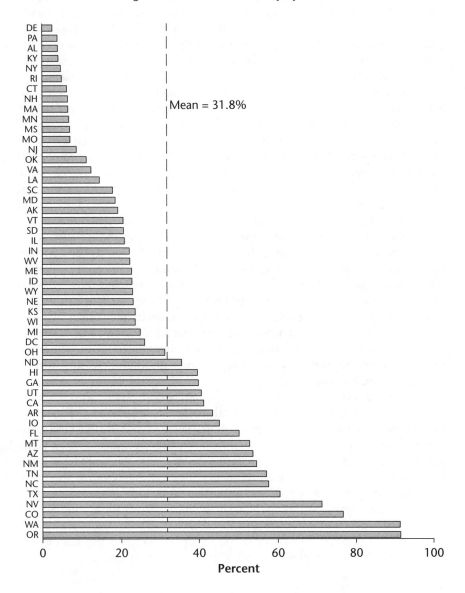

Source: U.S. Census Bureau, 2012 Current Population Study, November Supplement.

Note: Data are weighted.

To further compare voter turnout among various social groups, we rely on the 2012 American National Election Study (ANES) survey.[37]

Roughly 58 percent of the voting-eligible population turned out in 2012, but just over 85 percent of the respondents interviewed in the postelection survey reported that they voted. The ANES surveys commonly overestimate turnout for three reasons. First, even though the ANES respondents are asked a question that provides reasons for not voting, some voters falsely claim to have voted, perhaps owing to social pressure.[38] In past years, ANES has undertaken vote validation efforts, in which state voting and registration records were checked to authenticate respondents' claims—the 1988 presidential election was the last for which this was done. These validation efforts suggest that about 15 percent of the respondents who say that they voted did not do so, whereas only a handful of actual voters claim they did not vote. Importantly, for our purposes, most analyses that compare the results of reported voting with those measured by the validation studies suggest that *relative* levels of turnout among most social groups can be compared using reported turnout.[39] Second, the ANES surveys do not perfectly represent the voting-age population. Lower socioeconomic groups, which have very low turnout, are underrepresented. Discrepancies between the distribution of reported turnout in the ANES and actual turnout are exacerbated by low survey-response rates.[40] When response rates are low, surveys like the ANES tend to overrepresent higher socioeconomic groups and those who are interested in the survey's political subject matter. The response rate for the 2012 ANES was 38 percent, well below the rate associated with previous ANES surveys. Third, during presidential election years, the ANES attempts to interview respondents both before and after the election. Being interviewed before the election may provide a stimulus to survey respondents, thus increasing turnout among the ANES sample.

With this caveat in mind, we examine differences in voter turnout among various social groups. Nearly all empirical studies of turnout (as well as other forms of political participation) note the importance of individuals' social environments on their propensity to participate. Over forty years ago, Sidney Verba and Norman Nie articulated the "standard socioeconomic status model."[41] More recently, Verba, Brady, and Schlozman developed their "resource model of political participation," by which they argue that individuals' resources, particularly time, money, and civic skills, facilitate political participation.[42] Individuals high in socioeconomic status are also more likely to be located in social networks that encourage participatory norms. In the following sections, we examine patterns of voter participation among various social groups.

Race, Gender, Region, and Age

Table 4-3 compares reported turnout among social groups using the 2012 ANES survey. Our analysis begins by comparing African Americans and whites.[43] As was the case with the 2008 election study, the 2012 study shows that whites and blacks report voting at equal rates. But the reported rate of turnout for both groups is much higher in 2012 (87 percent) than four years earlier (78 percent).

Data from the CPS reveal that blacks were slightly more likely to report voting than whites, 66.2 percent to 64.1 percent. As noted earlier, this is the first time that black turnout has been estimated to be higher than white turnout, though the gap is not large. Nevertheless, increasing levels of participation among African Americans is a significant change in voting behavior. In 1964, the year prior to the passage of the Voting Rights Act, the CPS reported whites were 12.2 percentage points more likely to vote than blacks. By 2004, this difference was reduced to 5.4 percent.[44] According the CPS, turnout among non-Hispanic whites in 2012 was 64.1 percent, down from 2008 (66.1 percent) and 2004 (67.2) levels. The exit polls conducted for a consortium of news organizations suggest that black turnout in 2012 was equivalent to 2008; in both election years blacks composed 13 percent of the electorate. These numbers reflect an increase over 2004 values, which report that 11 percent of voters were black.

TABLE 4-3   Percentage of Electorate Who Reported Voting for President, by Social Group, 2012

Social group	Did vote	Did not vote	Total	(N)[a]
Total electorate	85	15	100	(1,588)
Electorate, by race				
African American	87	13	100	(201)
White	87	13	100	(1,128)
Other	72	28	100	(252)
Latinos (of any race)	74	26	100	(152)
Whites, by gender				
Female	89	11	100	(572)
Male	85	15	100	(556)
Whites, by region				
New England and Mid-Atlantic	89	11	100	(229)
North Central	88	12	100	(270)
South	87	13	100	(295)
Border	80	20	100	(82)
Mountain and Pacific	84	16	100	(220)
Whites, by birth cohort				
Before 1942	91	9	100	(166)
1943–1952	93	7	100	(200)
1953–1962	93	7	100	(224)
1963–1972	90	10	100	(180)
1973–1982	77	23	100	(151)
1983–1991	75	25	100	(145)

(Continued)

TABLE 4-3   (Continued)

Social group	Did vote	Did not vote	Total	$(N)^a$
1992–1995	50	50	100	(27)
Whites, by level of education				
Not high school graduate	85	15	100	(77)
High school graduate	77	23	100	(318)
Some college	88	12	100	(338)
College graduate	94	6	100	(252)
Advanced degree	95	5	100	(140)
Whites, by annual family income				
Less than $15,000	71	29	100	(120)
$15,000–34,999	81	19	100	(192)
$35,000–49,999	88	12	100	(113)
$50,000–74,999	84	16	100	(227)
$75,000–89,999	89	11	100	(112)
$90,000–124,999	96	4	100	(150)
$125,000–174,999	93	7	100	(81)
$175,000 and over	100	0	100	(80)
Whites, by union membership[b]				
Member	88	12	100	(200)
Nonmember	87	13	100	(914)

Source: Authors' analysis of the 2012 ANES survey.

[a] Numbers are weighted.

[b] Respondent or family member in union.

The 2012 ANES includes a nationally representative "oversample" of blacks, making it possible to make comparisons among blacks. As in earlier ANES surveys, blacks with higher levels of education are more likely to vote than those with lower levels of education. Blacks with college degrees were thirteen percentage points more likely to vote than those with only a high school diploma, and turnout among younger blacks continues to lag behind older generations. In 2008, black men and women voted at roughly the same rate, a marked difference from earlier elections.[45] In 2012, the ANES shows a slightly higher turnout for black women than men (only two percentage points); exit polls indicate that black women composed 8 percent of the electorate, while black men were 5 percent. The church continues to be an important mobilizer of black political participation.[46] Those African Americans who regularly attend church ("once a week") are twenty percentage points more likely to vote than those who never attend.

Table 4-3 reveals that turnout among Latinos was lower than that for whites and African Americans. This is consistent with the historical record. Low levels of Latino turnout have typically been attributed to lower levels of education, income, and English language skills, and some have demonstrated differences between native- and foreign-born Latinos—though evidence varies on this issue—as well as ethnic group.[47] ANES data reveal the importance of education among Latinos; college graduates were twenty-one percentage points more likely to vote than Latinos with only a high school degree. Yet, unfortunately, while the 2012 ANES includes a nationally representative oversample of Latinos, data regarding their ethnicity (e.g., Mexican American, Cuban American, Puerto Rican) were not publicly available at the time of this study. To examine differences among Latinos, we turn to the CPS. The Census data show that Hispanics (48.0 percent) were significantly less likely to vote than blacks (66.2 percent) and non-Hispanic whites (64.1 percent), but they were slightly more likely to vote than Asian Americans (47.3 percent). The data also show that foreign-born, naturalized Hispanics were six percentage points more likely to vote than native-born Hispanics. And ethnicity seems to matter as well, but these differences may be confounded by political geography. Only half of Mexican Americans participated in the 2012 election (the lowest among Latino groups), while roughly 75 percent of Cuban Americans voted. This difference is likely attributable to Mexican Americans—many of whom live in California and Texas—residing in uncompetitive states, while many Cuban Americans live in the battleground state of Florida. Overall, though, Latino turnout declined slightly in 2012, down roughly two percentage points.

In the 2008 election, white women were seven points more likely than white men to report voting, the largest female advantage in any of the presidential elections we studied prior to that year.[48] Women have voted at higher rates than men for some time now. The 1980 election was the last year in which the ANES surveys show white males to have a clear tendency to report voting more often than white females. Early ANES surveys show a clear decline in the turnout differential that advantaged men. In 1952, 1956, and 1960, the average male advantage was just over ten points, while in the 1964, 1968, 1972, and 1976 elections the gap narrowed to an average of just over five points. This pattern of a long period of male advantage in turnout followed by a long period of female advantage has also been evident in midterm elections.

The data for 2012 suggest the gender gap in voting may have declined since 2008. The ANES shows white women were only four points more likely to vote than white men. This gender difference is comparable to that found in the 2012 CPS, which estimates a three-percentage-point gap in turnout with non-Hispanic white women (64.5 percent) voting at a higher rate than non-Hispanic white men (61.5 percent). Exit polls also found a similar gender difference in turnout, estimating that white women composed 38 percent of the electorate and white men accounting for 44 percent.

Surveys are not needed to study turnout in the various regions of the country. Because we have estimates of both the voting-age population and the voting-eligible population for each state, we can measure turnout once we know the number of votes cast for president. According to McDonald's estimates, turnout among the voting-age population ranged from a low of

40 percent in Hawaii (44.2 percent of the voting-eligible population) to a high of 71.3 percent in Minnesota (75.7 percent of the voting-eligible population). But regional differences as a whole were small. According to our calculations, among the voting-age population in the South, 53.8 percent voted; outside the South, 56.4 percent did. Among the voting-eligible population, 58.3 percent of southerners voted; outside the South, 60.4 percent did. There are small regional differences among whites. As the data in Table 4-3 show, 87 percent of southern whites said they voted, and this estimate is the same for whites outside the South. We used CPS state-level estimates to calculate white non-Hispanic turnout in the eleven southern states. The CPS estimates turnout in the South to be 61.5 percent and 63.6 percent turnout outside the South. This relatively small difference reflects a fundamental change in postwar voting patterns since the Voting Rights Act of 1965. The one-party South was destroyed, electoral competition increased, and, with blacks enfranchised for the first time since the turn of the twentieth century, turnout increased among whites as well. Outside the South, turnout has declined.

Young Americans are more likely to have higher levels of formal education than their elders, and one might thus expect them to have higher levels of turnout. But they do not. Voter participation tends to increase with age. This is often attributed to changes in the life cycle; as people get older, settle down, and develop more community ties, they develop a greater appreciation for the role of government and politics in their lives, and they participate more.[49] Others argue that the effect of "life-changing" events may be overstated and that the greater likelihood of voter turnout with age is a product of greater political learning as people grow older.[50] Whatever the cause, the relationship between age and voter turnout is evident in each of the studies we examined.

In both 2008 and 2012, the Obama campaign expended great effort trying to mobilize young voters. But this effort had limited success at best. We reported turnout among voters eighteen and twenty-nine years old (the youngest two birth cohorts) in 2008 to be 67 percent. This was a slight increase over earlier ANES studies. Reported turnout among this age group was 74 percent among whites (80 percent among African Americans) in 2012, a sharp increase—but one that is contradicted by other available data. Exit polls for 2012 reported that eighteen- to twenty-nine-year-olds composed 19 percent of the electorate, a slight increase over 2008 (18 percent). Yet it is plausible that turnout among young people, while declining nationally, may not have declined at the same rate (or may have even increased) in battleground states, where voter mobilization efforts were more intense. Data from the CPS show that this geographic distinction is important. Turnout among eighteen- to twenty-nine-year-olds declined by 8.8 percentage points in non-battleground states in 2012. But in battleground states, turnout among young people declined only 6.2 percentage points, suggesting that mobilization efforts (or the closeness of the outcome in these states) partially offset youth disengagement in 2012. Interestingly, turnout among older Americans (fifty-five and older) was roughly six percentage points higher in

2012. Thus, age continues to be an important predictor of voter turnout rates in the United States.

Income and Union Membership

Jan Leighley and Jonathan Nagler argue that there is no better measure of an individual's social class than income, and income is strongly linked to voter participation.[51] The 2012 ANES shows that respondents' family income is related to reported turnout. White respondents with family incomes less than $15,000 were over twenty percentage points less likely to vote than those with incomes over $90,000. We found strong relationships between income and validated turnout in 1980, 1984, and 1988 and between income and reported turnout in all the presidential elections between 1982 and 2008. Earlier analyses of ANES data also demonstrate a strong relationship between family income and turnout in all the presidential elections between 1952 and 1976 and all the midterm elections between 1958 and 1978.[52] Previous CPS surveys have also shown a strong relationship between income and turnout, and the data for 2012 are no different. The CPS data show that turnout among all respondents with incomes less than $15,000 was 37.8 percent, while turnout among those with incomes greater than $100,000 was 74.8 percent.

Surveys over the years have found a weak and inconsistent relationship between union membership and turnout. Being in a household with a union member may create organizational ties that encourage voting. And unions have also been an important mobilizing agent for the Democratic Party, which for a significant portion of the postwar period relied on white working-class support as part of its electoral coalition. Yet Leighley and Nagler argue that the small and sporadic empirical association between union membership and turnout may result from union mobilization efforts increasing turnout among members and nonmembers alike. To support their claim, they provide evidence that the decline in union membership since 1964 has resulted in a decrease in voter turnout among lower- and middle-income groups regardless of membership. Exit polls show that voters from union households made up 18 percent of the electorate. But the 2012 ANES shows the effect of union membership to be negligible, with members and nonmembers participating at roughly the same rate—this is consistent with our findings from 2008.

Religion

Religion continues to play a powerful rule in American public life.[53] A 2013 survey by the Pew Research Center shows that 82 percent of Americans say that religion is an important part of their lives and over half say they attend religious services on at least a monthly basis.[54] Religious individuals tend to have strong social networks that facilitate the transmittal of political information and ease the costs of voting.[55] Churches also serve as direct and indirect vehicles for voter mobilization.[56]

In the earlier postwar years, Catholics were more likely to vote than Protestants, but these differences have declined.[57] The low turnout of Protestants, clearly documented by ANES surveys conducted between 1952 and 1978, resulted largely from two factors.[58] First, Protestants were more likely to live in the South, which was once a low-turnout region. Second, Protestants were more likely to be black, a group that had much lower turnout than whites. We have always compared turnout or reported turnout by comparing white Catholics with white Protestants. Except for the 1980 election, when there were no differences between Catholics and Protestants, Catholics were more likely to vote when vote validation measures were used (1984 and 1988). Catholics were also more likely to report voting in the five elections between 1992 and 2004, but in 2008 Protestants and Catholics were equally likely to turn out.

In our past studies, we used the ANES to examine differences in voter turnout among members of various religious denominations. Unfortunately, while the 2012 ANES inquired about respondents' religious affiliations and practices, the codes needed to classify respondents by religion and religiosity were not publicly available at the time of our writing. Thus, we are not able to update our analysis of religion and turnout for 2012. Exit polls, however, estimate that white Protestants composed 39 percent of the electorate, while white Catholics were 18 percent.[59] Overall, Protestants were 52 percent of the electorate, higher than their share of the U.S. population, while Catholics were 25 percent of the electorate, roughly equal to their population share.[60]

Between 1952 and 1996, Jews had higher reported turnout than either Protestants or Catholics in six of the seven presidential elections, as well as in five of the six midterm elections between 1958 and 1978. We found Jews to have higher levels of turnout or reported turnout in all seven elections between 1980 and 2008. In 2012, exit polls estimate that Jewish voters represented only 2 percent of the electorate in 2012.

For more than two decades, fundamentalist Protestants have been a pivotal actor in American politics. As we will see in Chapter 5, fundamentalist Protestants are conservative on social issues, such as abortion and same-sex marriage, and tend to throw their support overwhelmingly toward Republican presidential candidates. Indeed, Christian conservative churches and organizations expend considerable resources mobilizing voters through get-out-the-vote efforts and attempt to galvanize supporters through the circulation of voter information guides.[61]

In examining turnout among white fundamentalist Protestants since the 1992 election, we have found that the success of these groups in mobilizing their supporters has varied from election to election. In 2008, the last election for which we have data, we found no difference in reported turnout between Protestants who say they are born-again Christians and those who say they are not.[62]

Lyman A. Kellstedt argues that religious commitment is an important factor contributing to voting behavior.[63] In our previous studies, we were able to construct a measure of religious commitment using the ANES.[64] To score "very high" on this measure, respondents had to report praying several times a day and attending church at least once a week. In addition, they had to say that religion provided "a great deal" of guidance in their lives and to believe that the Bible is literally true or the "word of God." In 1992, 1996, 2000, and 2004, respondents who scored very high on this measure were the most likely to report voting, but in 2008 there was only a weak relationship between religious commitment and whether white Protestants said they voted. We lack the data necessary to measure religious commitment in 2012. However, the 2012 exit polls show that 15 percent of voters said they were Protestants who attended church weekly; 14 percent identified as Protestants who do not attend weekly. Eleven percent of voters identified themselves as Catholics who attend church weekly, and 13 percent were Catholics who do not attend weekly. While these exit poll results do not tell us directly about turnout differences between those who are devout and those who are not, they do suggest that these groups composed roughly equally sized segments of the electorate in 2012.

Most white Protestants can be classified into two categories, mainline and evangelical, which, according to Kenneth D. Wald, make up more than two-fifths of the total U.S. adult population.[65] As R. Stephen Warner has pointed out, "The root of the [mainline] liberal position is the interpretation of Christ as a moral teacher who told his disciples that they could best honor him by helping those in need." By contrast, says Warner, "the evangelical interpretation sees Jesus (as they prefer to call him) as one who offers salvation to anyone who confesses in his name." Liberal or mainline Protestants stress the importance of sharing their abundance with the needy, whereas evangelicals see the Bible as a source of revelation about Jesus.[66]

In classifying Protestants as mainline or evangelical, we rely on their denomination. For example, Episcopalians, Congregationalists, and most Methodists are classified as mainline, whereas Baptists, Pentecostals, and many small denominations are classified as evangelicals.[67] In 1992, 1996, 2000, and 2008, white mainline Protestants were more likely than white evangelicals to report voting. These results are scarcely surprising because mainline Protestants have higher levels of formal education than evangelicals. Only in 2004, when fundamentalist churches launched a massive get-out-the-vote effort, were white evangelicals as likely to report voting as white mainline Protestants.

Education

Surveys consistently reveal a strong relationship between formal education and electoral participation. The tendency for better-educated citizens to be more likely to vote is one of the most extensively documented facts in the study of politics. Indeed, in their classic study *Who Votes?*, Raymond E. Wolfinger and Steven J. Rosenstone note the "transcendent power of education" as a predictor of voter turnout.[68] Better-educated Americans have higher levels of political knowledge and political awareness; they also are more likely to possess the resources—money, time, and civic skills—that reduce the information costs of voting.[69]

The 2012 ANES reveals a strong relationship between formal education and voter turnout. Whites who did not graduate from high school were nearly ten percentage points less likely to report voting than those who graduated college. Yet reported voting among the least educated was remarkably high in 2012, 85 percent. This is much higher than in previous ANES surveys and is likely a product of the historically low response rate associated with the 2012 study. In 2008, for instance, whites without a high school diploma had a reported turnout rate of less than 50 percent, a relatively low rate but one that is more in line with previous studies than the rate reported in 2012.

The 2012 CPS also found a strong relationship between education and reported voter turnout. Among white citizens with less than a high school education, only 41.2 percent reported voting, and among those with only a high school diploma, 60.4 percent said they cast a ballot. Of those whites with some college-level education, 72.7 percent reported voting, and among college graduates, turnout was 87.9 percent. Among African Americans, education was also a strongly associated with voter turnout. Interestingly, less-educated African Americans were significantly more likely to vote than less-educated whites in 2012. Blacks with less than a high school education turned out at a reported rate of 61.8 percent, while those with a high school diploma reported turning out at a 72.6 percent rate. Turnout among African Americans with some college education was 81.9 percent, and among those with a college degree, it was 91.5 percent. Turnout differences among Latinos at varying levels of education were quite sharp. Latinos with less than a high school education turned out a rate of 35.5 percent; the rate was 39.4 percent among Latinos who are high school graduates. Turnout among Latinos with some college education was 54.2 percent, and for those with a college degree, turnout was 70.8 percent.

CHANGES IN TURNOUT AFTER 1960

The postwar turnout rate peaked in 1960. According to the U.S. Census Bureau, in that year, only 43.2 percent of whites and 20.1 percent of blacks twenty-five years and older were high school graduates. By 2010, 87.6 percent of whites and 84.2 percent of blacks were high school graduates. In 1960, only 8.1 percent of whites and 3.1 percent of blacks were college graduates. By 2010, 30.3 percent of whites and 19.8 percent of blacks had obtained college degrees. The growth in educational attainment is a remarkable change in American society, and this social transformation plays a central role in one of the longest standing empirical puzzles in the study of political behavior, a puzzle Richard A. Brody labels the "puzzle of political participation."[70] Given that education is a strong predictor of voter turnout at the individual level, why did national turnout levels decline between 1960 and 1980, and why did they stabilize, roughly speaking, thereafter, during a time when education levels rose dramatically?

Political scientists have studied the postwar changes in voter turnout extensively over the past several decades. Given the influence of education on turnout, one would expect increasing levels of education would lead to a substantial increase in turnout over this time, and certainly not a decline in voter participation of any degree, as happened between 1960 and 1980. This suggests that any stimulating effect of education on voter turnout was likely offset by other factors that depressed it. Some scholars argue that the decline in turnout was a function of social forces, such as the changing age distribution of the electorate and a decline in social institutions generally. Others point to institutional changes, such as the expansion of suffrage to eighteen-year-olds or to the ways in which the political parties conduct their campaigns as sources for the decline in voter turnout. Still others argue that the decline in voter turnout reflected changes in political attitudes that are fundamental for encouraging political participation.

The research by McDonald and Popkin provides one important part of the explanation for why turnout among the voting-age population has declined during the past half century. The percentage of noncitizens among the voting-age population in the United States has increased markedly from less than 2 percent in 1960 to 8.5 percent in 2010.[71] Moreover, in 1960, fewer than half a million people were incarcerated or were convicted felons, whereas in 2012 about five million were. This has resulted in an expansion in the number of ineligible voters in the United States. These changes would tend to reduce turnout among the voting-age population. Of course, neither the growth in noncitizens nor the increased number of disenfranchised felons is so large (large though these changes are) as to be sufficient for explaining the entire decline in turnout from 1960 onward. Moreover, these factors have increased at a higher rate in recent decades, but turnout no longer appears to be in decline.

In a comprehensive study of the decline in turnout between 1960 and 1988, Ruy Teixeira identifies three of the social forces that contributed to declining levels of voter participation.[72] After 1960, the electorate became significantly younger as the post–World War II "baby boomer" generation (those born between 1946 and 1964) came of age. Thus, the largest cohort in the electorate consisted of baby boomers, who were of an age when participation is lowest. Of course, boomers are considerably older today and now reside in the age cohort that is most likely to turn out, so they should be fueling an increase in participation. Teixeira also cites the decline in the percentage of Americans who were married, and married people are more likely to vote than those who are unmarried. He also points to declining church attendance as contributing to the decline in voter turnout.[73] Teixeira argues that the decline in church attendance, which reduces Americans' ties to their communities, was the most important of these three factors in reducing turnout and suggests that voter participation would have declined even further had education not been a countervailing force.[74]

Steven J. Rosenstone and John Mark Hansen also develop a comprehensive explanation for the decline in turnout. Using data from the ANES, they examine the effect of expanded suffrage (estimating that the inclusion of eighteen-, nineteen-, and twenty-year-olds in the 1972 elections likely caused about a one-percentage-point decline in turnout) and reduced voter registration requirements on voting. They found that reported turnout declined eleven percentage points from the 1960s to the 1980s. Yet their analysis also demonstrates that the increase in formal education was the most important factor preventing an even greater decline in voter participation. They estimate that turnout would have declined sixteen percentage points if it had not been for the combined effect of rising education levels and liberalized election laws.[75] Below, we discuss another institutional change that they argue contributed substantively to the decline in turnout—a change in the way political parties conduct electoral campaigns.

Most analysts agree that attitudinal changes contributed to the decline in electoral participation. Indeed, our own analysis has focused on the effects of attitudinal changes, particularly the influence of changes in party loyalties and the role of what George I. Balch and others have called feelings of "external political efficacy"—that is, the belief that political authorities will respond to attempts to influence them.[76] These are the same two fundamental attitudes analyzed by Teixeira in his first major study of turnout, and they are among the attitudes examined by Rosenstone and Hansen.[77] We found these attitudes contributed to the decline in turnout from 1960 through 1980, and they have remained influential in every presidential election we have studied from 1980 to 2012.[78]

To measure party identification, we use a standard set of questions to gauge individuals' psychological attachment to a partisan reference group.[79] In Chapter 8, we examine how party identification contributes to the way people vote. But party loyalties also contribute to *whether* people vote. Strong feelings of party identification contribute to one's psychological involvement in politics.[80] Moreover, party loyalties also reduce the time and effort needed to decide how to vote and thus reduce the costs of voting.[81] In every presidential election since 1952, the ANES studies have shown that strong partisans are more likely to vote than weaker partisans and independents who lean toward one of the parties. And in every election since 1960, independents with no partisan leanings have been the least likely to vote.

Partisanship is an important contributor to voters' decisions to turn out, but the strength of party loyalties in the United States has varied over time. Between 1952 and 1964, the number of self-identified "strong partisans" among the white electorate never fell below 35 percent. It then fell to 27 percent in 1966 and continued to fall, reaching its lowest level in 1978, when only 21 percent of voters identified strongly with one of the two major parties. In more recent years, party identification has risen; indeed, by 2004, it had returned to 1952–1964 levels. After a temporary decline in 2008 due to a decrease in Republican loyalties, the number of whites who were strong party identifiers rose to just over 30 percent in 2012.[82]

Feelings of political efficacy also contribute to voter participation. Citizens may expect to derive benefits from voting if they believe that government is responsive to their demands. Conversely, those who believe that political leaders will not or cannot respond to popular demands may see little reason to engage in political participation.[83] In thirteen of the fifteen elections between 1952 and 2008, Americans with high levels of political efficacy were more likely to vote than those at lower levels of efficacy.[84]

From 1960 to 1980, feelings of political efficacy dropped precipitously, and they remain low and in decline today. In 1956 and 1960, 64 percent of whites reported high levels of political efficacy, with only 15 percent scoring low. In 2012, few Americans felt that government responded to their needs. Indeed, efficacy was at an all-time low. Only 23 percent of whites scored high on our measure of political efficacy, and 45 percent scored low.

The steepest declines in partisan attachment and political efficacy occurred between 1960 and 1980, contemporaneous with the sharpest decline in voter participation. Our analysis of voter turnout during this two-decade period suggests that the combined impact of the decline in party identification and the decline in beliefs about government responsiveness account for roughly 70 percent of the decline of electoral participation. The ANES reports a decline in validated turnout among white voters of 10.3 percentage points between 1960 and 1980. By our estimates, if there had been no decline in either partisan attachments or external political efficacy, the decline in turnout would have been only 2.9 percentage points.[85] In previous volumes, we noted the persistent role these attitudes play in predicting voter turnout in subsequent election years. While party loyalties have rebounded to 1952–1964 levels, Americans' feelings of efficacy remain anemic, thus preventing a substantial increase in turnout levels. Using a rather simple algebraic procedure, we can estimate the percentage of whites in 2012 who would have reported voting for president had strength of partisanship and external political efficacy remained at 1960 levels.[86] Our estimate suggests that reported turnout among whites in 2012 would be three percentage points higher if not for these attitudinal changes.

In Table 4.4, we present the joint relationship between strength of party identification, feelings of efficacy, and reported electoral participation in the 2012 presidential election. As we have found in the past, strength of party identification and feelings of political efficacy are weakly related, but both contribute to turnout. Reading across each row reveals that strength of party identification is positively related to reported electoral participation, but the strength of this relationship is weaker in 2012 than in previous years. The difference in reported voting among whites with strong partisanship and those describing themselves as independents who lean toward a party is only two percentage points for those high in efficacy and eight points for those low in efficacy. In 2008, we reported differences of fifteen percentage points for those high in efficacy and thirty-four points for those low in efficacy. Yet given the low response rate and high level of overreporting of turnout associated with the 2012 ANES, it is difficult to establish whether this is a truly meaningful change in the nature of the relationship. Reading down each column, we see a strong and consistent relationship between feelings of political efficacy and reported voting within each partisan group—on the magnitude of ten- to sixteen-percentage-point differences. This suggests that the record-low level of political efficacy in 2012 was distributed among strong, weak, and nonpartisans alike and that efficacy had a strong relationship with decisions to turn out. In 2008, by comparison, we found a strong relationship between feelings of efficacy and reported turnout in only one partisan group, independents who lean toward a political party.

A comprehensive analysis of the role of attitudinal factors would have taken into account other factors that might have eroded turnout. For instance, as has been well documented, there has been a substantial decline in trust during the past four decades, a decline that appears to be occurring in a large number of democracies.[87] In 1964, when political trust among whites was highest, 77 percent of whites trusted the government to do what was right just about always or most of the time, and 74 percent of blacks endorsed this view.[88] Political trust reached a very low level in 1980, when only 25 percent of whites and 26 percent of blacks trusted the government. Trust rebounded during the Reagan years, but it fell after that, and by 1992 trust was almost as low as it had been in 1980. After that, trust rose in most elections, and by 2004, 50 percent of whites and 34 percent of blacks trusted the government. But trust dropped markedly among whites during the next four years, and it dropped somewhat among blacks also. In 2008, 30 percent of whites and 28 percent of blacks trusted the government.[89] In 2012, after the first term of the first black president, 19 percent of whites—a sharp decline—and 40 percent of blacks—a sharp increase—trusted the government in

TABLE 4-4   Percentage of Whites Who Reported Voting for President, by Strength of Party Identification and Sense of External Political Efficacy, 2012

Score on external political efficacy index	Strength of party identification							
	Strong partisan		Weak partisan		Independent who leans toward a party		Independent with no partisan leaning	
	%	(N)	%	(N)	%	(N)	%	(N)
High	98	(37)	90	(47)	96	(41)	[5]	(5)
Medium	97	(52)	77	(50)	87	(44)	82	(10)
Low	88	(57)	74	(76)	80	(125)	64	(19)

Source: Authors' analysis of the 2012 ANES survey.

Note: The numbers in parentheses are the totals on which the percentages are based. Numbers are weighted. The number in brackets is the total number reporting voting for president when there are fewer than ten total voters.

Washington to do what is right. Among Latinos, trust declined by six points over the course of Obama's first term from 36 to 30 percent.

Although the decline in trust in government would seem to be an obvious explanation for the decline in turnout, most scholarship shows little evidence supporting this. In most years, Americans who distrusted the government were as likely to vote as those who were politically trusting. For 2012, we find partial evidence for a relationship between trust in government and turnout. Respondents who trusted the government in Washington to do what is right were more than nine percentage points more likely to vote than those who expressed no trust in government. This relationship was not dependent on the race of the voter. Yet we see no difference in electoral participation between those who believe the government is run by a few big interests and those who believe it is run for the benefit of all.

ELECTION-SPECIFIC FACTORS

Focusing on long-term stable factors related to voting, such as social demographics and partisan attachments, might give one the impression that election-specific factors may not matter. Yet in any election there will be political and nonpolitical circumstances that affect voting. Among the nonpolitical factors shown to affect voter turnout is election day weather. Bad weather is likely to increase the physical costs of voting and make it more difficult for potential voters to get to the polls. A recent study, which examined county-level voter turnout in every presidential election from 1944 to 2000, showed that for every inch of rain a county received above its thirty-year average rainfall, turnout declined by nearly one percentage point.[90] In close elections, a nonpolitical factor like weather could have real political consequences by keeping voters in some localities away from the polls and potentially changing electoral outcomes.[91]

Politics matters, too, of course. Not all elections are competitive, and one factor that stimulates voter turnout is the expected closeness of the outcome.[92] According to the rational choice theory of voting developed by Anthony Downs and refined by William H. Riker and Peter C. Ordeshook, a person's expected benefit from voting increases in close elections, since the probability that one's vote will directly affect the outcome is higher.[93] Close elections also make it easier for potential voters to become politically informed as heightened media coverage, television advertising, and interpersonal discussion of politics help to create an information-rich environment. And parties and candidates are more likely to engage in get-out-the-vote efforts when election outcomes hang in the balance.

In Chapter 2, we identified the thirteen battleground states in the 2012 election.[94] Early predictions suggested these states might have close elections. According to the 2012 CPS, average voter turnout in these thirteen states was 75.1 percent, while the average in non-battleground states was 68.9 percent.

At the individual level, perceptions of the closeness of the presidential election may vary from person to person. These perceptions may be informed by the actual competitiveness of the election in the individual's state, or they may reflect the expected outcome of the Electoral College. But people sometimes espouse a distorted view of the competitive nature of the election. As Rosenstone and Hansen note, "[t]his may reflect ignorance, excitability, wishful thinking, accurate assessments of the leanings of friends and localities, or sober recollections of the inconstancy of public opinion polls."[95] Our analysis of the ANES shows that the percentage of people who think the election will be close varies greatly from election to election. For example, in 1996, only 52 percent of whites thought the election between Bill Clinton and Bob Dole would be close, but in 2000, 88 percent thought the contest between Gore and Bush would be close. In 2008, there were clear racial differences in individuals' perceptions of the competitiveness of the election. Among whites, 82 percent thought the election would be close; among blacks, only 69 percent did. These racial differences were remarkably persistent in 2012. Approximately 85 percent of whites believed the election between Obama and Romney would be close, while only 69 percent of blacks did. Among whites who thought the election would be close (n = 962), 88 percent said they voted; among those who though the winner would win by "quite a bit" (n = 145), 76 percent did. Among blacks, however, the perceived closeness of the election was not related to turnout.

The most direct way that campaigns attempt to influence turnout is through get-out-the-vote efforts. Modern campaigns expend exorbitant amounts of money and effort trying to bring their voters to the polls. Campaigns employ local phone banks and door-to-door canvassing; they use direct mail and social networking technology, and even old-fashioned political rallies, all in an effort to stimulate voter interests. But to what effect? Over a decade ago, political scientists Donald Green and Alan Gerber began a research agenda aimed at answering this question. Green and Gerber use field experiments to gauge the effectiveness of voter mobilization tactics.[96] The field experiments typically use voter registration rolls to randomly assign a subset of voters into "treatment" and "control" conditions. Those assigned to the treatment group are exposed to the specific get-out-the-vote tactic being tested, while those in the control group are not.[97] After the election, the voter rolls are reexamined to determine whether voter turnout was higher among those in the treatment group than those in control group, thus providing evidence of whether the mobilization tactic *caused* an increase in turnout. Green and Gerber's work, as well as that undertaken subsequently by others, suggests, among other things, that voters tend to respond best to personalized methods and messages, such as door-to-door canvassing, than impersonal techniques, such as "robocalls."[98] Pressure from one's social network is also important in mobilizing voters to the polls. In one of their most well-known experiments to date, Gerber and Green, joined by Christopher Larimer, found that voters are more likely to turn out—by an increased probability of 8.1 percentage points—when they are told prior to election day that their decision to vote will be publicized to their neighbors. This experiment not only demonstrates the effectiveness of social pressure in mobilizing voters, it provides supporting evidence for the argument that the historic decline in turnout could have been caused in part by the concomitant decline in Americans' willingness to join associational groups, such as fraternal organizations and churches.

Unlike these experimental designs, it is difficult to estimate the *causal* effect of mobilization on turnout using surveys. Consider the fact that campaigns often contact voters based on how likely they are to vote. Can we really say that mobilization causes turnout, or does the potential for turnout cause mobilization? Because the survey environment typically measures whether the individual was contacted by a political party and the individual's reported turnout contemporaneously, it is hard to establish for certain which variable came first. Thus, an analysis of the relationship between whether an individual was contacted by a political party and his or her reported turnout using the 2012 ANES is likely to establish only correlation, not causation.[99]

The longitudinal nature of the ANES does offer interesting insights into changes in the mobilization of the electorate, however. Most notably, the percentage of Americans who say they have been contacted by a political party increased after the 1960 election. In 1960, 22 percent of the electorate said a political party had contacted them.[100] By 1980, 32 percent said they had been contacted. The upward trend abated in 1992, when only 20 percent said they had been contacted by a political party. The percentage that said they had been contacted by a political party grew in 1996 and in 2000, and it increased slightly between 2000 and 2004. It grew again somewhat in 2008, when 43 percent said they had been contacted, with whites somewhat more likely to claim they had been contacted (45 percent) than blacks (38 percent). In 2012, 39 percent of the electorate said a political party had contacted them, a decrease from four years earlier. Interestingly, the race differences in party contact exhibited in 2008 were more pronounced than in 2012. Forty-four percent of whites claimed to have been contacted, roughly equivalent to 2008, but the contact rate among blacks in 2012 declined markedly to 26 percent. The study of party contact rates over time may shed further light on changes in turnout. Similar to education, increased levels of party contact over time may have prevented the decline from being even greater.

DOES LOW VOTER TURNOUT MATTER?

Many bemoan the low levels of turnout in U.S. elections. Some claim that low rates of voter participation undermine the legitimacy of elected political leaders. Seymour Martin Lipset, for instance, argues that the existence of a large bloc of nonparticipants in the electorate may be potentially dangerous because it means that many Americans have weak ties to the established parties and political leaders.[101] This may increase the prospects of electoral instability or perhaps political instability generally. Others argue that low levels of turnout, at minimum, increase the probability that American elections produce "biased" outcomes, reflecting the preferences of an active political class while ignoring those who may be alienated or disenfranchised.

Turnout rates may also increase the electoral fortunes of one party over the other. Conventional wisdom holds that since nonvoters are more likely to come from low-socioeconomic-status groups and ethnic minorities—groups that tend to vote Democratic—higher turnout benefits the Democrats. James DeNardo, using aggregate election data from 1932 to 1976, and Thomas Hansford and Brad Gomez, using aggregate data from 1948 to 2000, provide evidence that increases in turnout enlarge the vote share of Democratic candidates, though the nature of the relationship is more complex and weaker than one might assume.[102]

Elected officials appear convinced that their reelection fates depend on the level of turnout.[103] Over the past several decades, at both the national and state levels, legislators have debated a number of laws aimed at making it easier (or sometimes harder) for citizens to vote. Bills that make it easier to register to vote, such as the 1993 Motor Voter Law, and bills that promote convenience voting mechanisms, such as early voting or vote by mail, have typically divided legislators along strict party lines, with Democrats supporting efforts to expand the electorate and Republicans opposing them.

More recently, Republicans have led the push to require voter identification at the polls, typically by requiring the presentation of a government-issued identification card, such as a driver's license. Critics argue that voter identification laws disproportionately affect low-income and minority voters, who are likely to vote Democrat. At the time of the 2012 election, these bills had passed in thirty-three states.[104]

In our analyses of the 1980, 1984, and 1988 presidential elections, we argued that, among most reasonable scenarios, increased turnout would not have led to Democratic victories.[105] In 1992, increased turnout coincided with the Democratic victory, but not a higher share of the Democratic vote. Our analyses suggest that Bill Clinton benefited from increased turnout, but that he benefited more by converting voters who had supported George H. W. Bush four years earlier.[106] Despite the six-percentage-point decline in turnout between 1992 and 1996, Clinton was easily reelected. Even so, there is some evidence that the decline in turnout cost Clinton votes.[107]

In view of the closeness of the 2000 contest, it seems plausible that a successful get-out-the-vote effort by the Democrats could have swung the election to Al Gore. In 2004, turnout rose by over four percentage points, regardless of how it is measured. But Bush won with a majority of the popular vote, even though his margin over Kerry was small. Our analyses suggest that the Republicans were more successful in mobilizing their supporters than the Democrats. Some argue that the GOP gained because in eleven states proposals to ban same-sex marriage were on the ballot. But as we have shown, turnout was only one point higher in the states that had these propositions on the ballot than in the states that did not.[108] Bush won nine of the eleven states with such a proposition, but of those nine states only Ohio was closely contested, and turnout increased by nine percentage points there.

In 2008, many argued that Obama's victory was aided by the mobilization of new voters, particularly blacks, Latinos, and eighteen- to twenty-five-year-olds. But we found little evidence of turnout effects in 2008. The ANES data suggest that Republican identifiers were more likely to vote than Democrats in 2008, and Obama would have enjoyed an increase in support had Democrats and Republicans voted at the same rate. However, we found no additional evidence that higher turnout would have benefited Obama.[109]

As argued originally by the authors of *The American Voter*, if nonvoters and occasional voters hold preferences that differ from those of regular (or core) voters, then variation in turnout is likely to have meaningful electoral implications.[110] Thus, in Table 4-5, we examine whether respondents reported voting for president in 2012, according to their party identification, their positions on the issues (the "balance of issues" measure), and their evaluations of the performance of Barack Obama; which party is best able to handle the important problems facing the country; and their beliefs about whether the country is going in the right direction (the summary measure of "retrospective" evaluations).

As was the case in 2008, Obama was able to win the election in spite of Republican identifiers turning out at a higher rate than Democrats.[111] Table 4-5 shows that strong Republicans were somewhat more likely to report voting than strong Democrats, weak Republicans were more likely to vote than weak Democrats, and independents who felt close to the Republican Party were more likely to vote than those who leaned toward the Democrats. If we assume that each of the Democratic groups had turnout as high as each of the comparable Republican groups, and assume that the additional Democrats drawn to the polls voted the same way as the Democrats who did not, Obama would have gained about 1.5 percentage points.

In Chapter 6, we examine the issue preferences of the electorate. For every presidential election between 1980 and 2008, we built a measure of overall issue preferences based on the seven-point scales used by the ANES surveys to measure the issue preferences of the electorate.[112] But we have found little or no evidence of issue differences between those who vote and those who do not.

Our overall measure of issues preferences for 2012 is based on scales measuring the respondent's position on six issues: (1) reducing or increasing government services, (2) decreasing or increasing defense spending, (3) government health insurance, (4) government job guarantees, (5) government helping blacks, and (6) protecting the environment.[113] As Table 4-5 shows, respondents who are strongly Republican on the issues are much more likely to report voting than those who are strongly Democratic. However, the exact size of the difference here should be treated with caution since individuals who were strongly Democratic on the issues only made up 2.2 percent of the electorate. Respondents who were moderately Democratic and moderately Republican on the issues reported

TABLE 4-5   Percentage of Electorate Who Reported Voting for President, by Party Identification, Issue Preferences, and Retrospective Evaluations, 2012

	Voted	Did not vote	Total	(N)
Electorate, by party identification				
Strong Democrat	92	8	100	(331)
Weak Democrat	76	24	100	(208)
Independent, leans Democratic	78	22	100	(255)
Independent, no partisan leaning	65	35	100	(118)
Independent, leans Republican	84	16	100	(265)
Weak Republican	86	14	100	(188)
Strong Republican	97	3	100	(211)
Electorate, by scores on "balance of issues" measure				
Strongly Democratic	76	24	100	(35)
Moderately Democratic	85	15	100	(126)
Slightly Democratic	76	24	100	(204)
Neutral	84	16	100	(180)
Slightly Republican	83	17	100	(322)
Moderately Republican	85	15	100	(397)
Strongly Republican	92	8	100	(320)
Electorate, by scores on summary measure of retrospective evaluations of incumbent party				
Strongly opposed	96	4	100	(406)
Moderately opposed	82	18	100	(237)
Slightly opposed	73	27	100	(102)
Neutral	74	26	100	(154)
Slightly supportive	78	22	100	(174)
Moderately supportive	75	25	100	(171)
Strongly supportive	92	8	100	(313)

Source: Authors' analysis of the 2012 ANES survey.

Note: Numbers are weighted. Chapter 6 describes how the "balance of issues" measure was constructed, and Chapter 7 describes how the summary measure of retrospective evaluations was constructed. Both measures differ slightly from those presented in previous volumes of *Change and Continuity*, so care should be given when comparing to earlier election studies.

turnout at the same rate, while those who were slightly Republican on the issues were more likely to vote than those who lean toward the Democrats on the issues. Yet, on balance, differences in turnout based on issue preference had no effect on the percentage of Americans who voted for Obama and Romney.

In Chapter 7, we discuss the retrospective evaluations of the electorate. Voters, some analysts argue, make their decisions based not just on their evaluation of policy promises, but also on their evaluation of how well the party in power is doing. Between 1980 and 2000, we used a summary measure based on presidential approval, an evaluation of the job the government was doing dealing with the most important problem facing the country, and an assessment of which party would do a better job dealing with this problem. Due to changes in the ANES questionnaire, we were forced to construct alternative measures in both 2004 and 2008. Across each of the elections that we have studied, the relationship between retrospective evaluations and turnout has been weak, at best, and often nonexistent.

In 2012, we had to employ yet another measure—one based on the respondent's approval of the president, the respondent's evaluation of how good a job the government had been doing over the last four years, and the respondent's belief about whether things in the country are going in the right direction or are on the wrong track. Though voters were more likely to oppose the president than be supportive, differences in retrospective evaluations did not produce substantial turnout effects. If turnout differences between retrospective subgroups are eliminated, Obama would have gained only half of one percentage point.

Clearly, then, in most elections higher turnout is unlikely to affect the outcome. In our analyses, the largest and most consistent turnout effects that we see are associated with differences in voter participation among party identifiers. Consistent with other scholarship, we found that higher turnout benefits the Democrats but only to a small degree.[114] Moreover, we have found little evidence in our analyses to support the argument that the low voter turnout biases election outcomes on the basis of issue preferences or retrospective evaluations. Because in most presidential contests increased turnout would not have affected the outcome, some analysts might argue that low turnout does not matter.[115]

Despite this evidence, we do not accept the conclusion that low turnout is unimportant. We are especially concerned that turnout is low among the disadvantaged. Some observers believe this is so because political leaders structure political alternatives in a way that provides disadvantaged Americans with relatively little political choice. Frances Fox Piven and Richard A. Cloward, for example, acknowledge that the policy preferences of voters and nonvoters are similar, but they argue that this similarity exists because of the way that elites have structured policy choices:

> Political attitudes would inevitably change over time if the allegiance of
> voters from the bottom became the object of partisan competition, for
> then politicians would be prodded to identify and articulate the
> grievances of and aspirations of the lower-income voters in order to win

their support, thus helping to give form and voice to a distinctive political class.[116]

We cannot accept this argument either, mainly because it is highly speculative and there is little evidence to support it. The difficulty in supporting this view may in part stem from the nature of survey research itself, because questions about public policy are usually framed along the lines of controversy as defined by mainstream political leaders. Occasionally, however, surveys pose radical policy alternatives, and they often ask open-ended questions that allow respondents to state their own preferences. We find no concrete evidence that low turnout leads American political leaders to ignore the policy preferences of the electorate.

Nevertheless, low turnout can scarcely be healthy for a democracy. As we have shown, much of the initial decline in U.S. voter turnout following the 1960s could be attributed to decreases in partisan attachment and external political efficacy. Partisan identification has largely returned to 1960s levels, but turnout has not increased proportionally. Feelings of political efficacy have continued to decline and, as we reported, were at an all-time low in 2012. If turnout remains low because an ever-growing segment of the American public believes that "public officials don't care much what people like me think" and "people like me don't have any say about what the government does," then concern seems warranted.

Chapter 5

Social Forces and the Vote

More than 129 million Americans voted for president in 2012. Although voting is an individual act, group characteristics influence voting choices because individuals with similar social characteristics may share similar political interests. Group similarities in voting behavior may also reflect past political conditions. The partisan loyalties of African Americans, for example, were shaped by the Civil War; black loyalties to the Republican Party, the party of Lincoln, lasted through the 1932 election. The steady Democratic voting of southern whites, the product of those same historical conditions, lasted even longer, at least through 1960.

It is easy to see why group-based loyalties persist over time. Studies of pre-adult political learning suggest that partisan loyalties are often transmitted from generation to generation.[1] And because religion, ethnicity, and, to a lesser extent, social class are often transmitted from generation to generation, social divisions have considerable staying power. Moreover, the interactions of social group members may reinforce similarities in political attitudes and behaviors.

Politicians often make group appeals. They recognize that to win an election they need to mobilize the social groups that often supported them in the past and that it may be helpful to cut into their opponents' bases of support. Democrats tend to think in group terms more than Republicans because Democrats are a coalition of minorities that was formed in part by Franklin Roosevelt during the 1930s. For decades, Democrats have needed a high level of support from the social groups that had traditionally supported their broad-based coalition to win.

Roosevelt's New Deal coalition brought together sometimes disparate groups, including both union and nonunion working-class households, both African Americans and native white southerners, and both Jews and Catholics. Yet by the late twentieth century, the coalition had been fundamentally altered. While African Americans have maintained their loyalty to the Democrats, southern white conservatives have drifted to their more natural ideological home on the right and are now more likely to identify with the Republicans. Working-class voters are a cross-pressured group who sometimes side with the Democrats on economic issues, but sometimes agree with Republicans on social issues.[2] And union membership has declined greatly. Jewish voters remain loyal to the Democrats, but Catholic voters now support the two major parties at the roughly the same rate, and churchgoing Catholics now lean toward the Republican Party. And Latinos are a significant segment of the Democratic coalition.

The 1992 and 1996 presidential elections provide an example of the fragile nature of the Democratic coalition during the latter half of the twentieth century. Bill Clinton earned high levels of support from only two of the groups that made up the New Deal coalition formed by Roosevelt—African Americans and Jews. Most of the other New Deal coalition groups gave fewer than half of their votes to Clinton. Fortunately for him, in a three-way contest (it included independent candidate Ross Perot) only 43 percent of the vote was needed to win. Despite a second candidacy by Perot, the 1996 election was much more of a two-candidate fight, and Clinton won 49 percent of the popular vote. He gained ground among the vast majority of groups analyzed in this chapter, making especially large gains among union members and Latinos. In many respects, the Democratic losses after 1964 can be attributed to the party's failure to hold the loyalties of the New Deal coalition groups.

In 2008, Barack Obama's victory returned a Democrat to the White House. His victory marked the first time since 1976 that a Democrat won the presidency with a majority of the popular vote. But Obama did not restore the New Deal coalition. Instead, the Democrats currently rely on an electoral coalition in which African American and Latinos play a central role. Obama gained about a fourth of his total vote from black voters. This was possible because black turnout equaled white turnout and because blacks voted overwhelmingly Democratic. Yet among the groups that we examined, only blacks, Latinos, and Jews gave a clear majority of their vote to Obama. Obama had only a slight edge among white union members, and he split the white Catholic vote with John McCain. Among white southerners, a mainstay of the New Deal coalition, he won only a third of the vote.[3]

HOW SOCIAL GROUPS VOTED IN 2012

Table 5-1 presents the results of our analysis of how social groups voted in the 2012 presidential election.[4] Among the 1,420 respondents who said they voted for president, 52.2 percent said they voted for Obama, 46.2 percent for Romney, and 1.5 percent for other candidates—results that are within one percentage point of the actual results (see Table 3-1). The American National Election Studies (ANES) are the best source of data for analyzing change over time, but the total number of self-reported voters is small. This can make group-based analysis tenuous if the number of sample respondents within a group is exceedingly small. Therefore, we will often supplement (sometimes by necessity) our analysis with the exit polls (pool polls) conducted by Edison Research for a consortium of news organizations.[5] For the 2012 exit polls, 26,565 voters were interviewed. Most were randomly chosen as they left 350 polling places from across the United States on election day. Respondents who voted absentee or voted early were contacted via telephone. For the 2008 polls, 17,836 voters were surveyed at three hundred polling places around the nation, and 2,378 telephone interviews were conducted with absentee and early voters.[6]

Race, Gender, Region, and Age

Political differences between African Americans and whites are far sharper than any other social cleavage.[7] According to the ANES survey, 98 percent of black voters supported Obama (Table 5-1), whereas the pool poll indicates that 93 percent did. Obama's level of support among black voters in 2012 was similar to his 2008 levels. As one might expect, Obama did better among black voters than did the 2004 Democratic nominee, John Kerry, who won 88 percent of the black vote, according to both polls. Based on the ANES survey, we estimate that 24.4 percent of Obama's vote came from blacks; our analysis of the pool poll suggests that 23.7 percent did. In 2008, we estimated the percentage of the Obama electorate that was black to have been between 23 percent based on the ANES and 27 percent based on the pool poll. No other Democratic presidential winner has received as large a share of his vote from the black electorate as Obama. Even in the three-candidate contest of 1992, when the white vote was split among three candidates, Clinton received only a fifth of his votes from blacks. The large black contributions to the Democrats in 2008 and 2012 result from two factors: black turnout was as high (2008) as or higher (2012) than white turnout, and blacks voted overwhelmingly Democratic, equaling the black vote for two white Democrats, Lyndon Johnson in 1964 and Hubert Humphrey in 1968. Because only a handful of blacks voted for Romney, we cannot examine variation among black Romney voters.[8]

The Democrats continue to hold a decided edge among Latino voters. In 2004, Kerry won 67 percent of the Latino vote. Obama increased that vote share in 2008, garnering 75 percent of the Latino vote, and he did equally well with Latinos in 2012. The pool poll suggests that Obama won 71 percent of the Latino vote in 2012, a slight improvement over the 67 percent estimated by exit polls in 2008. Latinos, of course, are not a homogeneous group.[9] Cuban Americans in South Florida, for example, have traditionally voted Republican, though younger generations now lean Democratic. As noted in Chapter 4, the 2012 ANES included a nationally representative oversample of Latinos, but data regarding Hispanic ethnicity were not publically available at the time of our writing, so we cannot examine differences among Hispanic groups using the ANES. The pool poll, however, shows that Cuban American voters in South Florida split 50-47 percent in Romney's favor, a remarkably slim victory from a group long considered a reliable Republican voting bloc.[10]

TABLE 5-1   How Social Groups Voted for President, 2012 (percent)

Social group	Obama	Romney	Other	Total	(N)[a]
Total electorate	52	46	2	100	(1,420)
Electorate, by race					
African American	98	2	0	100	(189)
White	40	58	1	99	(1,034)
Other	70	26	5	101	(192)
Latino (of any race)	75	23	3	101	(121)
Whites, by gender					
Female	39	59	2	100	(544)
Male	42	58	1	101	(490)
Whites, by region					
New England and Mid-Atlantic	39	61	0	100	(205)
North Central	50	48	2	100	(247)
South	29	69	2	100	(272)
Border	45	55	0	100	(64)
Mountain and Pacific	45	54	1	100	(212)
Whites, by birth cohort					
Before 1942	34	66	0	100	(155)
1943–1952	43	57	0	100	(199)
1953–1962	42	57	1	100	(216)
1963–1972	39	59	2	100	(179)
1973–1982	41	55	4	100	(119)
1983–1991	42	56	2	100	(116)
1992–1995	44	55	1	100	(17)
Whites, by level of education					
Not high school graduate	44	54	2	100	(62)
High school graduate	39	60	1	100	(243)
Some college	37	61	2	100	(312)
College graduate	40	59	2	101	(260)
Advanced degree	49	51	1	101	(149)
Whites, by annual family income					
Less than $15,000	45	53	2	100	(88)
$15,000–$34,999	49	50	1	100	(153)
$35,000–$49,999	38	59	3	100	(111)
$50,000–$74,999	39	61	0	100	(197)
$75,000–$89,999	25	73	2	100	(108)
$90,000–$124,999	46	52	3	101	(149)
$125,000–$174,999	52	48	0	100	(85)
$175,000 and over	27	73	0	100	(89)

Social group	Obama	Romney	Other	Total	(N)[a]
Whites, by union membership[b]					
Member	53	47	1	101	(192)
Nonmember	38	61	1	100	(827)
Whites, by religion (exit polls)					
Jewish	71	29	0	100	(195)[c]
Catholic	40	59	1	100	(1752)
Protestant	30	69	1	100	(3795)
None	63	31	6	100	(876)
White Protestants, by whether born again (exit polls)					
Not born again	60	37	3	100	(3785)
Born again	21	78	1	100	(1330)
All voters, by religious denomination and church attendance (exit polls)					
Protestant/attend weekly	29	70	1	100	(770)
Protestant/not weekly	44	55	1	100	(718)
Catholic/attend weekly	42	57	1	100	(564)
Catholic/not weekly	56	42	2	100	(667)
All others	58	39	3	100	(2360)

Source: Authors' analysis of the 2012 ANES survey and the 2012 National Election Pool Exit Polls.

[a] Numbers are weighted.

[b] Respondent or family member in union.

[c] Ns for the exit polls are estimates based on the total number of respondents reported for each question

Based on data from the ANES and the pool polls, we estimate that Latinos (of all ethnicities) composed roughly 14 percent of Obama's 2012 electorate and between 4.7 and 5.7 percent of Romney's electorate. The U.S. Census predicts that the size of the Latino electorate could grow by as much as 40 percent in the next sixteen years. If Latinos' current rate of support for the Democrats were to continue, we estimate that nearly one in five Democratic votes will be cast by Latinos by 2028. This puts tremendous pressure on Republicans. The GOP already lags well behind Democrats in support among Latinos and African Americans; about 38 percent of Obama's voters came from these two groups, while somewhere between 5.3 and 7.4 percent of Romney's voters did. If Republicans cannot make inroads with these two minority groups, they will be forced to win a substantially larger share of the white vote.

Gender differences in voting behavior have been pronounced in some European societies, but they have been relatively weak in the United States.[11] Gender differences emerged in the 1980 election and have been found in every election since. According to the exit polls, the "gender gap" was eight percentage points in 1980, six points in 1984, seven points in 1988, four points in 1992, eleven points in 1996, twelve points in 2000, seven points in 2004, and seven points in 2008. According to the 2012 pool poll, 55 percent of women and 45 percent of men voted for Obama, a gap of ten points. Among white women, Obama received 42 percent of the vote; among white men he received 35 percent, for a gap of seven points.

As the gender gap began to emerge, some feminists hoped that women would play a major role in defeating the Republicans.[12] But as we pointed out more than three decades ago, a gender gap does not necessarily help the Democrats.[13] For example, in 1988, George H. W. Bush and Michael Dukakis each won half of the female vote, but Bush won a clear majority of the male vote. Thus Bush benefited from the gender gap in 1988. However, two decades later the role of gender was reversed. In 2008, Obama and McCain split the male vote, while Obama won a clear majority among women. By the same logic, then, Obama benefited from the gender gap in 2008. During the intervening elections, Clinton benefited from the gender gap in both 1992 and 1996, and George W. Bush benefited in 2000 and 2004.

Unlike the pool polls, the 2012 ANES reveals little evidence of a gender gap in voting. We find a small difference between white women and men in their support for Obama, but the gender gap here is in the opposite direction of that found in the exit polls. As seen in Table 5-1, the ANES suggests that white men were around three percentage points more likely to vote for Obama than white women, while white women were slightly more likely to support Romney than white men. This runs counter to expectations (and other evidence), but on balance the data suggest no candidate benefited from a gender gap. Indeed, among all voters in the ANES survey, roughly equal percentages of men and women voted for Obama (52 percent) and Romney (46 percent).

As for marital status, as in all of our analyses of ANES surveys between 1984 and 2008, we found clear differences between married women and single women.[14] Among all women voters who were married ($n = 475$), 39 percent voted for Obama; among those who were never married ($n = 147$), 83 percent did—a forty-four-point difference. This difference is similarly sized if we limit our analysis to white women. The marriage gap among men was substantially smaller. Among all men, married voters were nineteen points less likely to vote for Obama than men who had never been married, but this difference is largely attributable to the number of African American males who have never married. Among white men, married voters were only four percentage points less likely to vote for Obama than those who have never married.

Since the 2000 election, exit polls have shown that sexual orientation is related to the way people vote. In 2000, 70 percent of the respondents who said they were gay, lesbian, or bisexual voted for Gore; in 2004, 77 percent voted for Kerry; and in 2008, 70 percent voted for Obama. As president, Obama signed legislation repealing the "don't ask, don't tell" law, which allowed gays to serve in the military so long as they were not open about their sexual orientation, and in May 2012, he unexpectedly declared his support for the legalization of same-sex marriage.[15] While it is difficult to confirm, these actions may have allowed Obama to increase his vote share among gays, lesbians, and bisexuals, which rose in 2012 to 76 percent. In the four ANES surveys that have inquired about sexual orientation, self-acknowledged gay, lesbian, or bisexual voters made up approximately 4 percent of the electorate.[16] In 2012, 4.2 percent of the ANES respondents said they were gay, lesbian, or bisexual.[17] Among these voters ($n = 37$), 83 percent voted for Obama.

As described in Chapter 3, in the 2012 election the political variation among states was greater than in any election since 1964. And there were clear regional differences among white voters. As Table 5.1 shows, Mitt Romney garnered electoral majorities from white voters in all but one region. Romney, like all recent Republican nominees, fared best in the South, where he won 69 percent of the white vote. Obama won only 39 percent of the vote among white southerners. Exit polls show that he fared no better among whites in the two southern states he carried: 37 percent in Florida and 38 percent in Virginia. Obama's strongest support among whites came from the north central region, where he won 50 percent of the vote according to the ANES. Exit polls were taken in eight of the eleven states that define this region, and our analysis of these state-level results shows that Obama outpolled Romney among whites in only one of these states, Iowa, where a high turnout among white women and a larger gender gap (seventeen points) allowed Obama to capture the majority (51 percent) of the white vote.

Between Ronald Reagan's election in 1980 and Clinton's reelection in 1996, young voters were more likely to vote Republican than their elders, and the Democrats did best among Americans who came of age before World War II (born before 1924). This was not the case in the 2000, 2004, and 2008 elections. In these elections, the ANES surveys show that Republicans did well among white voters who entered the electorate in the 1980s, and who may have been influenced by the pro-Republican tide during the Reagan years. Yet among white voters who entered the electorate in the mid-1990s or later, Democrats outgained Republicans. If Democrats were optimistic about their future because of these trends among young voters, they were no doubt ecstatic about Obama's exceptional performance among young adults in 2008. According to the 2008 ANES surveys, Obama won 57 percent of the vote among whites born between 1979 and 2000 (those who were between the ages of eighteen and twenty-nine at the time of the election). The pool poll showed even larger gains for Democrats among young voters, estimating that Obama won 66 percent of voters aged eighteen to twenty-nine, a 12 percent increase over John Kerry's performance with that group in 2004.

The ANES shows Obama lost ground among young white voters in 2012. As seen in Table 5-1, Mitt Romney won majorities among white voters in every age group. But Obama remained quite strong among younger nonwhite voters. Indeed, among all voters, Obama won clear majorities with voters thirty-nine years old and younger. The pool polls also show Obama's lack of success with young white voters in 2012. Among whites age eighteen to twenty-nine, Romney won 51 to 44 percent. Obama fared worse among older whites.

Social Class, Education, Income, and Union Membership

Traditionally, the Democratic Party has fared well among the relatively disadvantaged. It has done better among the working class, voters with lower levels of formal education, and the poor. Moreover, since the 1930s most union leaders have supported the Democratic Party, and union members have been a mainstay of the Democratic presidential coalition. We are not able to measure social class differences using the 2012 ANES because the occupational codes we use to classify respondents as working class (manually employed) and middle class (non-manually employed) were not available at the time of this writing. But we do have substantial evidence that class differences as defined by occupation have been declining—a trend found in other advanced democracies.[18] Differences between the more educated and the less educated were also weak in 2012, but income effects were stronger, though inconsistent.

In 1992 and 1996, Bill Clinton fared best among whites who had not graduated from high school, whereas both George H. W. Bush and Bob Dole fared best among whites who were college graduates (but without advanced degrees). In 1992, Clinton won over half of the major-party vote among whites with advanced degrees, and in 1996 he won almost half the major-party vote among this group. In 2000, there was a weaker relationship between education and voting preferences, and in 2004, Kerry did best among whites in the highest and lowest educational categories. The 2008 ANES survey found only a weak relationship between level of education and the vote among whites. Moreover, the only educational group among which Obama won a majority of the vote was the small number who had not graduated from high school.

The 2012 ANES shows no discernible relationship between educational attainment and vote choice among whites. Romney won majorities among whites from all levels of education, but he did slightly better among those with a high school degree and those with some college. Romney was weakest among those whites who had not completed high school and those with advanced degrees. If nonwhites are added to the analysis, we see a stronger relationship between education and vote choice, with Obama winning a large majority among voters with a high school diploma or less and Romney winning among college graduates (but without advanced degrees). The 2012 pool poll, which is not broken down by race, shows a similar pattern. Obama won majorities among high school graduates (51 to 48 percent) and those who did not complete high school (64 to 35 percent). Obama also beat Romney 55 to 42 percent among those with a postgraduate education. Romney won 51 to 47 percent among college graduates without postgraduate training. Overall, these combined results strongly suggest that the effect of education on vote choice in 2012 was tied closely to differences in race and ethnicity.

Scholars such as Jeffrey M. Stonecash and Larry M. Bartels argue that voting differences according to income have been growing in the United States.[19] We find little to support this claim, however. Instead, we find evidence that the relationship between income and voting has varied considerably in recent decades and in no discernible pattern. In his victories in 1992 and 1996, for example, Clinton clearly fared much better among the poor than among the affluent. The relationship between income and voting preferences was weaker in both 2000 and 2004, although whites with an annual family income of $50,000 and above were more likely to vote for Bush. In 2008, the ANES data revealed a strong relationship between the respondent's family income and voting choice. Like Clinton's victories, Obama did better among those with lower incomes than those who were wealthier. Among whites with annual family incomes below $50,000 a majority voted for Obama. In all income groups above that level, a majority voted for McCain. Moreover, among whites with family incomes of $150,000 and above, over three in four voted Republican.

As seen in Table 5-1, the 2012 ANES shows a weak negative relationship between annual family income and voting for Obama. In fact, across all income categories except for those making between $125,000 and $174,999, Romney won a majority of the white vote. Obama's majority among this high-income group is a bit unexpected given the general nature of the relationship between income and vote choice in 2012. On average, Obama did better among those making less than $75,000 than he did among those making more—by our estimate, Obama received 43 percent support from the low-income groups and 38 percent among those with higher levels of income. As was the case with education, the relationship between family income and the vote is much stronger when we examine the full sample, regardless of race or ethnicity. The pool polls also show a strong relationship between income and vote choice among all voters. Indeed, Obama won comfortable majorities among voters making less than $50,000, while Romney garnered majorities among those with higher income. Again, it appears that much of the relationship between social class—in this case, measured by income and education—and the vote is conditioned by race and ethnicity.

According to the ANES surveys, Clinton made major gains among white union households between 1992 and 1996. But the 2000 ANES survey shows that Gore slipped twelve percentage points from Clinton's 1996 total, while George W. Bush gained sixteen points over Dole's. The 2004 ANES survey shows that Bush made no gains among union households, but gained six points among nonunion households. In 2008, the ANES survey shows a five-point loss for the Democrats among white union households, but a seven-point gain among nonunion households. According to the 2008 pool poll, Obama received the same share of the union vote as Kerry (59 percent), whereas Democratic support among nonunion households rose from 44 percent in 2004 to 51 percent in 2008.

Obama's vote share among white voters in nonunion households declined markedly between 2008 and 2012, a five-percentage-point drop. This allowed Romney to dominate Obama among nonunion households: 61 to 38 percent (see Figure 5-1). Obama maintained his support among white union voters, and beat Romney 53 to 47 percent in this group. The pool poll also shows a sizeable majority for Obama among voters in union households (for all races): 58 to 40 percent.

Religion

Religious differences have long played a major role in American politics.[20] In the postwar period, Catholics tended to support the Democrats, while white Protestants, especially those outside the South, tended to favor the Republicans. Jews consistently voted more Democratic than any other major religious group. Yet the religious cleavages of old, partly reflecting ethnic differences between Protestants and Catholics, do not necessarily hold today. As noted by David E. Campbell, "the last thirty years have seen a re-sorting of the parties' electoral coalitions along religious lines."[21] As ethnic differences have faded through assimilation and as social and moral issues have become more politically salient, religious denomination plays a smaller role in defining partisan loyalties. Indeed, the role of religion in modern politics is not so much about denomination as it is about what Campbell calls "religious devotional style" or religiosity. Today, Christian voters who classify themselves as devout in their beliefs and practices—regardless of denomination—tend to support the Republican Party.[22] This has allowed the Republicans to benefit electorally from a "coalition of the religious," which brings together groups that are sometimes theologically and politically disparate (if not antagonistic): evangelical Christians, traditionalist Catholics, and Mormons.[23]

In our past studies, we have used the ANES to examine differences in voting behavior based on religious denomination and devotion. Unfortunately, while the 2012 ANES inquired about voters' religious practices, the codes used to classify respondents by religion and religiosity were not publically available at the time of our writing. Thus, for 2012, we rely on data from the pool polls and report the results in Figure 5-1.

In the 2012 election, Barack Obama won a majority of the Catholic vote (50 to 48 percent), just as he had four years earlier against John McCain (54 to 45 percent). But Obama's majority support among *all* Catholics belies his relationship with *many* Catholic voters (and bishops) and says much about ethnic changes among American Catholics.[24] One in four voters in 2012 was a self-identified Catholic, but the "Catholic vote" is hardly a monolith. As Figure 5-1 shows, white Catholics voted decidedly in favor of Mitt Romney, awarding him 59 percent of the vote to Obama's 40 percent. Obama did better among white Catholic voters (47 percent) four years earlier, according to the pool poll, but he still earned fewer votes than McCain (52 percent). The 2008 ANES showed that white Catholics split evenly between Obama and McCain. Obviously, Obama's primary source of support among American Catholics is from Latinos, who represent about a third of all Catholics in the United States.[25] Latino Catholics tend to be younger and less affluent than white Catholics, and they also tend to be more likely to be liberal on social issues and self-identified Democrats.[26] Unfortunately, data limitations do not afford us the opportunity to analyze voting differences among Latino Catholics.

Although the Republican Party has been successful among white Protestants in general, it has been more successful among some than others. The Republican emphasis on traditional values may have special appeal to Protestants who share them. George W. Bush's policies, such as limiting funding for embryonic stem cell research, calling for an amendment to the U.S. Constitution to ban same-sex marriage, and appointing conservatives to the federal courts, may have appealed to Christian conservatives. But Romney's Mormon faith and previous support for abortion rights—though he has consistently opposed same-sex nuptials and stem cell research—may have given some socially conservative Evangelical Protestants cause for concern.

We focus here on differences among white Protestants. For example, for the 1992, 1996, 2000, and 2008 ANES surveys, we examined differences between white Protestants who said they were "born again" and those who had not had this religious experience.[27] In all four surveys, white born-again Protestants were more likely to vote Republican than those who were not. In 2008, nearly half the white Protestants who said they had not had this religious experience voted for Obama; among those who said they were born again, only one in four did. The 2012 pool poll also asked Protestants is they considered themselves born again or not. As shown in Table 5-1, Obama won 60 percent of the votes cast by white Protestants who do not say they have been born again. Among born-again Christians— roughly one-fourth of all Protestants—Romney outpolled Obama 78 to 21 percent.

As we noted earlier, Campbell argues that the role of religion in modern politics is not so much about denomination as it is about "religious devotional style" or religiosity. The point is similarly made by Lyman A. Kellstedt, who argues that religious commitment has an important effect on voting behavior.[28] Indeed, in our 2008 study, we showed that religious commitment was strongly associated with voting for the Republican nominee, John McCain.[29] Our ability to measure religious commitment in the 2012 pool poll is limited by the sparse number of questions asking about religious devotion. However, the pool poll does provide data indicating whether individuals who identified with a religion "attend weekly" services or "do not attend weekly."[30] Figure 5-1 presents the results for all Protestant and Catholic voters regardless of race, and religious commitment appears to have mattered in 2012. Protestants who attend weekly services were fifteen percentage points more likely to vote for Romney than those who do not attend regularly. Among Catholic voters who attend church weekly, the majority (57 percent) voted for Romney. Among those who do not attend regularly, Obama won 56 percent of the vote.

HOW SOCIAL GROUPS VOTED DURING THE POSTWAR YEARS

Though we found sharp racial and religious differences in voting, most other social differences in voting behavior were relatively small in 2012. How does this election compare with other presidential elections? Do the relationships between social variables and the vote found in 2012 result from long-term trends that have changed the importance of social factors? To answer these questions, we will examine the voting behavior of social groups that were an important part of the Democrats' New Deal coalition during the postwar years. Our analysis, which will begin with the 1944 election between Franklin Roosevelt and Thomas Dewey, uses a simple measure to assess the effect of social forces over time.

In his lucid discussion of the logic of party coalitions, Robert Axelrod analyzed six basic groups that made up the Democratic coalition: the poor, southerners, blacks (and other nonwhites), union members (and members of their families), Catholics and other non-Protestants such as Jews, and residents of the twelve largest metropolitan areas.[31] John R. Petrocik's more comprehensive study of the Democratic coalition identified fifteen groups and classified seven of them as predominantly Democratic: blacks, lower-status native southerners, middle- and upper-status southerners, Jews, Polish and Irish Catholics, union members, and lower-status border-state whites.[32] A more recent analysis by Harold W. Stanley, William T. Bianco, and Richard G. Niemi analyzes seven pro-Democratic groups: blacks, Catholics, Jews, women, native white southerners, members of union households, and the working class.[33] Our own analysis focuses on race, region, union membership, social class, and religion.[34]

The contribution that a social group can make to a party's coalition depends on three factors: the relative size of the group in the total electorate, its level of turnout compared with that of the total electorate, and its relative loyalty to the political party.[35] The larger a social group, the greater its contribution can be. For example, African Americans make up 12.6 percent of the electorate; the white working class makes up about 30 percent. Thus the potential contribution of blacks is smaller than that of the white working class. Historically, the electoral power of blacks was limited by their relatively low turnout. But black turnout has increased substantially in recent elections and in 2012 exceeded turnout among whites. Moreover, because blacks vote overwhelmingly Democratic, their contribution to the Democratic Party can be greater than their group size would indicate. And the relative size of their contribution grows as whites desert the Democratic Party.

Race

We begin by examining racial differences, which we can trace back to 1944 by using the National Opinion Research Center (NORC) study for that year.[36] Figure 5-1 shows the percentages of white and black major-party voters who voted Democratic for president from 1944 to 2012. (All six figures in this chapter are based on major-party voters.) Although most African Americans voted Democratic from 1944 to 1960, a substantial minority voted Republican. However, the political mobilization of blacks spurred by the civil rights movement and by the Republican candidacy of Barry Goldwater in 1964 ended that Republican voting, and the residual Republican loyalties of older blacks were discarded between 1962 and 1964.[37]

Although the Democrats made substantial gains among blacks, they lost ground among whites. From 1944 to 1964, the Democrats gained a majority of the white vote in three of six elections. Since then, they have never won a majority of the white vote. However, in a two-candidate contest a Democrat can win with just under half the white vote, as the 1960, 1976, 2008, and 2012 elections demonstrate. In the three-candidate contests of 1992 and 1996, Clinton was able to win with only about two-fifths of the white vote.[38]

The gap between the two trend lines in Figure 5-1 illustrates the overall difference in the Democratic vote between whites and blacks. Table 5-2 shows the overall level of "racial voting" in the six elections from 1944 to 1964, as well as four other measures of social cleavage.

From 1944 to 1964, racial differences in voting ranged from a low of twelve percentage points to a high of forty points. These differences then rose to fifty-

FIGURE 5-1   Major-Party Voters Who Voted Democratic for President, by Race, 1944–2012 (Percent)

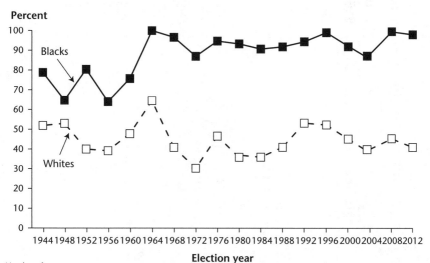

Number of:

Blacks   (52) (17) (51) (50) (75)   (94) (87) (138) (133) (105) (129) (122) (188) (102) (123) (111) (196) (189)

Whites   (1,564) (364) (1,257) (1,253) (1,340) (1,104) (816) (1,430) (1,459) (765) (1,220) (1,041) (1,134) (900) (851) (595) (1,250) (1,021)

Source: Authors' analysis of the ANES surveys.

TABLE 5-2   Relationship of Social Characteristics to Presidential Voting, 1944–2012

	Election year (percentage point difference)																	
	1944	1948	1952	1956	1960	1964	1968	1972	1976	1980	1984	1988	1992	1996	2000	2004	2008	2012
Racial voting[a]	27	12	40	25	23	36	56	57	48	56	54	51	41	47	47	49	54	57
Regional voting[b]																		
Among whites	—	—	12	17	6	-11	-4	-13	1	1	-9	-5	-10	-8	-20	-10	-14	-16
Among entire electorate (ANES surveys)	—	—	9	15	4	-5	6	-3	7	3	3	2	0	0	-10	1	-11	-2
Among entire electorate (official election results)	23	14	8	8	3	-13	-3	-11	5	2	-5	-7	-6	-7	-8	-8	-10	-9
Union voting[c]																		
Among whites	20	37	18	15	21	23	13	11	18	15	20	16	12	23	12	21	8	15
Among entire electorate	20	37	20	17	19	22	13	10	17	16	19	15	11	23	11	18	6	10
Class voting[d]																		
Among whites	19	44	20	8	12	19	10	2	17	9	8	5	4	6	-6	3	3	—

TABLE 5-2 (Continued)

| | Election year (percentage point difference) | | | | | | | | | | | | | | | | | |
	1944	1948	1952	1956	1960	1964	1968	1972	1976	1980	1984	1988	1992	1996	2000	2004	2008	2012
Among entire electorate	20	44	22	11	13	20	15	4	21	15	12	8	8	9	2	4	4	—
Religious voting[e]																		
Among whites	25	21	18	10	48	21	30	13	15	10	16	18	20	14	8	19	15	10
Among entire electorate	24	19	15	10	46	16	21	8	11	3	9	11	10	7	2	5	9	8

Sources: Authors' analysis of a 1944 NORC survey, official election results, ANES surveys, and the 2012 National Election Pool Exit Polls.

Notes: All calculations are based on major-party voters. — indicates not available.

[a] Percentage of blacks who voted Democratic minus percentage of whites who voted Democratic.

[b] Percentage of southerners who voted Democratic minus percentage of voters outside the South who voted Democratic. Comparable data for region were not available for the surveys conducted in 1944 and 1948.

[c] Percentage of members of union households who voted Democratic minus percentage of members of households with no union members who voted Democratic.

[d] Percentage of working class that voted Democratic minus percentage of middle class that voted Democratic. The data for occupation needed to classify respondents according to their social class for 2012 were not available as of this writing.

[e] Percentage of Catholics who voted Democratic minus percentage of Protestants who voted Democratic. Entries for 2012 are based on exit poll results.

six percentage points in 1968 (sixty-one points if Wallace voters are included with Nixon voters) and did not fall to the forty-percentage-point level until 1992.[39] Racial voting was higher in the 1996, 2000, and 2004 contests but increased markedly in the elections of Barack Obama. In 2008, there was a gap of fifty-four percentage points between blacks and whites, and in 2012 that gap increased to fifty-seven points, matching the record high level of racial voting found in 1972. Obama's elections exhibit the highest levels of racial voting in any elections in which the Democratic candidate has won.

Not only did African American loyalty to the Democratic Party increase sharply after 1960, but black turnout rose considerably from 1960 to 1968 because southern blacks were reenfranchised. And while black turnout rose, white turnout outside the South declined. Between 1960, when overall turnout was highest, and 1996, when postwar turnout was lowest, turnout fell by about fifteen percentage points among the voting-age population.[40] Since 1996, turnout in the United States has been rising. In the 2000 and 2004 election, turnout among whites and blacks increased at approximately the same rate. Yet in the 2008 and 2012 election, the groups moved in opposite directions, with black turnout continuing to rise and white turnout declining.

From 1948 to 1960, African Americans never accounted for more than one Democratic vote in twelve. In 1964, however, Johnson received about one in seven of his votes from blacks, and blacks contributed a fifth of the Democratic totals in both 1968 and 1972. In the 1976 election, which saw Democratic gains among whites, Jimmy Carter won only about one in seven of his votes from blacks, and in 1980 one in four. In the next three elections, about one in five Democratic votes were from blacks. In 1996, about one in six of Clinton's votes came from black voters, and in 2000 about one in five of Gore's votes did. In 2004 between a fifth and a fourth of Kerry's total vote was provided by black voters. Both Gore and Kerry came very close to winning, even with this heavy reliance on African American voters. In both 2008 and 2012, black voters accounted for about one-fourth of Obama's total vote. And, as we noted, no Democratic presidential winner had ever drawn this large a share of his total vote from these voters.

Region

White southerners' desertion of the Democratic Party is arguably the most dramatic change in postwar American politics. As we saw in Chapter 3, regional differences can be analyzed using official election statistics, but these statistics are of limited use in examining race-related differences in regional voting because election results are not tabulated by race. Consequently, we rely on survey data to document the dramatic shift in voting behavior among white southerners.

As Figure 5-2 reveals, white southerners were somewhat more Democratic than whites outside the South in the 1952 and 1956 contests between Dwight

Eisenhower and Adlai Stevenson and in the 1960 contest between John Kennedy and Richard Nixon.[41] But in the next three elections, regional differences were reversed, with white southerners voting more Republican than whites outside the South. In 1976 and 1980, when the Democrats fielded Jimmy Carter of Georgia as their standard bearer, white southerners and whites outside the South were very much alike. But since 1980, southern whites have been less likely than non-southern whites to vote Democratic, by an average difference of 11.5 percentage points. In 1984 and 1988, white southerners were less likely to vote Democratic than whites from any other region. In 1992 and 1996, Bill Clinton and his running mate, Al Gore, were both from the South. Even so, George H. W. Bush in 1992 and Bob Dole in 1996 did better among white southerners than among whites from any other region.[42] In 2000, the Democrats ran the southerner Gore, with Joseph Lieberman of Connecticut as his running mate. The Republican candidate, George W. Bush, the governor of Texas, was also a southerner, and his running mate, Dick Cheney, who had become a resident of Texas, moved back to Wyoming to reestablish his residence.[43] In 2004, the Democrats ran John Kerry, the junior senator from Massachusetts, although John Edwards, his running mate, was from North Carolina. But in both these contests, the Democratic vote in the South was low, and the Democrats did substantially better outside the South. In both 2008 and 2012, neither party ran a southerner on its ticket. In Obama's 2008 election, the Democrats made gains among both white southerners and whites outside the South. But as Figure 5-2 shows, the Democrats' support among whites in both regions receded in 2012.

Regional differences among whites from 1952 to 2012 are summarized in Table 5-2. The negative signs for 1964, 1968, 1972, and 1984–2012 reveal that the Democratic candidate fared better outside the South than he did in the South. As we saw in Chapter 3, in 1968 George Wallace had a strong regional base in the South. If we include Wallace voters with Nixon voters, regional differences change markedly, moving from –4 to –12.

Table 5-2 also presents regional differences for the entire electorate. Here, however, we present two sets of estimates: (1) the ANES results from 1952 to 2012 and (2) the results we computed using official election statistics. Both sets of statistics indicate that regional differences have been reversed, but these results are often different, and in many cases would lead to substantially different conclusions. The 2004 election provides a clear example. According to the 2004 ANES survey, voters in the South were as likely to vote Democratic as voters outside the South. But we know that this result is wrong. After all, Bush won all the southern states, whereas Kerry won nineteen states outside the South as well as the District of Columbia. In fact, the official statistics show that southerners were eight points more likely to vote Republican than voters outside the South. In this case, the ANES results, which are based on a sample of eight hundred voters, overestimated the number of Democratic voters in the South. This should remind us of a basic caution in studying elections: always turn to the actual election results before turning to the survey data.

FIGURE 5-2   White Major-Party Voters Who Voted Democratic for President, by
Region, 1952–2012 (Percent)

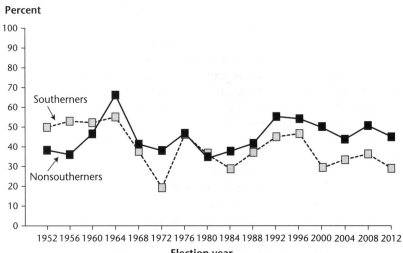

Percent

Number of:																
Southerners	(152)	(211)	(279)	(163)	(124)	(267)	(266)	(203)	(221)	(198)	(238)	(231)	(202)	(137)	(456)	(267)
Nonsoutherners	(975)	(1,002)	(1,061)	(851)	(692)	(1,163)	(1,193)	(562)	(999)	(843)	(897)	(669)	(649)	(458)	(795)	(724)

Source: Authors' analysis of the ANES surveys.

Surveys are useful in demonstrating the way in which the mobilization of southern blacks and the defection of southern whites from the Democratic Party dramatically transformed the Democratic coalition in the South.[44] According to our analysis of ANES surveys, between 1952 and 1960, Democratic presidential candidates never received more than one in fifteen of their votes in the South from blacks. In 1964, three in ten of Johnson's southern votes came from black voters, and in 1968 Hubert Humphrey received as many votes from southern blacks as from southern whites. In 1972, according to these data, George McGovern received more votes from southern blacks than from southern whites.

Black voters were crucial to Carter's success in the South in 1976; he received about a third of his support from African Americans. Even though he won ten of the eleven southern states, he won a majority of the white vote only in his home state of Georgia and possibly in Arkansas. In 1980, Carter again received about a third of his southern support from blacks. In 1984, Walter Mondale received about four in ten of his southern votes from blacks, and in 1988 one in three of the votes Michael Dukakis received came from black voters. In 1992 and 1996, Clinton won about a third of his southern support from African Americans. In 2000, four in ten of the southern votes Gore received came from blacks.

A southern running mate helped Kerry very little among southern whites in 2004. According to the ANES survey, about half of Kerry's votes in the South came from blacks.

Our analysis of the 2008 ANES survey indicates that about a third of Obama's votes in the South came from black voters. And blacks were crucial to the three southern states he carried, because he won a minority of the white vote in those states. In 2012, Obama's electorate in the South was roughly 38 percent black, an increase of five percentage points from his first election. This reflects a combination of factors, including increased turnout among blacks, lower turnout among whites, and a decrease in Obama's vote share among whites. Obama won two southern states; we estimate that a quarter of Obama's votes in Florida were from African Americans, while approximately 36 percent of Obama's votes in Virginia were from blacks.

Union Membership

Figure 5-3 shows the percentage of white union members and nonmembers who voted Democratic for president from 1944 to 2012. Over the course of the postwar period, Democrats have enjoyed a higher level of support from union members than nonmembers, but this has not always resulted in a majority of union votes. In all six elections between 1944 and 1964, the majority of white union members (and members of their households) voted Democratic. In 1968, Humphrey won a slight majority of the union vote, although his total would be cut to 43 percent if Wallace voters were included. The Democrats won about three-fifths of the union vote in 1976, when Jimmy Carter defeated Gerald Ford. In 1988, Dukakis appears to have won a slight majority of the white union vote, although he fell well short of Carter's 1976 tally. In 1992, Clinton won three-fifths of the major-party union vote and won nearly half the total union vote. In 1996, the ANES data show him making major gains and winning 70 percent of the major-party vote among union members. In 2000, Gore won a majority of the union vote, but he was well below Clinton's 1996 tally. In 2004, Kerry did slightly better than Gore among white union voters, but Bush did somewhat better among nonmembers. Because there are more nonmembers than members, this shift worked to Bush's advantage.

In 2008, the Democrats' support among white union members declined from 2004 levels, but Obama nonetheless won a small majority of white union voters. Obama made significant gains among nonmembers in 2008, obviously a net benefit for the Democrats. Obama maintained his majority support among white union members in 2012, again winning about 53 percent of the white union vote. But Obama's support from whites from nonmember households dropped precipitously, by roughly six points.

Differences in presidential voting between union members and nonmembers are presented in Table 5-2. Because in 1968 Wallace did better among union members than nonmembers, including Wallace voters with Nixon voters

FIGURE 5-3   White Major-Party Voters Who Voted Democratic for President, by
Union Membership, 1944–2012 (Percent)

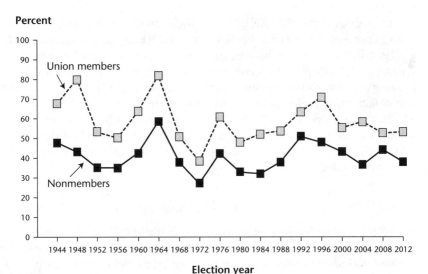

Percent

Number of:

Union members[a]   (332) (94) (305) (334) (342)[c] (259) (197) (366)   (347)[c] (193) (278) (209) (207)[c] (175)[c] (141)[c] (133)[c] (163)[c] (191)[c]
Nonmembers[b]   (1,215)(226) (815) (877) (979)[c] (775) (617)(1,049)(1,099)[c] (569) (941) (828) (925)[c] (723)[c] (706)[c] (461)[c](1,095)[c] (821)[c]

Source: Authors' analysis of the ANES surveys.

[a] Union member or in household with union member.

[b] Not a union member and not in household with union member.

[c] Numbers are weighted.

reduces union voting from thirteen percentage points to ten points. Union voting was highest in 1948, a year when Truman's opposition to the Taft-Hartley Act gained him strong union support.[45] Union voting was low in 1992 and 2000, when white union members were only slightly more likely to vote Democratic than nonmembers. Because Bush did better among nonmembers in 2004, the differences between members and nonmembers rose to twenty-one points. Differences between members and nonmembers were sharply reduced in 2008, reaching the lowest level in any of the preceding seventeen elections. Obama's loss of vote share among white nonunion members caused an increase in the member/nonmember voting differential. Table 5-2 also shows the results for the entire electorate, but because blacks are about as likely to live in union households as whites, including blacks has little effect in most years.

The percentage of the total electorate composed of white union members and their families has declined during the postwar years. White union members and their families made up 25 percent of the electorate in 1952; in 2012, according to the ANES survey, they made up only 17 percent.[46] Turnout among white union members has declined at about the same rate as turnout among nonunion whites. In addition, in many elections since 1964 the Democratic share of the union vote has been relatively low. All of these factors, as well as increased turnout by blacks, have reduced the contribution of white union members to the Democratic presidential coalition. Through 1960, a third of the total Democratic vote came from white union members and their families; between 1964 and 1984, only about one Democratic vote in four; in 1988, 1992, and 1996, only about one Democratic vote in five; and in 2000, only about one Gore vote in six. In 2004, with a drop in Democratic support among whites who did not live in union households, the share of Kerry's vote from union households rose back to one vote in five.

While Obama recorded a small majority among union voters in 2008, the ANES survey shows that only 10 percent of his votes in that year came from members of a white union household.[47] Union voters were a larger portion of Obama's electorate in 2012. Using the ANES, we estimate that 16.1 percent of Obama's votes nationally came from white union members, 17.8 percent based on the pool polls. Voters from union households were an important part of Obama's victories in the battleground states of Ohio and Wisconsin. Based on exit polls in those states and regardless of race, Obama won 60 percent of voters from union households in Ohio and 65 percent of union voters in Wisconsin.[48] This suggests that roughly 26 percent of the votes Obama won in Ohio and Wisconsin came from union membership. Among white union members, Obama's vote share declined in both states, though he still obtained sizeable majorities in each; he won 54 percent of white union voters in Ohio and 60 percent in Wisconsin. By our estimate, 18.5 percent of Obama's votes in Ohio and 20.5 percent in Wisconsin came from white union households.

Social Class

The broad social cleavage between manually employed workers (and their dependents) and nonmanually employed workers (and their dependents) is especially valuable for studying comparative behavior.[49] For this reason, we present the results of our analysis in Figure 5-4, even though we are not yet able to analyze the ANES results for 2012. The figure shows the percentage of white major-party voters who voted Democratic among the working class and the middle class in all the presidential elections between 1944 and 2008.

In all fourteen presidential elections between 1944 and 1996, the white working class voted more Democratic than the white middle class. But as Figure 5-4 shows, the percentage of white working-class voters who voted Democratic has varied considerably from election to election. It reached its lowest level in 1972 during the Nixon-McGovern contest. Carter regained a majority of the white working-class vote class in 1976, but he lost it four years later. Clinton won only

FIGURE 5-4   White Major-Party Voters Who Voted Democratic for President, by Social Class, 1944–2008 (Percent)

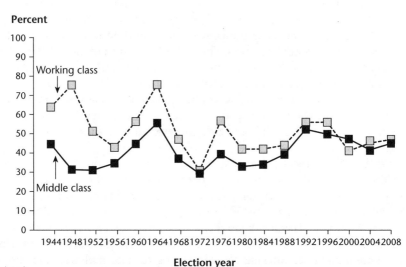

Source: Authors' analysis of a 1944 NORC survey and ANES surveys.

[a] Numbers are weighted.

two-fifths of the vote among working-class whites in the three-candidate race of 1992, although he did win a clear majority of the major-party vote among working-class whites. The 1996 election again featured a strong third-party candidate, but Clinton won half of the working-class vote and a clear majority of the major-party vote among this group. In 2000, Gore won only two-fifths of the vote among working-class whites, and 2000 is the only election during these years in which the Democratic presidential candidate did better among middle-class whites than among working-class whites. Support for the Democrats among the white working class increased slightly in 2004, but their vote share among the middle class declined, and John Kerry failed to win a majority among either group. The 2008 ANES is the last survey for which we have data on working-class and middle-class voting. Figure 5-4 shows that Obama improved his party's standing among working-class and middle-class voters in 2008, gaining around three percentage points among each group, but he failed to win a majority from either.

Although levels of class voting have varied over the last six decades, they have clearly followed a downward trend, as Table 5-2 reveals.[50] Class voting was even lower in 1968 if Wallace voters are included with Nixon voters, because 15 percent of white working-class voters supported Wallace, while only 10 percent of white middle-class voters did. Class voting was very low in 1972, mainly because many white working-class voters deserted McGovern. Only in 2000 do we find class voting to be negative.[51]

Class voting trends are affected substantially if African Americans are included in the analysis. Blacks are disproportionately working class, and they vote overwhelmingly Democratic. In all the elections between 1976 and 1996, class voting is higher when blacks (and other nonwhites) are included in the analysis. In 2000, class voting is positive (although very low) when blacks are included in our calculations. Class voting increased in 2004 and remained at that same level in 2008. The overall trend toward declining class voting is somewhat dampened when blacks are included. However, black workers vote Democratic because of the politics of race, not necessarily because they are working class. Obviously, there was no statistical relationship between social class and voting choice among blacks in 2008 because 99 percent of blacks voted Democratic.[52]

During the postwar years, the proportion of the electorate made up of working-class whites has remained relatively constant, while that of the middle class has grown. The percentage of whites in the agricultural sector has declined dramatically. Turnout fell among both the middle and working classes after 1960, but it fell more among the working class. Declining turnout and defections from the Democratic Party by working-class whites, along with increased turnout by blacks, have reduced the total white working-class contribution to the Democratic presidential coalition.

In 1948 and 1952, about half the Democratic vote came from working-class whites, and from 1956 through 1964 this social group supplied more than four in ten Democratic votes. Its contribution fell to just over a third in 1968 and then to under a third in 1972. In 1976, with the rise in class voting, the white working class provided nearly two-fifths of Carter's total, but it provided just over a third four years later in Carter's reelection bid. In 1984, over a third of Mondale's total support came from this group, and in 1988 Dukakis received more than two in five of his votes from this group. In both 1992 and 1996, working-class whites provided three in ten votes of Clinton's total, but in 2000 this group accounted for only about a fifth of Gore's votes. In 2004, with a drop in middle-class support for the Democratic candidate, Kerry received just under a fourth of his vote from working-class whites. Obama obtained only 15 percent of his votes from white working-class voters, a significant departure from 2004 and far below the group's contribution to the Democratic coalition in the early postwar years.

The white middle-class contribution to the Democratic presidential coalition amounted to fewer than three in ten votes in 1948 and 1952, and just under one-third in 1956, stabilizing at just over one-third in the next five elections. In 1984, Mondale received just under two in five of his votes from middle-class whites, and in 1988 Dukakis received more than two in five. In 1992, more than two in five of Clinton's total votes came from this group, rising to a half in 1996. In 2000, Gore received two-fifths of his total vote from middle-class whites, and in 2004 Kerry received just over two-fifths. In 2008, Obama received around 37 percent of his votes from middle-class whites. In all of the elections between 1984 and 2008, the Democrats received a larger share of their vote from middle-class whites than from working-class whites. The increasing middle-class contribution stems from two factors: (1) though objectively the middle class is shrinking, the percentage of individuals who classify themselves as "middle class" has increased, and (2) class differences are eroding.[53] The decline in class differences is a widespread phenomenon in advanced industrialized societies.[54]

Of course, our argument that class-based voting is declining depends on the way in which we have defined social class. Different definitions may yield different results. For example, in a major study depending on a far more complex definition that divides the electorate into seven social categories, Jeff Manza and Clem Brooks, using ANES data from 1952 to 1996, conclude that class differences are still important.[55] But their findings actually support our conclusion that the New Deal coalition has eroded. For example, they found that professionals were the most Republican class in the 1950s, but that by the 1996 election they had become the most Democratic.

Religion

Voting differences among major religious groups have also declined during the postwar years. Even so, as Figure 5-5 reveals, in every election since 1944 Jews have been more likely to vote Democratic than Catholics, and Catholics have been more likely to vote Democratic than Protestants.[56]

As Figure 5-5 shows, a large majority of Jews voted Democratic in every election from 1944 to 1968, and although the percentage declined in Nixon's landslide over McGovern in 1972, even McGovern won a majority of the Jewish vote. In 1980, many Jews (like many Gentiles) were dissatisfied with Carter's performance as president, and some resented the pressure he had exerted on Israel to accept the Camp David Accords, which returned the Sinai Peninsula—captured by Israel in 1967—to Egypt. A substantial minority of Jews supported third-party candidate John Anderson that year, but Carter still outpolled Reagan. Both Mondale in 1984 and Dukakis (whose wife is Jewish) in 1988 won a clear majority of the Jewish vote. The Jewish Democratic vote surged in 1992, with Clinton winning nine in ten major-party Jewish voters. With Lieberman, an observant Jew, as his running mate, Gore, too, won overwhelming Jewish support in 2000. Bush was strongly pro-Israel in his foreign policy, but Kerry won solid support among Jewish voters, although there may have been some Republican gains. In 2008, some Jews may have had reservations about Obama's commitment to Israel's security, but even so he may have made slight gains among Jewish voters. As noted earlier, religion codes for the 2012 ANES were not available at the time of our writing, so we supplement data from pool poll data for this election. The data show that Obama's support among white Jewish voters dropped significantly in 2012 to 71 percent. This decline is not necessarily a product of our switch from ANES to pool poll data. In fact, the 2008 exit polls were remarkably consistent

FIGURE 5-5　White Major-Party Voters Who Voted Democratic for President, by Religion, 1944–2012 (Percent)

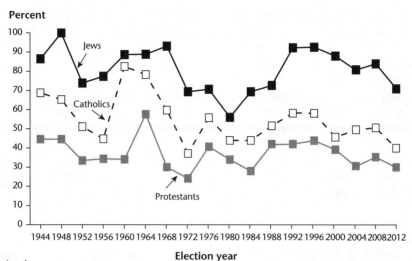

Number of:																			
Jews	(74)	(19)	(46)	(53)	(36)[a]	(29)	(29)	(36)	(41)[a]	(25)	(36)	(22)	(33)[a]	(25)[a]	(25)[a]	(21)[a]	(25)[a]	(195)[b]
Catholics	(311)	(101)	(284)	(288)	(309)[a]	(267)	(206)	(384)	(378)[a]	(188)	(360)	(287)	(301)[a]	(279)[a]	(269)[a]	(164)[a]	(259)[a]	(1752)[b]
Protestants	(1,183)	(222)	(770)	(841)	(957)[a]	(674)	(533)	(938)	(959)[a]	(490)	(709)	(641)	(642)[a]	(490)[a]	(454)[a]	(308)[a]	(720)[a]	(3795)[b]

Source: Authors' analysis of a 1944 NORC survey, ANES surveys and the 2012 National Election Pool Exit Polls.

[a] Numbers are weighted.

[b] Based on exit poll data.

with the 2008 ANES; the former estimated Obama's support among white Jewish voters at 83 percent, while the latter estimated it to be 84 percent. Obama had a rocky relationship with Israeli Prime Minister Benjamin Netanyahu during his first term, and the decline in his support among Jewish voters between 2008 and 2012 may reflect these tensions. Obviously, on the whole, Jewish voters' loyalty to the Democratic Party remains very strong.

A majority of white Catholics voted Democratic in six of the seven elections from 1944 to 1968. The percentage of Catholics voting Democratic surged in 1960, when the Democrats fielded a Catholic candidate, John Kennedy, but it was still very high in Johnson's landslide four years later.[57] In 1968, a majority of white Catholics voted Democratic, although Humphrey's total is reduced from 60 percent to 55 percent if Wallace voters are included. In 1976, Carter won a majority among white Catholics, but the Democrats did not win a majority of the major-party vote among white Catholics again until 1992. In his 1996 reelection, Clinton again won over half of the major-party vote among white Catholics. Four years later, George W. Bush outpolled Al Gore among white Catholics. Even in 2004, when the Democrats ran a Catholic presidential candidate, Bush outscored Kerry among white Catholic voters. Based on 2008 ANES data, Obama won half the vote among white Catholics. He won slightly less than half in the 2008 pool poll. Obama's vote share among white Catholics declined, however, in 2012, falling ten percentage points. As we noted earlier, much of the Democrats' support from white Catholics comes from those who are less devout in their religious practices, as well as the Latino Catholic population. But, on average, Democrats continue to do better among white Catholics than among white Protestants.

Our measure of religious voting shows considerable change from election to election, although there was a downward trend from 1968 to 2000, when religious differences reached their lowest level. Religious differences were somewhat higher in both 2004 and 2008 (see Table 5-2). Even though white Protestants were more likely than white Catholics to vote for Wallace in 1968, including Wallace voters in our total has little effect on religious voting (it falls from thirty points to twenty-nine points). Religious differences were small in the 1980 Reagan-Carter contest, but since then they have varied. Because the Latino Catholic electorate is projected to grow, religious voting may rise in future elections.

Including African Americans in our calculations reduces religious voting. Blacks are much more likely to be Protestant than Catholic, and including blacks in our calculations adds a substantial number of Protestant Democrats. In 2008, for example, religious voting is reduced from fifteen points to nine points when blacks (and other nonwhites) are included.

The Jewish contribution to the Democratic Party has declined, in part because Jews did not vote overwhelmingly Democratic in 1972, 1980, 1984, 1988, 2004, and 2012 and in part because Jews make up a small and declining share of the electorate. During the 1950s, Jews were about a twentieth of the electorate. But the most recent estimates suggest that only about one American in fifty is Jewish.[58]

Although Jews make up only about 2 percent of the population, three-fourths of the nation's Jews live in seven large states—New York, New Jersey, Massachusetts, California, Florida, Pennsylvania, and Illinois—which together had 178 electoral votes in 2012.[59] More important, two of these states are battleground states: Florida, where Jews make up 3.3 percent of the population, and Pennsylvania, where they make up 2.3 percent. Because exit polls suggest Jews made up 5 percent of the Florida electorate, and because Obama won the state by only 74,309 votes, Jews may have provided enough votes to swing the Sunshine State toward Obama. Overall, however, the electoral significance of Jews is lessened because five of these large states are not battleground states. For example, Jews make up 8.4 percent of the population in New York, far more than any other state. Although Jews could influence New York's 29 electoral votes, a Democratic candidate who does not win by a comfortable margin in New York is very likely to lose the election.[60]

According to our estimates based on ANES surveys, in 1948 Truman received about a third of his total vote from white Catholics. In 1952, Stevenson won three-tenths of his vote from white Catholics, but only one-fourth in 1956. In 1960, Kennedy, the first Catholic president, received 37 percent of his vote from Catholics, but the Catholic contribution fell—owing to an ebb in Catholic turnout—to just under three in ten votes when Johnson defeated Goldwater in 1964. In 1968, three-tenths of Humphrey's total vote came from white Catholics, but only a fourth of McGovern's vote in 1972. White Catholics provided just over a fourth of Carter's vote in his 1976 victory, but in his 1980 loss to Reagan just over a fifth came from this source. Mondale received just under three in ten of his votes from white Catholics, and Dukakis received a fifth of his vote from this group. According to our analysis based on ANES surveys, just over a fifth of Clinton's vote came from white Catholics in 1992, and just over a fourth in 1996. The ANES surveys suggest that both Kerry and Bush received about a fifth of their votes from white Catholics. In 2008, both the ANES survey and the pool poll suggest that less than a fifth of Obama's vote came from white Catholics. The 2012 pool poll suggests that only one in seven votes cast for Obama in 2012 came from white Catholics.

The contrast between the 1960 and 2004 elections is the most striking in these six-decade comparisons. In both elections, the Democrats fielded a Catholic presidential candidate. But Kennedy received over twice as large a share of the Catholic vote as Kerry. Religious differences were massive in 1960 and relatively modest in 2004. Well over a third of Kennedy's votes came from white Catholics, but only about one-fifth of Kerry's did, so that they made up barely more of Kerry's voter coalition than they made up of Obama's in 2008. Obviously, the social characteristics of the Catholic community changed over the span of forty-four years. And then there were social issues that may have led many Catholics to vote Republican in 2004 that were simply not on the political agenda four decades earlier.[61]

As the data reveal, in all of the elections between 1944 and 1996 the effects of class and religion were cumulative (Figure 5-6). In every one of these fourteen elections, working-class Catholics were more likely to vote Democratic than any other group. And in all these elections, middle-class Protestants were the most likely to vote Republican. In 2000, middle-class Catholics were the most likely to vote Democratic, and middle-class Protestants the most likely to vote Republican. In 2004 and 2008, as in the vast majority of past elections, working-class Catholics were the most Democratic group. Middle-class Protestants were somewhat more likely to vote Republican than middle-class Catholics. All the same, middle-class Protestants are the most consistent group, supporting the Republicans in all seventeen elections. We lack data on the effect of class and religion in the 2012 election.

The relative importance of social class and religion can be assessed by comparing the voting behavior of middle-class Catholics with that of working-class Protestants. Religion was more important than social class in predicting the vote in all elections between 1944 and 2008, except those in which social class was more important than religion—1948 (by a considerable margin), 1976, and

FIGURE 5-6   White Major-Party Voters Who Voted Democratic for President, by Social Class and Religion, 1944–2008 (Percent)

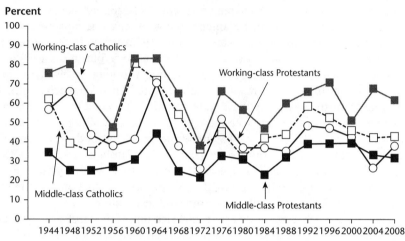

Percent

Working-class Catholics

Working-class Protestants

Middle-class Catholics

Middle-class Protestants

1944 1948 1952 1956 1960 1964 1968 1972 1976 1980 1984 1988 1992 1996 2000 2004 2008

Election year

Number of:
Catholics

Working class	(152)	(61)	(158)	(168)	(179)[a]	(126)	(83)	(176)	(163)[a]	(76)	(156)	(100)	(100)[a]	(86)[a]	(79)[a]	(41)[a]	(42)[a]
Middle class	(130)	(28)	(94)	(96)	(109)[a]	(121)	(96)	(176)	(179)[a]	(96)	(177)	(164)	(166)[a]	(167)[a]	(161)[a]	(108)[a]	(134)[a]

Protestants

Working class	(405)	(59)	(279)	(329)	(374)[a]	(280)	(198)	(383)	(367)[a]	(197)	(286)	(218)	(234)[a]	(159)[a]	(115)[a]	(79)[a]	(128)[a]
Middle class	(479)	(91)	(302)	(336)	(405)[a]	(287)	(254)	(430)	(457)[a]	(226)	(359)	(349)	(303)[a]	(256)[a]	(292)[a]	(185)[a]	(335)[a]

Source: Authors' analysis of a 1944 NORC survey and ANES surveys.

[a] Numbers are weighted.

1980—and the one, 1964, in which class and religion were equally important. However, all of these trend lines have been converging, suggesting that traditional sources of cleavage are declining in importance.

WHY THE NEW DEAL COALITION BROKE DOWN

The importance of race increased substantially after 1960, but all of the other factors we have examined have declined in importance. The effects of region on voting behavior have been reversed, with the Republicans now enjoying an advantage in the South, especially when we compare southern whites with whites outside the South. As the national Democratic Party strengthened its appeals to African Americans during the 1960s, party leaders endorsed policies that southern whites opposed, and many of them deserted the Democratic Party. The migration of northern whites to the South also may have reduced regional characteristics.

Although the Democratic Party's appeals to blacks may have weakened its hold on white groups that traditionally supported it, other factors were at work as well.[62] During the postwar years, these groups have changed. Although union members do not hold high-paying professional and managerial jobs, they have gained substantial economic advantages (however, these advantages may erode as the result of globalization). Differences in income between the working and the middle classes have diminished. And Catholics, who often came from more recent European immigrant groups than Protestants, have become increasingly middle class as the proportion of second- and third-generation Americans among Catholics has grown. This trend is only partially offset by the growing number of Catholic Latinos.

Not only have these social groups changed, but the historical conditions that led union members, the working class, and Catholics to become Democrats have receded further into the past. Although the transmission of partisan loyalties from generation to generation gives historically based coalitions some staying power, the ability of the family to transmit partisan loyalties has decreased as the strength of party identification among the electorate has weakened.[63] Moreover, with the passage of time the proportion of the electorate that directly experienced the Roosevelt years has progressively declined. By 2012, less than 2 percent of the voting-age population was old enough to have voted during the Roosevelt years. New policy issues, unrelated to the political conflicts of the New Deal era, have tended to erode party loyalties among traditionally Democratic groups. Edward G. Carmines and James A. Stimson provide strong evidence that race-related issues have been crucial in weakening the New Deal coalition.[64] And more recently, social issues such as abortion and same-sex marriage may have weakened Democratic Party loyalties among Catholic voters.

Despite the weakening of the New Deal coalition, the Democrats managed to win the presidency in 1992 and 1996, came very close to holding it in 2000, and came close to regaining it in 2004. In 2008, they did regain the presidency, winning a majority of the popular vote for the first time since 1976. And they won a popular-vote majority again in 2012. In his 1992 victory, Clinton boosted his share of the major-party vote among union members, the white working class, and even white southerners. He focused on appeals to middle America, and in both 1992 and 1996 he paid as low a price as possible to gain the black vote. Clinton was the first Democrat to win in an election in which blacks made up more than 15 percent of the Democratic vote. In 1996, Clinton once again won with over 15 percent of his votes provided by blacks. But the 1992 and 1996 elections were three-candidate contests. Our calculations suggest that, under typical levels of turnout among its various coalition groups, it would be exceedingly difficult for a Democrat to win a two-candidate contest in which blacks made up a fifth or more of his or her total coalition. Difficult, but not impossible.

With the 2008 and 2012 elections, we see the ingredients (and challenges) of building a modern Democratic coalition. Obama gained about a fourth of his total tally from black voters. This was possible because black turnout equaled or exceeded white turnout and because blacks voted overwhelmingly Democratic. The Democrats also enjoyed strong support from Latino voters, and population growth makes this group an increasingly larger share of the Democratic coalition. We began this chapter by noting that Democrats in the postwar period have been a "coalition of minorities"—increasingly, the minorities at the heart of this coalition are blacks and Latinos.

Obama has not restored the New Deal coalition. Among the groups we examined, apart from blacks only Jews gave a clear majority of their vote to Obama. Obama had only a slight edge among white union members, and he split the white Catholic vote with Romney, as he did with McCain. Among white southerners, a mainstay of the New Deal coalition, he won only a third of the vote.

Perhaps as James W. Ceaser and Andrew E. Busch argued after the 1992 election, future coalitions will be formed on the basis of common issue positions rather than on the demographic groups that both politicians and political scientists now employ.[65] Turning to the issue preferences of the electorate provides an opportunity to see how the Democrats can move from their 2012 victory to form a winning coalition and may provide insights into how the Republicans might regain political power.

Chapter 6

Candidates, Issues, and the Vote

In this chapter and the two that follow, we examine some of the concerns that underlie voters' choices for president. Even though scholars and politicians disagree about what factors voters employ and how they employ them, there is general consensus on several points. First, voters' attitudes or preferences determine their choices. There may be disagreement over exactly which attitudes shape behavior, but most scholars agree that voters deliberately choose to support the candidate they believe will make the best president. There is also general agreement that attitudes toward the candidates, the issues, and the parties are the most important in shaping the vote.[1] In these three chapters, we start with voters' considerations just before casting their ballots, and then turn to their earlier ones, ending with the most important long-term attitudinal force shaping the vote: party identification.

In this chapter, we look first at the relationship between several measures of candidate evaluation and the vote, beginning with the "feeling thermometers" used by the American National Election Studies (ANES) to measure affect toward the candidates. After this brief analysis, we examine aspects of the major components of these evaluations: voters' perceptions of the candidates' personal qualities and voters' perceptions of the candidates' professional qualifications and competence to serve as president.[2] As we will see, there is a very powerful relationship between thermometer evaluations of candidates and the vote, and an only somewhat less strong one between evaluations of candidate traits and the vote. It might seem obvious that voters support the candidate they like best, but in 1968, 1980, 1992, 1996, and 2000 the presence of a significant third candidate complicated decision making for many voters.[3]

We conceive of attitudes toward the candidates as the most direct influence on the vote itself, especially the summary evaluations encapsulated in the feeling thermometers. But attitudes toward the issues and the parties help to shape attitudes toward the candidates and thus the vote. With that in mind, we turn to the first part of our investigation of the role of issues. After analyzing the problems that most concerned the voters in 2012, we discuss the two basic forms of issue voting: that based on prospective issues and that based on retrospective issues. In this chapter, we investigate the impact of prospective issues. In doing so, we consider one of the enduring questions about issue voting: how much information does the public have on the issues and candidates' positions on them, and is this sufficient for casting an issues-based vote? Our analyses provide an indication of the significance of prospective issues in 2012, and we compare their impact as shown in earlier election surveys. Chapter 7 examines retrospective issues and the vote, and Chapter 8 examines partisan identification and assesses the significance of both parties and issues for voting in 2012 and in earlier elections.

ATTITUDES TOWARD THE CANDIDATES

Although the United States has a two-party system, there are still ways in which other candidates can appear on the ballot or run a write-in candidacy. The 2012 presidential election was a two-person race for all intents and purposes, but many other candidates were running as well. Four other political parties qualified for inclusion on at least ten state ballots. The Libertarian Party nominated Gary Johnson for president and qualified for forty-eight state ballots (and the District of Columbia's), winning about 1.3 million votes (just under 1 percent; Obama won about 65.9 million votes, by comparison). Jill Stein was the Green Party's presidential nominee, winning about one-third of 1 percent of the vote. Virgil Goode won just under one-tenth of 1 percent of the vote for the Constitution Party. Rocky Anderson and Tom Hoefling won about three-tenths of 1 percent for their parties (the Justice and America's Parties, respectively).

Here, though, we limit our attention to President Barack Obama and Governor Mitt Romney. We want to know why people preferred one candidate over the other, and therefore how they voted and, by extension, why Obama won the election. The obvious starting point in two-person races is to imagine that people voted for the candidate they preferred. This may sound obvious, but, as we noted above, in races with three or more candidates, people do not necessarily vote for the candidate they most prefer.[4]

Happily for understanding the 2012 presidential election, in a strictly two-person race people overwhelmingly vote for the candidate they prefer. This close relationship can be demonstrated by analyzing the feeling thermometer—a scale that runs from 0 to 100 degrees, with 0 indicating "very cold" or negative feelings, 50 indicating neutral feelings, and 100 indicating a "very warm" or positive evaluation.[5] Respondents who rank a major-party candidate highest among three candidates vote overwhelmingly for the major-party candidate. On the other hand, respondents who rank a third-party or independent candidate highest often desert that candidate to vote for one of the major-party candidates, which we believe may result from voters using strategic considerations to avoid "wasting" their vote on a candidate who has little chance of winning. The data for 2012 are reported in Table 6-1.

TABLE 6-1 Relative Ranking of Presidential Candidates on the Feeling
Thermometer: Response Distribution and Vote Choice, 2012

	Rated Obama higher than Romney on thermometer	Rated Obama equal to Romney on thermometer	Rated Romney higher than Obama on thermometer	Total	(*N*)
A. Distribution of responses					
Percent	55	7	38	100	(1,925)
B. Major-party voters who voted for Obama					
Percent	98	23	1	53	(1,286)
(*N*)	(683)	(58)	(544)		

Source: Authors' analysis of the 2012 ANES survey.

Note: The numbers in parentheses in Part B of the table are the totals on which the percentages are based. Only respondents who rated both candidates on the scale are included.

As the data in Part A of the table illustrate, 55 percent of the respondents rated Obama higher than Romney on the thermometer (in the pre-election wave of the survey), while 38 percent rated Romney higher, and the remaining 7 percent scored them equally. In 2008, 55 percent rated Obama higher than McCain. Part B shows why this lead in overall evaluations is so critical. In particular, it depicts the powerful relationship between these assessments and the vote, in which almost everyone supported the candidate they rated higher. Those who rated the candidates at the same score divided their votes three to one for Romney, but of course this is a very small percentage. This finding is particularly strong in 2012, but the general pattern of over nine in ten supporting their preferred candidates is commonplace, and so it is worth noting that, in other elections, we have shown that much smaller percentages report voting for third candidates, even among those who scored such candidates highest on these measures.[6] Overall, then, an important factor in Obama's victory was the larger proportion of the electorate who rated him more highly. These summary evaluations are quite proximate to the vote in a two-candidate race. They are, therefore, but a first, very close, step back from the vote to the discovery of underlying reasons that more voted for Obama.

That is to say that we are led to the next obvious question: why did more people rate Obama more warmly? The ANES asked a series of questions about how people view the candidates as people and as potential presidents, six of which are reported in Table 6-2A. These cover different aspects of attributes we might like a president to possess: morality, strong leadership, caring about people, being knowledgeable, intelligence, and honesty. What is striking is that citizens overall saw Obama as stronger on every one of these attributes. Sometimes, such as with morality and providing strong leadership, the edge is very small.

TABLE 6-2A   Distribution of Responses on Presidential Candidate Trait Evaluations, 2012 (percent)

	Extremely well	Very well	Moderately well	Slightly well	Not well at all	Total	(N)
Obama							
Moral	20	27	25	15	13	100	(1,989)
Provides strong leadership	16	25	25	15	18	99	(2,022)
Really cares about people like you	20	22	21	15	23	101	(2,025)
Knowledgeable	25	34	24	11	6	100	(2,027)
Intelligent	31	40	19	7	3	100	(2,032)
Honest	17	25	24	14	20	100	(2,023)
Romney							
Moral	17	23	27	17	17	101	(1,941)
Provides strong leadership	11	23	29	16	21	100	(1,947)
Really cares about people like you	6	14	22	19	40	101	(1,965)
Knowledgeable	12	31	30	15	11	99	(1,972)
Intelligent	18	37	27	11	8	101	(1,966)
Honest	8	18	26	19	29	100	(1,945)

Source: Authors' analysis of the 2012 ANES.

Note: Numbers are weighted.

Sometimes, perhaps especially with "really cares about people like me," intelligence, and honesty, the edge is quite a bit larger. Further, more people said that each trait describes Obama "very well" or "extremely well" than as only "slightly well" or "not well at all." The same was true only for morality and nearly so for providing strong leadership for evaluating Romney.[7]

In Table 6-2B, we report the percentage of major-party voters with differing assessments of the candidates who voted for Obama. It shows, for example, that among the 292 voters who said that "moral" described Obama extremely well, 91 percent voted for him; on the other hand, among the 245 voters who said that "moral" described Romney extremely well, only 13 percent voted for Obama. More generally, we can see that all of these evaluations are strongly related to the vote. Those who responded more positively than "moderately well" were very likely to vote for that candidate, while those who responded less positively than that were quite unlikely to support the candidate. Often, the "moderately well" category split their vote evenly, but so many believed that

TABLE 6-2B   Major-Party Vote for Obama and Romney by Presidential
Candidate Trait Evaluations, 2012 (percent)

	Extremely well	Very well	Moderately well	Slightly well	Not well at all
Obama					
Moral	91	75	45	12	5
(N)	(292)	(333)	(284)	(178)	(169)
Provides strong					
leadership	98	86	51	14	4
(N)	(217)	(317)	(320)	(174)	(251)
Really cares about					
people like you	98	86	46	18	5
(N)	(285)	(291)	(240)	(164)	(300)
Knowledgeable	87	67	27	6	6
(N)	(347)	(432)	(295)	(122)	(82)
Intelligent	81	53	20	12	6
(N)	(445)	(501)	(216)	(75)	(40)
Honest	95	84	50	11	2
(N)	(246)	(334)	(276)	(158)	(260)
Romney					
Moral	87	65	38	27	4
(N)	(245)	(296)	(326)	(196)	(174)
Provides strong					
leadership	91	75	54	19	2
(N)	(148)	(295)	(349)	(202)	(252)
Really cares about					
people like you	97	93	79	36	7
(N)	(84)	(193)	(273)	(236)	(475)
Knowledgeable	90	66	39	20	2
(N)	(162)	(376)	(407)	(194)	(120)
Intelligent	79	54	38	16	0
(N)	(253)	(465)	(326)	(130)	(83)
Honest	87	88	58	31	5
(N)	(123)	(235)	(336)	(199)	(354)

Source: Authors' analysis of the 2012 ANES.

Note: The numbers in parentheses are the totals on which the percentages are based. The numbers are weighted. The questions were asked of a randomly selected half of the sample.

Obama was knowledgeable and intelligent that saying they described him only "moderately well" was rather negative, and fewer of those voted for him. Conversely, so few thought that Romney cared about people like themselves that those who gave him moderate marks were actually rating him highly, compared to the rest of the public, and often supported him at the polls. Thus not only did the public's views of these candidate traits fit well with the candidates and their campaign themes, but the views were strongly related to the vote. But we would go even farther and conclude that Obama was seen by many as possessing in good measure a series of traits commonly desired in presidents, while Romney was not able to convince voters of the same thing. As a result, a significant part of the explanation of why Obama won the presidency was simply that more people thought he had the attributes and skills of a president than those who thought Romney did. Indeed, if choosing a president consisted exclusively of picking the candidate with the strongest set of skills and attributes, Obama would have won handily. Instead it is a choice of who would make the best president and what would he (or, someday, she) do with the office, and it is to one of these, acting to achieve various public policies, that we turn next.

PROSPECTIVE EVALUATIONS

Public policy concerns enter into the voting decision in two very different ways. In an election in which an incumbent is running, such as 2012, two questions become important: How has the incumbent president done on policy? And how likely is it that his opponent (or opponents) would do any better? Voting based on this form of policy appraisal is called retrospective voting and will be analyzed in Chapter 7.

The second form of policy-based voting involves examining the candidates' policy platforms and assessing which candidate's policy promises conform most closely to what the voter believes the government should be doing. Policy voting, therefore, involves comparing sets of promises and voting for the set that is most like the voter's own preferences. Voting based on these kinds of decisions is called prospective voting, because it involves examining the promises of the candidates about future actions. In this chapter, we examine prospective evaluations of the two major-party candidates in 2012 and how these evaluations relate to voter choice.

The last eleven elections show some remarkable similarities in prospective evaluations and voting. Perhaps the most important similarity is the perception of where the Democratic and Republican candidates stood on issues. In these elections, the public saw clear differences between the major-party nominees. In all cases, the public saw the Republican candidates as conservative on most issues, and most citizens scored the GOP candidates as more conservative than the voters themselves. And in all elections, the public saw the Democratic candidates as liberal on most issues, and most citizens viewed the Democratic candidates as more liberal than the voters themselves. As a result, many voters perceived a clear choice based on their understanding of the candidates' policy positions. The candidates, then, presented the voters with, as the 1964 Goldwater campaign slogan put it, "a choice, not an echo." The *average* citizen, however, faced a difficult choice. For many, the Democratic nominees were considered to be as far to the left as the Republicans were to the right. On balance, the net effect of prospective issues was to give neither party a clear advantage.

One of the most important differences among these elections was the mixture of issues that concerned the public. Each election presented its own mixture of policy concerns. Moreover, the general strategies of the candidates on issues differed in each election. In 1980 Jimmy Carter's incumbency was marked by a general perception that he was unable to solve pressing problems. Ronald Reagan attacked that weakness both directly (e.g., by the question he posed to the public during his debate with Carter: "Are you better off today than you were four years ago?") and indirectly. The indirect attack was more future-oriented. Reagan offered a clear set of proposals designed to convince the public that he would be more likely to solve the nation's problems because he had his own plan to end soaring inflation, to strengthen the United States militarily, and to regain respect and influence for the United States abroad.

In 1984 the public perceived Reagan as a far more successful president than Carter had been. Reagan chose to run his reelection campaign by focusing primarily on the theme that things were much better by 1984 (as illustrated by his advertising slogan "It's morning in America"). Walter Mondale attacked that claim by arguing that Reagan's policies were unfair and by pointing to the rapidly growing budget deficit. But Reagan countered that Mondale was another "tax and spend" Democrat, and the "Great Communicator," as some called him, captured a second term.

The 1988 campaign was more similar to the 1984 campaign than to the 1980 campaign. George H. W. Bush continued to run on the successes of the Reagan-Bush administration and promised no new taxes. ("Read my lips," he said. "No new taxes!") Michael S. Dukakis initially attempted to portray the election as one about "competence" rather than "ideology," arguing that he had demonstrated his competence as governor of Massachusetts and that Bush, by implication, was less competent. Bush countered that it really was an election about ideology and that Dukakis was just another liberal Democrat from Massachusetts.

The 1992 election presented yet another type of campaign. Bush used the success of the 1991 Persian Gulf War to augment his claim that he was a successful world leader, but Bill Clinton attacked the Bush administration on domestic issues, barely discussing foreign affairs at all. He sought to keep the electorate focused on the current economic woes and argued for substantial reforms of the health care system, hoping to appeal to Democrats and to spur action should he be the first Democrat in the White House in twelve years. At the same time, he sought to portray himself not as another "tax and spend" liberal Democrat, but as a moderate "New Democrat."

In 1996 Clinton ran a campaign typical of a popular incumbent; he focused on what led people to approve of his handling of the presidency and avoided mentioning many specific new programs. His policy proposals were a lengthy series of relatively inexpensive, limited programs. Bob Dole, having difficulties deciding whether to emphasize Clinton's personal failings in the first term or to call for different programs for the future, decided to put a significant tax cut proposal at the center of his candidacy under either of those campaign strategies.

In 2000 the candidates debated a broad array of domestic issues—education, health care, social security, and taxes the most prominent among them—often couched in terms of a newfound "problem": federal government budget surpluses. Typically, these issues (except for taxes) have favored Democratic contenders, and Republicans often avoided detailed discussions of all except taxes, on the grounds that doing so would make the issues more salient to voters and would highlight the Democratic advantages. George W. Bush, however, spoke out on education, in particular, as well as health care and Social Security to a lesser extent, believing he could undercut the traditional Democratic advantage. For his part, Al Gore had the advantage of his belief (backed by public opinion polls) that the public was less in favor of tax cuts than usual and more in favor of allocating budget surpluses to buttress popular domestic programs.

In 2004, by contrast, Bush and Kerry had less choice about what issues to consider. With wars under way in Iraq and Afghanistan, and against terrorism, neither candidate could avoid foreign policy considerations. Bush preferred to emphasize that Iraq was part of the war on terrorism, while Kerry argued that it was not, and indeed that it was a costly distraction from it. Similarly, 2004 opened with the economy slumping. The Democrats, including Kerry, attacked the Bush administration policies, while Bush countered by saying that the economy was actually improving—in large part because of his successful policies. As the year wore on, the economy did in fact improve, although not so much as to remove all criticism.

The 2008 campaign began as one in which the Democrats tried to emphasize their opposition to the Bush policies in Iraq and their concern about the war in Afghanistan. On the domestic front, Obama emphasized health care reform, improved environmental policies, and other aspects of his agenda that called for "change." McCain, conversely, began with a spirited defense of the war in Iraq, and especially the "surge" in the war effort there. By fall, however, the economy had swept aside virtually every other issue but war from consideration, and replaced war as topic number one. Indeed, so worrisome were the economic events of the fall that candidates could ill afford to do anything but relate any domestic issue to their plans for fighting the economic downturn.

As we saw in Chapter 2, both the Obama and Romney camps anticipated a close contest in 2012. Romney's side wanted to make the campaign be about Obama and his successes or failures in office—retrospective voting concerns— on the grounds that the economy had not recovered sufficiently to justify returning Obama to office. This was made problematic first by Romney's "47 percent of the electorate" remarks (undoubtedly related to why the public viewed him skeptically with respect to "really cares about people like me") and then by Hurricane Sandy and the appearance—reinforced by a leading Republican figure, New Jersey Gov. Chris Christie—that Obama was doing his job very well. Obama, for his part, approached issues rather more like Clinton had in 1996, offering a series of popular but relatively small domestic initiatives ("small ball" as it was called at times), and his emphasis on how the economy was not where everyone hoped but it was improving and would do so quicker with Democrats in office.

What about the public's views? From 1972 to 2004, we were able to use ANES surveys to assess this question. In 2008, we examined exit polls, conducted as voters were leaving the pooling place, and the various interested parties (news media and so on) formed a pool to conduct that poll (called a "pool poll"). We did so again for 2012.

In the four elections preceding the one in 2004, the great majority of responses revolved around domestic issues rather than foreign policy, perhaps because of the end of the Cold War (although concerns about foreign policy were also low in 1976, during the Cold War). In the eight elections prior to 2004, two major categories of domestic issues dominated. From 1976 to 1992, in good times and bad, by far the more commonly cited issue was the economy. In 1972, 1996, 2000, and then in 2004 as well, the most frequently cited problems were in the social issues category, such as either social welfare issues or concerns about pubic order. In 2004, for example, nearly half (49 percent) cited social issues, while 29 percent (the highest since 1984, that is, since the Cold War) cited a foreign and defense issue. Mostly that was the war in Iraq in particular (18 percent). In 2008 (shifting now from the ANES to the pool poll) 63 percent of voters said the economy was most important, with the war in Iraq selected by 10 percent and the war on terror by 9 percent.

Table 6-3 reports the results of the pool poll for 2012. Foreign policy continued to drop in concern, as U.S. involvement in Iraq was over and the war in Afghanistan was diminishing. Only 5 percent selected foreign policy as most important. It was the economy that remained dominant, as 56 percent selected it as their chief concern, while 15 percent more said it was the deficit. The latter had been a key part of the Tea Party and Republican leadership concerns through 2010 and into 2012 (it is of course an issue that touches on the economy and on the role of the government and so is not purely about either the economy or the government). Another large portion, 18 percent, said that health care was the most important problem, while selection of other options was rare. As might

TABLE 6-3 Most Important Problem as Seen by the Electorate, 2012

Problem	Percent
The economy	59
Health care	18
Federal budget deficit	15
Foreign policy	5

Source: The 2012 National Election Exit Polls. The question asked 10,798 respondents about which of the four issues was the most important issue facing the country.

be expected, those who thought the deficit most important were very likely to vote for Romney, while those who cared most about health care were even more likely to support Obama. Obama also held a substantial lead among those most concerned about foreign policy. Romney held a small but real lead among those who thought the economy was the most important problem facing the country. Still, being concerned about a problem does not directly indicate which candidate voters intend to back. A vote, after all, is a choice among alternatives. To investigate these questions, we must look at the voters' issue preferences and their perceptions of where candidates stood on the issues.

ISSUE POSITIONS AND PERCEPTIONS

Since 1972, the ANES surveys have included issue scales designed to measure the preferences of the electorate and voters' perceptions of the positions the candidates took on the issues. The questions are therefore especially appropriate for examining prospective issue evaluations. We hasten to add, however, that voters' perceptions of where the incumbent party's nominee stands may well be based in part on what the president has done in office, as well as on the campaign promises he made as the party's nominee. The policy promises of the opposition party candidate may also be judged in part by what that candidate's party did when it last held the White House. And these may be especially so for 2012, as Obama had a four-year record dealing with the economic crisis, while memories of 2008 had not faded, so that Romney might have been a hostage of memories of the Bush administration's policies. Nevertheless, the issue scales generally focus on prospective evaluations and are very different from those used to make the retrospective judgments that we will examine in Chapter 7.

The issue scales will be used to answer several questions: What alternatives did the voters believe the candidates were offering? To what extent did the voters have issue preferences of their own and relatively clear perceptions of candidates' positions? Finally, how strongly were voters' preferences and perceptions related to their choice of candidates?

Figure 6-1 shows the seven-point issue scales used in the 2012 ANES survey. The figure presents the average (median) position of the respondents (labeled S for self) and the average (median) perceptions of the positions of Obama and Romney (labeled O and R). The issues raised in 2012 probed the respondents' own preferences and perceptions of the major-party nominees on whether government should spend more or less on social services; whether defense spending should be increased or decreased; whether health insurance should be provided by the government or by private insurance; whether the government should see to it that everyone has a job and a good standard of living or let citizens get ahead on their own; whether the government should provide aid to blacks or whether they should help themselves; and whether the government should protect the environment at the cost of jobs and a good standard of living.

FIGURE 6-1   Median Self-Placement of the Electorate and the Electorate's
             Placement of Candidates on Issue Scales, 2012

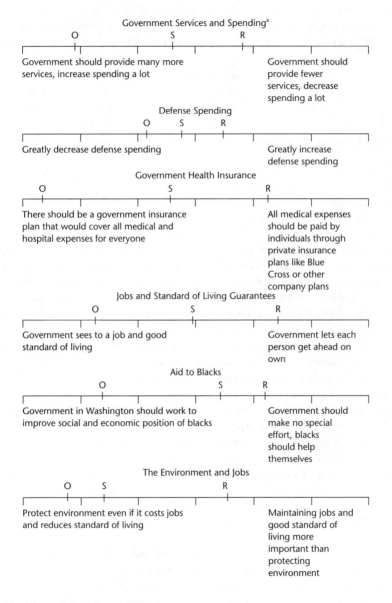

Source: Authors' analysis of the 2012 ANES.

Note: S = median self-placement of the respondents; O = median placement of Obama; R = median placement of Romney.

[a] Reversed from actual scoring to make a "liberal" response closer to point 1 and a "conservative" response closer to point 7.

These issues were selected for inclusion in the ANES survey because they are controversial and generally measure long-standing partisan divisions. As a result, the average citizen comes out looking reasonably moderate on these issues. In every case, the average citizen falls between the positions corresponding to the average placements of the two candidates. On many issues asked in 2012, the typical citizen was near the center of the scale, generally falling between one-half point to the left and one-half point to the right of the midpoint of four. Only on the environment scale was the average citizen more than a full point—in this case a bit more than a point and a half to the left—of the center. The basic message is that, on average, the public in 2012 was mostly moderate on these long-standing issues.

Note that, on five of six of the scales, all but the aid-to-blacks measure, the average citizen was at least very slightly to the liberal end of the scale. Because we use the median as our measure of "average," that means that over half of the respondents were at least slightly liberal and may have been very liberal on those five issues. That is actually a change from 2008 (in which all six of these issue scales were also included).[8] In that year, the average citizen was to the left on every issue scale. On health care, the average citizen was somewhat more liberal in 2008 than 2012 (i.e., less than a half a point farther to the left in 2008), so while the Republican concerns about "Obamacare" may indeed have had an effect on public opinion, that effect did not change opinion greatly. One might also imagine that the Republican and Tea Party appeals to reduce the size of the federal government might have made a difference on the government services and spending scale. If so, they had effects very similar to health care, as the average citizen moved about a half point closer to 4, but remained on the liberal side of the scale, in 2012. The only really large change is on the environment scale, in which, in 2008, the average person was close to 3.5, but moved a full point to the left in 2012. We might imagine this larger change reflects base support for environmental concerns that had been tempered by the depths of recession and consequent job losses in 2008, which were at least partially attenuated due to the modest economic recovery. Thus, by 2012, people's core preferences for action on environmental issues reemerged. Indeed, this issue question has been asked since 1996, and the average citizen was at or near 3 in all elections before 2008, further suggesting that the recession moved people to be more moderate on the environment that year—but not in 2012, indicating that at least the extent of dissatisfaction with the economy had waned.

Generally, on issue scales used between 1980 and 2012, the public has viewed the Democratic candidate as more liberal and the Republican candidate as more conservative than the average member of the public.[9] Indeed, these differences are often quite large, and as it happens, this was especially so in 2012. Except for defense spending, they exceed 2 points (with a maximum difference of 6 points) on every issue scale. And on most the difference was nearly 3 points or even greater (with an average difference of 2.8 points). This set of differences is perhaps the greatest we have yet measured.

That effect appears to be due more to perceptions on the Republican side. Perceptions of Obama generally (but not invariably) became just a bit more liberal (especially on the environment, but also on health care), but these differences were reasonably slim. What really changed from 2008 to 2012 was the perception of the Republican nominee. McCain, for example, was seen to be very slightly to the left of the midpoint on government services, defense spending, aid to blacks, and virtually at 4 on the environment issue in 2008. On defense spending, the jobs scale, and health care, he was seen as close to 5. Romney, by contrast, was seen as anywhere from a half to a full point more conservative on every domestic issue, appearing about a half point less conservative than McCain only on defense spending. Overall, the public saw quite large differences between the offerings of the two candidates. No matter how much or how little the public may have been polarized in 2012, it saw that alleged polarization dividing the two candidates, even more so than in preceding elections.

While voters saw clear differences between the candidates, the average voter faced a difficult choice. Obama was seen to the left of the average respondent and Romney was seen to the right on every issue. Of course, we cannot at this point go much further on these overall figures. The choice is made not by a mythical average voter choosing based on what the respondents as a whole thought the candidates offered, but by individual voters considering what they think about these issues. To consider a voter's choices, we must look inside these averages to assess the individual behavior that makes up those averages.

ISSUE VOTING CRITERIA

The Problem

Because voting is an individual action, we must look at the preferences of individuals to see whether prospective issues influenced their votes. In fact, the question of prospective voting is controversial. In their classic study of the American electorate, *The American Voter,* Angus Campbell and his colleagues pointed out that the public is often ill informed about public policy and may not be able to vote on the basis of issues. They asked themselves what information voters would need before an issue could influence the decision on how to vote, and they answered by posing three conditions. First, the voters must hold an opinion on the issue; second, they must learn what the government is doing on the issue; and third, they must perceive a difference between the policies of the two major parties. According to the authors' analysis, only about one-quarter to one-third of the electorate in 1956 could meet these three conditions, and they therefore concluded that relatively few were likely to vote on the basis of issues.

Although it is impossible to replicate the analysis in *The American Voter,* we can adapt the authors' procedures to the 2012 electorate. ANES data, in fact, focus even more directly on the actual choice citizens must make—the choice among the candidates. The first criterion is whether respondents claim to have an opinion on the issue. This is measured by whether they placed themselves on the issue scale, the same way as measured by Campbell et al. Second, the respondents should have some perception of the positions taken by the candidates on an issue. This is measured by whether they could place both major-party candidates on that issue. Although some voters might perceive the position of one candidate and vote on that basis, prospective voting involves a comparison between or among alternatives, so the expressed ability to perceive the stands of the contenders seems a minimal requirement of prospective issue voting. Third, the voter must see a difference between the positions of the candidates. Failing to see a difference means that the voter perceived no choice on the issue, perhaps because he or she failed to detect actual distinctions between the candidates. This failure might arise from lack of attention to the issue in the campaign. It also may arise from instances in which the candidates actually did take very similar positions on the issue, and respondents were thus, on average, reflecting that similarity, as we believe was truer of the candidates on most issues in 1976 than in other campaigns.

A voter might be able to satisfy these criteria but misperceive the offerings of the candidates. This leads to a fourth condition, which we were able to measure more systematically than was possible in 1956: did the respondents accurately perceive the relative positions of the two major-party candidates—that is, did they see Romney as more conservative than Obama? This criterion does not demand that the voter have an accurate perception of what the candidate proposes, but it does expect the voter to have recognized that Obama, for example, favored spending more on social services than did Romney.

In Table 6-4, we report the percentages of the sample that met the four criteria on the seven issue scales used in 2012.[10] We also show the average proportion that met these criteria for all scales and compare those averages to comparable averages for all issue scales used in the ten preceding elections.[11] Column I of Table 6-4 reveals that most people felt capable of placing themselves on the issue scales, and this capability was common to all election years.[12]

Nearly as many of the public also placed both candidates on the scales. Indeed, the drop off in placing one's self compared to placing one's self, Obama, and Romney is slightly less than in any other election year survey and considerably smaller in 2012 (nine percentage points) than in, say, 1972 (twenty-five points) or 1976 (twenty-six points). While there is a decline in the percentage also seeing differences between Obama and Romney on these issues, the main point is that 2012 shares the high watermark in this regard, tied with the Clinton elections. In 2012, on average, two out of three respondents placed themselves, both candidates, and saw a difference between the stances of the two candidates.

Finally, a high percentage met all four issue voting criteria, with nearly three in five doing so on average. That puts 2012 as the survey with the highest percentage meeting all four criteria. Compare 2012 with 1976. In the earlier election, only one in four met these criteria on average. In that year, relatively few

TABLE 6-4   Four Criteria for Issue Voting, 2012, and Comparisons with 1972–2008 Presidential Elections

| | Percentage of sample who . . . | | | |
| | I | II | III | IV |
Issue scale	Placed self on scale	Placed both candidates on scale[a]	Saw differences between Obama and Romney	Saw Obama more "liberal" than Romney
Government spending/services	84	77	71	63
Defense spending	80	71	60	42
Government health insurance	90	83	74	68
Jobs and standard of living	89	82	71	67
Aid to blacks	84	73	63	57
Jobs and the environment	80	70	59	53
Average[b]				
2012 (6)	85	76	66	58
2008 (7)	88	78	61	51
2004 (7)	89	76	62	52
2000 (7)	87	69	51	41
1996 (9)	89	80	65	55
1992 (3)	85	71	66	52
1988 (7)	86	66	52	43
1984 (7)	84	73	62	53
1980 (9)	82	61	51	43
1976 (9)	84	58	39	26
1972 (8)	90	65	49	41

Source: Authors' analysis of ANES surveys.

Note: Columns II, III, and IV compare the Democratic and Republican nominees. Third-party or independent candidates John Anderson (1980), Ross Perot (1992 and 1996), and Ralph Nader (2000 and 2004) were excluded.

[a] Until 1996, respondents who could not place themselves on a scale were not asked to place the candidates on that issue scale. Although they were asked to do so in 1996, 2000, 2004, 2008, and 2012, we excluded them from further calculations to maintain comparability with prior surveys.

[b] Number in parentheses is the number of issue scales included in the average for each election year survey.

could see differences between Gerald Ford and Jimmy Carter on issues, and therefore could hardly have also gotten them in the correct order! But by 2012,

the idea of polarization seems to have fully settled into the presidential electorate. That is to say, they saw the candidates as taking consistently and starkly
different positions on just about every major issue (or at least every one of these
six), and there was very little disagreement or confusion about that point in the
electorate. They saw the Republican and the Democratic nominees as polarized,
more so than ever before in the last eleven elections.

The data in Table 6-4 suggest that the potential for prospective issue voting
was high in 2012. Therefore, we might expect these issues to be rather closely
related to voter choice. We will examine voter choice on these issues in two ways.
First, how often did people vote for the closer candidate on each issue? Second,
how strongly related to the vote is the set of all issues taken together?

APPARENT ISSUE VOTING IN 2012

Issue Criteria and Voting on Each Issue

The first question is to what extent did people who were closer to a candidate on
a given issue actually vote for that candidate—that is, how strong is apparent issue
voting?[13] In Table 6-5, we report the proportion of major-party voters who voted
for Obama by where they placed themselves on the issue scales. We divided the
seven points into the set of positions that were closer to where the average citizen
placed Romney and Obama (see Figure 6-1).[14] Note that, while the average perceptions of the two candidates did vary from issues to issue, the net effect of that
variation did not make a great deal of difference. In particular, on each of the six
issues, respondents who placed themselves to the left of the midpoint, that is, at
1, 2, or 3, were closer to where the electorate as a whole thought Obama stood.
Similarly, those to the right of the midpoint were always closer to the perception
of Romney. And on each of the six issues, those who placed themselves at the
midpoint, that is, at 4, were invariably closer to Romney than to Obama, but only
between slightly so and very slightly so. The midpoint between the placements of
the two candidates was always between 3 and 4, and half the time not far at all
from 4, that is, not far at all from an equal balancing of Obama and Romney, one
just about as far to the left as the other was to the right. We see this as support for
the idea that the two parties and their candidates and officeholders have achieved
a balanced polarization with consistent deviation for the policy center toward
their party's extreme (liberal for Democrats, conservative for Republicans) on
issue after issue, and that, by 2012, the public saw clearly even the presidential
candidates being consistent with their parties' positions.

Table 6-5 reveals the clear relationship between the voters' issue positions and
the candidate they supported on the six scales. Those who adopted positions at
the liberal end of each scale were very likely to vote for Obama. If we define
liberal as adopting position 1 or 2, Obama received at least three in four votes or
even more on each scale. Indeed, that was even true for those at point 3, the most

TABLE 6-5 Major-Party Voters Who Voted for Obama, by Seven-Point Issue Scales, 2012 (percent)

Issue scale	Closer to median perception of Obama				Closer to median perception of Romney			(N)
	1	2	3	4	5	6	7	
Government spending/services[a]	81	93	78	63	31	18	6	
(N)	(66)	(68)	(213)	(312)	(239)	(143)	(101)	(1,143)
Defense spending	79	89	71	56	33	34	29	
(N)	(39)	(83)	(154)	(379)	(247)	(137)	(78)	(1,118)
Government health insurance	86	79	79	66	38	18	15	
(N)	(147)	(128)	(162)	(210)	(205)	(208)	(145)	(1,206)
Jobs and standard of living	85	79	79	70	53	25	18	
(N)	(78)	(84)	(114)	(282)	(210)	(231)	(179)	(1,177)
Aid to blacks	96	91	81	63	55	24	28	
(N)	(55)	(57)	(88)	(306)	(169)	(184)	(259)	(1,118)
Jobs and the environment	84	76	51	37	10	14	17	
(N)	(224)	(230)	(231)	(178)	(132)	(79)	(43)	(1,118)

Source: Authors' analysis of the 2012 ANES.

Note: Numbers in parentheses are the totals on which percentages are based. Numbers are weighted.

[a] Reversed from actual scoring to make a "liberal" response closer to 1 and a "conservative" response closer to 7.

slightly liberal position, on every issue except the environment. Obama only once received as much as one in three votes on any issue scale from those at the two most conservative positions, and that exception was defense spending, and it was the issue on which voters saw by far the least difference between the two candidates' stances. One point to keep in mind to understand the outcome of 2012 is that Obama carried noticeable majorities among those who placed themselves at 4 on every issue but the environment and jobs, and on that issue the preferences of the public were strongly skewed toward the left. Recall that voters at 4 on the other five issues were slightly closer to Romney than to Obama. We might imagine that this slight degree of greater proximity to Romney on a single issue was outweighed by other factors. In any event, with that slight exception, there are very strong relationships between the public's opinions and their perceptions of candidates on prospective issues, and that is true for virtually each issue scale.

The information on issues can be summarized, as it is in Table 6-6, to illustrate what happens when voters met the various conditions for issue voting. In the first column of Table 6-6, we report the percentage of major-party voters who placed themselves closer to the average perception of Romney or Obama and who voted for the closer candidate. To be more specific, the denominator is the total number of major-party voters who placed themselves closer to the electorate's perception of Romney or Obama. The numerator is the total number of major-party voters who were both closer to Obama and voted for him plus the total number of major-party voters who were both closer to Romney and voted for him.

If voting were unrelated to issue positions, we would expect 50 percent of voters to vote for the closer candidate on average. In 2012, on average 63 percent voted for the closer candidate, very similar to the percentage doing so in most elections—not as high as in 2004, but slightly higher than in 2008, for example. These figures do not tell the whole story, however, because those who placed themselves on an issue but failed to meet some other criterion were unlikely to have cast a vote based on that issue. In the second column of Table 6-6, we report the percentage of those who voted for the closer candidate on each issue among voters who met all four conditions on that issue. The third column reports the percentage that voted for the closer candidate among voters who placed themselves but failed to meet all three of the remaining conditions.

Those respondents who met all four conditions were more likely to vote for the closer candidate on any issue. Indeed, there is relatively little difference, on average, across all elections, although 2012 and 2000 tied for the lowest percentage. In each case, however, including 2012, about seven in ten such voters supported the closer candidate. By contrast, for those respondents who failed to meet the last three of the conditions on issue voting, voting was essentially random with respect to the issues, although surprisingly high in 2012, at 58 percent.

The strong similarity of all election averages in the second and third columns suggests that issue voting seems more prevalent in some elections than others

TABLE 6-6   Apparent Issue Voting, 2012, and Comparisons with 1972–2008
Presidential Elections

Issue scale	Percentage of voters who voted for closer candidate and . . .		
	Placed self on issue scale	Met all four issue voting criteria	Placed self but failed to meet all three other criteria
Government spending/ services	66	67	65
Defense spending	53	65	42
Government health insurance	66	73	55
Jobs and standard of living	60	60	61
Aid to blacks	75	84	67
Jobs and the environment	56	57	55
Averages[a]			
2012 (6)	63	68	58
2008 (7)	62	71	47
2004 (7)	67	75	51
2000 (7)	60	68	40
1996 (9)	63	74	41
1992 (3)	62	70	48
1988 (7)	62	71	45
1984 (7)	65	73	46
1980 (9)	63	71	48
1976 (9)	57	70	50
1972 (8)	66	76	55

Source: Authors' analysis of ANES surveys.

Note: An "apparent issue vote" is a vote for the candidate closer to one's position on an issue scale. The closer candidate is determined by comparing self-placement to the median placements of the two candidates on the scale as a whole. Respondents who did not place themselves or who were equidistant from the two candidates are excluded from the calculations. In 2008, analyses conducted on the randomly selected half-sample asked questions with the traditional wording, except "aid to blacks," which was asked of the full sample with the same (traditional) wording.

[a] The number in parentheses is the number of seven-point issue scales included in the average for each election year survey.

because elections differ in the number of people who clearly perceive differences between the candidates. In all elections, about seven in ten who satisfied all four conditions voted consistently with their issue preferences; in all elections, those who did not satisfy all the conditions on perceptions of candidates voted essentially randomly with respect to individual issues. As we saw earlier, the degree to which such perceptions vary from election to election depends more on the strategies of the candidates than on the qualities of the voters. Therefore, the relatively low percentage of apparent issue voting in 1976, for example, results from the perception of small differences between the two rather moderate candidates. The larger magnitude of apparent issue voting in 2012, as in most other elections, stems primarily from the greater clarity with which most people saw the positions of the two nominees. One must add that, in 2012, the clarity and consistency of such perceptions was what stood out.

The Balance-of-Issues Measure

In prospective issue voting, voters compare the full set of policy proposals made by the candidates. Because nearly every issue is strongly related to the vote, we might expect the set of all issues to be even more strongly so. To examine this relationship, we constructed an overall assessment of the issue scales to arrive at what we call the balance-of-issues measure. We give individuals a score of +1 if their positions on an issue scale were closer to the average perception of Romney, a score of –1 if their positions were closer to the average perception of Obama, and a score of 0 if they had no preference on an issue. The scores for all six issue scales were added together, creating a measure that ranged from –6 to +6. For example, respondents who were closer to the average perception of Obama's positions on all six scales received a score of –6. A negative score indicated that the respondent was, on balance, closer to the public's perception of Obama, while a positive score indicated the respondent was, overall, closer to the public's perception of Romney. We collapsed this thirteen-point measure into seven categories, running from strongly Democratic through neutral to strongly Republican. We have used this scale since 1980.[15] The 2012 election has an odd feature, in which all those at point 4 on any issue were slightly closer to Romney than to Obama, but the emphasis should be on "slight." As is often the case, more people put themselves at 4 than any other position on most of the issues scales. As a result, many people get a +1 for being slightly closer to Romney than to Obama, on issue after issue. And as a result, the balance of opinion in the electorate ends up looking more pro-Republican than in other elections. In any event, the results are reported in Table 6-7.

As can be seen in Part A of Table 6-7, 11 percent of respondents were in the two most strongly Democratic positions, while 43 percent were in the two most strongly Republican positions. Just under one in four was moderately or slightly Democratic, while over four in ten fell in the two comparable Republican categories. Thus the balance-of-issues measure tilted noticeably in the Republican direction, even though the respondents were often just slightly closer to Romney than Obama on specific issues. The balance-of-issues measure, however, was strongly related to the vote, as the findings for the individual issues would suggest

TABLE 6-7 Distribution of Electorate on Net Balance of Issues Measure and Major-Party Vote, 2012 (percent)

| | Net balance of issues | | | | | | | | |
	Strongly Democratic	Moderately Democratic	Slightly Democratic	Neutral	Slightly Republican	Moderately Republican	Strongly Republican	Total	(N)
	A. Distribution of responses								
Percent	3	8	14	12	21	24	19	101	(2,041)
	B. Major-party voters who voted for Obama								
Percent	100	92	89	78	66	38	8	53	(1,283)
(N)	(26)	(106)	(151)	(145)	(254)	(323)	(278)		

Source: Authors' analysis of the 2012 ANES.

Note: Numbers are weighted. The numbers in parentheses in Part B of the table are the totals on which the percentages are based.

(see Table 6-7 Part B). Obama won the vast majority of the votes from those in the three Democratic categories. He won a bit more than three in four votes from those in the neutral group and then about two in three from those in the slightly Republican category. His support dropped off dramatically from that point. Indeed, the decline in Democratic voting across the net balance-of-issues categories was about as strong in 2008 as it was in 1984, 1996, 2000, and 2004.

The Abortion Issue

Clearly, abortion was not the major issue in the 2012 election. Even so it has been in most elections; it did play a significant, even if smaller, role in 2012 and it is likely to remain consequential in future elections. Part of the reason for this is the partisan divisions on this issue. The Republican national platform has taken a strong pro-life stand since 1980, while the Democratic Party has become increasingly pro-choice. In addition, it is one of a complex of issues that define much of the social issues dimension, one of two major dimensions of domestic policy (economics being the second) into which most domestic policies—and most controversial issues—fall. Abortion has been central to the rise of social conservatism in America, virtually back to its modern emergence in the wake of the Supreme Court decision in *Roe v. Wade* (1973), which made abortion legal throughout the United States.

The second reason for examining this issue is that it is another policy question about which respondents were asked their own views as well as what they thought Romney's and Obama's positions were—a battery that has been asked for the last several elections. It differs from (and is therefore hard to compare directly with) the seven-point issue scales, however, because respondents were given only four alternatives, but each was a specified policy option:

1. By law, abortion should never be permitted.

2. The law should permit abortion only in case of rape, incest, or when the woman's life is in danger.

3. The law should permit abortion for reasons *other than* rape, incest, or danger to the woman's life, but only after the need for the abortion has been clearly established.

4. By law, a woman should always be able to obtain an abortion as a matter of personal choice.

Table 6-8 reports percentages voting for Obama for various groups of respondents. For example, seven in ten who believed that abortion should be a matter of personal choice voted for Obama, whereas one in three who thought it should never be permitted nonetheless voted for him. Substantial numbers of voters (slightly more than eight in ten) met all four conditions on this issue and, for

TABLE 6-8   Percentage of Major-Party Voters Who Voted for Obama, by Opinion about Abortion and What They Believe Romney's and Obama's Positions Are, 2012

	Abortion should never be permitted		Abortion should be permitted only in the case of rape, incest, or danger to health of the woman		Abortion should be permitted for other reasons, but only if a need is established		Abortion should be a matter of personal choice	
	%	(N)	%	(N)	%	(N)	%	(N)
All major-party voters	33	(120)	33	(346)	53	(226)	70	(584)
Major-party voters who placed both candidates, who saw a difference between them, and who saw Obama as more pro-choice than Romney	20	(92)	27	(276)	48	(174)	75	(499)
Major-party voters who did not meet all three of these conditions	73	(28)	55	(71)	69	(52)	38	(86)

Source: Authors' analysis of the 2012 ANES.

Note: Numbers in parentheses are the totals on which the percentages are based. Numbers are weighted.

them, their position was even more strongly related to the vote, as three in four who thought abortion should be a matter of personal choice voted for Obama, but only one in five who thought it should not be permitted did so. Thus, the abortion issue adds to our previous findings, indeed stands as one of the strongest voting issues we have measured.

CONCLUSION

Our findings suggest that, for major-party voters, prospective issues were important in the 2012 election. In fact, 2012 stands out as an election in which prospective issues played about as strong a role in shaping people's vote as any others. Prospective issues are particularly important for understanding how citizens voted. They cannot account for Obama's victory in the popular vote. Those for whom prospective issues gave a clear choice voted consistently with those issues. But not only were more voters at least slightly closer to Romney than to Obama, but also most people were located between the candidates as the electorate saw them. Indeed, on most issues the majority of people were relatively moderate, and the candidates were perceived as more conservative and more liberal, respectively. Moreover, when the conditions for issue voting are present, there can be a strong relationship between the position voters hold and their choice between the major-party candidates. And it appears that, perhaps due to the lengthening period for which the two parties have polarized on most important policies facing the electorate, a remarkably high proportion of the electorate met the conditions for casting an issue-based vote on many of the issues considered here. For these reasons, we conclude that voters took prospective issues into account in 2012, but it is also our conclusion that they considered other factors as well. In the next chapter, we will see that the second form of policy voting, that based on retrospective evaluations, was among those other factors, as it has been in previous presidential elections.

Chapter 7

Presidential Performance
and Candidate Choice

Just as in 2008, the presidential candidates in 2012 focused mostly on the economy. Although both candidates took very different stances on these concerns in 2012, as their counterparts did in 2008, the 2012 campaign *differed* from that of 2008 and, in important respects, had similarities to the strategies pursued by the contenders in 2004. In particular, what made 2012 different from 2008 was that Obama was running for reelection and thereby was justifying and defending his actions as president. In that regard, 2012 differed from 2008, because not only was the incumbent president, George W. Bush, not running for reelection (he was constitutionally ineligible) but his partisan counterpart, John McCain, did not spend great effort in defending the Bush administration, but instead sought to convey what he would seek to accomplish if elected to solve the recent, stunning economic crisis. Thus, Obama's reelection bid was more similar to Bush's effort in 2004, in that Bush campaigned in 2004 on the record of his administration, claiming that his policies were working. His relatively close reelection owed much to the somewhat more positive than negative evaluations of those policies. Of course, 2004 was an election conducted during the Iraq and Afghanistan wars, thus evaluations were heavily about how voters perceived the war efforts. In 2012, the president was more likely to be evaluated on his economic policies, but even so, he hoped that he, like Bush in 2004, would find evaluations of his performance in office sufficiently positive to yield reelection, whether close or not.

But these were hardly the first elections in which candidates thought carefully about how they would present themselves with respect to the successes or failures of the incumbent president and his party. In the aftermath of the very close election in 2000, for example, many Democrats and pundits had criticized Al Gore for his failure to campaign on the successes of the Clinton-Gore administration. They believed that, by doing so, he could have reminded voters of the positive performance of the American economy in the late 1990s.[1] These criticisms were easy to understand because there has often been a close correspondence between the performance of the economy and the electoral fortunes of the incumbent president's party, both directly and indirectly. A strong economy enhances the incumbent's approval ratings, thereby strengthening his party's support among the electorate. Indeed, in 1988 George H. W. Bush was aided in his bid to rise from vice president to president by the strong economy during the Reagan-Bush administration.[2] But by 1992 the voters had concluded that it was time to "throw the rascals out," and Bush the incumbent lost to Bill Clinton.[3] To the extent that voters were considering the successes and failures of the incumbent president and his party in these cases, perhaps in comparison to what they thought his opponent and the opponent's party would have done had they been in office, voters were casting a retrospective vote.

Retrospective evaluations are concerns about policy, but they differ significantly from the prospective evaluations considered in the last chapter. Retrospective evaluations are, as the name suggests, concerns about the past. These evaluations focus on outcomes, with what actually happened, rather than on the policy means for achieving outcomes, which are at the heart of prospective evaluations. For example, after his reelection in 2004, George W. Bush argued that there was a looming problem in Social Security and proposed private accounts as a solution. Even though other events soon intervened to draw attention away from this policy, some Democrats argued against the president on the grounds that creating private accounts would actually make the problem worse. These Democrats agreed with Bush that there was a problem, but they were focusing on concerns they had about the policy means that Bush proposed to solve that problem, a classic response in terms of prospective evaluations. Other Democrats argued that there really was no serious problem with Social Security in the first place. Such arguments focused on policy outcomes, which are the basis of retrospective judgments. This scenario illustrates the difference between prospective and retrospective judgments, but also illustrates that the two are often different sides of the same policy coin.

WHAT IS RETROSPECTIVE VOTING?

A voter who casts a ballot for the incumbent party's candidate because the incumbent was, in the voter's opinion, a successful president or votes for the opposition because, in the voter's opinion, the incumbent was unsuccessful is said to have cast a retrospective vote. In other words, retrospective voting decisions are based on evaluations of the course of politics over the last term in office and on evaluations of how much the incumbent should be held responsible for what good or bad occurred. V. O. Key Jr. popularized this argument by suggesting that the voter might be "a rational god of vengeance and of reward."[4]

The more closely a candidate can be tied to the actions of the incumbent, the more likely it is that voters will decide retrospectively. The incumbent president cannot escape such evaluations, and the incumbent vice president is usually identified with (and often chooses to identify himself with) the administration's performance. The electorate has frequently played the role of Key's "rational god," because an incumbent president or vice president has stood for election in twenty-four of the twenty-nine presidential elections since 1900 (all but 1908, 1920, 1928, 1952, and 2008).

Key's thesis has three aspects. First, retrospective voters are oriented toward outcomes rather than the policy means to achieve them. Second, these voters evaluate the performance of the incumbent only, all but ignoring the opposition. Finally, they evaluate what has been done, paying little attention to what the candidates promise to do in the future. Does this kind of voting make sense? Some suggest an alternative, as we discuss next, but note that if everyone did in fact vote against an incumbent whose performance they thought insufficient, then incumbents would have very strong incentives to provide such sufficiently high levels of performance to avoid the wrath of the electorate.

Anthony Downs was the first to develop in some detail an alternative version of retrospective voting.[5] His account is one about information and its credibility to the voter. He argues that voters look to the past to understand what the incumbent party's candidate will do in the future. According to Downs, parties are basically consistent in their goals, methods, and ideologies over time. Therefore, the past performances of both parties' nominees may prove relevant for making predictions about their future conduct. Because it takes time and effort to evaluate campaign promises and because promises are just words, voters find it faster, easier, and safer to use past performance to project the administration's actions for the next four years. Downs also emphasizes that retrospective evaluations are used in making comparisons among the alternatives presented to the voter. Key sees a retrospective referendum on the incumbent's party alone. Downs believes that retrospective evaluations are used to compare the candidates as well as to provide a guide to the future. Even incumbents may use such Downsian retrospective claims. In 1996, for example, Clinton attempted to tie his opponent, Sen. Bob Dole, to the performance of congressional Republicans because they had assumed the majority in the 1994 election. Clinton pointedly referred to the 104th Congress as the "Dole-Gingrich" Congress.

Morris P. Fiorina elaborates on and extends Downs's thesis. For our purposes, Fiorina's major addition to the Downsian perspective is his argument that party identification plays a central role. He argues that "citizens monitor party promises and performances over time, encapsulate their observations in a summary judgment termed 'party identification,' and rely on this core of previous experience when they assign responsibility for current societal conditions and evaluate ambiguous platforms designed to deal with uncertain futures."[6] We return to Fiorina's views on partisanship in Chapter 8.

Retrospective voting and voting according to issue positions, as analyzed in Chapter 6, differ significantly. The difference lies in how concerned people are with societal outcomes and how concerned they are with the policy means to achieve desired outcomes. For example, everyone prefers economic prosperity. The disagreement among political decision makers lies in how best to achieve it. At the voters' level, however, the central question is whether people care only about achieving prosperity or whether they care about, or even are able to judge, how to achieve this desired goal. Perhaps they looked at high inflation and interest rates in 1980 and said, "We tried Carter's approach, and it failed. Let's try something else—anything else." They may have noted the long run of relative economic prosperity from 1983 to 1988 and said, "Whatever Reagan did, it worked. Let's keep it going by putting his vice president in office." In 1996 they may have agreed with Clinton that he had presided over a successful economy, and so they decided to remain with the incumbent. In 2012 just how these concerns would play was uncertain. Would the public judge the economy as improving sufficiently, or was its improvement too little, too late?

Economic policy, along with foreign and defense policies, are especially likely to be discussed in these terms because they share several characteristics. First, the outcomes are often quite clear, and most voters can judge whether they approve of the results. Inflation and unemployment are high or low; the economy is growing or it is not. The country is at war or at peace; the world is stable or unstable. Indeed, one thing that made 2012 unusual was that economic conditions, though improving, were still a mixture of good and bad results. Thus voters might differ from one another in whether they thought the economy was sufficiently better than in 2008. Second, there is often near consensus on the desired outcomes; no one disagrees with peace or prosperity, with world stability, or with low unemployment. Third, the means to achieving these ends are often very complex, and information is hard to understand; experts as well as candidates and parties disagree over the specific ways to achieve the desired ends. How should the economy be improved, and how could terrorism possibly be contained or democracy established in a foreign land?

As issues, therefore, peace and prosperity differ sharply from policy areas such as abortion, in which there is vigorous disagreement over ends among experts, leaders, and the public. On still other issues, people value both ends *and* means. The classic cases often revolve around the question of whether it is appropriate for government to take action in a particular area at all. Ronald Reagan was fond of saying, "Government isn't the solution to our problems; government *is* the problem." For example, should the government provide national health insurance? After decades of trying, Democrats under the Obama administration finally succeeded in passing the Affordable Care Act, a program labeled "Obamacare" by the Republicans. Republicans continued to try to roll back the law or keep it from being implemented. Few disagree with the end of better health care, but they disagree over the appropriate means to achieve it. The choice of means touches on some of the basic philosophical and ideological differences that have divided Republicans and Democrats for decades.[7] For example, in the 1984 presidential campaign, Walter Mondale agreed with Reagan that the country was in a period of economic prosperity and that prosperity was a good thing, but he also argued that Reagan's policies were unfair to the disadvantaged. In the 1992 campaign, Bill Clinton and Ross Perot claimed that Reagan's and George H. W. Bush's policies, by creating such large deficits, were creating the conditions for future woes. Clearly, then, disagreement was not over the ends, but over the means and the consequences that would follow from using different means to achieve them.

Two basic conditions must be met before retrospective evaluations can affect voting choices. First, individuals must connect their concerns with the incumbent and the actions the president and his party took in office. This condition would not be present if, for example, a voter blamed earlier administrations with sowing the seeds that become the "Great Recession," blamed an ineffective Congress or Wall Street, or even believed that the problems were beyond anyone's control. Second, individuals, in the Downs-Fiorina view, must compare their evaluations of the incumbent's past performance with what they believe the nominee of the opposition party would do. For example, even if they thought Obama's performance on the economy was weak, voters might have compared that performance with programs supported by Romney in 2012 and concluded that his efforts would not result in any better outcome and might even make things worse.

In this second condition, a certain asymmetry exists, one that benefits the incumbent. Even if the incumbent's performance has been weak in a certain area, the challenger still has to convince voters that he or she could do better. It is more difficult, however, for a challenger to convince voters who think the incumbent's performance has been strong that the challenger would be even stronger. This asymmetry advantaged Republican candidates in the 1980s, but worked to Bob Dole's disadvantage in 1996 and to Bush's in 2000 and his putative successor in 2008. Would this asymmetry apply to 2012? Or perhaps, would both sides have the more difficult problem of convincing the electorate they could handle important problems when current performance was judged as neither especially strong nor especially weak?

We examine next some illustrative retrospective evaluations and study their impact on voter choice. In Chapter 6 we looked at issue scales designed to measure the public's evaluations of candidates' promises. For the incumbent party, the public can evaluate not only its promises but also its actions. We compare promises with performance in this chapter, but one must remember that the distinctions are not as sharp in practice as they are in principle.[8] The Downs-Fiorina view is that past actions and projections about the future are necessarily intertwined.

EVALUATIONS OF GOVERNMENT
PERFORMANCE ON IMPORTANT PROBLEMS

"Do you feel things in this country are generally going in the right direction, or do you feel things have pretty seriously gotten off on the wrong track?"[9] This question is designed to measure retrospective judgments, and the responses are presented in Table 7-1. In the Appendix to this book, we report responses to the question the American National Election Studies (ANES) had asked in prior surveys, comparing the respondents' evaluations of government performance on the problem that each respondent identified as the single most important one facing the country.[10] The most striking finding in Part A of Table 7-1 is that in 2012 few (only one in three) thought the country was on the right track. These questions are asked by many polling agencies to gauge the feelings of the public, and RealClearPolitics reports an averaging across these many polling outfits. Using their aggregated data, we find that, overall, the public has viewed things as being on the wrong track since June 2009, and the election period in 2012 was roughly typical of the perceptions of the country since then.[11]

If the voter is a rational god of vengeance and reward, we can expect to find a strong relationship between the evaluation of government performance and the vote. Such is indeed the case (see Part B of Table 7-1). More than nine out of ten people who thought the country was on the right track voted for Obama, while three in ten who thought the country was on the wrong track voted for him.

TABLE 7-1   Evaluation of Government Performance and Major-Party Vote, 2012 (percent)

A. Evaluation of government performance during the last four years	
Right track	33
Wrong track	67
Total	100
(*N*)	(1,958)
B. Percentage of major-party vote for incumbent party's nominee	
Right track	94
(*N*)	(430)
Wrong track	30
(*N*)	(804)

Source: Authors' analysis of the 2012 ANES survey.

Note: The numbers in parentheses in Part B are the totals on which the percentages are based. The numbers in Parts A and B are weighted.

According to Downs and Fiorina, it is important for voters not only to evaluate how things have been going but also to assess how that evaluation compares with the alternative. In most recent elections, including 2012, respondents have been asked which party would do a better job of solving the problem they named as the most important. Part A of Table 7-2 shows the responses to these questions (also see the Appendix for comparison to earlier elections). These questions are clearly oriented toward the future, but they may call for judgments about past performance, consistent with the Downs-Fiorina view. Respondents were not asked to evaluate policy alternatives, and thus responses were most likely based on a retrospective comparison of how the incumbent party handled things with a prediction about how the opposition would fare. We therefore consider these questions to be a measure of comparative retrospective evaluations.

Part A in Table 7-2 shows that the public had different views about which party was better at handling their important concerns. In particular, there is pretty close to an even three-way split among those thinking that one party or the other was better or that there was no difference between the two parties in this regard. To be sure, there were more who said the Democrats were better, but the seven-point difference between the two parties is rather slighter than usual.

In prior elections, slightly more than one in four had thought the Republicans were better able to handle their most important concern. This included major

TABLE 7-2   Evaluation of Party Seen as Better on Most Important Political Problem and Major-Party Vote, 2012 (percent)

Better party	2012
A. Distribution of responses on party better on most important political problem	
Republican	31
No difference	31
Democratic	38
Total	100
(*N*)	(1,884)
B. Major-party voters who voted Democratic for president	
Republican	7
(*N*)	(436)
No difference	56
(*N*)	(405)
Democratic	98
(*N*)	(429)

Source: Authors' analysis of the 2012 ANES.

Note: The numbers in parentheses are the totals on which the percentages are based. Numbers are weighted. Question wording: "Which political party do you think would be the most likely to get the government to do a better job in dealing with this problem?"

Republican defeats (such as in 1996), solid victories (such as in 1988), and major landslide victories (such as in 1972). In 2008, by contrast, very few selected the "neither party" option, and still only one in four selected the Republican Party. Thus the Democratic Party held a huge advantage on this measure, one of the rare instances in which a clear majority thought one party would be better. So by 2012 the Democrats had clearly lost their advantage, but the Republicans had not really gathered a major advantage either. Indeed, it looks a bit like a missed opportunity for Republicans, with a large majority of respondents thinking the country was on the wrong track, but with the Republicans unable to convince very many that they were better able to solve the most important problems, presumptively putting the United States back on the right track.

Part B of Table 7-2 reveals that the relationship between the party seen as better on the most important political problem and the vote is very strong. Obama won nearly all the votes from those who thought the Democrats would be better. Romney was able to hold nearly all of those who thought the Republican Party better able to handle the most important problem. The candidates essentially split the "no difference" category evenly.

The data presented in Tables 7-1 and 7-2 have an important limitation. The first question analyzed in Table 7-1 refers to how the country is going, not the incumbent president, nor even the government. The question examined in Table 7-2 refers to which political party would handle the problem better and does not directly refer to the incumbent—and we believe it is the assessment of the incumbent that relates most directly to voters' evaluations of the candidates for president. Thus we will look more closely at the incumbent and at people's comparisons of his and the opposition's performance where the data are available to permit such comparisons.

ECONOMIC EVALUATIONS AND THE VOTE FOR THE INCUMBENT

More than any other, economic issues have been highlighted as suitable retrospective issues. The impact of economic conditions on congressional and presidential elections has been studied extensively.[12] Popular evaluations of presidential effectiveness, John E. Mueller has pointed out, are strongly influenced by the economy.[13] A major reason for Jimmy Carter's defeat in 1980 was the perception that economic performance had been weak during his administration. Reagan's rhetorical question in the 1980 debate with Carter, "Are you better off than you were four years ago?" indicates that politicians realize the power such arguments have over the electorate. Reagan owed his sweeping reelection victory in 1984 largely to the perception that economic performance by the end of his first term had become, after a deep recession in the middle, much stronger.

If people are concerned about economic outcomes, they might start by looking for an answer to the sort of question Reagan asked. Part A of Table 7-3 presents

ANES respondents' perceptions of whether they were financially better off than one year earlier. From 1972 to 1980, about a third of the sample felt they were better off. Over that period, however, more and more of the remainder felt they were worse off. By 1980, "worse now" was the most common response. But by 1984 many respondents were feeling the economic recovery, and more than two in five said they were better off than in the previous year; only a little more than one in four felt worse off. But because 1984 was only two years after a deep recession, many may have seen their economic fortunes improve considerably over the prior year or so. By 1988 that recovery had been sustained, and the distribution of responses to this question in 1988 was very similar to that of 1984. By 1992 there was a return to the feelings of the earlier period, and responses were nearly evenly divided between "better now," "same," and "worse now." In 1996 the responses were like those of the 1984 and 1988 elections—and even slightly more favorable than in those years. In 2000 about a third felt better off, similar to responses through 1980. However, far fewer felt worse off in 2000 than in any of the seven preceding elections. Over half responded in 2000 that they were about the same as a year ago. In 2004 we see a return to the pattern more typical of the 1984, 1988, and 1996 elections, with over two in five feeling better off, the most popular response. It was a different story, however, in 2008 because half the respondents said they were worse off, with only a third saying they were better off (the same as in 1992), and very few feeling their finances were the same. The situation in 2012 presented little to help or harm either side. A few more thought they were better off than worse off, but each view was held by close to two in five. Only one in four did not claim their situation was the same as in 2008. Thus, while 2008 presented a very strong advantage for Democrats, neither side had much of one in 2012. If anything, there was slightly good news for Democrats.

In Part B of Table 7-3, we see how the responses to this question are related to the two-party presidential vote. In 2008, that relationship was not particularly strong. McCain was able to win just over half the votes of those who felt better off, just as he did among those relatively few who felt neither better nor worse off. Obama won support from a clear majority of that half of the electorate who felt worse off, winning over three in five of their votes. But in 2012 that relationship strengthened. Indeed, it was one of the strongest, similar in magnitude (such as the difference in the proportions voting for the incumbent between the better and worse off categories) to 1984 and 2004. That is, the extent that the family's financial situation shaped the vote was as strong as in the Reagan and Bush reelection contests, and the Clinton reelection campaign was not far behind. It thus appears that incumbents have a good chance of winning reelection when people can say they are mostly better off than worse off (as in these four elections) and personal economic circumstances are rather strongly related to the vote.

People may "vote their pocketbooks," but they are even more likely to vote retrospectively based on their judgments of how the economy as a whole has been faring. And personal and national economic experiences can be quite different. In

TABLE 7-3   Public's Assessment of Personal Financial Situation and Major-Party Vote, 1972–2012 (percent)

"Would you say that you (and your family) are better off or worse off financially than you were a year ago?"

Response	1972[a]	1976	1980	1984	1988	1992	1996	2000[a]	2004	2008	2012
					A. Distribution of responses						
Better now	36	34	33	44	42	31	46	33	43	32	42
Same	42	35	25	28	33	34	31	53	25	18	23
Worse now	23	31	42	27	25	35	24	14	32	50	35
Total	101	100	100	99	100	100	101	100	100	100	100
(N)	(955)	(2,828)[b]	(1,393)	(1,956)	(2,025)	(2,474)[b]	(1,708)[b]	(907)[b]	(1,203)[b]	(2,307)[b]	(2,035)[b]
				B. Major-party voters who voted for the incumbent party nominee for president							
Better now	69	55	46	74	63	53	66	56	65	53	69
(N)	(247)	(574)[b]	(295)	(612)	(489)	(413)[b]	(462)[b]	(164)[b]	(354)[b]	(491)[b]	(532)[b]
Same	70	52	46	55	50	45	52	51	50	52	53
(N)	(279)	(571)[b]	(226)	(407)	(405)	(500)[b]	(348)[b]	(291)[b]	(207)[b]	(280)[b]	(306)[b]
Worse now	52	38	40	33	40	27	47	45	28	38	34
(N)	(153)	(475)[b]	(351)	(338)	(283)	(453)[b]	(225)[b]	(56)[b]	(219)[b]	(778)[b]	(441)[b]

Source: Authors' analysis of ANES surveys.

Note: Numbers in parentheses are the totals upon which percentages are based.

[a] This question was asked of a randomly selected half-sample in 1972 and 2000.

[b] Numbers are weighted.

1980, for example, about 40 percent of respondents thought their own financial situation was worse than the year before, but responses to the 1980 ANES survey revealed that twice as many (83 percent) thought the national economy was worse off than the year before. In 1992 the public gave the nation's economy a far more negative assessment than they gave their own financial situations. That was not the case in 1996 and 2000, when respondents gave broadly similar assessments of their personal fortunes and those of the nation. But then in 2004 the public had much more negative views of the economy as a whole, although (naturally) the public saw the economy in 2008 in the most negative terms ever observed in these surveys. Fully nine in ten respondents believed that the economy was worse off. That changed substantially again in 2012. Here the views leaned slightly negatively, but it was not too far from an even three-way split between "better," "same," "and worse," with "better" trailing "worse" by only four points.

In Part B of Table 7-4, we show the relationship between responses to these items and the major-party vote for president. The relationship between these measures and the vote is always strong. Moreover, a comparison of Part B of Table 7-3 and Part B of Table 7-4 reveals that, in general, the vote is more closely associated with perceptions of the nation's economy than it is with perceptions of one's personal economic well-being. In 2012, the relationship was as strong as any we have been able to assess. The difference in votes cast for Obama between the "better" and "worse" categories was nearly seventy percentage points, with the "same" category essentially splitting their votes evenly. Thus, both personal and national economic circumstances mattered a great deal in this election.

To this point, we have looked at personal and national economic conditions and the role of the government in shaping them. We have not yet looked at the extent to which such evaluations are attributed to the incumbent. In Table 7-5, we report responses to the question of whether people approved of the incumbent's handling of the economy from the elections of 1980–2012. Although a majority approved of Reagan's handling of the economy in both 1984 and 1988, fewer than one in five held positive views of the economic performance of the Carter administration. In 1992 evaluations of George H. W. Bush were also very negative. In 1996 evaluations of Clinton's handling of the economy were stronger than those of incumbents in the previous surveys. By 2000 evaluations of Clinton's handling of the economy were even stronger, with three of every four respondents approving. Evaluations of George W. Bush's handling of the economy in 2004 were more negative than positive, although not nearly as negative of those of Jimmy Carter or of Bush's father. By 2008 evaluations of Bush's handling of the economy were very negative. But in 2012, evaluations of Obama's handling of the economy were quite like those of Bush in 2004; on balance negative but only moderately so.

The bottom-line question is whether these views are related to voter choice. According to the data in Part B of Table 7-5, the answer is yes. Those who held positive views of the incumbent's performance on the economy were very likely to vote for that party's candidate, while those who did not were just as likely to

TABLE 7-4 Public's View of the State of the Economy and Major-Party Vote, 1980–2012 (percent)

Response	1980	1984	1988	1992	1996	2000[b]	2004[b]	2008[b]	2012
"Would you say that over the past year the nation's economy has gotten . . . ?"									
A. Distribution of responses									
Better	4	44	19	4	40	39	24	2	30
Stayed same	13	33	50	22	44	44	31	7	37
Worse	83	23	31	73	16	17	45	90	34
Total	100	100	100	99	100	100	100	99	101
(N)	(1,580)	(1,904)	(1,956)	(2,465)[a]	(1,700)[a]	(1,787)[a]	(1,196)[a]	(2,313)[b]	(2,037)[a]
B. Major-party voters who voted for the incumbent party nominee for president									
Better	58	80	77	86	75	69	87	69	88
(N)	(33)	(646)	(249)	(62)[a]	(458)[a]	(408)[a]	(211)[a]	(34)[a]	(407)[a]
Stayed same	71	53	53	62	45	45	88	57	52
(N)	(102)	(413)	(568)	(318)[a]	(443)[a]	(487)[a]	(243)[a]	(109)[a]	(468)[a]
Worse	39	21	34	32	33	31	20	44	20
(N)	(732)	(282)	(348)	(981)[a]	(130)[a]	(154)[a]	(319)[a]	(1,425)[a]	(406)[a]

Source: Authors' analysis of ANES surveys.

Note: Numbers in parentheses are the totals on which percentages are based.

[a] Numbers are weighted.

[b] We combined the results using standard and experimental prompts that contained different word ordering in 2000, 2004, and 2008

TABLE 7-5 Evaluations of the Incumbent's Handling of the Economy and Major-Party Vote, 1980–2012 (percent)

Response	Approval of incumbent's handling of the economy								
	1980[a]	1984[b]	1988[b]	1992[b]	1996[b]	2000[b]	2004[b]	2008[b]	2012[b]
A. Distribution of responses									
Positive view	18	58	54	20	66	77	41	18	46
Balanced view	17	b	b	b	b	b	b	b	b
Negative view	65	42	46	80	34	23	59	82	54
Total	100	100	100	100	100	100	100	100	100
(N)	(1,097)	(1,858)	(1,897)	(2,425)[c]	(1,666)[c]	(1,686)[c]	(1,173)[c]	(2,227)[c]	(1,923)[c]
B. Major-party voters who voted for the incumbent party nominee									
Positive view	88	86	80	90	79	67	91	89	93
(N)	(130)	(801)	(645)	(310)[c]	(688)[c]	(768)[c]	(341)[c]	(313)[c]	(585)[c]
Balanced view	60	b	b	b	b	b	b	b	b
(N)	(114)								
Negative view	23	16	17	26	13	11	17	33	15
(N)	(451)	(515)	(492)	(1,039)[c]	(322)[c]	(233)[c]	(431)[c]	(1,200)[c]	(642)[c]

Source: Authors' analysis of ANES surveys.

[a] In 1980 the questions asked whether the respondent approved or disapproved of Carter's handling of inflation [unemployment]. A positive [negative] view was approve [disapprove] on both; balanced responses were approve on one, disapprove on the other.

[b] In 1984, 1988, 1992, 1996, 2000, 2004, 2008, and 2012, the question asked whether the respondent had a positive or a negative view (balanced view was omitted) of the [president's] handling of the economy.

[c] Numbers are weighted.

vote against him. More than nine in ten of those holding a positive view voted for Obama; only about one in seven who disapproved of his handling of the economy supported him. This relationship is once again as strong as we have yet observed. In this case, 2012 looks very much like 2004, both in the approval rates and in the strong relationship to the vote. The economy was a vitally important factor in the 2012 election, as all three retrospective evaluations of the economy are clearly and strongly related to the vote.

FOREIGN POLICY EVALUATIONS AND THE VOTE FOR THE INCUMBENT

Foreign and economic policies are, as we noted earlier, commonly evaluated by means of retrospective assessments. These policies share the characteristics of consensual goals (peace and prosperity, respectively, plus security in both cases), complex technology, and difficulty in ascertaining relationships between means and ends. Foreign policy differs from economic policy in one practical way, however. As we noted in the last chapter, economic problems are invariably a major concern, but foreign affairs are salient only sporadically. Indeed, foreign affairs are of sufficiently sporadic concern that most surveys, including the ANES, only occasionally have many measures to judge their role in elections.

Three questions included in the 2004 and 2008 ANES surveys examined evaluations of foreign affairs over the recent past. One question asked whether the standing of the United States in the world had become stronger or weaker or stayed the same, and thus called for a general assessment about how well things had gone for the nation in the world. The other two asked respondents to evaluate aspects of the war in Iraq, specifically whether that war was worth the cost and whether it had increased or decreased the threat of terrorism—a point of particular partisan contention. These were repeated in 2012 except that, in place of Iraq, the latter two questions asked about our involvement in Afghanistan. The responses to these questions are reported in Table 7-6.

Part A of Table 7-6 reveals that a majority of the respondents thought the United States had become weaker in the world, up from the nearly half (46 percent) who thought so in 2004, but noticeably down from the two-thirds who thought so in 2008. Conversely, the 26 percent in 2004 who thought the United States had become stronger had dropped to only 8 percent in 2008, and barely rebounded to 15 percent in 2012. This was hardly good news for the incumbent party, and we can see in part B of Table 7-6 that Romney won three of four votes of those who thought the United States had weakened, whereas Obama won every vote of those few who thought the United States had strengthened and one in three of those who saw little change. This relationship is roughly similar to the relationships found in 2004 and 2008.[14]

In 2004, 40 percent of respondents thought the war in Iraq was worth the cost; the rest thought it was not. In 2008 this measure, too, became more negative,

TABLE 7-6   Evaluations of Three Foreign Policy Issues and Major-Party Vote, 2012 (percent)

	U.S. standing in the world over the past year	Afghanistan war worth the cost		Afghanistan war increased or decreased the threat of terrorism	
		A. Evaluations of issues			
Stronger	15	Worth it	28	Decreased	24
Stayed the same	32			Stayed the same	46
Weaker	53	Not worth it	72	Increased	30
Total	100		100		100
(N)	(2,014)		(1,928)		(2,025)
	B. Major-Party voters holding these views who voted Republican for president				
Stronger	100	Worth it	53	Decreased	47
(N)	(192)		(330)		(319)
Stayed the same	76			Stayed the same	42
(N)	(394)				(592)
Weaker	27	Not worth it	44	Increased	53
(N)	(686)		(874)		(366)

Source: Authors' analysis of the 2012 ANES.

Note: Numbers are weighted. The numbers in parentheses in Part B are the totals on which the percentages are based.

with exactly one-quarter thinking the war was worth the cost, and three-quarters thinking it not. It so happens that this is quite similar to the feelings about the war in Afghanistan. Part B of Table 7-6 shows that those opinions were only weakly related to the vote. The question about war and terrorism was not asked in 2004. In 2008 it was asked about Iraq and there was a balanced relationship, with nearly half of respondents saying that the war in Iraq had neither increased nor decreased the threat of terrorism; the rest were nearly evenly divided between the war increasing and decreasing the threat. Again, even though it was a different war, the relationship between the war in Afghanistan and terrorism was quite similar in 2012. What was different from 2008, however, was that responses to this question were entirely unrelated to the vote. So while opinion about Iraq in 2008 and Afghanistan in 2012 was quite similar, neither of the two questions had any important relationship to the vote. It appears that the winding down of our involvement in Afghanistan had allowed the public to turn its attention to more domestic matters.

Table 7-7 presents data on two measures of approval of Obama's performance: how well he handled the war in Afghanistan and foreign relations more generally. Part A of Table 7-7 demonstrates that moderate and slight majorities approved of Obama on these two measures, respectively. These ratings are more

TABLE 7-7   President's Handling of Two Foreign Policy Issues and Major-Party Vote, 2012 (percent)

"Do you approve or disapprove of the way Barack Obama is handling . . . ?"		
	War in Afghanistan	Foreign relations
A. Distribution of responses		
Approve	59	54
Disapprove	41	46
Total	100	100
(*N*)	(1,831)	(1,838)
B. Major-party voters who voted for the incumbent party's nominee		
Approve	75	86
(*N*)	(700)	(652)
Disapprove	23	15
(*N*)	(463)	(532)

Source: Authors' analysis of the 2012 ANES.

Note: Numbers are weighted. The numbers in parentheses in Part B are the totals on which the percentages are based.

positive than those given to Bush in 2004 and 2008 (albeit about Iraq). As evident in Part B of Table 7-7, these measures, but especially overall approval of foreign relations, were strongly related to the vote, with Obama winning 86 percent support on the foreign relations measure, for example, about the same percentage McCain had won in 2008.

The key points in all of these data seem to be the following. First, as we saw in Chapter 6, foreign policy was just not seen as especially important to the public. This tempered all of the findings and made 2012 quite different from, say, 2004, when foreign policy and evaluations of the wars were near the top of almost everyone's list of political concerns. Second, even though people appeared to be disenchanted with the status of the war in Afghanistan, they did not appear to hold the incumbent responsible. It was apparently still understood either as a shared responsibility between the Bush and Obama administrations or as not Obama's fault at all.

EVALUATIONS OF THE INCUMBENT

Fiorina distinguishes between "simple" and "mediated" retrospective evaluations. By simple, Fiorina means evaluations of the direct effects of social outcomes on the person, such as one's financial status, or direct perceptions of the nation's economic well-being. Mediated retrospective evaluations are evaluations seen through or mediated by the perceptions of political actors and institutions.[15] Approval of Obama's handling of the economy and the assessment of which party would better handle the most important problem are examples.

As we have seen, the more politically mediated the question, the more closely the responses align with voting behavior. Perhaps the ultimate in mediated evaluations is the presidential approval question: "Do you approve or disapprove of the way [the incumbent] is handling his job as president?" From a retrospective voting standpoint, this evaluation is a summary of all aspects of the incumbent's service in office. Table 7-8 reports the distribution of overall evaluations and their relationship to major-party voting in the last eleven elections.[16]

Part A of Table 7-8 reveals that incumbents Richard Nixon (1972), Gerald Ford (1976), Ronald Reagan (1984), and Bill Clinton (1996) enjoyed widespread approval, whereas only two respondents in five approved of Jimmy Carter's and George H. W. Bush's handling of the job in 1980 and 1992, respectively. This situation presented Carter and Bush with a problem. Conversely, highly approved incumbents, such as Reagan in 1984 and Clinton in 1996—and their vice presidents as beneficiaries in 1988 and 2000, respectively—had a major advantage. Clinton dramatically reversed any negative perceptions held of his incumbency in 1994, so that by 1996 he received the highest level of approval in the fall of an election year since Nixon's landslide reelection in 1972. Between 1996 and 2000, Clinton suffered through several scandals, one of which culminated in his impeachment in 1998. Such events might be expected to lead to substantial declines in his approval ratings, but instead his ratings remained high—higher even than Reagan's at the end of his presidency. The evaluations in 2004 present a more varied picture. For the first time in nine elections, the proportions approving and disapproving of George W. Bush were almost exactly the same. In view of what we have seen so far, it should come as no surprise that evaluations of Bush turned dramatically by 2008, so that he was by far the least approved incumbent during this period, with nearly three in four respondents disapproving of his handling of the office. Obama's approval ratings were, again, much like Bush's in 2004, coming out with slightly more approving than disapproving.[17]

If it is true that the more mediated the evaluation, the more closely it seems to align with behavior, and if presidential approval is the most mediated evaluation of all, then we would expect a powerful relationship with the vote. As part B of Table 7-8 illustrates, that is true over the full set of elections for which we have the relevant data. As we have seen before, the approval ratings in 2012 are at least as strongly or generally even more strongly related to the vote than in any preceding election—again, nearly matched only by 2004. More than nine in ten people who approved of Obama's performance voted for him, only 7 percent who disapproved voted for him.

TABLE 7-8   President's Handling of Job and Major-Party Vote, 1972–2012 (percent)

"Do you approve or disapprove of the way [the incumbent] is handling his job as president?"

	1972[a]	1976	1980	1984	1988	1992	1996	2000	2004	2008	2012
A. Distribution of responses											
Approve	71	63	41	63	60	43	68	67	51	27	54
Disapprove	29	37	59	37	40	57	32	33	49	73	46
Total	100	100	100	100	100	100	100	100	100	100	100
(N)	(1,215)	(2,439)[b]	(1,475)	(2,091)	(1,935)	(2,419)[b]	(1,692)[b]	(1,742)[b]	(1,182)[b]	(2,245)[b]	(1,930)[b]
B. Major-party voters who voted for the incumbent party's nominee											
Approve	83	74	81	87	79	81	84	74	91	88	93
(N)	(553)	(935)[b]	(315)	(863)	(722)	(587)[b]	(676)[b]	(662)[b]	(408)[b]	(441)[b]	(651)[b]
Disapprove	14	9	18	7	12	11	4	13	6	26	7
(N)	(203)	(523)[b]	(491)	(449)	(442)	(759)[b]	(350)[b]	(366)[b]	(372)[b]	(1,075)[b]	(582)[b]

Source: Authors' analysis of ANES surveys.

Note: In Part B, numbers in parentheses are the totals on which percentages are based.

[a] Question was asked of a randomly selected half-sample in 1972.

[b] Numbers are weighted.

THE IMPACT OF RETROSPECTIVE EVALUATIONS

Our evidence strongly suggests that retrospective voting has been widespread in all recent elections. Moreover, as far as data permit us to judge, the evidence is clearly on the side of the Downs-Fiorina view. Retrospective evaluations appear to be used to make comparative judgments. Presumably, voters find it easier, less time-consuming, and less risky to evaluate the incumbent party based on what its president did in the most recent term or terms in office than on the nominees' promises for the future. But few people base their votes on judgments of past performance alone. Most use past judgments as a starting point for comparing the major contenders with respect to their likely future performances. Furthermore, it appears that voters were nearly as willing to apply their judgments about what proved to be a generally unpopular incumbent administration to McCain, who shared a party with the incumbent but was not a part of his administration, as they were to apply their judgments of incumbent performance to predecessors who were either the incumbent president or vice president.

In analyzing previous elections, we constructed an overall assessment of retrospective voting and compared that overall assessment across elections. We then compared that net retrospective assessment with our balance-of-issues measure. Our measure was constructed by combining the question asking whether the United States is on the right or on the wrong track, the presidential approval measure, and the assessment of which party would better handle the problem the respondent thinks is the single most important.[18] The combination of responses to these three questions creates a seven-point scale ranging from strongly negative evaluations of recent and current conditions to strongly positive evaluations of performance in these various areas. For example, those who thought the nation was on the right track approved of Obama's job performance, and thought the Democratic Party would better handle the most important problem are scored as strongly supportive of Obama in their retrospective evaluations in 2012.

In Table 7-9, we present the results of this measure.[19] The figures indicate that there was a substantial diversity of responses, but that the measure was skewed somewhat against the incumbent. By this measure, roughly one in four was strongly opposed to the performance of the Obama administration, with nearly another quarter moderately or slightly opposed. One in ten was neutral, while a bit more than one in five were slightly or moderately supportive, and another one in five was strongly supportive of the Obama administration. Part B of Table 7-9 presents a remarkably clear example of a very strong relationship between responses and votes, with over 90 percent of those in any of the three supportive categories voting for Obama, and very few of those moderately or strongly opposed voting for him. The slightly opposed split their votes about evenly, while Obama held the votes of eight in ten of those scored neutral on this measure. Thus for five of the seven categories, the valence of evaluations alone tells you everything you need to know about respondents' voting choices. Perhaps because

TABLE 7-9 Summary Measure of Retrospective Evaluations of the Obama Administration and Major-Party Vote, 2012

	Strongly opposed	Moderately opposed	Slightly opposed	Neutral	Slightly supportive	Moderately supportive	Strongly supportive	Total (N)
				A. Distribution of responses				
Percent	26	16	7	10	11	12	19	101 (1,892)
				B. Major-party voters who voted for Obama				
Percent	0	13	49	83	95	92	100	53
(N)	(374)	(179)	(67)	(109)	(135)	(121)	(285)	(1,270)

Source: Authors' analysis of the 2012 ANES.

Note: Numbers are weighted. The numbers in Part B are the totals on which the percentages are based.

there appears to be some belief that, even though the country may not be on the right track and even though the economy (the most common choice of most important problem) is not as strong as many would like, many voters appeared to hold Obama less responsible for the problems and be more generous in their evaluations of his performance in terms of the responses to these concerns, due perhaps to remembrances of Bush's highly negatively evaluated handling of the economy in 2008, and attribution of the problems to Bush or even those outside the government.

We cannot really compare 2012 with any other election on this measure, but we can at least make broad generalizations.[20] In earlier years, it was reasonable to conclude that the 1980 election was a clear and strong rejection of Carter's incumbency. In 1984 Reagan won in large part because voters perceived that he had performed well and because Mondale was unable to convince the public that he would do better. In 1988 George H. W. Bush won in large part because Reagan appeared to have performed well—and people thought Bush would stay the course. In 1992 Bush lost because of the far more negative evaluations of his administration and of his party than had been recorded in any election since 1980. In 1996 Clinton won reelection in large part for the same reasons that Reagan had won in 1984: he was viewed as having performed well on the job, and he was able to convince the public that his opponent would not do any better. In 2000 Gore essentially tied George W. Bush, because the slightly pro-incumbent set of evaluations combined with a very slight asymmetry against the incumbent in translating those evaluations into voting choices. In 2004 there was a slight victory for the incumbent because more thought he had performed well than poorly. And 2008 was most like 1980, with a highly skewed distribution working against the Republicans (likely the most skewed measure of all). In 2012, evaluations, once again, paralleled those (with a different measure) from 2004, with an outcome not substantially different—slightly negative evaluations overall, but not so negative as to cost the incumbent reelection.

How do retrospective assessments compare with prospective judgments? As described in Chapter 6, prospective issues, especially our balance-of-issues measure, have become more strongly related to the vote over the last few elections, perhaps peaking in 2012. There appears to be a significant extent of partisan polarization in the electorate in terms of their evaluations of the choices and their vote, even if not in terms of their own opinions about issues. Table 7-10 reports the impact of both types of policy evaluation measures on the major-party vote in 2012. Both policy measures were collapsed into three categories: pro-Democratic, neutral, and pro-Republican. Reading down each column, we see that, controlling for retrospective evaluations, prospective issues are modestly related to the vote in a positive direction. Or to be more precise, they are modestly related to the vote among those whose retrospective evaluations are nearly or actually neutral. It is thus only among those whose retrospective evaluations did not even moderately incline them toward either party that prospective evaluations are related to the vote, but even here, Obama received

TABLE 7-10   Major-Party Voters Who Voted for Obama, by Balance of Issues and Summary of Retrospective Measures, 2012

	Summary retrospective							
	Strongly or moderately Democratic		Slightly supportive or slightly opposed or neutral		Strongly or moderately Republican		Total	
Net balance of issues	%	(*N*)	%	(*N*)	%	(*N*)	%	(*N*)
Democratic	99	(177)	93	(81)	18	(20)	91	(279)
Neutral	98	(66)	87	(55)	6	(26)	78	(146)
Republican	96	(167)	74	(176)	[4]	(508)	37	(850)
Total	98	(410)	81	(312)	[5]	(554)	54	(1,275)

Source: Authors' analysis of the 2012 ANES survey.

Note: Numbers are weighted. Numbers in parentheses are the totals on which percentages are based. For the condensed measure of retrospective voting, we combine respondents who are strongly positive (or negative) toward Barack Obama and the Democratic Party with respondents who are moderately positive (or negative). We combine respondents who are slightly positive (or negative) with those who are neutral (see Table 7-9). For the condensed balance-of-issues measure, any respondent who is closer to Romney is classified as pro-Republican. The neutral category is the same as the seven-point measure (see Table 6-7). For the one entry with fewer than ten major-party voters, the number of them who voted for Obama is in brackets.

the votes of nearly three in four who were neutral on retrospective issues and pro-Republican on policy issues.

Reading across each row, we see that retrospective evaluations are very strongly related to the vote. This is true no matter what prospective evaluations respondents held. Thus we can conclude that in 2012 retrospective evaluations shaped voting choices to a great extent. Prospective evaluations were still important, but only for those without a moderate or strong partisan direction to their retrospective judgments.

Together, the two kinds of policy measures take us a long way toward understanding voting choices. Essentially everyone whose retrospective and prospective evaluations inclined them toward the same party voted for the candidate of that party. This accounting of voting choices is stronger when considering both forms of policy evaluations than when looking at either one individually.[21]

CONCLUSION

In this and the previous chapter, we have found that both retrospective and prospective evaluations were strongly related to the vote in 2012. Indeed, 2012 presents an unusually clear case of retrospective evaluations being a very powerful reason for Obama's victory. While they are always strong, they genuinely stand out in 2012. In 1992, for example, dissatisfaction with George H. W. Bush's performance and with his and his party's handling of the most important problem— usually an economic concern in 1992 (see Table 6-3)—goes a long way toward explaining his defeat, while satisfaction with Clinton's performance and the absence of an advantage for the Republicans in being seen as able to deal with the most important concerns of voters go a long way toward explaining his 1996 victory. In 2000 prospective issues favored neither candidate, because essentially the same number of major-party voters were closer to Bush than to Gore. The Democrat had a modest advantage on retrospective evaluations, but Bush won greater support among those with pro-Republican evaluations than did Gore among those with pro-Democratic evaluations. The result was another even balance and, as a result, a tied outcome. Although Kerry was favored on prospective evaluations in 2004, his advantage was counterbalanced by Bush's slight advantage based on retrospective evaluations, leading to a Bush reelection victory with only a slight gain in the popular vote. By 2008, the public had turned quite negative on Bush's performance, and that led to a major advantage for the Democrats. In 2012, there was a return, essentially, to the 2004 patterns, except with a Democrat as incumbent and with retrospective judgments focusing more heavily on the economy and less heavily on international affairs. Even so, our explanation remains incomplete. For example, why did so many of those in the middle or neutral category on retrospective evaluations support Obama, even those inclined toward Romney on prospective policies? Even more important, we have not accounted for *why* people hold the views they expressed on these two measures. We cannot provide a complete account of the origins of people's views, of course, but there is one important source we can examine: party identification. Party identification provides a powerful way in which the typical citizen can reach preliminary judgments on issues, whether prospective or retrospective, and on evaluations of the candidates themselves. As we will see, partisanship is strongly related to these judgments, especially to retrospective evaluations.

Chapter 8

Party Loyalties, Policy Preferences, and the Vote

In Chapter 5 we discussed the influence of social forces such as race and ethnicity on voting behavior. We noted that, for example, African Americans do not vote Democratic simply because of their race. Instead, race and other social forces provide the context for electoral politics and thus influence how voters reach their decisions. In Chapters 6 and 7, we studied the effects of various perceived traits of the candidates and of both prospective and retrospective evaluations on the vote. The question for here is why, for example, did some voters approve of Obama's performance, while others did not? Partisanship is an important part of the answer, indeed perhaps the single most important part of the answer, because it is the most important factor connecting voters' backgrounds, social settings, and their more immediate assessments of issues and the candidates. Thus a major part of the explanation of why African Americans vote overwhelmingly Democratic are the various events and actions that made the Democratic Party attractive (and the Republican Party unattractive) to them. The reason why some people approved of Obama's performance while others did not is largely because some are Democrats and some are Republicans. Party is therefore the third of the triumvirate of candidates, issues, and parties—that is, evaluations of the parties are one of three major forces that shape voting behavior, and it may be even more foundational than that. Party identification is likely to have indirect effects as well as direct ones, helping us understand why voters have the evaluations of candidates and of issues they do.

Partisanship is not the only force that helps connect context and evaluation, but it has proven to be by far the most important for understanding elections. Its dual role in directly and indirectly affecting voting makes it unusually critical for understanding why U.S. citizens vote as they do. Most Americans identify with a political party, which is one reason why it is so central. Their identification then influences their political attitudes and, ultimately, their behavior. In the 1950s and 1960s, Angus Campbell and his co-authors of *The American Voter*, along with other scholars, began to emphasize the role of party loyalties.[1] Although today few people deny that partisanship is central to political attitudes and behavior, many scholars question the interpretation of the evidence gathered during that period. Here we ask two questions: What is party identification? And how does it actually structure other attitudes and behavior? We then examine the role that party identification played in the 2012 presidential election.

PARTY IDENTIFICATION: THE ORIGINAL VIEW

According to Angus Campbell and his colleagues, party identification is "the individual's affective orientation to an important group-object in his environment," in this case a political party.[2] In other words, an individual recognizes that two major political parties are playing significant roles in elections and develops an affinity for one of them. Partisanship, therefore, represents an evaluation of the two parties, but its implications extend to a wider variety of political phenomena. Campbell and his colleagues measured partisanship by asking individuals which party they identified with and how strong that identification was.[3] If an individual did not identify with one of the parties, he or she may have either "leaned" toward a party or been a "pure" independent. Individuals who could not answer the party identification questions were classified as "apolitical."[4] Most Americans develop a preference for either the Republican or Democratic Party. Very few identify with any third party. The rest are mostly independents, who, according to this classic view, are not only unattached to a party but also relatively unattached to politics in general. They are less interested, less informed, and less active than those who identify with a party.

Partisan identification in this view becomes an attachment or loyalty similar to that between the individual and other groups or organizations in society, such as a religious body, a social class, or even a favorite sports team.[5] As with loyalties to many of these groups, partisan affiliation often begins early. One of the first political attitudes children develop is partisan identification, and it develops well before they acquire policy preferences and many other political orientations. Furthermore, as with other group loyalties, once an attachment to a party develops, it tends to endure.[6] Some people do switch parties, of course, but they usually do so only if their social situation changes dramatically, if there is an issue of overriding concern that sways their loyalties, or if the political parties themselves change substantially.

Party identification, then, stands as a base or core orientation to electoral politics. Once formed, this core orientation, predicated on a general evaluation of the two parties, affects many other specific orientations. Democratic loyalists tend to rate Democratic candidates and officeholders more highly than Republican candidates and officeholders, and vice versa. In effect, one is predisposed to evaluate the promises and performance of one's party leaders relatively more favorably. It follows, therefore, that Democrats are more likely to vote for Democratic candidates than are Republicans, and vice versa.

PARTY IDENTIFICATION: AN ALTERNATIVE VIEW

In *The Responsible Electorate*, published in 1966, V. O. Key Jr. argued that party loyalties contributed to electoral inertia and that many partisans voted as "stand-patters" from election to election.[7] In other words, in the absence of any information to the contrary, or if the attractions and disadvantages of the candidates are fairly evenly balanced, partisans are expected to vote for the candidate of their party. It is voters' "standing decision" until and unless they are given good reasons not to follow it. More recently, scholars have reexamined the bases of such behavior. In this new view, citizens who consider themselves Democrats have a standing decision to vote for the Democratic nominee because of the past positions of the Democrats and the Republicans and because of the parties' comparative past performances while in office. In short, this view of partisan identification presumes that it is a "running tally" of past experiences (mostly in terms of policy and performance), a sort of summary expression of political memory, according to Morris P. Fiorina.[8]

Furthermore, when in doubt about how, for example, a Democratic candidate is likely to handle a civil rights issue in comparison with the Republican opponent, voters can reasonably assume that the Democrat will be more liberal than the Republican—until and unless the candidates indicate otherwise. Political parties tend to be consistent with their basic historical policy cleavages for long periods of time, changing in any fundamental ways only rarely. Naturally, therefore, summary judgments of parties and their typical candidates do not change radically or often.[9] As a result, a citizen's running tally serves as a good first approximation, changes rarely, and can be an excellent device for saving time and effort that would be spent gathering information in the absence of this "memory."

Many of the major findings used in support of the original interpretation of party identification are completely consistent with this more policy-oriented view. We do not have the evidence to assert that one view is superior to the other. Indeed, the two interpretations are not mutually exclusive. Moreover, they share the important conclusion that party identification plays a central role in shaping voters' decisions and make many of the same predictions.

These two views are still widely studied today, with adherents of each view enriching and extending the core positions on each side. For example, Robert S. Erikson, Michael B. MacKuen, and James A. Stimson argued that an updated version of the Key-Downs-Fiorina view of partisanship is one of the central concepts for understanding what they call the "macro polity"—that is, an explanation of how political leaders, institutions, and policy respond to changes in aggregate public opinion.[10] They argue that partisanship in the electorate changes, as do macro-level conditions such as inflation and unemployment rates, akin to the Key-Downs-Fiorina view. In turn, political elites react to changes in this "macropartisanship," among other aspects of public opinion and beliefs. On the other side, Donald Green, Bradley Palmquist, and Eric Schickler developed an equally elegant account of the affective base of partisan identification and its stability over time.[11] This view is therefore the modern version of the original account by Campbell et al. And, as their exchanges have shown, the two sets of authors differ substantially in their interpretations of what partisanship means, but empirical differences are slighter.[12]

Both views agree that partisan identifications are long-term forces in politics. Both agree that, for most people, such identifications are formed early in life; children often develop a partisan loyalty, which they usually learn from their parents, although these loyalties are seldom explicitly taught. Both views recognize that partisan loyalties contribute to voter participation, as we demonstrated in Chapter 4. Partisan choices also are often closely associated with social forces, as discussed in Chapter 5, especially when a social group is actively engaged in partisan politics. An important illustration of this point is the affiliation of evangelical and other religious groups on the right with the Republican Party today, reinforcing the tendency of those who share such religious beliefs to identify with the Republican Party, much as members of labor and civil rights groups have long affiliated with the Democrats. Finally, both views agree that partisanship is closely associated with more immediate evaluations, including assessments of candidates and their traits, and both prospective and retrospective evaluations of the issues and candidates, as analyzed in Chapters 6 and 7.

The two views disagree over the nature of the linkage between partisanship and other attitudes, such as those toward the candidates and issues. The standard view argues that partisanship, as a long-term loyalty, affects the evaluations of issues and candidates by voters, but that it, in turn, is largely unaffected by such evaluations, except in such dramatic circumstances as realigning elections. In this sense, partisanship is a "filter" through which the concerns relevant to the particular election are viewed. In the alternative view, partisanship as a running tally may affect, but also is affected by, more immediate concerns. Indeed, Fiorina's definition of partisanship makes clear that the running tally includes current as well as past assessments. Distinguishing empirically between these two views is therefore quite difficult. Although the alternative view may believe that partisan identification is affected by retrospective and prospective assessments of the issues and candidates in the current election, such assessments rarely change an individual's identification because of that person's past experiences and the impact of initial socialization. We will analyze the role of partisan identification in 2012 and other recent elections in ways consistent with both major views of partisan identification.

PARTY IDENTIFICATION IN THE ELECTORATE

If partisan identification is a fundamental orientation for most citizens, then the distribution of partisan loyalties is crucial. The American National Election Study (ANES) surveys have monitored the party loyalties of the American electorate since 1952. In Table 8-1, we show the basic distributions of partisan loyalties in presidential election years from 1980 to 2012, and the results for 1952 to 1976 can be found in Appendix Table A8-2. As the table shows, most Americans identify with a political party. In 2012, 57 percent claimed to think of themselves as a Democrat or as a Republican, and another 33 percent, who initially said they were independent or had no partisan preference, nevertheless said they felt closer to one of the major parties than to the other.[13] One in ten was purely independent of party. One of the biggest changes in partisanship in the electorate began in the mid-1960s, when more people claimed to be independents.[14] This growth stopped, however, in the late 1970s and early 1980s. There was very little change in partisan loyalties between the 1984 and 1992 surveys.

There were signs in 1996 of reversals of the trends in party identification toward greater independence. All partisan groups increased slightly in 1996 compared with 1992, and the percentage of "pure" independents (i.e., those with no partisan leanings) was at its lowest level, 8 percent, since 1968. That dip in independence stopped, however, so that the percentages of independents in 2004, 2008, and 2012 were at about the same levels as during the 1980s.

Table 8-1 also shows that people are rather evenly divided between the two parties. The Democrats retained a small lead over Republicans in the 2012 survey. They lead 33 to 24 among strong and weak identifiers. Including leaners puts them just short of an outright majority, and they hold an eight-point lead over Republicans using this measure. Over the last forty years, the balance between the two parties had favored the Democrats by a range of about 55/45 to about 60/40. The results from the last six presidential election years before 2012 still fell within that range, although more often at the lower part of the range. From 1984 to 2000, there was a clear shift toward the Republicans. In 1980, 35 percent of partisans were Republicans; in 2000 Republicans accounted for 42 percent. The inclusion of independents who leaned toward a party would increase the percentage of Republicans to 38 percent in 1980 and 43 percent in 2000. The high point was 47 percent in 1988. In 2004 the (strong and weak) Democrats led comparable Republicans in the ANES survey with 33 percent to 29 percent (or 54/46). The Democratic advantage increased in 2008, as the percentage of Republicans declined while there was a one-point increase on the Democratic side. These two small differences nevertheless brought the ratio of Democrats to Republicans to 57/43. The percentage of independents who leaned toward a party remained the same as in 2004, and as a result, including them maintained the Democrats' edge over Republicans at 57/43, keeping the partisan balance within the historical range of a noticeable Democratic lead. By 2012, however, that edge had slid just below the 55/45 boundary, at 54.4 percent

TABLE 8-1 Party Identification in Presidential Years, Pre-election Surveys, 1980–2012 (percent)

Party identification	1980	1984	1988	1992	1996	2000	2004	2008	2012
Strong Democrat	18	17	18	17	18	19	17	19	20
Weak Democrat	24	20	18	18	20	15	16	15	13
Independent, leans Democratic	12	11	12	14	14	15	17	17	16
Independent, no partisan leanings	13	11	11	12	8	12	10	11	10
Independent, leans Republican	10	13	14	13	12	13	12	12	17
Weak Republican	14	15	14	15	16	12	12	13	11
Strong Republican	9	13	14	11	13	12	17	13	13
Total	100	100	101	100	101	98	101	100	100
(N)	(1,577)	(2,198)	(1,999)	(2,450)[a]	(1,696)[a]	(1,777)[a]	(1,193)[a]	(2,301)[a]	(2,039)[a]
Apolitical	2	2	2	1	1	1	[b]	[b]	[c]
(N)	(35)	(38)	(33)	(23)	(14)	(21)	(3)	(2)	[c]

Source: Authors' analysis of ANES surveys.

[a] Numbers are weighted.

[b] Less than 1 percent.

[c] The ANES survey did not use the apolitical category in 2012.

Democrat, 45.6 percent Republican. The Democrats will take that edge, although one should understand that it is reduced in most cases, due to the slightly higher percentage of those somewhat fewer Republicans who turn out in most years.

Gary C. Jacobson has provided two excellent analyses of the shift in party loyalties away from the Republican Party from a high watermark in 2003 to a low-water mark in 2009. His analyses strongly suggest that the decline was driven largely by the decline in approval of George W. Bush's performance as president.[15] Jacobson relies mainly on Gallup data, which probably capture more short-term variation than the standard Michigan Survey Research Center question.[16]

A variety of other data sets can be analyzed, some of which are more attuned to long-term changes in partisanship. The most useful is the General Social Survey (GSS) conducted by the National Opinion Research Center at the University of Chicago. These national samples are based on in-person interviews, use the standard ANES party identification questions, and usually have a sample size of 1,500 (nearly 2,000 in 2012). The GSS has measured party identification since 1972.[17] Like the ANES surveys, the GSS reveals some Republican gains. From 1972 to 1982, the percentage of party identifiers supporting the Republicans never rose above 37 percent, and even if independents who lean toward a party are included, the percentage of Republicans never rose above 38 percent. In 1984, party identifiers who were Republicans rose to 40 percent, and Republican strength peaked in the 1990 GSS, which showed 48 percent of all party identifiers as Republicans. If independents who leaned toward a party are included, that percentage increases to 49. But the Republicans made no further gains, even in the 1991 survey conducted during and after the Persian Gulf War. In the February–April 2000 GSS survey, 43 percent of all party identifiers were Republicans, and the total is unchanged if independent leaners are included. In 2004, 47 percent of all party identifiers were Republicans (a similar percentage with leaners included). And like the 2004 ANES, the 2004 GSS registered the highest percentage of strong Republicans ever recorded: 14 percent. The overall percentage of Republicans was virtually the same in the 2006 GSS, although strong Republicans fell to 11 percent. But there was a clear drop in the percentage of Republicans in 2008. Among party identifiers only 42 percent were Republicans, and that percentage stayed the same when independent leaners were included. Thus there was a five-point drop in the percentage of Republicans in only four years. The percentage of strong Republicans remained at 11.

In 2012, the GSS data were quite similar to the ANES results. The GSS reported about 34 percent of the sample saying they think of themselves as Democrats, with another one in eight "leaning" in that direction, for a total of 46 percent Democrat. Twenty-four percent were strong or not-so-strong Republicans in the GSS, and 8 percent more leaned toward the GOP, giving Republicans a total of 32 percent. Thus, the Democrats retained a slight lead in the GSS in 2012, but the substantial difference was the one in five who reported themselves to be purely independent of parties. The GSS is not conducted during or immediately after the general election campaign as the ANES is, which may account for at least some of the difference due to the heat of a partisan campaign. Still, there are twice as many "pure" independents in the spring as compared to the fall, which suggests some extent of real change. Most of this change appears to have come from those who claim to "lean" to a party, and it is at least possible that the heat of the election campaign transforms those who report themselves to be purely independent of the two parties to reflect their attraction to one of the parties or its candidates in the election race by saying they lean in that direction.

Surveys conducted by Gallup are also useful, because they have a very long history (longer even than the ANES) and because in recent years they include the same question tapping "leaners" (which they did not originally do).[18] Gallup's last pre-election survey (November 1–4, 2012) found that Democrats led Republicans 35 to 30 percent, while including "leaners" yielded 50 percent Democrats and 42 percent Republicans, with 8 percent "pure" independents. This was almost exactly the same division as in late September 2012. In mid-April (at a time reasonably close to when the GSS was in the field), the divisions were 47 Democrat, 43 Republican, and hence 10 percent "pure" independents.

Our analysis of prior ANES surveys reveals that the earlier shift toward the Republican Party was concentrated among white Americans.[19] As described in Chapter 5, the sharpest social division in U.S. electoral politics is race, and this division has been reflected in partisan loyalties for decades. Moreover, the racial gap has appeared to be widening, with a sharp increase in 2004.

Although the distribution of partisanship in the electorate as a whole has changed only somewhat since 1984, this stability masks the growth in Republican identification among whites through 2004, and the compensating growth of already strong Democratic loyalties among African Americans. In Tables 8-2 and 8-3, we report the party identification of whites and blacks, respectively, between 1980 and 2012. In Tables A8-2 and A8-3 in the Appendix, we report the party identification of whites and of blacks between 1952 and 1978. As these four tables show, black and white patterns in partisan loyalties were very different from 1952 to 2012. There was a sharp shift in black loyalties in the mid-1960s. Before then, about 50 percent of African Americans were strong or weak Democrats. Since that time, 60 to 70 percent—and even more—of blacks have considered themselves Democrats.

The party loyalties of whites have changed more slowly. Still, the percentage of self-professed Democrats among whites declined during the Reagan years, while the percentage of Republicans increased. In the five elections that followed, partisanship among whites changed. If independents who lean Republican are included, there was close to an even balance among whites between the two parties in 1984. By 1988 the numbers of strong and weak Democrats and strong and weak Republicans were virtually the same, with more strong Republicans than strong Democrats for the first time. Adding in the two groups of independent leaners gave Republicans a clear advantage in identification among whites. In 1992, however, there were slightly more strong and weak Democrats than strong and weak Republicans. In 1996 all four of the partisan categories were larger, by one to three points, than in 1992. The result was that the balance

TABLE 8-2 Party Identification among Whites, 1980–2012 (percent)

Party identification[a]	1980	1982	1984	1986	1988	1990	1992
Strong Democrat	14	16	15	14	14	17	14
Weak Democrat	23	24	18	21	16	19	17
Independent, leans Democratic	12	11	11	10	10	11	14
Independent, no partisan leanings	14	11	11	12	12	11	12
Independent, leans Republican	11	9	13	13	15	13	14
Weak Republican	16	16	17	17	15	16	16
Strong Republican	9	11	14	12	16	11	12
Apolitical	2	2	2	2	1	1	1
Total	101	100	101	101	99	99	100

TABLE 8-2 (Continued)

(N)	(1,405) 1994	(1,248) 1996	(1,931) 1998	(1,798)[b] 2000	(1,693) 2002	(1,663) 2004	(2,702)[b] 2008	2012
Strong Democrat	12	15	15	15	12	13	14	13
Weak Democrat	19	19	18	14	16	12	14	10
Independent, leans Democratic	12	13	14	15	14	17	17	15
Independent, no partisan leanings	10	8	11	13	8	8	12	10
Independent, leans Republican	13	12	12	14	15	13	13	22
Weak Republican	16	17	18	14	17	15	15	13
Strong Republican	17	15	11	14	17	21	16	17
Apolitical	1	1	2	1	1	a	a	c
Total	100	100	101	100	100	99	101	100
(N)	(1,510)[b]	(1,451)[b]	(1,091)[b]	(1,404)[b]	(1,129)[b]	(859)[b]	(1,824)[b]	(1,441)[b]

Source: Authors' analysis of ANES surveys.

[a] The percentage supporting another party has not been presented; it usually totals less than 1 percent and never totals more than 1 percent.

[b] Numbers are weighted.

[c] The ANES survey did not use the apolitical category in 2012.

TABLE 8-3 Party Identification among Blacks, 1980–2012 (percent)

Party identification[a]	1980	1982	1984	1986	1988	1990	1992
Strong Democrat	45	53	32	42	39	40	40
Weak Democrat	27	26	31	30	24	23	24
Independent, leans Democratic	9	12	14	12	18	16	14
Independent, no partisan leanings	7	5	11	7	6	8	12
Independent, leans Republican	3	1	6	2	5	7	3
Weak Republican	2	2	1	2	5	3	3
Strong Republican	3	0	2	2	1	2	2
Apolitical	4	1	2	2	3	2	2
Total	100	100	99	99	101	101	100

TABLE 8-3 (Continued)

(N)	(187)	(148)	(247)	(322)	(267)	(270)	(317)ᶜ	
	1994	1996	1998	2000	2002	2004	2008	2012
Strong Democrat	38	43	48	47	53	30	47	55
Weak Democrat	23	22	23	21	16	30	23	17
Independent, leans Democratic	20	16	12	14	17	20	15	17
Independent, no partisan leanings	8	10	7	10	6	12	9	4
Independent, leans Republican	4	5	3	4	2	5	3	5
Weak Republican	2	3	3	3	4	2	1	0
Strong Republican	3	1	1	0	2	1	1	1
Apolitical	3	0	2	1	ᵇ	ᵇ	ᵇ	ᵈ
Total	101	100	99	100	100	100	99	99
(N)	(203)ᶜ	(200)ᶜ	(149)ᶜ	(225)ᶜ	(161)ᶜ	(193)ᶜ	(281)ᶜ	(242)ᶜ

Source: Authors' analysis of ANES surveys.

ᵃ The percentage supporting another party has not been presented; it usually totals less than 1 percent and never totals more than 1 percent.

ᵇ Less than 1 percent.

ᶜ Numbers are weighted.

ᵈ The ANES survey did not use the apolitical category in 2012.

of Republicans to Democrats changed very slightly, and the near parity of identifiers with the two parties among whites remained. By 2000 the parity was even more striking. But 2002 revealed a substantial increase in Republican identification among whites, one that was constant in terms of the three Republican groups in 2004. Democratic identification declined slightly, so that from 2000 to 2004 strong and weak Democrats fell by four points, partially balanced by a two-point gain among independent leaners. Pure independents declined sharply, to 8 percent, in both 2002 and 2004, a sign (along with the growth in strong Republicans) that the white electorate was polarizing somewhat on partisanship. As a result, the three Republican groups constituted very nearly half of the white electorate and led Democrats by a 49 percent to 42 percent margin. That changed in 2008.[20] Democratic identification (over the three Democratic categories) increased three percentage points to 45 percent, while strong Republicans fell from 21 to 16 percent, dropping their three-category total to 44 percent. Thus in 2008 Democrats had at least regained parity with Republicans among white identifiers. And pure independents increased four points, to 12 percent, the highest level in over a decade.

That changed again in 2012. The Democrats lost ground in all three Democratic categories in 2012 compared to 2008, with a slight decrease in pure independents. That change seemed to move to the category of independents who lean toward the Republicans, as the strong and weak Republican categories changed little. As a result, the GOP held a seven-point advantage over Democrats in terms of strong and weak identifiers, but a fourteen-point advantage if adding in those who lean toward a party.[21]

Party identification among blacks is very different. In 2012 there were very few black Republicans. Indeed, the percentage of black Republicans fell to near trace levels, with only 6 percent choosing any Republican option and a mere 1 percent being strong and weak Republicans. Because the Democrats were the first major party to choose an African American presidential candidate, we would expect this choice to exert a strong pull of blacks toward the party, perhaps limited only by blacks' already strong standing as Democrats. In 2008 nearly half of the blacks said they were strong Democrats, a very high proportion, although not as high as in 1964, 1968 (see Table A8-3), or 2002. Another 23 percent were weak Democrats, with 15 percent more leaning toward the party. As a result, seven in every eight blacks chose one of the three Democratic options, with most of the rest claiming to be purely independent of either party. In 2012, the Democrats made even more gains, as a full 55 percent of African Americans said they were strong Democrats, the highest yet recorded in these surveys, and Democrats held the loyalties of nearly nine in ten African Americans over all three Democratic groups, essentially the same as in 1982 and 2002. These 2012 results from the ANES are similar to those from the GSS. Republicans received the support of about 2 percent of African Americans, which increased only another 2 percent, including leaners. The three Democrat groups totaled 81 percent in the GSS.

These racial differences in partisanship are long-standing, and they have increased over time. Between 1952 and 1962, blacks were primarily Democratic, but about one in seven supported the Republicans. Black partisanship shifted massively and abruptly even further toward the Democratic Party in 1964. In that year, over half of all black voters considered themselves strong Democrats. Since then, well over half have identified with the Democratic Party. Black Republican identification fell to barely a trace in 1964 and edged up only slightly since then, only to fall back even further in recent years.

The abrupt change in black loyalties in 1964 reflects the two presidential nominees of that year: Democrat Lyndon Johnson and Republican Barry Goldwater. President Johnson's advocacy of civil rights legislation appealed directly to black voters, and his Great Society and War on Poverty programs made only slightly less direct appeals. Arizona senator Barry Goldwater voted against the 1964 Civil Rights Act, a vote criticized even by many of his Republican peers. In 1968 Republican nominee Richard Nixon began to pursue systematically what was called the "southern strategy"—that is, an attempt to win votes and long-term loyalties among white southerners. This strategy unfolded slowly but consistently over the years, as Republicans, particularly Ronald Reagan, continued to pursue the southern strategy. Party stances have not changed appreciably since then.[22]

In 1964 the proportion of blacks considered apolitical dropped from the teens to very small proportions, similar to those among whites. This shift resulted from the civil rights movement, the contest between Johnson and Goldwater, and the passage of the Civil Rights Act. The civil rights movement stimulated many blacks, especially in the South, to become politically active. Furthermore, the 1965 Voting Rights Act enabled many of them to vote for the first time. Party and electoral politics suddenly were relevant, and blacks responded as all others by becoming engaged with the political—and party—system.

HISPANIC PARTISANSHIP IN 2008 AND 2012

One of the most important changes in American society and its politics has been the growth of the Latino/a community. They are now the largest ethnic or racial minority in the United States, and the results of the 2012 election spurred a vast commentary on the future of the Republican Party based on whether and how it might be able to appeal to the Latino/a vote or seek a majority in some other way, such as through voter identification laws. We have not been able to assess their attitudes and behavior until recently due to the small numbers who appear in ANES and other survey opinion polls. Fortunately, in 2008 and 2012, the ANES included a supplemental sample of such citizens so that we have access to sufficiently large numbers to support at least a modicum of analysis. Table 8-4 reports the distribution of partisan loyalties among Latinos in Part A and their voting patterns in Part B, which we consider below. As can be seen there, Latino/a partisanship may not be as massively Democratic as that of African Americans, but

TABLE 8-4   Party Identification and Vote Choice among Latinos, 2008–2012 (percent)

	2008	2012
A. Party Identification among Latinos		
Strong Democrat	23	27
Weak Democrat	21	23
Independent, leans Democrat	17	16
Independent, no partisan leanings	16	15
Independent, leans Republican	9	7
Weak Republican	6	6
Strong Republican	7	5
Total	99	99
(*N*)	(192)	(221)
B. Latino Major-Party Voters Who Voted Democratic for President, by Party Identification		
Strong Democrat	95	100
Weak Democrat	90	87
Independent, leans Democrat	94	99
Independent, no partisan leanings	61	82
Independent, leans Republican	35	39
Weak Republican	24	4
Strong Republican	20	1
Total	79	78
(*N*)	(104)	(107)

Source: Authors' analysis of the ANES Surveys.

Note: Numbers are weighted. The numbers in parentheses in Part B are the totals on which the percentages are based.

Republicans do very poorly among Latinos (less than one in five identify as a Republican, including "leaners"), whereas by 2012, the Democratic Party had secured the loyalties of a majority of them, and essentially two of three identified as one of the three Democratic categories. With movement, even if slight, in the Democratic direction from 2008 to 2012, and with growth of the American population concentrated heavily among Latinos, the Republicans were right to indicate that they needed to think carefully about their strategies with respect to race and ethnicity. It is likely that their ability to win majorities into the future depends on it.

PARTY IDENTIFICATION AND THE VOTE

As we saw in Chapter 4, partisanship is related to turnout. Strong supporters of either party are more likely to vote than weak supporters, and independents who lean toward a party are more likely to vote than independents without partisan leanings. Republicans are somewhat more likely to vote than Democrats. Although partisanship influences whether people vote, it is more strongly related to how people vote.

Table 8-5 reports the percentage of white major-party voters who voted for the Democratic candidate across all categories of partisanship since 1980, and Table A8-5 in the Appendix reports the same for earlier ANES studies.[23] Clearly, there is a strong relationship between partisan identification and choice of candidate. In every election except 1972, the Democratic nominee has received more than 80 percent of the vote of strong Democrats and majority support from both weak Democratic partisans and independent Democratic leaners. In 1996 these figures were higher than in any other election in this period, with nine in ten white Democratic identifiers voting for their party's nominee. Although the figures fell somewhat in 2000, especially in the independent-leaning Democrat category, that reversed in 2004, with John Kerry holding on to very large majorities of those who identified with the Democratic Party, including nearly nine in ten independents who were leaning toward the Democratic Party. In 2008 this very high level of Democratic voting continued, with slight declines among strong Democrats balanced by comparable increases among weak Democrats. The 2012 election looks similar to 2008 in this regard, with substantial support for Obama among all Democrats.

Since 1952 strong Republicans have given the Democratic candidate less than one vote in ten. In 1988 more of the weak Republicans and independents who leaned toward the Republican Party voted for Michael Dukakis than had voted for Walter Mondale in 1984, but, even so, only about one in seven voted Democratic. In 1992 Clinton won an even larger percentage of the two-party vote from these Republicans, and he increased his support among Republicans again in 1996. In 2000 George W. Bush held essentially the same level of support among the three white Republican categories as his father had in 1988 and 1992, and if anything increased his support among Republicans in 2004. In 2008 over 90 percent of the strong and weak Republicans voted for McCain, just as they had for Bush four years earlier. The 2012 data look rather similar to 2004 and 2008, with Romney doing a little better in holding weak Republican votes but doing a little worse than McCain among Republican leaners.

The pure independent vote, which fluctuates substantially, has been more Republican than Democratic in eleven of these sixteen elections and was strongly Democratic only in 1964. Clinton did well among major-party voters in 1992. John F. Kennedy won 50 percent of that vote in 1960, but Bill Clinton won nearly two-thirds of the pure independents' vote (between the two parties) in 1992.[24] Kerry was able to win 54 percent of the pure independent vote. Obama, like Kennedy, won exactly half of the vote among whites who were pure independents in 2008. However, that 50-50 vote in 1960 was the same as the overall vote, whereas Obama won a higher proportion from the full electorate than from white pure independents. He fell back slightly in 2012, winning 46 percent of the "pure" independent vote among whites.

TABLE 8-5 White Major-Party Voters Who Voted Democratic for President, by Party Identification, 1980–2012 (percent)

Party identification	1980	1984	1988	1992	1996	2000	2004	2008	2012
Strong Democrat	87	88	93	96	98	96	97	92	99
Weak Democrat	59	63	68	80	88	81	78	83	84
Independent, leans Democratic	57	77	86	92	91	72	88	88	87
Independent, no partisan leanings	23	21	35	63	39	44	54	50	46
Independent, leans Republican	13	5	13	14	26	15	13	17	12
Weak Republican	5	6	16	18	21	16	10	10	14
Strong Republican	4	2	2	2	3	1	3	2	4

Source: Authors' analysis of ANES surveys.

Note: To approximate the numbers on which these percentages are based, see Table 8-2. Actual *N*s will be smaller than those that can be derived from these tables because respondents who did not vote (or voted for a non-major-party candidate) have been excluded from the calculations. Numbers also will be lower because the voting report is provided in the postelection interviews, which usually contain about 10 percent fewer respondents than the pre-election interviews in which party identification is measured.

Thus, at least among major-party white voters, partisanship is very strongly related to the vote. In recent elections, the Democrats have been better able to hold support among their partisans, perhaps because the loss of southern white support has made the party more homogeneous in its outlook. Their partisan base has become essentially as strong as the Republicans', which has been consistently strong except in the very best years for the Democrats. Partisanship, then, has become more polarized in its relationship to the vote. Obama won because he broke relatively even among independents and because he held his base well, about as well as Republicans held theirs.

Part B of Table 8-4 shows that there is a very powerful relationship between Latino/a party identification and their vote. Nearly all Democratic Latinos voted for Obama in 2008 and 2012. Obama was able to hold about a quarter of the relatively small number of Hispanics who identified with the GOP in 2008, but Romney won nearly all of the by-now very small number of strong and weak Republican Latino/a votes in 2012. The pure independent vote broke strongly for Obama in 2008 but increased dramatically in 2012.

Although nearly all blacks vote Democratic regardless of their partisan affiliations (most are, however, Democratic identifiers), among Latinos and whites partisanship leads to loyalty in voting. Between 1964 and 1980, the relationship between party identification and the vote was declining, but in 1984 the relationship between party identification and the presidential vote was higher than in any of the five elections from 1964 to 1980. The relationship remained strong in 1988 and continued to be quite strong in the two Clinton elections and the Gore-Bush election, at least among major-party voters. The question of whether the parties are gathering new strength at the presidential level could not be answered definitively from the 2000 election data, but the 2004, 2008, and 2012 election data now make it clear that these growing signs have become a strong trend, to the point that party identification is as strongly related to the presidential vote as it has been since the 1950s and early 1960s. The relationship between party identification and voting in general will be reconsidered in Chapter 10, when we assess its relationship to the congressional vote.[25]

Partisanship is related to the way people vote. The question, therefore, is why do partisans support their party's candidates? As we shall see, party identification affects behavior because it helps structure (and, according to the understanding of partisanship as a running tally of experiences, is structured by) the way voters view both policies and performance.

POLICY PREFERENCES AND PERFORMANCE EVALUATIONS

In their study of voting in the 1948 election, Bernard R. Berelson, Paul F. Lazarsfeld, and William N. McPhee discovered that Democratic voters attributed to their nominee, incumbent Harry S Truman, positions on key issues that were consistent with their beliefs—whether those beliefs were liberal, moderate, or conservative.[26]

Similarly, Republicans tended to see their nominee, Gov. Thomas E. Dewey of New York, as taking whatever positions they preferred. These tendencies toward projection (projecting one's own preferences on to what one thinks the favored candidate prefers) are discomforting for those who hope that, in a democracy, issue preferences shape candidate assessment and voting choices rather than the other way around. These authors did find, however, that the more the voters knew, the less likely they were to project their preferences onto the candidates. Research since then has emphasized the role of party identification not only in projection, but also in shaping the policy preferences in the public in the first place.[27] In this section, we use four examples to illustrate the strong relationship between partisan affiliation and perceptions, preferences, and evaluations of candidates.

Partisanship and Approval of President's Job Performance

Most partisans evaluate the job performance of a president from their party more highly than do independents and, especially, more highly than do those who identify with the other party. Figure 8-1A shows the percentage of each of the seven partisan groups that approved of the way the incumbent has handled his job as president (as a proportion of those approving or disapproving) in the last four presidential elections in which there was a Democratic president (1980, 1996, 2000, and 2012). Figure 8-1B presents similar results for the seven elections in which there was a Republican incumbent (1972, 1976, 1984, 1988, 1992, 2004, and 2008).[28] Strong partisans of the incumbent's party typically give overwhelming approval to that incumbent (Table A8-2 in the Appendix presents the exact values for each year.) It is not guaranteed, however. In 1980 only 73 percent of strong Democrats approved of Jimmy Carter, which is just about the same percentage of strong Republicans who approved of George W. Bush's job performance in 2008.

We can draw two conclusions about 2012 from the data in Figures 8-1A and 8-1B. First, just as in every election, there was a strong partisan cast to evaluations of the president in 2012. Democrats are very likely to approve of any Democratic incumbent and very unlikely to approve of any Republican incumbent, and vice versa for Republicans. This fact was even more true in 2012 than in prior elections, as the degree of partisan polarization in approval of Obama's handling of his job was more dramatic than any other. Virtually all strong Democrats approved, and virtually no strong Republicans did. Even independent leaners were divided 80-20 in each party, Democrats approving, Republicans disapproving, with pure independents falling directly in between.

Partisanship and Approval of President's Handling of the Economy

Our second illustration extends the connection we have drawn between partisanship and approval of the incumbent's job performance. In this case, we examine the relationship between partisanship and approval of the incumbent's handling of the economy. Table 8-6 shows the relationship among all seven partisan categories and approval of incumbent presidents' handling of the economy from 2000 through 2012, while Table A8-6 in the Appendix provides data back to 1984.[29]

In 1984 and 1988, more than three-quarters of each of the three Republican groups approved of Reagan's handling of the economy, while more than half—and often more than two-thirds—of the three Democratic groups disapproved. Independents generally approved of Reagan's economic efforts, albeit more strongly in 1984 than in 1988. The 1992 election was dramatically different, with overwhelming disapproval of George H. W. Bush's handling of the economy among the three Democratic groups and the pure independents. Even two-thirds of the weak and Republican-leaning independents disapproved. Only strong Republicans typically approved, and even then one in three did not. The relationship in 1996 is most like that of 1984. In 2000 the vast majority of Democrats and even three in four of the pure independents approved of Clinton's economic performance—by far the highest economic approval mark independents have given. But then most Republicans also approved. In 2004 the weak but improving economy meant that George W. Bush was approved by "only" nine in ten strong Republicans and about seven in ten weak Republicans and those independents who leaned toward the Republicans. Democratic disapproval reached very high levels, and once again pure independents did not favor Bush, only one in three approving of his handling of the economy. In 2008 the Wall Street meltdown occurred in the midst of the campaign, and its effects were devastating to President Bush's approval ratings. Only 18 percent of respondents approved of Bush's handling of the economy. Even though these ratings were lower than the overall approval ratings, they displayed a clear partisan effect. Strong Republicans still approved more than they disapproved, and one in four in the other two Republican categories approved. These are very low percentages to be sure, but they are higher than among pure independents (note, however, that more pure independents approved in 2008 than in 1992) and much higher than the mere trace levels of any type of Democrat, with about one in twenty approving.

The relationship between partisanship and approval of Obama's handling of the economy in 2012 was very strong. Of the three Democrat categories of partisanship, from six in ten to nine in ten approved of Obama's performance. Ninety-five percent of strong Republicans disapproved, with seven in eight of weak and of leaning Republicans also disapproving. And pure independents disapproved of Obama's performance by nearly a two-to-one ratio. Thus, as in so many other cases we have examined, evaluations and voting in 2012 were quite polarized by party even in the electorate. In this case, it might well be because, unlike 2008 with its economic collapse during the campaign or, say, 1996 with an ongoing boom, the neither too positive nor too negative economic news made it possible for partisans to disagree across party lines on the economic performance of the incumbent. Perhaps there are other reasons for this, but it is undeniable that these evaluations differed dramatically across party lines.

FIGURE 8-1A   Approval of Democratic Incumbents' Handling of Job, by Party Identification, 1980, 1996, 2000, and 2012

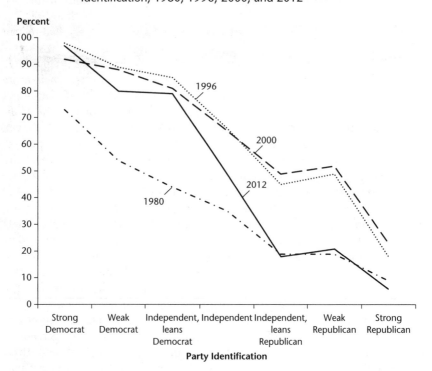

Source: Authors' analysis of ANES surveys.

Prospective Issues

The third example of the impact of partisanship on attitudes and beliefs is its relationship to positions on policy issues. In Table 8-7 and Table A8-7, we report this relationship among the seven partisan categories and our balance-of-issues measure developed in Chapter 6, collapsed into a three groupings: pro-Republican, neutral, pro-Democratic.[30] As we saw in Chapter 6, these issues favored the Republicans in 1972, 1976, and 1980, worked slightly to the Democratic advantage in 1984, 1988, and 1992, then once again favored the Republicans in the elections from 1996 to 2012. In all cases, the balance-of-issues measure had only moderately favored one party over the other, but in 2008 it clearly favored the Republicans, and in 2012 it did so primarily because the most popular issue position was only slightly closer to Romney's position, but was so on essentially every issue included in the measure.

As Table 8-7 and Table A8-7 show for 1976–2012, there has been a steady, clear, moderately strong relationship between partisanship and the balance-of-issues measure, and it is one that, by 2000, had strengthened considerably and continued

FIGURE 8-1B   Approval of Republican Incumbents' Handling of Job, by Party
Identification, 1972, 1976, 1984, 1988, 1992, 2004, and 2008

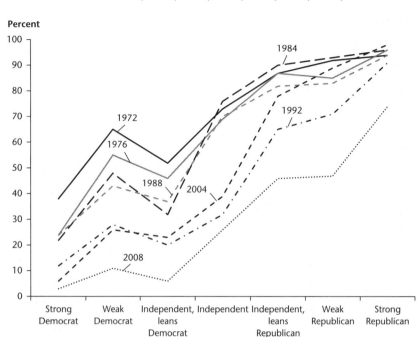

Source: Authors' analysis of ANES surveys.

to strengthen into 2008, with only modest weakening in 2012. Until 1984 the
relationship had been stronger among Republicans than among Democrats. In
1984 and 1988 (and also in 1992, but that measure depends on only three issues
and is therefore less useful), the relationship was, if anything, stronger among
Democrats than Republicans. That change very likely stemmed from the political
context. In 1980, for example, more people, Democrats as well as Republicans,
were closer to Reagan's median position than to Carter's on important issues such
as defense spending and income tax cuts. However, after Reagan pushed increases
in defense spending and cuts in income taxes through Congress in his first term,
the electorate no longer favored as great an increase in defense spending and was
more amenable to higher spending on some domestic programs.

Thus in the next three elections, issues tended to divide the electorate along
party lines, with Democrats closer to their party's nominee. The result was a
sharper and more balanced relationship between partisanship and the balance-
of-issues measure. In 1996, although the balance-of-issues measure favored the
Republicans, its relationship to party identification was stronger. It was almost
as strong in 2000 and was moderately strong on both sides of the competition.

TABLE 8-6 Approval of Incumbent's Handling of the Economy among Partisan Groups, 2000–2012 (percent)

		Party identification							
Year	Attitudes toward handling of the economy	Strong Democrat	Weak Democrat	Independent, leans Democrat	Independent	Independent, leans Republican	Weak Republican	Strong Republican	Total
2000	Approve	95	90	84	73	60	70	47	77
	Disapprove	5	10	16	27	40	30	53	23
	Total	100	100	100	100	100	100	100	100
	(N)	(342)	(265)	(264)	(198)	(206)	(184)	(200)	(1,659)
2004	Approve	5	18	10	34	68	72	89	40
	Disapprove	95	82	90	66	32	28	11	60
	Total	100	100	100	100	100	100	100	100
	(N)	(197)	(176)	(204)	(107)	(139)	(141)	(194)	(1,158)
2008	Approve	4	7	5	16	27	25	58	18
	Disapprove	96	93	95	84	73	75	42	82
	Total	100	100	100	100	100	100	100	100
	(N)	(428)	(338)	(381)	(240)	(255)	(274)	(291)	(2,208)
2012	Approve	92	74	62	37	15	13	5	46
	Disapprove	8	26	38	63	85	87	95	54
	Total	100	100	100	100	100	100	100	100
	(N)	(400)	(244)	(295)	(163)	(349)	(205)	(258)	(1,914)

Source: Authors' analysis of ANES surveys.

Note: Numbers are weighted

TABLE 8-7   Balance-of-Issues Positions among Partisan Groups, 2000–2012 (percent)

				Party identification				
Issue positions closer to[a]	Strong Democrat	Weak Democrat	Independent, leans Democrat	Independent	Independent, leans Republican	Weak Republican	Strong Republican	Total
2000[b]								
Democratic candidate	30	26	25	20	8	10	2	19
Neutral	47	48	46	49	40	33	25	43
Republican candidate	23	25	29	31	51	57	73	38
Total	100	101	100	100	99	100	100	100
(N)	(188)	(161)	(157)	(113)	(134)	(101)	(99)	(953)
2004[b]								
Democratic candidate	72	55	57	40	19	21	9	40
Neutral	8	11	9	10	9	6	5	8
Republican candidate	21	33	34	50	73	73	86	52
Total	100	99	101	100	100	99	100	100
(N)	(168)	(157)	(180)	(100)	(124)	(136)	(179)	(1,046)
2008[b,c]								
Democratic candidate	60	46	47	28	16	14	8	34
Neutral	6	9	14	10	17	9	[2]	9
Republican candidate	34	45	40	63	67	77	90	56
Total	100	100	101	101	100	100	99	99
(N)	(219)	(163)	(203)	(135)	(143)	(148)	(142)	(1,153)

(Continued)

TABLE 8-7 (Continued)

Issue positions closer to[a]	Party identification							
	Strong Democrat	Weak Democrat	Independent, leans Democrat	Independent	Independent, leans Republican	Weak Republican	Strong Republican	Total
2012[b]								
Democratic candidate	48	37	31	23	7	7	5	24
Neutral	15	18	17	10	10	6	4	11
Republican candidate	36	44	53	67	83	88	92	64
Total	99	99	101	100	100	101	101	99
(N)	(406)	(256)	(321)	(206)	(354)	(214)	(267)	(2,024)

Source: Authors' analysis of ANES surveys.

Note: In the one instance when the category included fewer than ten observations, we show the total number of people in that category in brackets.

[a] The Democratic category on the condensed balance-of-issues measure includes any respondent who is at least slightly Democratic; the Republican category includes any respondent who is at least slightly Republican. The neutral category is the same as the neutral category on the seven-point issue scale (see Table 6-5).

[b] Numbers are weighted.

[c] In 2008, the issues questions used to form the balance-of-issues scale were asked of a randomly selected half-sample.

Prospective issues appear to be increasingly polarized by party, strikingly so by 2000. The data for the 2000 through 2012 elections are quite similar in that there is a strong relationship between party identification and the balance-of-issues measure. In 2012, more strong Democrats were closer to Obama's position than to Romney's, while more than nine out of ten strong Republicans were closer to where the electorate placed Romany. Thus the degree of polarization on this measure continues to be quite strong in recent elections.

Partisan polarization characterizes not only prospective issues but also most other factors we have examined. In our balance-of-issues measure, "polarization" really means "consistency"—that is, partisans find their party's candidate closer to them than the opposing party's nominee on more and more issues. On these measures, then, what we observe as growing polarization stems from the increased differentiation and consistency of positions of the candidates and not as much from changes in the issue positions among the public.

Retrospective Evaluations

Finally, we find a strong relationship between party identification and our measure of retrospective evaluations in 2012. We cannot directly compare this measure in the 2012 election with those for earlier elections, because the questions that make up the summary retrospective measure in the last seven presidential elections differ from those available in 2004, and both differ from those available in 2008 and again in 2012.[31] Still, it is worth noting that this measure was very strongly related to partisanship in those earlier elections. Table 8-8 shows the relationship in 2012, collapsing the summary retrospective measure into the three categories of pro-Democratic, neutral, and pro-Republican. The relationship is very strong. All strong Republicans had negative retrospective evaluations, for example, while nearly three in four strong Democrats held positive ones. We conclude that retrospective evaluations are invariably strongly related to partisanship, and if comparable measures were available, we suspect that 2012 would be among the most strongly related to the partisanship.[32]

Not only are party identification and retrospective evaluations consistently and strongly related to the vote, but these two measures also are strongly related to each other in every election. Do they both still contribute independently to the vote? As we learn from the data in Table 8-9 about the 2012 election, the answer is yes.[33] In Table 8-9, we examine the combined impact of party identification and retrospective evaluations on voting choices. To simplify the presentation, we use the three groupings of the summary retrospective evaluations, and we collapse party identification into the three groups: strong and weak Republicans, all three independent categories, and strong and weak Democrats.

Table 8-9 shows the percentage of major-party voters who voted Democratic by both party identification and retrospective evaluations in 2012. Reading down the columns reveals that party identification is strongly related to the vote,

TABLE 8-8 Retrospective Evaluations among Partisan Groups, 2012 (percent)

Summary measure of retrospective evaluations[a]	Party identification							
	Strong Democrat	Weak Democrat	Independent, leans Democrat	Independent	Independent, leans Republican	Weak Republican	Strong Republican	Total
Pro-Democratic	74	46	39	19	9	5	0	31
Neutral	23	40	49	38	17	21	11	28
Pro-Republican	3	14	12	43	73	74	89	41
Total	100	100	100	100	99	100	100	100
(N)	(384)	(239)	(291)	(177)	(335)	(206)	(251)	(1,883)

Source: Authors' analysis of the 2012 ANES.

Note: Numbers are weighted.

[a] The Democratic category on the condensed measure of retrospective evaluations includes any respondent who is at least slightly opposed to the incumbent's party; the Republican category includes any respondent who supports the incumbent's party at least slightly. The neutral category is the same as the neutral score on the full seven-point measure (see Table 7-9).

TABLE 8-9   Percentage of Major-Party Voters Who Voted for Obama, by Party Identification and Summary of Retrospective Evaluations, 2012

| | Summary of retrospective evaluations[a] | | | | | | | |
| | Pro-Democratic | | Neutral | | Pro-Republican | | Total | |
Party identification	%	(N)	%	(N)	%	(N)	%	(N)
Democratic	99	(299)	95	(124)	30	(27)	94	(450)
Independent	95	(98)	80	(137)	8	(228)	48	(463)
Republican	76	(9)	49	(48)	[0]	(297)	9	(354)
Total	98	(406)	81	(309)	5	(552)	53	(1,267)

Source: Authors' analysis of the 2012 ANES.

Note: Numbers are weighted. The numbers in parentheses are the totals on which the percentages are based. The sample is restricted to respondents who were randomly assigned to the old version of issue questions.

[a] The Democratic category on the condensed measure of retrospective evaluations includes any respondent who is at least slightly opposed to the incumbent's party; the Republican category includes any respondent who supports the incumbent's party at least slightly. The neutral category is the same as the neutral score on the full seven-point measure (see Table 7-9).

regardless of the voter's retrospective evaluations, a pattern found in the nine elections before 2012. Not enough people assessed the Republicans positively on retrospective evaluations to say much about that column, but the other two columns illustrate a very strong relationship. Reading across each row reveals that in all elections retrospective evaluations are related to the vote, regardless of the voter's party identification, and once again a pattern was discovered in all nine earlier elections. Moreover, as in all nine elections between 1976 and 2008, party identification and retrospective evaluations had a combined impact on how people voted in 2008. For example, in 2012 all Republicans with pro-Republican evaluations reported voting for Romney; among Democrats with pro-Democratic evaluations, 99 percent voted for Obama.

Finally, partisanship and retrospective assessments appear to have roughly equal effects on the vote (although retrospective evaluations might, if anything, outweigh partisanship in 2012), and certainly both are strongly related to the vote, even when both variables are examined together. For example, the effect of retrospective evaluations on the vote is not the result of partisans having positive retrospective assessments of their party's presidents and negative ones when the opposition holds the White House. Republicans who hold pro-Democratic retrospective judgments were much more supportive of Obama than other Republicans. Overall, then, we can conclude that partisanship is a key component for understanding evaluations of the public and their votes, but the large changes in outcomes over time must be traced to retrospective and prospective evaluations, simply because partisanship does not change substantially over time.

In summary, partisanship appears to affect the way voters evaluate incumbents and their performances. Positions on issues have been a bit different. Although partisans in the 1970s and early 1980s were likely to be closer to their party's nominee on policy, the connection was less clear than between partisanship and retrospective evaluations. It is only recently that prospective evaluations have emerged as being nearly as important a set of influences on candidate choice as retrospective evaluations. It may well be that the strengthening of this relationship is a reflection of the increasingly sharp cleavages between the parties.[34] Still, policy-related evaluations are influenced in part by history and political memory and in part by the candidates' campaign strategies. Partisan attachments, then, limit the ability of a candidate to control his or her fate in the electorate, but such attachments are not entirely rigid. Candidates have some flexibility in the support they receive from partisans, especially depending on the candidates' or their predecessors' performance in office and on the policy promises they make in the campaign.

CONCLUSION

Party loyalties affect how people vote, how they evaluate issues, and how they judge the performance of the incumbent president and his party. In recent years, research has suggested not only that party loyalties affect issue preferences, perceptions, and evaluations, but that preferences, perceptions, and evaluations may also may affect those loyalties in turn. There is good reason to believe that the relationship between partisanship and these factors is more complex than any model that assumes a one-way relationship would suggest. Doubtless, evaluations of the incumbent's performance may also affect party loyalties.[35]

As we saw in this chapter, there was a substantial shift toward Republican loyalties during the 1980s; among whites, the clear advantage Democrats had enjoyed over the last four decades appeared to be gone. While the 2008 election suggests that there was at least a chance that the Democrats would enjoy a resurgence, that advantage was at least temporarily stemmed in 2012, when the two parties were near parity. To some extent, the earlier shift in party loyalties in the 1980s must have reflected Reagan's appeal and his successful performance in office, as judged by the electorate. It also appears that he was able to shift some of that appeal in George H. W. Bush's direction in 1988 both directly, by the connection between performance judgments and the vote, and indirectly, through shifts in party loyalties among white Americans. Bush lost much of the appeal he inherited, primarily because of negative assessments of his handling of the economy, and he was not able to hold on to the high approval ratings he had attained in 1991 after the success in the Persian Gulf War. In 1996 Clinton demonstrated that a president could rebound from a weak early performance as judged by the electorate and benefit from a growing economy.

The 1996 election stood as one comparable to the reelection campaigns of other recent successful incumbents, although Clinton received marks as high as or higher than Nixon's in 1972 and Reagan's in 1984 for his overall performance and for his handling of the economy. With strong retrospective judgments, the electorate basically decided that one good term deserved another.

The political landscape was dramatically different after the 1996 election compared with the time just before the 1992 election. Although the proportion of Democrats to Republicans in the electorate had been quite close for over a decade, the general impression was that Republicans had a "lock" on the White House, while the Democrats' forty-year majority in the U.S. House was thought to be unbreakable. The 1992 election demonstrated that a party has a lock on the presidency only when the public believes that party's candidate will handle the office better than the opposition. The 1994 election so reversed conventional thinking that some then considered Congress a stronghold for the Republican Party. Conventional wisdom, a lengthy history of such outcomes, and the apparent strength of the Republican delegation seemed to ensure that the GOP would gain seats in the 1998 congressional elections, but they actually lost five House seats. A Democratic resurgence seemed to be in the making. The Republicans' handling of the impeachment and Senate trial of President Clinton seemed to further set the stage for Democratic gains. Perhaps the single most surprising fact leading into the 2000 presidential race was the high approval ratings an impeached, but not convicted, Clinton held.

The question for the 2000 campaign was why Vice President Al Gore was unable to do better than essentially tie George W. Bush in the election (whether counting by popular or electoral votes). We must remember, however, how closely balanced all other key indicators were. Partisanship among whites was essentially evenly split between the two parties, with a Republican advantage in turnout at least partially offsetting the Democratic partisanship of blacks. Prospective issues, as in most election years, only modestly favored one side or the other. Retrospective evaluations, however, provided Gore with a solid edge, as did approval ratings of Clinton on the economy. The failure, then, was in Gore's inability to translate that edge in retrospective assessments into a more substantial lead in the voting booth. Retrospective evaluations were almost as strongly related to the vote in 2000 as in other recent elections, but Gore failed to push beyond that slight popular vote plurality and turn a virtual tie into an outright win.

George W. Bush, it appears, learned some lessons from 2000 for his 2004 reelection. In 2004, he faced an electorate that, like its immediate predecessors', was almost evenly balanced in its partisanship, with a slight Democratic edge in numbers of identifiers balanced by their lower propensity to turn out than Republican identifiers. Meanwhile, because of the continuing decline in the proportion of pure independents, there were fewer opportunities to win over those not already predisposed to support one party or the other. Furthermore, although Bush held an edge in prospective evaluations, Kerry held an advantage on retrospective assessments, but in both cases the edges were small. Thus with fewer independents to woo and such an even balance, the contest became a race for both the remaining independents and the weakly attached and an effort to strengthen the base—by motivating supporters to, in turn, motivate the base to actually turn out. Perhaps for this reason, we observed a strengthening of the affective component of partisan attachments—that is, a growth in strong partisans at the expense of the more weakly attached, at least during the campaign itself.

All of this was lost in 2008. Partisanship shifted toward the Democrats. The Bush administration was the least popular we have yet been able to measure. The public rejected his incumbency in general and his handling of the economy in particular. As a result, John McCain faced an unusually steep uphill battle. It is no wonder that he and Sarah Palin emphasized their "maverick" status as independent of the Bush administration. They did not, however, cut themselves loose from their partisan base. McCain might have been able to do so, but his selection of Palin as running mate indicated that his administration would be distinct from Bush's administration but nevertheless just as Republican. In view of the edge he held on prospective issues, that was a plausible choice. But the financial meltdown in the fall of 2008 probably sealed his fate. The election came down to being a partisan one, on which the Democrats turned out to hold an increased advantage, and a retrospective one, on which the Democrats held an overwhelming advantage. These two factors translated into a comfortable victory for Obama—and many other Democrats.

Much had changed between 2008 and 2012. The Democratic hold on the House and Senate was lost in a disastrous congressional election in 2010. The legislative victories of the Obama administration and Democrats in 2009 and early 2010 yielded controversy and what was originally a rather popular-based outpouring of protest that became the Tea Party. As we will see in subsequent chapters, this movement pushed Republican congressional candidates and officeholders toward the right wing of their party, deepening polarization. In any event, the last two years of Obama's first term were fundamentally altered as Republicans assumed control of the House and acquired an effective veto in the Senate through the use of the provisions surrounding filibustering. Legislative victories proved extraordinarily difficult to achieve, and partisan controversy and even bickering and name-calling added more emotion to partisan polarization in Washington. The result was that voters increasingly saw and acted on that partisan polarization among political elites. Public opinion on partisanship and evaluations of all kinds, that is, reflected the polarization they perceived, even if the public was more or less evenly balanced in their views and not evidently deeply polarized in their own issue opinions. When given a menu of polarized campaigns, the public responded with polarized choices, making partisanship and its relationship to evaluations and choices as strong an influence as ever.

Despite the shifts in partisan identification during the past half century, we should not exaggerate the change. The same two parties hold the loyalties of three-fifths of the electorate, and because at least some self-professed independents may actually be partisans, the share is probably higher. Moreover, the share of strong party identifiers, who form the most reliable core of supporters for each party, has grown from a low point of only about one in five in 1978 to about one in three in 2012. And the relationship between party identification and the vote was very strong in 2000, 2004, 2008, and 2012. Although none of these changes demonstrates that either party has won the "hearts and minds" of the electorate, they do call into question the thesis that a partisan dealignment has occurred.

Chapter 9

Candidates and Outcomes in 2012

In 1994 the Republicans unexpectedly won control of both chambers of Congress, the first time the GOP had won the House since 1952. (The only time they had controlled the Senate during that period was 1980–1986.) The electoral earthquake of 1994 shaped all subsequent Congressional contests. From 1996 on, as each subsequent election season began, there was at least some doubt about who would control the Congress after the voters chose, and there were some additional changes of control. In the next five elections after 1994 the GOP retained control of the House, although they lost seats in the first three and gained in the next two. In the Senate, the Republicans added to their majority in 1996, broke even in 1998, and then lost ground in 2000, leaving the chamber evenly divided. Then in 2002 the GOP made small gains to get a little breathing room, and in 2004 they gained a bit more. Going into the elections of 2006, the GOP still had control of Congress, but that year their luck ran out. The GOP suffered a crushing defeat, losing 30 seats in the House and 6 in the Senate, shifting control of both bodies to the Democrats, and in 2008 the Democrats achieved a second substantial gain in a row, adding 21 seats in the House and 8 seats in the Senate. Then in 2010, party fortunes reversed again: in the wake of the Great Recession the Democrats lost the House, with the Republicans picking up a net gain of 63 seats. In the Senate the GOP fell short of control, but they did gain 6 seats. In 2012 the Republicans had hoped to continue to make gains, but that was not to be. Instead the Democrats regained some ground. In the House, they won 201 seats to the Republicans' 234, a gain of 8 seats. In the Senate, the result was a 53 to 45 division in favor of the Democrats, with two independents (both of whom sided with the Democrats on control).[1] That was a gain of 2 seats.

In this chapter, we examine the pattern of congressional outcomes for 2012 and see how it compares to previous years. We explain why the 2012 results took the shape they did—what factors affected the success of incumbents seeking to return and what permitted some challengers to run better than others. We also discuss the likely impact of the election results on the politics of the 113th Congress.

Finally, we consider the implications of the 2012 results for the 2014 midterm elections and for other subsequent elections.

Patterns of Incumbency Success

One of the most dependable generalizations about American politics is that most congressional races involve incumbents and most incumbents are reelected. While this statement has been true for every set of congressional elections since World War II, the degree to which it has held varied from one election to another. Table 9-1 presents information on election outcomes for House and Senate races involving incumbents between 1954 and 2012.[2] During this period, an average of 93 percent of House incumbents and 84 percent of Senate incumbents who sought reelection were successful.

The proportion of representatives reelected in 2012 (about 90 percent) was below the thirty-election average, while the 91 percent success rate for senators was seven points above the average for that chamber. The results for the House were significantly affected by this having been the first election after the 2010 census, and so most districts had been redrawn, some substantially. This forced a number of representatives to face another incumbent in the same district, boosting the number of incumbent defeats.[3] In the Senate, there were a disproportionate number of Democratic seats up, and as we will see later the Republicans performed substantially below their expectations.

During the period covered by Table 9-1, House and Senate outcomes have sometimes been similar, and in other instances have exhibited different patterns. For example, in most years between 1968 and 1988, House incumbents were substantially more successful than their Senate counterparts. In the three elections between 1976 and 1980, House incumbents' success averaged over 93 percent, while senators averaged only 62 percent. By contrast, the success rates in the last five elections before 2000 were fairly similar. More recently, in all but two of the seven elections beginning with 2000, we have again seen some divergence with House incumbents being more successful.

These differences between the two bodies stem from at least two factors. The first is primarily statistical: House elections routinely involve around 400 incumbents, while Senate contests usually have fewer than 30. A smaller number of cases is more likely to produce volatile results over time. Thus, the proportion of successful Senate incumbents tends to vary more than that for the House. In addition, Senate races are more likely to be vigorously contested than House races, making incumbents more vulnerable. In many years a substantial number of representatives had no opponent at all, or had one who was inexperienced, underfunded, or both. Senators, on the other hand, often had strong, well-financed opponents. Thus representatives were electorally advantaged relative to

TABLE 9-1   House and Senate Incumbents and Election Outcomes, 1954–2012

Year	Incumbent running (N)	Primary defeats %	Primary defeats (N)	General election defeats %	General election defeats (N)	Reelected %	Reelected (N)
House							
1954	(407)	1.5	(6)	5.4	(22)	93.1	(379)
1956	(410)	1.5	(6)	3.7	(15)	94.9	(389)
1958	(394)	0.8	(3)	9.4	(37)	89.8	(354)
1960	(405)	1.2	(5)	6.2	(25)	92.6	(375)
1962	(402)	3.0	(12)	5.5	(22)	91.5	(368)
1964	(397)	2.0	(8)	11.3	(45)	86.6	(344)
1966	(411)	1.9	(8)	10.0	(41)	88.1	(362)
1968	(409)	1.0	(4)	2.2	(9)	96.8	(396)
1970	(401)	2.5	(10)	3.0	(12)	94.5	(379)
1972	(392)	3.3	(13)	3.3	(13)	93.4	(366)
1974	(391)	2.0	(8)	10.2	(40)	87.7	(343)
1976	(383)	0.8	(3)	3.1	(12)	96.1	(368)
1978	(382)	1.3	(5)	5.0	(19)	93.7	(358)
1980	(398)	1.5	(6)	7.8	(31)	90.7	(361)
1982	(393)	2.5	(10)	7.4	(29)	90.1	(354)
1984	(411)	0.7	(3)	3.9	(16)	95.4	(392)
1986	(393)	0.5	(2)	1.5	(6)	98.0	(385)
1988	(409)	0.2	(1)	1.5	(6)	98.3	(402)
1990	(407)	0.2	(1)	3.7	(15)	96.1	(391)
1992	(368)	5.4	(20)	6.3	(23)	88.3	(325)
1994	(387)	1.0	(4)	8.8	(34)	90.2	(349)
1996	(384)	0.5	(2)	5.5	(21)	94.0	(361)
1998	(401)	0.2	(1)	1.5	(6)	98.3	(394)
2000	(403)	0.7	(3)	1.5	(6)	97.8	(394)
2002	(398)	2.0	(8)	1.8	(7)	96.2	(383)
2004	(404)	0.5	(2)	1.7	(7)	97.8	(395)
2006	(404)	0.5	(2)	5.4	(22)	94.1	(380)
2008	(403)[a]	0.9	(4)	4.7	(19)	94.2	(380)
2010	(396)	1.0	(4)	13.6	(54)	85.4	(338)
2012	(391)	4.6	(18)	5.6	(22)	89.8	(351)
Senate							
1954	(27)	—	(0)	15	(4)	85	(23)
1956	(30)	—	(0)	13	(4)	87	(26)
1958	(26)	—	(0)	35	(9)	65	(17)
1960	(28)	—	(0)	4	(1)	96	(27)
1962	(30)	—	(0)	10	(3)	90	(27)
1964	(30)	—	(0)	7	(2)	93	(28)
1966	(29)	7	(2)	3	(1)	90	(26)
1968	(28)	14	(4)	14	(4)	71	(20)

Year	Incumbent running (N)	Primary defeats %	Primary defeats (N)	General election defeats %	General election defeats (N)	Reelected %	Reelected (N)
1970	(28)	4	(1)	11	(3)	86	(24)
1972	(26)	4	(1)	19	(5)	77	(20)
1974	(26)	4	(1)	8	(2)	88	(23)
1976	(25)	—	(0)	36	(9)	64	(16)
1978	(22)	—	(1)	27	(6)	68	(15)
1980	(29)	—	(4)	31	(9)	55	(16)
1982	(30)	—	(0)	7	(2)	93	(28)
1984	(29)	—	(0)	10	(3)	90	(26)
1986	(27)	—	(0)	22	(6)	78	(21)
1988	(26)	—	(0)	12	(3)	88	(23)
1990	(30)	—	(0)	3	(1)	97	(29)
1992	(27)	4	(1)	11	(3)	85	(23)
1994	(26)	—	(0)	8	(2)	92	(24)
1996	(20)	—	(0)	5	(1)	95	(19)
1998	(29)	—	(0)	10	(3)	90	(26)
2000	(27)	—	(0)	22	(6)	78	(21)
2002	(26)	4	(1)	8	(2)	88	(23)
2004	(25)	—	(0)	5	(1)	96	(24)
2006	(28)	—	(0)	21	(6)	79	(22)
2008	(29)	—	(0)	17	(5)	93	(24)
2010	(25)	12	(3)	8	(2)	84[a]	(21)
2012	(22)	5	(1)	5	(1)	91	(20)

Source: Compiled by the authors.

[a] In 2010 Senator Lisa Murkowski (R-AL) was defeated in the primary and then won the general election as a write-in candidate. Thus she is counted both as a primary defeat and as reelected.

senators. In the early 1990s, the competitiveness of House elections increased, reducing the relative advantage for representatives, although the election cycles since then still have seen competition in House contests confined to a more narrow range of constituencies than Senate races. We will consider this issue in more detail later in the chapter.

Having considered incumbency, we now consider political parties. Figure 9-1 shows the percentage of seats in the House and Senate held by the Democrats after each election since 1952. It graphically demonstrates how large a departure from the past the elections of 1994 through 2004 were. In House elections before 1994, the high percentage of incumbents running and the high rate of incumbent success led to fairly stable partisan control. Most important, the Democrats won a majority in the House in every election since 1954 and had won twenty consecutive national elections. This was by far the longest period of dominance of the

House by the same party in American history.[4] This winning streak was ended by the upheaval of 1994, when the GOP made a net gain of fifty-two representatives, winning 53 percent of the total seats. They held their majority in each subsequent election through 2004, although there were small shifts back to the Democrats in 1996, 1998, and 2000. Then in 2006, the Democrats took back the House and expanded their margin in 2008. The huge GOP success of 2010 restored their control, and 2012 returned them as the majority with a reduced margin.

In the Senate, previous Republican control was much more recent. They had taken the Senate in the Reagan victory of 1980 and retained it in 1982 and 1984. When the class of 1980 faced the voters again in 1986, however, the Democrats made significant gains and won back the majority. They held it until the GOP regained control in 1994, and then the Republicans expanded their margin in 1996. Then in 2000, fortune turned against them, resulting in the 50-50 division of the chamber. (This was followed a few months later by the decision of Sen. James Jeffords of Vermont to become an independent and to vote with the Democrats on organizing the chamber, shifting majority control to them until after the 2002 elections.) In 2004, the GOP gained four seats, and again reached their high watermark of 55 percent. Finally, the combined Democratic gain of fourteen seats in 2006 and 2008 restored solid control for that party, which they have retained since despite the difficult election of 2010.

The combined effect of party and incumbency in the general election of 2012 is shown in Table 9-2. Overall, the Democrats won 46 percent of the races for House seats and 57 percent of the Senate contests. Despite the sharp partisanship of both the presidential and congressional races, incumbents of both parties did well in House races. Ninety-seven percent of House Democratic incumbents in

FIGURE 9-1   Democratic Share of Seats in House and Senate, 1953–2013

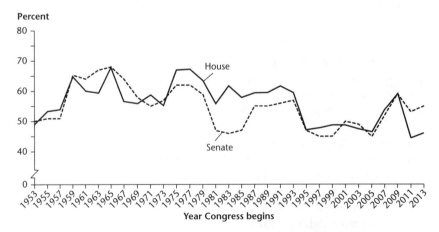

Source: 1953–1997: Norman J. Ornstein, Thomas E. Mann, and Michael J. Mlbin, *Vital Statistics on Congress 2008* (Washington, D.C.: Brookings Institution, 2008); 2009–2013: compiled by the authors.

the general election won reelection, and 93 percent of House Republicans were successful. In Senate races, all sixteen Democratic incumbents won, as did four of five GOP incumbents.

Regional Bases of Power

The geographic pattern of the 2012 outcomes in the House and Senate can be seen in the partisan breakdowns by region in Table 9-3.[5] For comparison, we also present corresponding data for 1981 (after the Republicans took control of the Senate in Reagan's first election) and for 1953 (the last Congress before 1995 in which the Republicans controlled both chambers). This series of elections reveals the enormous shifts in the regional political balance that have occurred over the last six decades. In the House, comparing 2013 to 1981, we see that the GOP share declined in the East and West, while it increased in the Midwest, South, and Border states. (In 2009, with the initial election of Obama, the Midwest had also been a region of decline for the GOP, but they bounced back substantially in the Republican landslide of 2010.) The most pronounced shifts were in the East, the Border states, and the South, with the Republican share decreasing by twelve percentage points in the first region while increasing by thirty-two and thirty-five points, respectively, in the latter two. Overall, the Democrats won a majority of House seats in all regions but the South in 2008. With the exception of the Midwest, the pattern is roughly similar in the Senate. Between 1981 and 2013, GOP gains were limited to two regions (the South and Border), while they lost ground in the West, Midwest, and East.

TABLE 9-2   House and Senate General Election Outcomes, by Party and Incumbency, 2012 (percent)

	Democratic incumbent	No incumbent			Two incumbents	Republican incumbent	Total
		Democratic seat	New seat	Republican seat			
House							
Democrats	98	78	63	5	0	7	46
Republicans	2	22	37	95	100	93	54
Total	100	100	100	100	100	100	100
(N)	158	23	19	20	2	213	435
Senate							
Democrats	100	86		40		20	76
Republicans	0	14		60		80	24
Total	100	100		100		100	100
N	16	7	0	5	0	5	33

Source: Compiled by the authors.

TABLE 9-3   Party Shares of Regional Delegations in the House and Senate, 1953, 1981, and 2013 (percent)

	1953			1981			2013		
Region	Dems (%)	Reps (%)	(N)	Dems (%)	Reps (%)	(N)	Dems (%)	Reps (%)	(N)
House									
East	35	65	(116)	56	44	(105)	68	32	(79)
Midwest	23	76	(118)	47	53	(111)	38	62	(86)
West	33	67	(57)	51	49	(76)	62	38	(102)
South	94	6	(106)	64	36	(108)	29	71	(138)
Border	68	32	(38)	69	31	(35)	37	63	(30)
Total	49	51	(435)	56	44	(435)	46	54	(435)
Senate									
East	25	75	(20)	50	50	(20)	85	15	(20)
Midwest	14	86	(22)	41	59	(22)	50	50	(22)
West	45	55	(22)	35	65	(26)	62	38	(26)
South	100	0	(22)	55	45	(22)	27	73	(22)
Border	70	30	(10)	70	30	(10)	50	50	(10)
Total	49	51	(96)	47	53	(100)	45	55	(100)

Source: Compiled by the authors.

The 2013 results are even more interesting when viewed from the longer historical perspective. In 1953 there were sharp regional differences in party representation in both houses. These differences diminished significantly by 1981, but new and substantial deviations developed subsequently. The most obvious changes occurred in the East and the South. In 1953 the Republicans held nearly two-thirds of the House seats in the East, but by 2013 their share had fallen to less than one-third. Indeed, in New England, historically a bastion of Republican strength, the GOP did not win even one of the twenty-one seats in 2012. The Republican decline in eastern Senate seats over the period was even greater, down from 75 percent to only 15 percent. In the South, on the other hand, the percentage of House seats held by Democrats declined from 94 percent in 1953 to 29 percent in 2013. In 1953 the Democrats held all twenty-two southern Senate seats, but in 2013 they controlled only six.

This change in the partisan share of the South's seats in Congress has had an important impact on that region's influence within the two parties. The South used to be the backbone of Democratic congressional representation. This, and the tendency of southern members to build seniority, gave southerners disproportionate power within the Democratic Party in Congress. Because of declining Democratic electoral success in the region, the numerical strength of southern Democrats within their party in Congress has waned. In 1953, with the Republicans in control of both chambers, southerners accounted for around 45 percent of Democratic seats in the House and Senate. By the 1970s, southern strength had declined, to stabilize at between 25 and 30 percent of Democratic seats. In 2013, southerners accounted for 20 percent of Democratic House seats, and only 11 percent of Democratic senators.

The South's share of Republican congressional representation presents the reverse picture. Minuscule at the end of World War II, it steadily grew, reaching about 20 percent in the House after the 1980 elections and 42 percent after 2012. As a consequence of these changes, southern influence has declined in the Democratic Party and grown in the GOP, to the point that southerners have often held a disproportionate share of the Republican leadership positions in both houses of Congress. Because southerners of both parties tend to be more conservative than their colleagues from other regions, these shifts in regional strength have tended to make the Democratic Party in Congress more liberal and the Republican Party more conservative.[6]

Other regional changes since 1953, while not as striking as those in the South and East, are also significant. In the 1953 House, the Republicans controlled the West by a two-to-one margin, and the Midwest by three to one. In 2013 they were a 38 percent minority in the West, and had a 62 percent share in the Midwest. The Senate also exhibited shifts away from substantial Republican strength in the West and Midwest. On the other hand, with the increased Republican control of the South and Democratic dominance in the East, regional differences in party shares are more prominent in 2013 than they were in 1981, and partisan representation is only a little more regionally homogeneous in the Congress of 2013 than it was in the Congress of 1953.

National Forces in the Congressional Elections

The patterns of outcomes discussed above were shaped by a variety of influences. As with most congressional elections, the most important among these were the resources available to individual candidates and how those resources were distributed between the parties in specific races. We will discuss those matters shortly, but first we consider potential and actual national-level influences particular to 2012.

The first national force to assess is whether there was a pattern in public opinion that advantaged one party or the other. Such *national tides* may occur in presidential years or in midterms, and they can have a profound impact on the outcomes of congressional elections. Often these tides flow from reaction to presidents or presidential candidates. For example, in 1964 the presidential landslide victory of Lyndon B. Johnson over Barry M. Goldwater carried over to major Democratic gains in both congressional chambers, and Ronald Reagan's ten-point margin over Jimmy Carter in 1980 helped Republicans achieve an unexpected majority in the Senate and major gains in the House. Similarly, negative public reactions to events in the first two years of Bill Clinton's presidency played a major part in the Republicans' congressional victories in 1994, and dissatisfaction with President Bush significantly enhanced the Democrats' campaign to retake the House in 2006.

Clearly, 2012 was an election without a significant national tide working in favor of either the Democrats or the Republicans. This is not surprising after three wave elections in a row in 2006–2010. We saw in Chapter 2 that the presidential race was close all year and that the president's approval rating was mediocre but not terrible. Many House and Senate races were deemed up for grabs, but the proportion of each party's seats that were projected as competitive was similar. Moreover, unlike what would be usual for an election with a partisan wave, the number of seats that were classified as close remained fairly stable over the election cycle. Figure 9-2 presents the number of Democratic and Republican House seats that political analyst Charlie Cook estimated to be highly competitive at various points in the 2011–2012 period.[7] The total number of competitive seats increased only a small amount, from fifty-five to sixty-five, between August 2011 and November 2012. Moreover, the ratio between the parties was also fairly constant: in August 2011, 55 percent of the competitive seats were held by Republicans, while in November of the following year it was 58 percent.

FIGURE 9-2   Competitive House Districts, 2011–2012

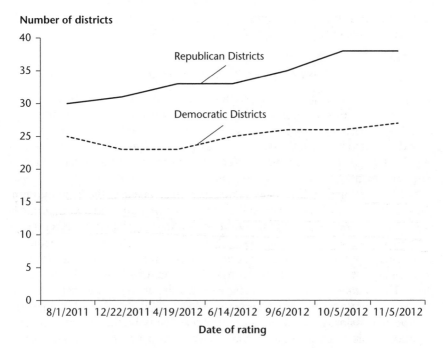

Source: Compiled by the authors from editions of the *Cook Political Report* on listed dates.

Another potential national influence is public reaction to the performance of Congress. In the 1996 presidential race, for example, Clinton and the Democrats tried to focus public attention on what they claimed was the extremism and excesses of the new GOP congressional majority, albeit with only very limited success.[8] In 2012 public opinion toward Congress had turned very negative. In almost every major survey taken during the year leading up to the election, approval of the job Congress was doing was below 20 percent. However, given that congressional control in the two chambers was split between the parties, neither appeared in benefit electorally; attitudes were negative toward both parties. For example, in a CNN/ORC poll conducted just before the elections, 37 percent of respondents said they approved of the job Democratic leaders in Congress were doing, while 59 percent disapproved. The parallel figures for Republican leaders were 28 percent approved and 66 percent disapproved.[9]

Efforts of National Parties and Their Allies

One important national-level influence is the efforts of congressional party leaders and their allies to influence the races. Before the 1980s, the activities of national parties in congressional elections were very limited. Individual candidates were mostly self-starters who were largely on their own in raising money and planning strategy. More recently, this situation has changed substantially, and party leaders and organizations are now heavily involved in recruiting and funding their candidates.[10] As we will see below, the quality of candidates and their level of funding are two of the central determinants of election outcomes. Thus both the short-term and long-term fates of the parties in Congress provided incentives for them to be active in efforts to improve their circumstances in these respects.

Recruiting Candidates

National party organizations are now continually active in candidate recruiting and fund-raising. As soon as the voting in one election ends, activity for the next begins. Democrats' main concern after their huge defeat in the 2010 midterms was that many of their senior members would become frustrated by their minority status (and the expectation that it would continue) and retire. The situation was exacerbated by the fact that many districts were disrupted by the national redistricting that followed the 2010 census. National campaign leaders and their staffs were active in 2011 and 2012 trying to stave off possible retirements and to entice other candidates to seek office. The plans of individual candidates were monitored and possible strategies for eventually taking back the majority were discussed. The perceived prospects of success were key elements of the strategic calculations of potential recruits. It is much easier for a party to persuade a prospect to run if that party's national prospects look bright.

In the end both parties were moderately successful in staving off House retirements, with only twenty-five representatives (eleven Republicans and fourteen Democrats) opting to leave office entirely, although thirteen additional members sought higher office. Proportionately, retirements were greater in the Senate. There were thirty-three seats up in 2012, nine held by Republicans and twenty-four by Democrats. In twelve of these the sitting senator (five Republicans and seven Democrats) declined to run.

Both the Democratic and Republican party campaign organizations asserted that they had the chance to make gains in 2012, and they diligently searched for candidates. The vice chairman of recruitment of the National Republican Congressional Committee (NRCC) contended in July 2011: "Not only did we already do well last year, but we'll have more opportunities to win more seats next year." Another recruiter indicated that he had spoken to twenty-five potential candidates and seven had already announced.[11] The Democratic Congressional Campaign Committee (DCCC) faced a more demanding mission than their opponents. To maintain their majority, the GOP needed only to minimize net losses. To regain majority status, the Democrats had to gain twenty-five seats, a daunting task when one recognizes that the last time the president's party had gained that many seats was in 1964, forty-eight years earlier. To have a chance, the DCCC decided to cast a wide net. In January 2012 they announced a target list of fifty-seven Republican seats, more than twice the size of previous cycles.[12] One source of candidates they targeted was those who had run in 2010 but failed because of the Republican tide. Another included people from outside the political arena, with the idea that they might be appealing to voters unhappy with traditional politicians. For example, DCCC chairman Rep. Steve Israel of New York approached Orlando, Florida, police chief Val Demings about running; she indicated she had never thought of seeking a congressional seat. "Then you're the perfect candidate," he said.[13] (Demings ran, but fell short with over 48 percent of the vote.) Two other examples were former astronaut Jose Hernandez and emergency room doctor Raul Ruiz. Both faced GOP incumbents in California; the former lost and the latter won.

With regard to Senate seats, the prestige of the office, coupled with greater competitiveness on average, tends to draw a lot of strong candidates without the effort of party leaders. But they still play a significant role, especially in races that look like they may be difficult. For example, in 2012 Democratic Sen. Kent Conrad of North Dakota announced he was retiring. Given that the state had a strong tilt to the Republicans in presidential contests, many observers thought that any Democrat would be an underdog for the Senate. However, the national Democrats persuaded former state Attorney General Heidi Heitkamp to run, and she narrowly won.

The Republicans had a particular problem with recruiting. In 2010 party leaders had endorsed a number of candidates based on perceptions of their electability. But many conservatives aligned with the Tea Party movement objected to what they saw as the establishment trying to dictate to the people. In states like

Delaware, Nevada, and Colorado, insurgents defeated the leadership-backed choices in primaries, but went on to lose the general election. Hoping to avoid a repeat of that pattern, Sen. John Cornyn of Texas, the chairman of the National Republican Senatorial Committee (NRSC), promised that his group would remain neutral until any primary contests were resolved.[14] This promise, however, did not keep party leaders from seeking to persuade strong candidates to run, and they believed that they had done well. Senate Minority Leader Mitch McConnell (R-KY) touted the recruitment of three members of the House and former governors in North Dakota, Montana, New Mexico, and Hawaii.[15] This case also demonstrates that success in recruiting does not guarantee general-election success; all four of those candidates lost.

Sometimes party leaders even try to persuade potential candidates not to run, usually to clear the way for another whom they perceive to be stronger. For example, in Arizona the former state Democratic party chairman had announced his candidacy and raised money, but he withdrew when Richard Carmona, former Surgeon General of the United States, also announced. Carmona had been an independent and was recruited by Obama and Democratic Senate Majority Leader Harry Reid, among others.[16] (Carmona ended up losing in a close race.) Another such effort occurred among the Republicans even after their candidate had been chosen. Rep. Todd Akin of Missouri won a contested primary for the right to face Democratic Sen. Claire McCaskill, who was regarded as extremely vulnerable. However, during the campaign Akin was talking about abortion policy and he claimed that an exception for rape in an abortion ban was unnecessary because, in instances of what he termed "legitimate rape," women's bodies blocked pregnancy. The remark created a storm of criticism, and Republican strategists worried that the controversy would undermine other of the party's candidates. As a consequence many party leaders called on Akin to withdraw from the race, and Karl Rove's Super PAC and the NRSC indicated they would withhold funding. Akin refused to withdraw, and in November McCaskill was reelected with almost 55 percent of the vote.[17]

Money and Other Aid

In addition to recruitment, party leaders have grown increasingly active in fund-raising, pursuing many alternative strategies. For example, top party leaders solicit donations to the congressional campaign committees like the NRCC and the DCCC, and they appear at fund-raisers for individual candidates in their districts. The amounts they raise are considerable. From the beginning of 2011 until May 1, 2012, Minority Leader Nancy Pelosi of California brought in $43.4 million, even more than she had raised two years earlier as Speaker. But majority status is an asset for fund-raising, and Speaker John Boehner of Ohio did substantially better than Pelosi, amassing $70 million in contributions for the Republicans.[18]

In both parties, raising campaign funds for the party has become a prominent obligation for members who hold or want leadership posts and committee chairmanships, and the amounts they raise are a significant portion of money spent in campaigns. For example, during the two years leading up to the 2008 elections, Rep. Charles Rangel of New York, then the Democratic chairman of the tax-writing Ways and Means Committee, raised an impressive $5 million. He transferred over $1.1 million of this to other Democratic candidates, including $435,000 to the DCCC.[19] Indeed the parties set contribution targets for their incumbents (which they term "dues"). Of course, many members would prefer to retain the money they raise for their own use, and sometimes party leaders must pressure their colleagues to meet their obligations. In March 2012, for example, the DCCC warned Democratic representatives that members who had failed to pay their dues would not be guaranteed a hotel reservation at the Democratic national convention later in the year.[20]

Party leaders are able to do more to help candidates' reelection efforts than just raise or spend campaign money, at least for the House majority. Because the majority party has almost total control over the floor agenda and the content of bills, it can add or remove provisions in bills that will enhance their members' reelection chances, or permit vulnerable colleagues to bring their popular bills to the floor, thus enhancing their reputations.

In addition to funding by the formal party organizations like the NRCC, the parties' congressional candidates are receiving increasing support from Super PACs.[21] Between June 1 and September 8, 2012, about $130 million was spent on television advertising in Senate contests, and 39 percent of that was spent by outside groups. That was an increase from the 22 percent spent during the same period in the 2010 contests.[22] While the lion's share of the Super PAC funding went to Senate contests, money from those sources was increasingly going to House races as well.

Reapportionment and Redistricting

After every census, the new population figures are used to calculate how many House seats each state is entitled to. This leads to some redistribution of seats among the states (called reapportionment). Then all forty-three states with more than one seat must draw new district lines to make the district populations as equal as possible (redistricting). It might seem odd to term a process that takes place separately within each individual state "national," but because of the electoral tide in favor of the GOP in 2010, it is appropriate this time.

Each state determines how it will draw its district lines, but most have maintained the traditional historical format of having the lines drawn by their legislatures and codified in a state law. Because of the Republicans' 2010 triumph, they dominated the redistricting process leading up to 2012, and they sought to use their position to create districts that would protect representatives from their party. The common historical term for this seeking of partisan advantage is *gerrymandering*. Of the forty-three states with two or more districts, the GOP controlled the process in eighteen (with 202 House seats), while the Democrats controlled only six states (with 47 seats). This substantial advantage for the GOP permitted them to maintain control of the House by a comfortable margin even though Democratic candidates won the national House vote by 49.2 percent to 48.0 percent for the GOP.[23] Twelve states had divided partisan control; they had 87 seats. Finally, seven states (with 92 seats) used some form of commission instead of the legislature to draw lines.

As one would expect, these different contexts provided differential advantages to the two parties. In the states where Republicans were in control, the net change was a loss of two Democrats and a gain of six Republicans. (The difference in the partisan totals is because nine of the eighteen states gained or lost seats in the reapportionment.) In the states where Democrats were in control, on the other hand, they gained three seats and the GOP lost five. So each party was able to secure gains where it controlled the districting process. This was particularly true in larger states with more total seats because that gave the designers more options. For example, in North Carolina (with thirteen seats) the Republicans gained three representatives and the Democrats lost three. In Illinois, on the other hand, with eighteen seats after a loss of one in the reapportionment and the Democrats in control, the process cost the GOP five seats and the Democrats gained four. An example of the potential magnitude of the advantage that gerrymandering can offer comes from Pennsylvania, where the Republicans controlled the process. Before reapportionment they held twelve of the state's nineteen seats. Then Pennsylvania lost one seat due to slow population growth and the GOP drew the new district lines. The 2012 result was five Democrats and thirteen Republicans even though the Democrats received 50.3 percent of the statewide House vote to the GOP's 48.8 percent.[24]

In the states where partisan control was divided, the Democrats gained two seats and the Republicans lost four. And in the commission states, the Republican total declined by five, while the number of seats for the Democrats increased by the same number. The most striking and consequential state in this context was California, which had chosen by referenda passed in 2008 and 2010 to create a state commission (made up of a mix of Republicans, Democrats, and independents) that would draw lines for both congressional and state legislative districts. In addition, the plan instituted a so-called jungle primary system, in which all candidates for a particular office run together in a combined primary, and the top two finishers (regardless of party) move on to the general election. Supporters of this process argued that it would yield more moderate candidates who would not be so constrained by the extremes in the parties' bases.

The new commission produced a plan for the congressional districts that (as many supporters of the referenda had hoped) substantially changed the pattern of district lines and disrupted the political fortunes of many incumbents. California congressional election results had been remarkably stable during the previous decade. In the five election cycles from 2002 to 2010, only one incumbent had been defeated for reelection. That changed in 2012. When the districting plan was initially announced in May 2011, twelve of the fifty-three districts contained two or more incumbents, although most of those conflicts were rectified by candidates changing districts or deciding not to seek reelection. Even so, the primary in June 2012 yielded two districts with two Democratic incumbents and six other districts where both finalists were from the same party. Overall the new districting plan resulted in fourteen new representatives from California. Seven incumbents were defeated: two Democrats by other Democratic incumbents, two other Democrats by non-incumbents from the same party, and three Republicans by Democratic challengers. In addition, seven members decided not to run again; one of them (Democrat Bob Filner) ran for mayor of San Diego and won. And beyond the incumbent defeats, six other members were reelected with less than 55 percent of the vote. Thus the new districting regime succeeded in producing significantly more turnover and competition for Congress. It will be a while before we can tell whether it will induce more moderation among the members chosen.

In summary, except for a few states, the impact of redistricting was limited, at least in the context of a national election with no strong trend toward either party. The substantial advantage the Republicans had in controlling the process permitted them to strengthen the positions of many of their freshman members who might otherwise have been much more vulnerable, but they were not able to turn that advantage into a substantial increase in GOP seats. For the Democrats, their entire gain of eight seats can be accounted for by districting in two states: California and Illinois. Without those two, the entire national House contest would have been a wash. We will discuss some future implications of the new districts below.

CANDIDATES' RESOURCES AND ELECTION OUTCOMES

Seats in the House and Senate are highly valued posts for which candidates compete vigorously. In contests for these offices, candidates draw on every resource they have. To explain the results of congressional elections, we must consider the comparative advantages and disadvantages of the various candidates. In this section we will discuss the most significant resources available to candidates and the impact of those resources on the outcomes of congressional elections.

Candidate Quality

The personal abilities that foster electoral success can be a major political asset. Many constituencies today do not offer a certain victory for one of the two major parties, and for those that do strongly tilt to one party there is often a contested primary, so election outcomes usually depend heavily on candidate quality. A strong, capable candidate is a significant asset for a party; a weak, inept one is a liability that is difficult to overcome. In his study of the activities of House members in their districts, Richard F. Fenno Jr., described how members try to build support within their constituencies, establishing bonds of trust between constituents and their representative.[25] Members attempt to convey to their constituents a sense that they are qualified for their job, that they identify with their constituents, and that they empathize with constituents and their problems. Challengers of incumbents and candidates for open seats must engage in similar activities to win support. The winner of a contested congressional election will usually be the candidate who is better able to establish these bonds of support among constituents and to convince them that he or she is the person for the job (or that the opponent is not).

One indicator of candidate quality is previous success at winning elective office. The more important the office a candidate has held, the more likely it is that he or she has overcome significant competition to obtain the office. Moreover, the visibility and reputation for performance that usually accompany public office can also be a significant electoral asset. For example, state legislators running for House seats can claim that they have experience that has prepared them for congressional service. State legislators may also have built successful organizations that are useful in conducting congressional campaigns. Finally, previous success in an electoral arena suggests that experienced candidates are more likely to be able to run stronger campaigns than candidates without previous success or experience. Less adept candidates are likely to have been screened out at lower levels of office competition. For these and other reasons, an experienced candidate tends to have an electoral advantage over a candidate who has held no previous elected office.[26] Moreover, the higher the office previously held, the stronger the candidate will tend to be in the congressional contest.[27]

In Table 9-4, we present data showing which candidates were successful in 2012, controlling for office background, party, and incumbency.[28] In House contests, the vast majority of candidates who challenged incumbents lost regardless of their office background or party, although those with office experience did better than those who had none. The impact of candidate quality is stronger in races without incumbents. Here candidates who had been state legislators were very successful, and those with other elective experience won at a higher rate than those without any elective office experience. In Senate races, because there was only a single incumbent loss, no pattern is visible. For non-incumbent candidates, those with stronger office backgrounds generally did better.

Given the importance of candidate quality, it is worth noting that there has been substantial variation in the proportion of experienced challengers over time. During the 1980s the proportion of House incumbents facing challengers who had previously won elective office declined. In 1980, 17.6 percent of incumbents faced such challenges; in 1984, 14.7 percent did; in 1988, only 10.5 percent did. In 1992, due largely to perceptions of incumbent vulnerability because of redistricting and scandal, the proportion rose to 23.5 percent, but in 1996 it was back down to 16.5 percent and it remained at that level in 2000.[29] In 2004, however, there was a substantial resurgence in the number of experienced candidates in both parties, with 22.4 percent of the total challengers having previously held elective office, followed by a decline again in 2008 to 14.8 percent. In 2012, the proportion rebounded again to 20 percent.[30]

TABLE 9-4   Success in House and Senate Elections, Controlling for Office Background, Party, and Incumbency, 2012 (percent)

	Candidate is opponent of . . .		No incumbent in district	
	Democratic incumbent	Republican incumbent	Democratic candidate	Republican candidate
House				
State Legislature/U.S. House	0 (5)	7.8 (13)	64.3 (14)	70 (10)
Other Elected	12 (25)	15.2 (33)	68 (25)	54.5 (22)
No Elected	.8 (128)	5.4 (167)	19 (21)	40 (30)
Senate				
U.S. House	0 (4)	0 (1)	100 (5)	25 (4)
Statewide elected	0 (1)	NA	100 (3)	20 (5)
Other Elected	0 (4)	0 (2)	0 (1)	100 (1)
No elected	0 (7)	33.3 (3)	0 (1)	0 (1)

Source: Data on office backgrounds were taken from issues of the *Cook Political Report*, supplemented by other sources. Compiled by the authors.

Whether experienced politicians actually run for the House or Senate is not an accident. These are significant strategic decisions made by politicians, and they have much to lose if they make the wrong choice. The choices will be governed by factors related to the perceived chance of success, the potential value of the new office compared to what will be lost if the candidate fails, and the costs of running.[31] The chances of success of the two major parties vary from election to election, both locally and nationally. Therefore, each election offers a different mix of experienced and inexperienced candidates for the House and Senate from the two parties.

The most influential factor in whether a potential candidate will run is whether there is an incumbent in the race. High reelection rates tend to discourage potentially strong challengers from running, which in turn makes it even more likely that the incumbents will win. In addition to the general difficulty of challenging incumbents, factors related to specific election years (both nationally and in a particular district) will affect decisions to run. For example, the Republican Party had particular difficulty recruiting strong candidates in 1986 because of fears about a potential backlash from the Iran-Contra scandals. And the 2008 decline in experienced candidates just cited was likely mainly due to the minority Republicans being unable to recruit strong candidates in many districts because the electoral environment was perceived to be negative for their party. On the other hand, recent research indicates that potential House candidates are most strongly influenced in their decision by their perceived chances of winning their party's nomination.[32] Moreover, the actions of incumbents may influence the choices of potential challengers. For example, building up a large reserve of campaign funds between elections may dissuade some possible opponents, although analysis of Senate contests (which usually involve experienced challengers) indicates that this factor does not have a systematic impact in those races.[33]

As we have seen, most congressional races do not involve challengers who have previous office experience. Given their slight chance of winning, why do challengers without experience run at all? As Jeffrey S. Banks and D. Roderick Kiewiet pointed out, although the chances of success against incumbents may be small for such candidates, such a race may still be their best chance of ever winning a seat in Congress.[34] If inexperienced challengers were to put off their candidacies until a time when there is no incumbent, their opposition would likely include multiple experienced candidates from both parties. Moreover, as David Canon demonstrated, previous office experience is an imperfect indicator of candidate quality, because some candidates without such experience can still have significant political assets and be formidable challengers.[35] For example, four former television journalists who had never previously held office won House seats in 1992, and three of them defeated incumbents. They were able to build on their substantial name recognition among voters to win nomination and election.[36] For more recent examples, consider two 2000 contests, one from each chamber. The Republican candidate for the House in Nebraska's third district was Tom Osborne, the extremely popular former head coach of the University of Nebraska's football team. Osborne was elected to an open seat with a phenomenal 82 percent of the vote. In the New York Senate race, the very visible (and ultimately successful) Democratic candidate was then first lady, Hillary Rodham Clinton.

Incumbency

One reason most incumbents win is that incumbency itself is a significant resource. To be more precise, incumbency is not a single resource, but rather a status that usually gives a candidate a variety of benefits. In some respects, incumbency works to a candidate's advantage automatically. For example, incumbents tend to be more visible to voters than their challengers.[37] Less automatic, but very important, incumbents usually tend to be viewed more favorably than challengers. Moreover, at least a plurality of the electorate in most districts will identify with the incumbent's political party, and this pattern has become stronger over the last couple of decades. Incumbents can also use their status to gain advantages. Incumbents usually raise and spend more money than challengers, and they usually have a better developed and more experienced campaign organization. They also have assets, provided at public expense, such as a staff and franking privileges (free postage for mail to their constituents), that both help them perform their jobs and provide electoral benefits.

Increasing Electoral Margins

From the mid-1960s through the late 1980s, the margins by which incumbents were reelected increased (the pattern was less clear and more erratic in Senate elections than in House elections).[38] These changing patterns interested analysts primarily because they believed that the disappearance of marginal incumbents means less congressional turnover and a House that would be less responsive to the electorate.

Edward R. Tufte offered an early explanation for the increased incumbency margins by arguing that redistricting had protected incumbents of both parties.[39] This argument seemed plausible because the increase in margins occurred about the same time as the massive redistrictings required by Supreme Court decisions of the mid-1960s. But other analysts showed that incumbents had won by larger margins both in states that had redistricted and in those that had not, as well as in Senate contests.[40] Thus redistricting could not be the major reason for the change.

Another explanation offered for the increase in incumbents' margins was the growth in the perquisites of members and the greater complexity of government. Morris P. Fiorina noted that in the post–New Deal period the level of federal services and the bureaucracy that administers them had grown tremendously.[41] More complex government means that many people will encounter problems in receiving services, and people who have problems frequently contact their representative to complain and seek help. Fiorina contended that in the mid-1960s new members of Congress emphasized such constituency problem solving more than their predecessors. This expanded constituency service developed into a reservoir of electoral support. Although analyses of the impact of constituency services have produced mixed conclusions, it is likely that the growth of these services offers a partial explanation for changing incumbent vote margins and for the incumbency advantage generally.[42]

The declining impact of party loyalties provided a third explanation for the growth in incumbent vote margins, either alone or in interaction with other factors. Until the mid-1960s there was a very strong linkage between party identification and congressional voting behavior. Most Americans identified with a political party, many identified strongly, and most voters supported the candidate of their chosen party. Subsequently, however, the impact of party identification decreased, as we will see in Chapter 10. John A. Ferejohn, drawing on data from the National Election Studies, showed that the strength of party ties weakened and that within any given category of party identification the tendency to support the candidate of one's party declined.[43] An analysis by Albert D. Cover showed that between 1958 and 1974 voters who did not identify with the party of a congressional incumbent were increasingly more likely to defect from their party and support the incumbent, while there had been no increase in defections from party identification by voters of the same party as incumbents.[44] Thus weakened party ties produced a substantial net benefit for incumbents,[45] although, as we saw in Chapter 8 (and will discuss further in Chapter 10), party loyalties among the electorate have grown stronger in recent years.

The Trend Reversed

Whatever the relative importance of these factors, and the others we will discuss, in explaining the increase in incumbents' victory margins, the increase continued through the 1980s, as the data in Table 9-5 show, peaking at 68.2 percent in 1986 and 1988. These data are only for races in which both parties ran candidates. Thus they exclude contests where an incumbent ran unopposed. Such races were also increasing in number during this period; therefore, the data actually understate the growth in incumbents' margins.

Then, in 1990, something changed. The average share of the vote for incumbents declined by nearly five percentage points. The decline was, moreover, not a result of a shift of voters toward one party, as with the decline from 1980 to 1982; both parties' incumbents suffered. Rather, the shift in incumbents' electoral fortunes was

TABLE 9-5   Average Vote Percentages of House Incumbents, Selected Years, 1974–2012

Year	Democrats	Republicans	All incumbents
1974	68.5	55.2	61.7
1980	64.0	67.9	65.5
1982	67.9	59.9	64.1
1984	64.2	68.2	65.9
1986	70.2	65.6	68.2
1988	68.8	67.5	68.2
1990	65.8	59.8	63.5
1992	63.3	62.9	63.1
1994	60.0	67.6	62.8
1996	66.6	60.7	63.3
1998	65.0	61.6	63.3
2000	67.2	62.9	65.1
2002	66.4	66.1	66.3
2004	67.8	63.9	65.4
2006	71.5	60.0	65.0
2008	69.0	61.0	65.0
2010	60.9	72.0	64.7
2012	67.8	62.7	64.9

Source: 1974–1990: "House Incumbents' Average Vote Percentage," *Congressional Quarterly Weekly Report*, November 10, 1990, 3800; 1994: *New York Times*, November 10, 1994; 1992 and 1996: *USA Today*, November 8, 1996, 4A; 1998–2012: compiled by the authors.

Note: These figures include only races where both major parties ran candidates. Thus they exclude contests in which an incumbent ran unopposed.

apparently the result of what was called the "anti-incumbent mood" among the voters. Early in 1990 pollsters and commentators began to perceive stronger anti-Congress sentiments in the electorate.[46] For the first time, analysts began to question whether incumbency remained the asset it used to be.

There was, of course, nothing new about Congress being unpopular; Congress had long suffered ups and downs in approval, just as the president had. What changed in 1990 was that Congress's unpopularity appeared to be undermining the approval of individual members by their own constituents. Yet as the data presented in Table 9-1 show, even though there was a drop in the average percentage of the vote received by incumbents in 1990, the rate of reelection still reached 96 percent. The decline in vote margins was not great enough to produce a rash of defeats. Many observers wondered, however, whether 1990 was the beginning of a new trend: would incumbents' electoral drawing power continue to decline?

In 1992, scandals damaged many representatives of both parties, and among the public the evaluation of Congress was very low. Opponents of incumbents emphasized that they were "outsiders" and not "professional politicians" (even when they had substantial political experience). The results from 1992 show that incumbents' share of the vote dropped a bit more. Republicans rebounded a little from their bad 1990 showing, while Democrats fell more than two percentage points. Yet again, however, the casualty rate among incumbents who ran in the general election was lower than many expected: 93 percent were reelected. (It is important to note, however, that a substantial number of incumbents had already been defeated in the primaries, and many weak incumbents had retired.) Then in 1994, although there was only a slight additional drop in incumbents' share of the vote overall, the drop was greater (and concentrated) for Democrats, and their casualty rate was high. The result was the loss of their majority. Next in 1996, there was a slight rebound in incumbents' vote share, with Democrats increasing sharply while the GOP fell. That vote shift translated into eighteen Republican incumbents defeated, but only three Democrats. Finally, the results from 2000 through 2012 fall in between the highs of the mid-1980s and the lows of 1994 and 1996. Indeed, during those years the average incumbent vote percentage was virtually identical each year, although the averages for the parties have varied with the electoral climate.

This discussion illustrates that incumbents' vote margins and incumbents' reelection success are related but distinct phenomena.[47] When—as was true in the 1980s—the average share of the vote received by incumbents is very high, they can lose a lot of ground before a large number of defeats occur. What appears to have occurred in 1990 is that many incumbents were subjected to vigorous contests for the first time in years. Such challenges were then repeated or extended to additional incumbents in 1992, 1994, and 1996. Potential candidates apparently looked at the political situation and concluded that incumbents who had previously looked unbeatable could now potentially be defeated, and there was a substantial increase in the number of candidates for Congress. These vigorous contests by challengers who were stronger than usual resulted in a decrease in the share of the vote received by many incumbents. Over the years, however, the increased competition caught up with a greater number of incumbents. Now, in the twenty-first century, the aggregate level of competition varies from election to election, largely due to the political context and to the deliberate crafting of safe districts for both parties' incumbents.

Campaign Spending

A third resource that strongly affects congressional elections is campaign spending. Campaign spending has received a great deal of attention in the last four decades because researchers gained access to more dependable data than had previously been available.[48] The data on spending have consistently shown that incumbents usually outspend their challengers, often by large margins, and that through the early 1990s, the disparity had increased.[49] (As we shall see shortly, more recent data show significant changes.)

Disparities in campaign spending are linked to the increase in incumbents' election margins. Beginning in the 1960s, congressional campaigns relied more heavily on campaign techniques that cost money—for example, media time, campaign consulting, and direct mailing—and these became increasingly expensive. At the same time, candidates were progressively less likely to have available pools of campaign workers from established party organizations or from interest groups. This made using expensive media and direct mail strategies relatively more important. Most challengers are unable to raise significant campaign funds. Neither individuals nor groups interested in the outcomes of congressional elections like to throw money away; before making contributions they usually need to be convinced that the candidate has a chance. Yet we have seen that in most election years few incumbents have been beaten. Thus it is often difficult to convince potential contributors that their money will produce results, and contributions are often not forthcoming. Most challengers are thus at a strategic disadvantage, and they are unable to raise sufficient funds to wage a competitive campaign.[50]

It is the ability to compete, rather than the simple question of relative amounts of spending, that is at the core of the issue. We have noted that incumbents have many inherent advantages that the challenger must overcome if he or she hopes to win. But often the money is not there to overcome them. In 2012, for example, over 33 percent of challengers spent $25,000 or less, and exactly half spent $75,000 or less. With so little money available, challengers are unable to make themselves visible to the electorate or to convey a convincing message.[51] Under such circumstances, most voters—being unaware of the positions, or perhaps even the existence, of the challenger—vote for the incumbent.

Data from 2012 on campaign spending and election outcomes seem consistent with this argument, and they show patterns similar to those exhibited in other recent elections.[52] Linking spending to outcomes, Table 9-6 shows the relationship between the incumbent's share of the vote in the 2012 House elections and the amount of money spent by the challenger. Clearly, there is a strong negative relationship between how much challengers spend and how well incumbents do. In races where challengers spent less than $26,000, 97 percent of the incumbents received 60 percent or more of the vote. At the other end of the spectrum, in races where challengers spent $800,000 or more, 92 percent of the incumbents received less than 60 percent of the vote, and more than half got less than 55 percent. These results are consistent with those in earlier House elections for which comparable data are available.[53]

These findings are reinforced by other research that shows that challenger spending has a greater influence on election outcomes than does incumbent spending.[54] This generalization has been questioned on methodological grounds,[55] but further research by Gary C. Jacobson reinforced his earlier findings. Using both aggregate and survey data, he found that "the amount spent by the challenger is far more important in accounting for voters' decisions than is the amount of spending by the incumbent."[56] More recently Jacobson emphasized the importance of incumbent spending. Comparing successful House challenges to those who are unsuccessful, he noted that the successful candidates were more likely to be familiar to voters. He wrote, "It is no mystery why winning challengers reached so many voters and were so much more familiar to them. They ran much better financed campaigns than did the losers."[57] Analysis of Senate elections has also resulted in conflicting conclusions.[58]

Of course, challengers who appear to have good prospects will find it easier to raise money than those whose chances seem slim. Thus one might wonder whether these data simply reflect the fulfillment of expectations, in which money

TABLE 9-6   Incumbents' Share of the Vote in the 2012 House Elections, by Challenger Campaign Spending (percent)

| Challenger spending | Incumbents' share of two-party vote | | | | | |
	70% or more	60%–69%	55%–59%	Less than 55%	Total	N
$0–$25,000	65.5	31.9	2.5	0.0	99.9	119
$26,000–$75,000	35.7	53.6	10.7	0.0	100.0	56
$76,000–$199,000	19.1	66.0	14.9	0.0	100.0	47
$200,000–$399,000	10.7	53.6	32.1	3.6	100.0	28
$400,000–$799,000	11.5	38.5	42.3	7.7	100.0	26
$800,000 and up	1.34	6.9	37.5	54.2	100.0	72
All	34.8	36.1	17.8	11.3	100.0	348

Source: Federal Election Commission, http://www.fec.gov. Compiled by the authors

Note: Races without a major-party opponent are excluded and challenger spending that is unavailable was coded in the $0–25,000 row.

flows to challengers who would have done well regardless of spending. Other research, however, indicates that that is probably not the case. In an analysis of the 1972 and 1974 congressional elections, Jacobson concluded, "Our evidence is that campaign spending helps candidates, particularly non-incumbents, by bringing them to the attention of the voters; it is not the case that well-known candidates simply attract more money; rather money buys attention."[59] From this perspective, adequate funding is a necessary but not a sufficient condition for a closely fought election contest, a perspective consistent with the data in Table 9-6. Heavily outspending one's opponent is not a guarantee of victory; the evidence does not indicate that elections can simply be bought. If an incumbent outspends the challenger, the incumbent can still lose if the challenger is adequately funded and runs a campaign that persuades the voters.[60] The 2012 elections, for example, offer clear evidence of this. In eleven of the twenty-one races in which incumbents faced a non-incumbent challenger from the other party and the incumbent lost, the loser outspent the winner.[61] Indeed, in three of these contests the losing incumbent spent more than twice as much. In the most extreme example, Republican incumbent Allen B. West of Florida spent over $19 million but lost to challenger Patrick Murphy, who spent $4.6 million. Perhaps most important, however, no victorious challenger spent less than $1.2 million.

On the other hand, a spending advantage is not a guarantee to a challenger. In an extreme example from 2000, losing Republican challenger Phil Sudan spent $3.247 million against incumbent Ken Bentsen of Texas, who spent $1.354 million. Despite being outspent by over two to one, Bentsen won more than 60 percent of the vote. A somewhat less extreme case occurred in 2008, when Republican Sandy Treadwell spent over $7 million compared to incumbent Democrat Kristen Gillibrand of New York's $4.49 million. The Democrat was reelected with over 61 percent of the vote. Based on this analysis, our view can be summarized as follows: if a challenger is to attain visibility and get his or her message across to the voters—neutralizing the incumbent's advantages in name recognition and perquisites of office—the challenger needs to be adequately funded. If both sides in a race are adequately funded, the outcome will tend to turn on factors other than just money, and the relative spending of the two candidates is unlikely to control the outcome.

This argument carries us full circle back to our earlier discussion and leads us to bring together the three kinds of resources that we have considered: candidate experience, incumbency, and campaign spending. Table 9-7 presents data showing the impact of these three factors in the 2012 House elections. We categorize challenger experience as strong or weak depending on previous elective-office experience; challenger spending was classified as low or high depending on whether it was below or above $200,000.[62] The data show that each element exerts some independent effect, but the impact of spending seems to have been more consequential in 2012 (as was also true in 2008). When challengers had weak experience and low spending (58 percent of the races), all incumbents won, and 94 percent won with more than 60 percent of the vote. In the opposite situation, when the challenger had both strong experience and substantial spending, 84 percent of the races were relatively competitive. The combined results for the two intermediate categories fall between the extremes. In addition, incumbent defeats occurred with greater frequency in situations where the challenger was experienced and had strong spending. Yet note how few such races there were in 2012. Table 9-7 also reveals that 75 percent of the challengers with strong experience were able to raise substantial funds (fifty-six of seventy-five), whereas only 25 percent of challengers with little experience were able to do so.

This combination of factors also helps to explain the greater volatility of outcomes in Senate races we talked about earlier. Previous analysis has shown that the effects of campaign spending in Senate contests are consistent with what we have found true for House races: if challenger spending is above some threshold, the election is often quite close; if it is below that level, the incumbent is likely to win by a large margin.[63] In Senate races, however, the mix of well-funded and poorly funded challengers is different. Senate challengers are more likely to be able to raise significant amounts of money than their House counterparts. Indeed in recent elections, a number of challengers (and open-seat candidates) have been wealthy individuals who could provide a large share of their funding from their own resources. The most extreme example comes from 2000, when Jon Corzine, the Democratic candidate for the open New Jersey Senate seat, spent more than $60 million of his own money to defeat his opponent by 50 to 47 percent. Corzine spent a total of $63 million; the Republican spent $6.4 million.[64] Corzine was elected by a three-percentage-point margin.

Senate challengers, moreover, are also more likely to possess significant office experience. Thus, in Senate contests incumbents often face well-funded and experienced challengers, and the stage is then set for their defeat if other circumstances work against them. The lesson from the evidence presented here is captured by the words of David Johnson, the director of the Democratic Senatorial Campaign Committee, to Rep. Richard C. Shelby of Alabama, who was challenging Republican Sen. Jeremiah Denton in 1986. Shelby, who eventually won, was concerned that he did not have enough campaign funds, since Denton was outspending him two to one. Johnson responded: "You don't have as much money, but you're going to have enough—and enough is all it takes to win."[65]

THE 2012 ELECTIONS: THE IMPACT ON CONGRESS

The elections of 1994 produced huge consequences for politics and governing, and each subsequent election over the next decade was seen in relation to that event: would GOP control be maintained or lost, strengthened or weakened? The GOP retained control in five elections, then their luck ran out in 2006. A significant electoral tide gave the Democrats control of both chambers, which they improved on in 2008. That was followed by the Republican congressional landslide of 2010, and the return of divided government when the GOP took the

TABLE 9-7   Incumbents' Share of the Vote in the 2012 House Elections, by Challenger Experience and Spending (percent)

Challenger experience/ spending	Incumbents' share of two-party vote					
	70% or more	60%–69%	55%–59%	Less than 55%	Total	N
Weak/low	49.49 (101)	44.44 (90)	6.06 (12)	0 (0)	99.99	203
Strong/low	31.58 (6)	47.37 (9)	21.05 (4)	0 (0)	100	19
Weak/high	10.14 (7)	30.43 (21)	30.43 (21)	28.98 (20)	100	69
Strong/high	0 (0)	15.78 (9)	45.61 (26)	38.59 (22)	100	57

Source: See Tables 9-4 and 9-6. Compiled by the authors.

Note: Percentages read across. Strong challengers have held a significant elected office (U.S. representative; statewide office; countywide or citywide office such as mayor, prosecutor, and so on). High-spending challengers spent more than $200,000. Races without a major-party opponent are excluded.

House. Divided government was maintained in 2012, with modest Democratic gains in both chambers. The House "class of 2012" brought 84 new members, 19.3 percent of the body. In the Senate, 12 of the 100 members were newly elected in 2012.

The small Democratic gains maintained roughly the same political balance as in the previous Congress, a close division in which moderate members were still important. This should be seen in the context of a long-term decline of such members in the Congress, and an increase in the number of conservative Republicans and liberal Democrats. Thirty to thirty-five years ago, there was considerable ideological overlap between the parties. The Democrats had a substantial conservative contingent, mostly from the South, that was as conservative as the right wing of the Republican Party. Similarly, the GOP had a contingent (primarily northeasterners) whose members were as liberal as northern Democrats. In addition, each party had a significant number of moderate members. During the intervening years, however, because of changes in the electorate and in the Congress, this overlap between the parties began to disappear.[66] By the mid-1980s, both parties in both houses of Congress had become more politically homogeneous, and that homogeneity continued to increase in subsequent elections. In each chamber there was little departure from a complete ideological separation of the two parties.[67] Thus in the 113th Congress that resulted from the 2012 elections, substantial majorities of each party had sharply different policy preferences from those in the other party, with a small but potentially influential group of members in the middle.

The House: Testing Majority Party Control

In 1995, the new Republican majority instituted major institutional changes in the House.[68] By comparison, the changes in House organization for the 111th

Congress were modest. The House granted the majority leadership somewhat more flexibility regarding a floor procedure called *suspension of the rules* (which blocks all amendments on a bill but requires a two-thirds majority to pass). The majority's steering committee also chose six new committee chairs to replace members who had left the House or had reached the six-year term limit on Republican committee leaders. By and large, however, the GOP retained the previous congress's set of rules that centralized power in the majority party and its leadership.

The leadership's difficulties with the party's rank and file persisted. The landslide of 2010 brought to the House a large Republican freshman class that was dominated by populist insurgents who were identified with the Tea Party movement. This group was suspicious of establishment Republicans, and especially of speaker John Boehner and the House leadership.[69] During the 112th Congress the leadership had significant difficulty in persuading the Tea Party wing to follow their lead, and this led to frequent problems with passing bills the leaders deemed necessary. The newcomers wanted major changes in national policy (such as the complete repeal of "Obamacare") and they were disinclined to compromise in order to get things passed. The GOP's internal conflicts brought the government close to a shutdown and a near default on the national debt, and these led to a downgrade of the nation's debt rating.

After the 2012 election the Congress reconvened in a "lame-duck" session to complete unfinished business before the newly elected members took office. At the beginning of this session, the Republicans met to endorse their candidate for Speaker (Boehner) and to assign members to committees. As part of that process they expanded the number of votes the top party leaders had on the Republican Steering Committee (which makes assignments) and reduced the number of votes cast by the class of 2010.[70] Then the greater leadership leverage was used to remove four dissident Republicans from major committee assignments they had held in the previous Congress—a virtually unheard of action. These were members who had often vigorously opposed the leadership on both substance and strategy. Sources indicated that the decision was made after reviewing a spreadsheet detailing the frequency with which members voted with the leadership. One GOP leadership aide indicated the message being sent: "You want good things in Congress and to have a good career? Better play along nicely."[71]

A major focus of the lame-duck session was the so-called fiscal cliff, a set of expiring tax rates that would result in substantial income tax increases and significant spending cuts for both defense and domestic programs known as the *sequester*. Regarding taxes, Obama had proposed in his reelection campaign to renew the tax cuts only for families who earned less than $250,000 per year, while the Republicans wanted them renewed for everyone. Poll data indicated that a majority of Americans favored the president's views and that if the Congress failed to reach agreement that they would primarily blame the GOP.[72] Believing that his party would be damaged politically by a deadlock, Boehner acquiesced in a Senate-passed compromise that gave the Democrats most of what they wanted.

This deal passed on January 1, two days before the new Congress took over. House Democrats overwhelmingly backed it, but 64 percent of the Republicans voted no, including the GOP Majority Leader (Eric Cantor of Virginia) and the party's Whip (Kevin McCarthy of California). This was a violation of what is known as the Hastert Rule, named after the former GOP House Speaker Dennis Hastert of Illinois. Hastert had contended that the House should only take up bills that were backed by a majority of the majority party, and he followed this rule the vast majority of the time. Boehner, however, had violated the rule three times earlier in the 112th Congress[73] and then again in the new Congress with the passage of the bill to provide relief for victims of Hurricane Sandy and the renewal of the Violence Against Women Act.[74] Each of these occasions prompted strong negative reactions from the GOP's Tea Party wing. The speaker sought to reassure the conservatives by saying that this was "not a practice that I would expect to continue long term."[75] But the conservatives were not mollified, and some members proposed enshrining the Hastert Rule in the rules of the House Republican Conference.

The vote for the compromise averting the fiscal cliff had immediate consequences for Boehner. The first vote of a new Congress is to elect the Speaker, and a group of conservative representatives, angered by the removal of the dissidents from committees and the fiscal cliff deal, organized an effort to deny Boehner the absolute majority of votes he needed for election. The hope was that if a second ballot were forced, someone more acceptable might come forward to contest the election. And even if that did not happen, it would be a strong blow to Boehner's stature. In the event, enough Republican members initially pledged not to vote for Boehner, but the morning of the vote a few changed their minds. As it was, twelve GOP members abstained or voted for others (as did all the Democrats), and Boehner narrowly won reelection. The other top leaders, Cantor and McCarthy, were reelected without a contest.

Another issue raised at the beginning of the Congress was the representation of women in the Republican leadership. The number of female GOP representatives had declined from twenty-four to nineteen in the 2012 elections. This was less than 10 percent of the membership. (Among Democrats, women accounted for 29 percent of their Caucus). Rep. Cathy McMorris Rogers was elected to be chair of the Republican Conference, and two other women were picked for lower-ranking leadership posts, but the Steering Committee's decisions did not include any women among the committee chairs. Boehner remedied this by choosing Candice Miller of Michigan to be the chair of House Administration, one of the three committees on which the Speaker picks the chair himself. These actions illustrate the party leader's concern for the reputation[76] of the GOP among voters. In recent elections women have been more supportive of the Democrats than the Republicans, and the latter recognize they need to be seen as open to women's participation and concerns. (We will say more about the efforts to enhance the party's reputation later in this chapter.)

The Democratic Caucus experienced less conflict than the Republicans. Immediately after the election there was speculation about whether Nancy

Pelosi of California would continue as Minority Leader, but she quickly put that to rest. She announced that she would continue in order to help get more women elected and to pursue progress on issues of concern to her. Steny Hoyer of Maryland was reelected as Minority Whip, and Steve Israel of New York agreed to serve another term as chair of the party's campaign committee.

The Senate: How Effective Is Majority Control?

The surprising success of the Democrats in the Senate elections offered no pressure for a leadership change, and Harry Reid of Nevada and Dick Durbin of Illinois were reelected as Majority Leader and Majority Whip, respectively, posts they have both held since January 2007. On the Republican side, Mitch McConnell of Kentucky was reelected as Minority Leader and John Cornyn of Texas was chosen to be the new Minority Whip.

The Senate has always been predominantly a men's club, but that has been gradually changing. As in the House, the Senate makeup from the 2012 elections varied significantly in gender diversity. The number of female Democrats increased from twelve to sixteen, while the number of female Republicans dropped from five to four. As a result, 20 percent of the senators were women, 29 percent of the Democrats and 9 percent of the Republicans.

The central organization issue was whether there would be a change in the rules regarding the Senate's distinctive practice of the filibuster. Also known as *extended debate*, the filibuster refers to an effort to prevent resolution of a measure under consideration in the Senate by refusing to end discussion of it. Unlike the House, where debate can be ended by a simple majority vote at any time, Senate consideration can be terminated against the will of those who would continue only by invoking cloture. Under Senate rules, cloture requires sixty votes except on a proposal to change Senate rules, when the support of two-thirds of those voting is needed.[77]

The incidence of filibusters and cloture efforts, and their relevance to the legislative process, has increased greatly over the last six decades. In the seven congresses from 1947 through 1960, motions to invoke cloture were filed only 4 times, and none were approved. Filibusters were rare and were almost always employed by southerners to seek to block civil rights bills. Then gradually, as partisan polarization came to characterize the Senate, the scope of topics for filibusters broadened and their frequency increased. In the three congresses from 2007 through 2012, 388 cloture motions were filed and cloture was successfully invoked 164 times.[78] Another perspective on the increase comes from analysis offered by Barbara Sinclair. She gathered data on action on major bills over time. Her evidence shows that in the 1960s, only 8 percent of bills involved extended-debate problems (i.e., a filibuster or the threat of one). From 2007 through 2010, on the other hand, over 70 percent of major bills experienced such problems.[79]

The increased use of filibusters has made it more difficult and costly for the majority party to secure passage of the bills it favors. As a consequence, some senators in the majority have sought to alter the Senate's rules to place limits on what could be filibustered or how many votes would be required to impose cloture. Of course, members of the minority would be unlikely to support such efforts, and they would be likely to use the filibuster to block them. As noted above, Senate rules specify that motions to impose cloture on attempted rules changes required even more votes than such efforts on regular legislation. But some members and outside observers contend that the rule does not apply at the opening of a Congress, and that only the vote of a majority is then necessary to end debate and adopt an alternative rule. Whether such an interpretation (dubbed the "nuclear option" by participants) would be applied in a particular instance would depend on whether the presiding officer of the Senate, the vice president, so ruled and whether that ruling was upheld by a majority of senators. A significant proportion of the senators of both parties have accepted the view that a simple majority was sufficient to impose cloture on a rules change when they were in the minority (and the same people have often taken the opposite view when in the majority).

After the GOP Senate gains of 2010, there was talk among Democrats about seeking to changes the cloture rules by a majority vote, but a confrontation was avoided by a "gentleman's agreement" between the two party leaders that purported to limit the scope of filibusters. Harry Reid and many Democrats were unhappy with the operation of that agreement, and after the 2012 elections Democrats again raised the specter of a rules change. Indeed, in late November Reid flatly predicted that Senate Democrats would vote to limit Republican use of the filibuster in the new Congress, although many observers questioned whether he actually had the votes to effect the change.[80]

When the new Senate convened, a confrontation over the nuclear option was again avoided by negotiations between the party leaders and other members. The agreement included two sets of rules changes, both of which were adopted. The first set applied only to the new 113th Congress. It said that a motion for the Senate to consider a bill (formally known as the *motion to proceed*) could not be filibustered as long as the majority leader permitted four amendments, two from each party, to be debated and voted on. The package also tightened the limits on the amount of debate that was permitted after cloture was adopted. The second set of changes permanently altered the Senate rules. Now the Senate could hold a cloture vote on a motion to proceed the day after it was filed (reducing the previous wait by a day) and after adoption there would be no more debate before voting (saving another day).

None of the changes adopted affected the ability of senators to filibuster final passage votes on bills or nominations, so the strength of that tactic for blocking action is unabated. Rather, the revisions reduced the use of the filibuster as a delaying tactic, thus expediting action. This all fell far short of the changes that most liberal Democrats wanted, and it is unclear how much difference they made. Indeed, in May 2013 Harry Reid complained that despite the rules changes and another gentleman's agreement between him and Mitch McConnell, "Republican obstruction on nominees continues unabated, no different than it was in the last Congress."[81] As a result of continued conflicts over confirmations, on November 21, 2013, Reid exercised the nuclear option. By a 52-48 vote the Senate adopted new rules for cloture on all executive branch nominations and federal court nominations other than those for the Supreme Court. Now debate on those nominations could be terminated by a simple majority vote rather than the sixty votes previously needed.

The Obama Administration and Divided Government

Obama's reelection, coupled with the small changes in the partisan balance in Congress, maintained the divided government pattern of the previous two years. Political scientists have debated whether unified party control results in more or different significant legislation compared to divided government.[82] Whatever the implications of divided government had been in the past, however, in the period of great partisan polarization (roughly from the 1980s to the present) it has meant significantly reduced legislative productivity. And that trend has grown stronger over the years.

Consider the record of the 112th Congress that ended on January 3, 2013. That Congress passed 283 public laws. That is the fewest of any Congress at least since 1947. Indeed, the next lowest total was the 333 laws passed in the 104th Congress (1995–1997); that was 18 percent more laws that the 112th Congress.[83] (During the 104th, the government was also divided, with the GOP in control of the House and Senate, and Democrat Bill Clinton in the White House.) Whether this pattern is good or bad for the country is, of course, a question for individual citizens to answer. But there is no question that less is getting done, and office-holders of both parties and citizens of all ideologies complain about that.

The 113th Congress began with hopes and promises that things would be different. President Obama renewed previous pledges to reach out to congressional Republicans, and GOP leaders indicated a willingness to cooperate—conditionally. For example, Speaker Boehner said: "Mr. President, this is your moment. Let's challenge ourselves to find the common ground that has eluded us."[84] And Mitch McConnell said that the president had to move to the center, where Republicans would "be there to meet him halfway."[85] And even as strong a critic of Congress as Norman Ornstein of the American Enterprise Institute perceived some hopeful signs, saying that he was "modestly hopeful that we might have a productive 113th Congress."[86]

The first major bill considered in the new Congress provided relief funds for the victims of Hurricane Sandy. The Senate had passed a relief bill in the previous Congress, but Boehner declined to take it up after the exhausting resolution of the fiscal cliff deal. This decision produced a torrent of criticism of the Speaker from Republican members from New York and New Jersey who had expected completion of the bill before adjournment. GOP Rep. Peter King of New York called the failure to resolve the bill a "disgrace" and "immoral." He also said: "anyone from New York and New Jersey who contributes one penny to congressional Republicans is out of their minds."[87]

Recognizing that this was an issue of the highest salience to part of his membership, as well an issue of importance to the electorate, Boehner knew he had to act. But other, more conservative GOP representatives were against passing an aid bill unless the funds were offset by cuts elsewhere in the budget. The Speaker knew that such a proposal would be unacceptable to affected Republicans as well as Democrats, so he had to bring to the floor a bill that gave aid without offsets. When an amendment was proposed to require offsets, about two-thirds of Republicans voted for it, but with only five Democrats joining them, it failed. Then on passage of the bill, 79 percent of GOP members voted no, but the remaining Republicans plus all but one Democrat supported the bill and it passed. Thus the GOP leadership began the new year with a violation of the Hastert Rule after ending the previous Congress with another. The defection of Republicans for affected states was not surprising, of course. The issue was too important to their constituents to do otherwise. But the fight illustrated the continuing fissure in the party between members aligned with the Tea Party and more conventional conservatives, and the problems of the leadership in accommodating both.

Circumstances improved a bit briefly for the Republicans when Congress was able to clear a bill suspending the debt ceiling, which had been reached. This avoided another crisis, but GOP members were pleased because the suspension lasted only until May 19, when the matter would have to be revisited. And Boehner promised conservatives that the House Budget Committee would draft a plan to eliminate the deficit within a decade. And then in late March the Congress and the administration were able to agree on a continuing resolution to provide appropriations for the remainder of the fiscal year, eliminating for a while any threat of a government shutdown.

Other matters did not go as well, however. On March 1, the large automatic cuts of the sequester went into effect despite great efforts to avoid them. Then in mid-April, hopes for a new gun control law were dashed. In the wake of an elementary school shooting in Newtown, Connecticut, that took the lives of twenty children and six adults, members of Congress and the administration sought to create a bipartisan proposal that would overcome the resistance that had blocked new gun laws for almost two decades. But when the Senate took up the bill, only fifty-four votes (just four of which came from Republicans) were marshaled for the main proposal focused on expanding background checks for gun sales. While this was a majority, the Senate had set a requirement of sixty votes to approve proposals. This is a common practice in the body when a filibuster is threatened, as was true in this case. When other provisions also failed to pass, Harry Reid suspended consideration of the bill, and it is unlikely that it will be taken up again.

As of the middle of July 2013, many other proposals dealt with by the Congress had not been resolved and faced uncertain fates. While both chambers had passed initial budget plans (this was the first time in four years the Senate had been able to do so), no resolution of the differences between them had been worked out because the Republicans refused to permit a conference committee to be created. Most of the resistance came from senators aligned with the Tea Party who were worried about compromises that would be reached. John McCain (R-AZ) urged going to conference, saying those who were worried should trust House Budget Committee chairman Paul Ryan (R-WI) to protect the party's interests. But Senator Ted Cruz (R-TX) responded: "Let me be clear: I don't trust the Republicans, and I don't trust the Democrats. . . . [I]t is the leadership of both parties that has gotten us in this mess."[88]

Then in late June the House rejected the farm programs bill. This had usually been a bipartisan bill that combined agriculture subsidies with funding for food stamps. But this time Democrats overwhelmingly opposed the bill because of cuts in food stamp funds, while sixty-two Republican conservatives voted no because they wanted greater cuts. In July a new bill that included only agriculture programs and ignored food stamps entirely was adopted on a close party-line vote, but it was unclear how this approach would fare in the Senate. Finally, the top priority of the Obama administration, comprehensive immigration reform, produced a brief return of somewhat bipartisan cooperation when the Senate passed 68-32, with the support of every Democrat and fourteen of the forty-six Republicans voting. But here, too, future prospects are uncertain. The House Republican leadership indicated that they would not take up the Senate bill, nor would they seek to pass any comprehensive proposal. Instead they intended to approach the issue piecemeal, focusing first on improving border security.

Thus despite the optimism on the part of some at the opening of the 113th Congress, one-fourth of the way through the government is mired in the same kind of gridlock that characterized the 112th. Indeed, it may be a bit worse. At the six-month mark in 2011 the Congress had passed twenty-three laws. At the same point in 2013, the equivalent number was fifteen.[89] Nor did there seem to be much reason to expect the pattern to reverse in the next year and a half.

THE 2014 ELECTIONS AND BEYOND

Expectations about midterm elections are usually shaped by a strong historical pattern: the party of the president lost strength in the House in twenty-four of the twenty-eight midterm elections since the beginning of the twentieth century. The first column in Table 9-8 shows the magnitude of these losses in midterms since World War II. They average 25.9 seats for the president's party. There was, however, considerable variation in the outcomes, from the 63-seat loss by the Democrats in 2010 to the 6-seat Republican gain in 2002. Another consideration

TABLE 9-8   House Seat Losses by the President's Party in Midterm Elections, 1946–2010

All elections	First term of administration	Later term of administration
1946: 55 Democrats	1954: 18 Republicans	1946: 55 Democrats
1950: 29 Democrats	1962: 4 Democrats	1950: 29 Democrats
1954: 18 Republicans	1970: 12 Republicans	1958: 47 Republicans
1958: 47 Republicans	1978: 11 Democrats	1966: 47 Democrats
1962: 4 Democrats	1982: 26 Republicans	1974: 43 Republicans
1966: 47 Democrats	1990: 9 Republicans	1986: 5 Republicans
1970: 12 Republicans	1994: 52 Democrats	1998: (+5) Democrats
1974: 43 Republicans	2002: (+6) Republicans	2006: 30 Republicans
1978: 11 Democrats	2010: 63 Democrats	
1982: 26 Republicans		Average: 31.4
1986: 5 Republicans	Average: 21.0	
1990: 9 Republicans		
1994: 52 Democrats		
1998: (+5) Democrats		
2002: (+6) Republicans		
2006: 30 Republicans		
2010: 63 Democrats		
Average: 25.9		

Source: Compiled by the authors.

related to the president, however, clarifies the context for analysis. During the first midterm election of his presidency, the president may be able to make a plausible appeal that he has not had enough time to bring about substantial change or to solidify many achievements. Moreover, even if things are not going very well, voters may not be inclined to blame a president who has served for such a short time. But four years later (if the president is fortunate enough to face a second midterm), appeals of too little time are unlikely to be persuasive. After six years, if the economy or foreign policy is not going well, voters may seek a policy change by reducing the number of the president's partisans in Congress.

The second and third columns in Table 9-8 indicate that this is what has usually happened in the past. Losses by the president's party in the first midterm election of a presidency have tended to be much smaller than losses in subsequent midterms.[90] Indeed, with the exception of the results in 1986, 1994, 1998, 2002, and 2010, the two categories yield two sets of outcomes that are sharply different from one another. In the six midterm elections besides 1994, 2002, and 2010 that took place during a first term, the president's party lost between four and twenty-six seats, with an average loss of thirteen. In the six elections after the first term (excluding 1986 and 1998), the range of losses was between twenty-nine and fifty-five seats, with an average loss of forty-two. (We will discuss the atypical years later.) But one potential mitigating factor for 2014 regarding this pattern is that the Democrats' huge losses in the 2010 midterm leaves them with many fewer vulnerable seats than had been true before that.

Models of House Elections

In the 1970s and 1980s, a number of scholars constructed and tested models of congressional election outcomes, focusing especially on midterms, seeking to isolate the factors that most strongly influenced the results. The earliest models, constructed by Tufte and by Jacobson and Kernell, focused on two variables: presidential approval and a measure of the state of the economy.[91] Tufte hypothesized a direct influence by these forces on voter choice and election outcomes. The theory was that an unpopular president or a poor economy would cause the president's party to lose votes and, therefore, seats in the House. In essence, the midterm elections were viewed as a referendum on the performance of the president and his party. Jacobson and Kernell, on the other hand, saw more indirect effects of presidential approval and the economy. They argued that these forces affected election results by influencing the decisions of potential congressional candidates. If the president is unpopular and the economy is in bad shape, potential candidates will expect the president's party to perform poorly. As a consequence, strong potential candidates of the president's party will be more inclined to forgo running until a better year, and strong candidates from the opposition party will be more inclined to run because they foresee good prospects for success. According to Jacobson and Kernell, this mix of weak candidates from the president's party and strong opposition candidates will lead to a poor election performance by the party occupying the White House. To measure this predicted relationship, their model related the partisan division of the vote to presidential approval and the economic situation early in the election year. This, they argued, is when decisions to run for office are being made, not at the time of the election, so it is not appropriate to focus on approval and the economy at that time. This view has come to be called the *strategic politicians hypothesis.*[92]

Subsequent research built from this base. One model, developed by Alan I. Abramowitz, Albert D. Cover, and Helmut Norpoth, considered a new variable: short-term party evaluations.[93] They argued that voters' attitudes about the economic competence of the political parties affect the impact of presidential approval and economic conditions on voting decisions. If the electorate judges that the party holding the presidency is better able to deal with the problems voters regard as most serious, the negative impact of an unpopular president or a weak economy will be reduced. The authors concluded from their analysis of both aggregate votes and responses to surveys in midterm elections that there is evidence for their party competence hypothesis.

All of these models used the division of the popular vote as the variable to be predicted, and they focused only on midterm elections. Later work merged midterm results with those of presidential years, contending that there should be no conceptual distinction between them. These efforts sought to predict changes in seats without reference to the division of the vote. For example, a study by Bruce I. Oppenheimer, James A. Stimson, and Richard W. Waterman argued that the missing piece in the congressional election puzzle is the degree of "exposure," or "the excess or deficit number of seats a party holds measured against its long-term norm."[94] If a party wins more House seats than normal, those extra seats will be vulnerable in the next election, and the party is likely to suffer losses. Thus the party that wins a presidential election does not automatically benefit in House elections. But if the president's party does well in the House races, it will be more vulnerable in the subsequent midterm elections. Indeed, the May 1986 article by Oppenheimer and his colleagues predicted only small Republican losses for 1986 because Reagan's large 1984 victory was not accompanied by substantial congressional gains for his party. The actual result in 1986 was consistent with this prediction, for the GOP lost only five seats.

Another model of House elections was constructed by Robin F. Marra and Charles W. Ostrom Jr.[95] They developed a "comprehensive referendum voting model" of both presidential year and midterm elections, and included factors such as foreign policy crises, scandals, unresolved policy disputes, party identification, and changes in the level of presidential approval. The model also incorporated measures reflecting hypothesized relationships in the models we discussed earlier: the level of presidential approval, the state of the economy, the strategic politicians hypothesis, exposure, and party competence. The model was tested on data from all congressional elections from 1950 through 1986.

The Marra-Ostrom analysis showed significant support for most of the predicted relationships. The results indicated that the most powerful influences affecting congressional seat changes were presidential approval (directly and through various events) and exposure. The model was striking in its statistical accuracy: the average error in the predicted change was only four seats. The average error varied little whether presidential or midterm years were predicted, and the analysis demonstrated that the usually greater losses for the president's party in second midterm years resulted from negative shifts in presidential approval, exposure, and scandals. However, when the empirical analysis was extended by Ostrom and Brian Newman to include the election years from 1988 through 1998, the accuracy of the model declined.[96] They produced a revised model that included some additional variables. In particular they found that the relative number of open seats held by the two parties was important in determining losses. Moreover, once that variable was taken into account, the importance of the exposure variable decreased. That is, the most important form of exposure was open seats; incumbents were less vulnerable.

Drawing on the insights of these various models, we can see how these factors may influence outcomes in the 2014 House elections. How well the economy is doing and what proportion of the voters approve of Obama's performance early in the year may encourage or discourage high-quality potential challengers. The same variables close to election time may lead voters to support or oppose Democratic candidates based on their judgments of the job the Obama administration is doing. The usual midterm losses happen for reasons; they are not part of the laws of nature. Therefore, if the usual reasons for such losses (such as a recession or an unpopular president) are not present in 2014, we should not expect the consequent losses to occur, or at least not the magnitude of losses that history might lead us to expect.[97] This is why the president's party gained seats in the midterms of 1998 and 2002. If, on the other hand, those reasons are present, the context will be quite different.

In the summer of 2013, Obama's approval was similar to the situation before the 2012 election: weak but not terrible. An average of eight polls from June 10 to 25 yielded a mean approval rating of 45.9 percent, with only two of the polls showing approval higher than disapproval.[98] Moreover, there were signs that the slow economic recovery was continuing to gain ground. If the economy improves further and Obama's popularity moves back above 50 percent, Democrats could be somewhat insulated from significant losses. On the other hand, recent scandals in the administration (like IRS scrutiny of Tea Party groups' tax status and the discovery that the National Security Agency was collecting data on a wide range of telephone traffic) may further undermine the president's approval rating. In addition, the models we discussed indicate that other considerations are also important. Democratic exposure is relatively low due to the large losses of 2010, and to this point it appears that few Democratic members of the House are planning to retire. This could leave the Democrats with fewer vulnerable seats than usual.

With regard to high-quality candidates coming forward to run, Republicans are at least as aware of the pattern of midterm losses as are political scientists, so potential candidates may regard the political landscape as encouraging. For Democrats, on the other hand, that same landscape may be daunting and so recruiting may be somewhat difficult. Moreover, the analysis of short-term party evaluations reminds us that highly salient issues may offset the negative effects of poor economic conditions. Finally, the impact of events like crises and scandals in the Marra-Ostrom model reminds us that there are many unforeseeable events that may influence the 2014 congressional election results.

Some Additional Considerations About House Races

A few further points related to the previous discussion are necessary to complete our analysis of the prospects for 2014 House races. The vulnerability of individual members varies between parties and across other attributes, and we should not expect those distributions necessarily to be similar from election to election. For example, in one year a party may have a relatively high percentage of freshmen or of members who won by narrow margins in the preceding election, while in another year the party's proportion of such potentially vulnerable members may be low. As Table 9-9 shows, both parties have a roughly similar (and relatively small) number of members who won with less than 55 percent of the vote. Twenty-three Republicans and twenty-eight Democrats fell into this category. This is fewer close races for each party than the number that resulted from the 2000 elections, and it is substantially fewer than the total of ninety-five after 1996 (also two years after a Republican landslide). It is in this type of district that strong challengers are most likely to come forward and where the challengers who do run are most able to raise adequate campaign funds. Thus based solely on these election-margin figures, the political landscape doesn't present a very attractive prospect for challengers of either party.

As our earlier analysis indicates, the parties' respective success in recruiting strong candidates for open seats and to oppose the other party's incumbents can be expected to play a significant role in shaping outcomes for 2014. Both Democratic and Republican campaign organizations were actively pursuing recruits during 2013, with some successes and some failures. The personal and financial costs of candidacies and the difficulty of defeating an incumbent often make recruitment difficult, and the special problems of each party made the task harder. For the Democrats this included minority status and the difficulty of winning enough seats to take control, while for the Republicans troubles included personal divisions and a damaged reputation. We will return to these issues at the end of this section. Both parties focused on encouraging losing candidates who came close to try again, and analyst Stewart Rothenberg predicted that 2014 may see more than a dozen rematches.[99]

Moreover, even successful recruitment efforts bring no guarantee of success. For example, in a New York special House election in April 2009 (to replace Democrat Gillibrand, who had been appointed to succeed Hillary Clinton in the Senate), the GOP candidate was a member of the state legislature from the area. Moreover, the district had a historically Republican tilt, and the Democrat was a

TABLE 9-9   Percentage of Vote Received by Winning House Candidates, by Party and Type of Race, 2012

	Republican			Democrat		
	Reelected incumbent	Successful challenger	Open seat winner	Reelected incumbent	Successful challenger	Open seat winner
55 or less	15	4	4	8	11	7
55.1-60	44	1	12	22	2	3
60.1-70	90	0	13	44	2	14
70.1-100	49	0	3	79	0	8
Total	198	5	32	153	15	32

Source: Compiled by the authors.

Note: Table shows the number of districts that meet the criteria for each cell. Open seats include races in which an incumbent lost a primary.

young businessman with no experience in public office. Yet the Democrat won.[100] Then in 2012, the GOP recruited a popular mayor, Mia Love, to face Democratic incumbent Jim Matheson in the heavily Republican fourth district of Utah. Even though the district voted for Mitt Romney for president by a margin of 67 to 30 percent, Matheson narrowly survived.[101]

Worth noting here is the continuing impact of term limits in the states. Although the term limits movement failed to impose restrictions on members of Congress, it succeeded in imposing them on state legislators in fifteen states, and those limits continue to have an impact. One potential outlet for a state legislator who cannot run for reelection is to seek a congressional seat. This may lead to a greater number of strong challengers in House races than would otherwise be the case. For example, California limits state legislators to twelve years combined in the two chambers, and a number of legislators will have to leave their current positions shortly. Some of them are contemplating races for a U.S. House seat.[102]

As we have discussed, the potential number of open seats is also relevant to questions of candidate recruitment and district vulnerability. Our analysis above shows that open seats are more likely to switch parties than are those with incumbents, and that both parties are more likely to field strong candidates. As of June 2013, there was only a single confirmed retirement: Republican Michele Bachman of Minnesota. However, there were concerns that a number of representatives will leave the House to seek Senate seats or governorships, and by June 2013 eleven members (six Democrats and five Republicans) had committed to races.[103]

Finally, one should remember that the rules that shape elections are subject to change and that such changes can have a substantial impact on the pattern of election outcomes. One source of such change is the courts. In 2013 the U.S. Supreme Court struck down a provision of the Voting Rights Act that requires many state and local governments, mainly in the South, to seek permission from the U.S. Justice Department or a federal court before they can make changes to certain voting procedures. The provision, which had been reauthorized by Congress in 2006, had been challenged on the grounds that such restrictions on the rights of states were no longer required. Five justices joined in an opinion by Chief Justice John Roberts in which he said that Congress was able to impose federal restrictions on states where voting rights were at risk, but it must do so based on contemporary data on discrimination, which was not the case in this instance. Thus Congress could pass a new law, but it is unlikely that this will occur given the polarization and divided control in Congress. This case is likely to have substantial consequences in the near term because many Republican-controlled state governments were preparing new voting regulations.[104]

A couple of weeks earlier, the Court delivered another election-law decision, this one related to an Arizona law that added a proof-of-citizenship requirement to a federal voter registration form. The Court ruled that a state could not substitute its judgment for a federal decision on what could be required.[105] This was a limited ruling (e.g., the Court did not say a state could not create its own parallel form), but it does illustrate that even without the preclearance provision of the Voting Rights Act there are many avenues for substantive litigation related to new election laws.

As a consequence of all of the factors we have discussed, Democrats may have more reason for concern than Republicans, and the road to the seventeen-seat net gain the party needs to win a majority looks particularly difficult. In the thirty-four congressional elections since World War II, the president's party has gained that many seats only three times, and all were in presidential election years. Yet our analysis also indicates that GOP success is not certain. We have seen that it is possible for the historical pattern to be broken under certain conditions. Probably the most relevant one for 2014 relates to the Republican party's reputation with voters. Poll data from the Pew Research Center (supported by similar analyses in other polls) shows that the party's ratings stand at the lowest point in twenty years, with only 33 percent of respondents indicating that they have a favorable view of the GOP and 58 percent seeing it unfavorably. (The parallel numbers for the Democrats were 47 percent favorable and 46 percent unfavorable.)[106]

Within this context, the Democrats will continue to portray the Republicans as extreme and blame that extremism for the gridlock over policy in Washington. If the Democrats are successful, the public may decide to place the blame for their unhappiness with the national government on the GOP rather than on the president's party, as happened in 1996 when the Democrats gained seats in the midterm. The Republicans, in the wake of their unexpected failures in the 2012 presidential and Senate races, are aware of this problem and are considering ways to deal with it. We will say more about this effort at the end of this chapter.

Senate Races in 2014

Because there are few Senate races and because they are relatively independent of one another, we have focused our discussion of 2014 on the House. We will now close with a few comments about the upper chamber's contests. Due to the six-year Senate terms, and the fact that these terms are staggered, the number of seats to be defended by each party varies from election to election. As was true in 2012, the Democrats hold the most seats of the thirty-five that will be contested in 2014, with twenty seats compared to the Republicans' fifteen. (These totals include the thirty-three seats normally scheduled to be contested, plus special elections in Hawaii and New Jersey to fill the remainder of the terms of two members who died.) Thus the GOP has more targets for gains, and some features of the landscape make the situation look even more attractive for them. For example, seven of the seats will be open, and five of those currently are held by Democrats. Moreover, three of those five are in states (Montana, South Dakota, and West Virginia) that Romney carried by at least ten points. However, as we discussed above, the playing field looked attractive for the Republicans in 2012, but they failed to gain ground, and even in their great year of 2010 they lost a number of seats they thought would be theirs.

We have seen that the kinds of candidates seeking office have a major influence on the outcome and that parties, therefore, try to get the strongest candidates to come forward. In this cycle, however, both parties are having difficulty. In "Iowa, for example, the state's lieutenant governor, agriculture secretary, secretary of state and two prominent congressmen all declined to seek the Republican nomination" for the seat being vacated by Democrat Tom Harkin.[107] Prominent Republicans have also declined to run for the Senate in Alaska, Michigan, Georgia, and Nebraska. Similarly, Democrats who were regarded as strong contenders have passed on the opportunity in Georgia and South Dakota. Of course, some strong contenders have announced, like Democratic Rep. Bruce Braley in Iowa, but many analysts have remarked about recruitment difficulties for 2014. And to many of them the reason is quite simple: "rarely has the thought of serving in the Senate seemed so unappealing" because the chamber "is so riven by partisanship and gummed up by its own arcane rules."[108] This reflects the impact of the polarization we discussed earlier.

This recruitment problem appears to be more serious for the Republicans because of the difficulties experienced in 2010 and 2012 with conflicts over Senate nominations between the Tea Party and establishment wings. Prominent Republican leaders have become increasingly concerned that these conflicts may continue to undermine the effort to recover GOP control of the Senate, and they sought to deal with the problem. GOP strategist Karl Rove and a number of others formed the Conservative Victory Project to influence the choice of candidates in Republican primaries. Steven Law, president of American Crossroads (a super PAC started by Rove), said: "There is broad concern about having blown a significant number of races because the wrong candidates were selected."[109] This effort, however, has stimulated a great deal of resistance from more ideological segments of the party. For example, Chris Chocola of the Club for Growth (an anti-tax group that opposes Republicans they deem too moderate) said that electability is a "false standard,"[110] and that Rove "is focused on the (Republican) brand. We are not party builders. We are trying to improve the gene pool of Congress based on principle." And Todd Akin, the defeated Republican nominee for the Senate in Missouri, said of the Rove effort: "If they were successful, it basically helps kill the grassroots heart of the party."[111]

The conflict was visible when Republican party leaders successfully encouraged GOP Rep. Shelley Moore Capito of West Virginia to seek the party's Senate nomination to replace retiring Democrat Jay Rockefeller. On the first day of her candidacy she was criticized by Chocola of the Club for Growth and by the head of the Senate Conservatives Fund, a group founded by former South Carolina Sen. Jim DeMint. The latter indicated that if a strong challenger to Capito came forward, their group would seriously consider supporting that challenger.[112] Democrats, on the other hand, have exhibited more pragmatism in Senate recruiting and appear to be emphasizing electability in seeking 2014 candidates.[113]

To summarize, then, House results are likely to depend heavily on the political context that exists both late in 2013 (when many candidate decisions will be made) and in November 2014. The context will probably determine whether the historical pattern of losses by the president's party occurs again or is broken as it was in the 1998 and 2002 midterms. For the Senate seats, on the other hand, the results probably depend more on the circumstances in individual races, largely fought independently of one another.

Beyond 2014: Polarization and the Struggle for the Control of Congress

Just as every election has implications for those that follow, the elections of 2014 will have an impact on subsequent contests. We do not know those results, so we cannot yet describe the effects, but a few general considerations are likely to have an impact on future congressional contests.

The national demographic changes we have touched on in Chapter 2, and that we will discuss further in Chapter 11 will continue to be important. While these shifts slowed somewhat due to reduced immigration during the economic slump, the proportion of the population that is made up of Latinos and other minorities will continue to grow. The Democrats are currently advantaged among these groups, and they will pursue strategies that seek to retain that advantage and that improve the activation of those constituencies, as demonstrated by the strong efforts to pass a comprehensive immigration bill in the 113th Congress. Republicans, on the other hand, will look for ways to improve their standing among minorities, particularly Latinos. Indeed, they will have to succeed to a degree if they are to remain competitive as the population distribution changes. (We will return to this subject in Chapter 11.)

The impact of the shifting demographics will be shaped by the Republican party's efforts to improve its reputation. The soul searching that followed the unexpected failures of 2012 led the chairman of the Republican National Committee (RNC), Reince Priebus, to commission a task force to conduct a self-analysis of the GOP. The task force issued an extremely critical report in March 2013. It stated: "Public perception of the party is at record lows. . . . Young voters are increasingly rolling their eyes at what the party represents, and many minorities wrongly think that Republicans do not like them or want them in the country."[114] The report focused mainly on competing for the presidency, but it spoke more broadly of the problems of the party's "federal wing," saying: "We have become expert in how to provide ideological reinforcement to like-minded people. . . . But devastatingly, we have lost the ability to be persuasive with, or welcoming to, those who do not agree with us on every issue."[115] And while it concentrated mainly on tactical considerations rather than changes in the party's positions, the report did signal a need and willingness to change the nation's immigration system.

As with the Senate recruitment conflicts we just considered, the party was split in reactions to the report. Congressional leaders like John Boehner and Eric Cantor praised the arguments for modernizing campaign techniques, but Tea Party groups and their allies offered cautions and criticisms. For example, talk show host Rush Limbaugh said Republicans were "totally bamboozled" and lacking in confidence.[116] And in response to the report's statement that on social issues the party would never win over young voters if it were seen as "totally intolerant of alternative points of view," the leader of the conservative Family Research Council said: "If the RNC abandons marriage, evangelicals will either sit the elections out completely—or move to create a third party."[117] This will be a precarious path for the party to tread.

Even in this context, however, the Democrats have their own problems, at least in the near term. To be sure, they are in a good position relative to competing for the presidency, and for the 2016 Senate elections they will be defending only ten of the thirty-four seats, most in solidly Democratic states. But the legacy of the redistricting plans the Republicans were able to impose after the 2010 census is that the difficulties of obtaining a majority in 2014 will at best only gradually subside as the decade wears on. Success would probably require winning the national vote for the House by about the same substantial margin they did in 2008. While not impossible, this is surely a difficult task. Thus the remainder of the decade would seem likely to offer a good chance of a continuation of divided government and the gridlock that now accompanies it.

Chapter 10

The Congressional Electorate in 2012

In the preceding chapter we viewed congressional elections at the district and state levels and saw how they formed a national result. In this chapter we consider congressional elections from the point of view of the individual voter, using the same American National Election Studies (ANES) surveys we employed to study presidential voting. We discuss how social forces, issues, partisan loyalties, incumbency, and evaluations of congressional and presidential performance influence the decisions of voters in congressional elections. We also try to determine the existence and extent of presidential coattails.

SOCIAL FORCES AND THE CONGRESSIONAL VOTE

In general, social forces relate to the congressional vote similarly to the way they do to the presidential vote (Table 10-1).[1] This has been true in our previous analyses of national elections, but the relationship was somewhat tighter in 2012 than in the 1980s and 1990s. While the aggregate vote for Democratic House candidates and the vote for Obama vary somewhat, in most of the categories we used in the presidential vote analysis, the relative performances are fairly similar (see Table 5-1).[2] This may reflect the closer relationship between party identification and the vote in recent elections for both the president and Congress demonstrated in analyses by Larry M. Bartels.[3]

Consider, for example, the relationship between voting and gender. In the total electorate, Barack Obama received 52 percent of the vote and House Democrats got 47 percent. Among white female voters, Democrats ran six points better for the presidency than for the House, and they did four points better among white males. (Except for the discussion of voting and race, the analysis here, as in Chapter 5, focuses on white voters.) The gender results are interesting when compared to the past. In 1988, there was a small gender gap in the presidential vote (about three points), with women more likely to vote Democratic

TABLE 10-1   How Social Groups Voted for Congress, 2012 (percent)

Social group	Democratic	Republican	Total	(N)
Total electorate	47	53	100	(934)
Electorate, by race				
African American	95	5	100	(106)
White	37	63	100	(716)
Other	63	37	100	(108)
Latinos (of any race)	66	34	100	(66)
Whites, by gender				
Female	35	65	100	(372)
Male	40	60	100	(343)
Whites, by region				
New England and Mid-Atlantic	42	59	101	(165)
North Central	46	54	100	(162)
South	23	77	100	(194)
Border	41	59	100	(43)
Mountain and Pacific	41	59	100	(126)
Whites, by birth cohort				
Before 1942	26	74	100	(107)
1943–1952	47	54	101	(138)
1953–1962	38	62	100	(171)
1963–1972	39	61	100	(128)
1973–1982	44	56	100	(83)
1983–1991	20	80	100	(61)
1992–1995	[0]	[4]	100	(4)
Whites, by level of education				
Not high school graduate	36	64	100	(36)
High school graduate	29	71	100	(183)
Some college	35	65	100	(211)
College graduate	39	61	100	(175)
Advanced degree	52	48	100	(108)
Whites, by annual family income				
Less than $15,000	35	65	100	(55)
$15,000–$34,999	39	61	100	(105)
$35,000–$49,999	38	62	100	(68)
$50,000–$74,999	33	67	100	(148)
$75,000–$89,999	30	70	100	(85)
$90,000–$124,999	51	49	100	(112)
$125,000–$174,999	40	60	100	(58)
$175,000 and over	37	63	100	(55)

Social group	Democratic	Republican	Total	(N)
Whites, by union membership [a]				
Member	51	49	100	(147)
Nonmember	34	66	100	(562)

Source: Authors' analysis of the 2012 American National Election Studies (ANES) survey.

Note: The numbers in parentheses are the totals on which the percentages are based. Numbers are weighted. The number in brackets is the total number in that category when there are fewer than ten total voters.

[a] Respondent or family member in union.

than men, but there was no gap in the House vote. By 2000, however, the gender gap was more pronounced in the vote both for the president and for representatives; the major-party share of the vote was nine points more Democratic for women in the former case and ten points more Democratic in the latter. In 2004, gender differences were reduced in both types of races, with the Democratic advantage among women down to seven points for president and three points in House contests. And in 2012, the differences declined even further. There was no gender gap in the presidential vote, and in the House vote Democrats ran five points better among white men than among white women.

The presidential and congressional voting patterns are similar within many other social categories, including race, education, and income. For both the presidential and the congressional vote, African Americans were substantially more likely to vote Democratic. The difference was fifty-eight points for both the presidential race and the House contests. Another similarity was regarding union member voters, who were seventeen points more Democratic than nonunion voters in the House vote, while they were fifteen points more Democratic for president. In 2008 the pattern for the two offices was also similar, but it was smaller: eleven percentage points better for the House and nine points better for the presidency. In 2004, on the other hand, the relative performances were quite different, with the Democrats faring only seven points better among union members in House contests, but nineteen points better in the presidential race.

There are some differences in the ways the presidential and congressional vote relate to income categories. The presidential data in Chapter 5 showed that the tendency among whites to vote Democratic was stronger in both the lowest income categories and the categories near (but not at) the top of the income ladder. In the House vote, however, the Democratic vote among low-income voters was weaker. Moreover, this is a great reversal from the past. As recently as the 2000 election, the tendency to vote Democratic tended to increase as income declined across the whole income spectrum, and in the three lowest income categories white voters gave the party between 50 and 60 percent of the vote.

As for education, Democratic performance was only slightly variable across categories except for advanced degrees, where they did thirteen percentage points better than any other category. For the presidency, on the other hand, the party's candidates did best in both the top and bottom category. It should be remembered, however, that all of these differences involve categories with relatively small numbers of respondents, so the results may simply be due to sampling variation. The bottom line is that, overall, presidential and congressional voting among social groups were fairly similar in 2012.[4]

ISSUES AND THE CONGRESSIONAL VOTE

In Chapter 6 we analyzed the impact of issues on the presidential vote in 2012. Any attempt to conduct a parallel analysis for congressional elections is hampered by limited data. One interesting perspective on issues in the congressional vote is gained by asking whether voters are affected by their perceptions of where candidates stand on the issues. For a considerable time, previous analyses demonstrated a relationship between a voter's perception of House candidates' position on a liberal-conservative issue scale and the voter's choice,[5] and we found similar relationships in 2012. For example, among self-identified liberals in the NES survey who viewed the Democratic House candidate as more liberal than the Republican candidate ($N = 102$), 94 percent voted Democratic; among self-identified conservatives who saw the Republican House candidate as more conservative than the Democrat ($N = 158$), 92 percent voted Republican. This is a similar, but stronger, relationship than what we have observed over the last three decades.

Research by Alan I. Abramowitz sheds additional light on this question. In two articles he used NES surveys to demonstrate a relationship between candidate ideology and voter choice in both House and Senate elections.[6] For the 1978 Senate election, Abramowitz classified the contests according to the clarity of the ideological choice the two major party candidates offered to voters. He found that the higher the ideological clarity of the race, the more likely voters were to perceive some difference between the candidates on a liberalism-conservatism scale, and the stronger the relationship was between voters' positions on that scale and the vote. Indeed, in races with a very clear choice, ideology had approximately the same impact on the vote as party identification. In an analysis of House races in 1980 and 1982, Abramowitz found that the more liberal the voter was, the more likely the voter was to vote Democratic; but the relationship then was statistically significant only in 1982. Furthermore, work by Michael Ensley indicates that the degree of ideological divergence between candidates conditions the magnitude of the impact of ideology on vote choice.[7]

Another perspective was offered in analyses by Robert S. Erikson and Gerald C. Wright.[8] They examined the positions of 1982 House candidates on a variety of issues (expressed in response to a CBS News/*New York Times* poll) and found that, on most issues, most of the districts had the choice between a liberal Democrat and a conservative Republican. They also found that moderate candidates did better in attracting votes than more extreme candidates. In a subsequent study, involving the 1994 House elections, Erikson and Wright showed that both the issue stands of incumbents (measured by positions on roll call votes) and the district's ideology (measured by the district's propensity to vote for Michael S. Dukakis in the previous presidential election) are strongly related to the congressional vote.[9] The same authors, in a study of the 2002 elections, employed a measure of candidate ideology that was derived from candidates' responses to questions about issues rather than from roll calls. That analysis confirms that incumbent ideology has a substantial effect on vote share, with moderates gaining more votes relative to more extreme members. Challenger ideology does not have a consistent effect, reflecting the lesser visibility of their positions to the electorate.[10]

We examined the relationships between issues and congressional voting choices in 2012, analyzing the issues we studied in Chapter 6. For the most part, the relationship between issue preferences and congressional vote choices were weak and inconsistent, and these relationships were even weaker when we controlled for the tendency of Democratic identifiers to have liberal positions on these issues and of Republicans to have conservative issue preferences. However, partisan loyalties clearly affect congressional voting, even when we take issue preferences into account. Therefore, before considering the effects of other factors we will provide more information about the effects of party identification on House voting.

PARTY IDENTIFICATION AND THE CONGRESSIONAL VOTE

As our previous discussion demonstrates, party identification has a significant effect on voters' decisions. Table 10-2 (corresponding to Table 8-5 on the presidential vote) reports the percentage of whites voting Democratic for the House across all categories of partisanship from 1952 through 2012.[11] The data reveal that the proportion of voters who cast ballots in accordance with their party identification declined substantially over time through the 1980s. During the 1990s and later, however, there was a resurgence of party voting for the House, especially among Republican identifiers.

Consider first the strong identifier categories. In every election from 1952 through 1964, at least nine out of ten strong party identifiers supported the candidate of their party. After that, the percentage dropped, falling to four out of five in 1980, and then fluctuating through 1992. But in the last four elections, strong identifiers showed levels of loyalty similar to those in the late 1960s. The relationship between party and voting among weak party identifiers shows a more erratic pattern, although defection rates tend to be higher in most years between 1970 and 1992 than earlier. (Because we present the percentage of major-party

TABLE 10-2 Percentage of White Major-Party Voters Who Voted Democratic for the House, by Party Identification, 1952–2012

Party Identification	1952	1954	1956	1958	1960	1962	1964	1966	1968	1970	1972	1974	1976	1978	1980
Strong Democrat	90	97	94	96	92	96	92	92	88	91	91	89	86	83	82
Weak Democrat	76	77	86	88	85	83	84	81	72	76	79	81	76	79	66
Independent, leans Democrat	63	70	82	75	86	74	78	54	60	74	78	87	76	60	69
Independent, no partisan leanings	25	41	35	46	52	61	70	49	48	48	54	54	55	56	57
Independent, leans Republican	18	6	17	26	26	28	28	31	18	35	27	38	32	36	32
Weak Republican	10	6	11	22	14	14	34	22	21	17	24	31	28	34	26
Strong Republican	5	5	5	6	8	6	8	12	8	4	15	14	15	19	22

Party Identification	1982	1984	1986	1988	1990	1992	1994	1996	1998	2000	2002	2004	2008	2012
Strong Democrat	90	87	91	86	91	87	87	87	88	88	93	92	92	89
Weak Democrat	73	66	71	80	80	81	73	70	60	69	73	74	82	86
Independent, leans Democrat	84	76	71	86	79	73	65	70	62	71	75	74	81	75
Independent, no partisan leanings	31	59	59	66	60	53	55	42	45	50	42	46	43	21
Independent, leans Republican	36	39	37	37	33	36	26	19	23	27	28	30	21	8
Weak Republican	20	33	34	29	39	35	21	19	25	15	26	19	22	12
Strong Republican	12	15	20	23	17	16	6	2	8	11	6	8	7	4

Source: Authors' analysis of the ANES surveys.

Note: To approximate the numbers on which these percentages are based, see Table 8-2 in Chapter 8 and Table A8-2 in the Appendix. Actual *N*s are smaller than those that can be derived from these tables because respondents who did not vote (or who voted for a minor party) were excluded from these calculations. Numbers also are lower for the presidential election years because the voting report is provided in the postelection interviews that usually contain about 10 percent fewer respondents than the pre-election interviews in which party identification was measured. Except for 1954, the off-year election surveys are based on a postelection interview. Note that no ANES Time Series survey was conducted in 2006 and 2010.

voters who voted Democratic, the defection rate for Democrats is the reported percentage subtracted from 100 percent.) Note that during this period the tendency to defect was stronger among Republicans, which reflected the Democrats' greater number of incumbents, as discussed in Chapter 9. Probably reflecting the effects of the Republicans' majority status and the corresponding increase in the number of Republican incumbents, from 1996 through 2000 the tendency of Democrats to defect rose, whereas among Republicans it fell. In the last four listed elections, however, the Democratic defection rate was lower in all three Democratic categories (and the GOP defection rate was lower among strong Republicans) compared to the 1998 and 2000 elections. We consider these matters further in the next section.

Despite the increase in defections from party identification from the mid-1960s through the end of the century, strong party identifiers continued to be notably more likely to vote in accord with their party than weak identifiers. In most years, weak Republicans were more likely to vote Republican than independents who leaned toward the Republican Party, although in 1996, 1998, and 2002 these groups were about equally likely to vote Republican. Weak Democrats were more likely to vote Democratic than independents who leaned Democratic in most of the elections from 1952 through 1978, but in a number of elections since then this pattern has been reversed by a small margin. In general, then, the relationship between party identification and the vote was strongest in the 1950s and early 1960s, less strong for a while thereafter, and it shows a substantial recent rebound.

If party identifiers were defecting more frequently in House elections over recent decades, to whom have they been defecting? As one might expect from the last chapter, the answer is: to incumbents.

INCUMBENCY AND THE CONGRESSIONAL VOTE

In Chapter 9 we mentioned Albert D. Cover's analysis of congressional voting behavior from 1958 through 1974.[12] Cover compared the rates of defection from party identification among voters who were of the same party as the incumbent and those who were of the same party as the challenger. The analysis showed no systematic increase over time in defection among voters who shared identification with incumbents, and the proportions defecting varied between 5 percent and 14 percent. Among voters who identified with the same party as challengers, however, the rate of defection—that is, the proportion voting for the incumbent instead of the candidate of their own party—increased steadily from 16 percent in 1958 to 56 percent in 1972, then dropped to 49 percent in 1974. Thus the declining relationship between party identification and House voting resulted largely from increased support for incumbents. Because there were more Democratic incumbents, this tendency was consistent with the higher defection rates among Republican identifiers, as seen in Table 10-2.

Controlling for party identification and incumbency, in Table 10-3 we present data on the percentage of respondents who voted Democratic for the House and Senate in 2012 that confirm this view. In both House and Senate voting we find the same relationship as Cover did. (Recall that because we present the percentage of major-party voters who voted Democratic, the defection rate for Democrats is the reported percentage subtracted from 100 percent. Among Republicans, the percentage reported in the table is the defection rate. By definition, independents cannot defect.) For the House, the proportion of voters defecting from their party identification is low when that identification is shared by the incumbent: 3 percent among Democrats and 1 percent among Republicans.[13] However, when the incumbent belongs to the other party, the rates are much higher: 25 percent among Democrats and 21 percent among Republicans. Note also that the support of the independents is skewed sharply in favor of the incumbent. When there was an incumbent Democrat running, 59 percent of the independents voted Democratic; when there was an incumbent Republican, 74 percent of the independents voted Republican.

The analogous pattern is quite similar in the data on Senate voting. When given the opportunity to support a Republican House incumbent, 25 percent of the Democratic identifiers defected. Faced with the opportunity to support an incumbent Republican senator, 14 percent defected. Similarly, 21 percent of Republicans supported a Democratic House incumbent, while 17 percent

TABLE 10-3   Percentage Who Voted Democratic for the House and Senate, by Party Identification and Incumbency, 2012

	Party identification					
	Democrat		Independent		Republican	
Incumbency	%	(N)	%	(N)	%	(N)
House						
Democrat	97	(156)	59	(140)	21	(71)
None	95	(46)	29	(45)	11	(57)
Republican	75	(86)	26	(120)	1	(152)
Senate						
Democrat	96	(201)	70	(177)	17	(150)
None	89	(54)	37	(65)	10	(65)
Republican	86	(16)	20	(71)	0	(36)

Source: Authors' analysis of the 2012 ANES survey.

Note: The numbers in parentheses are the totals on which the percentages are based. Numbers are weighted. In this table and in subsequent tables in this chapter, strong and weak Democrats and strong and weak Republicans are combined. Independents include those who lean toward either party and "pure" independents.

backed an incumbent Democratic senator. Because the proportion of the electorate that has the chance to vote for Democratic and Republican senatorial candidates will vary greatly from election to election, it is difficult to generalize about the overall effects of incumbency in Senate contests from this type of data. In the remainder of this chapter we continue to explore this relationship among party identification, incumbency, and congressional voting.

THE CONGRESSIONAL VOTE AS REFERENDUM

In Chapter 7 we analyzed the effect of perceptions of presidential performance on the vote for president in 2012, more or less viewing that election as a referendum on Obama's job performance. A similar approach can be applied here, employing different perspectives. On the one hand, a congressional election can be considered a referendum on the performance of a particular member of Congress; on the other hand, it can be viewed as a referendum on the president's performance. We will consider both possibilities here.

As we noted in Chapter 9, for some time, public opinion surveys have shown that the approval ratings of congressional incumbents by their constituents are very high, even when judgments on the performance of Congress as an institution are not. While traveling with House incumbents in their districts, Richard F. Fenno Jr. noted that the people he met overwhelmingly approved of the performance of their own representative, although at the time the public generally disapproved of the job the institution was doing.[14] Data in the 2012 NES survey again indicate widespread approval of House incumbents: among respondents who had an opinion, 70 percent endorsed their member's job performance. Approval was widespread, regardless of the party identification of the voter or the party of the incumbent. Indeed, as Table 10-4 shows, approval is well above 50 percent even among identifiers of the party opposite that of the incumbent.

Further evidence indicates, moreover, that the level of approval has electoral consequences. Table 10-4 presents the level of pro-incumbent voting among voters who share the incumbent's party and among those who are of the opposite party, controlling for whether they approve or disapprove of the incumbent's job performance. If voters approve of the member's performance and share his or her party identification, support is nearly 100 percent. At the opposite pole, among voters from the opposite party who disapprove, support is low. In the mixed categories, the incumbents receive intermediate levels of support. Because approval rates are very high even among voters of the opposite party, most incumbents are reelected by large margins, even in a difficult year such as 2010 for the Democrats or 2008 for the Republicans.

In Chapter 9 we pointed out that midterm congressional elections are influenced by public evaluations of the president's job performance. Voters who think the president is doing a good job are more likely to support the congressional candidate of the president's party. Less scholarly attention has been given to this

TABLE 10-4   Percentage of Voters Who Supported Incumbents in House Voting, by Party Identification and Evaluation of Incumbent's Performance, 2012

| | Voters' evaluation of incumbent's job performance | | | |
| | Approve | | Disapprove | |
	%	(N)	%	(N)
Incumbent is of same party as voter	98	(242)	96	(25)
Incumbent is of opposite party	76	(226)	13	(121)

Source: Authors' analysis of the 2012 ANES survey.

Note: The numbers in parentheses are the totals on which the percentages are based. Numbers are weighted. The total number of cases is somewhat lower than for previous tables because we excluded respondents who did not evaluate the performance of the incumbent and those who live in a district that had no incumbent running.

phenomenon in presidential election years, but the 2012 NES survey provides us with the data needed to explore the question.

On the surface at least, there would appear to be a strong relationship. Among voters who approved of Obama's job performance ($N = 312$), 82 percent voted Democratic for the House; among those who disapproved of the president's performance ($N = 240$), only 13 percent supported Democrats. In 1980 there was a similar relationship between the two variables, but when controls were introduced for party identification and incumbency, the relationship all but disappeared.[15] Approval of Carter increased the Democratic House vote by a small amount among Democrats, but had virtually no effect among independents and Republicans. In 2012, however, the results were different. Table 10-5 presents the relevant data on House voting, controlling for party identification, incumbency, and evaluation of Obama's job performance. The data show that even with these controls, evaluations of the president's job had an impact on House voting by all groups of identifiers. To be sure, Democrats were still more likely both to approve of Obama and to vote Democratic rather than Republican. Yet even after controlling for the pull of incumbency, within all three party identification categories those who disapproved of Obama's job performance were less likely to vote Democratic for the House than were those who approved.

PRESIDENTIAL COATTAILS AND THE CONGRESSIONAL VOTE

Another perspective on the congressional vote, somewhat related to the presidential referendum concept we just considered, is the impact of the voter's presidential vote decision, or the length of a presidential candidate's "coattails."

TABLE 10-5   Percentage Who Voted Democratic for the House, by Evaluation of Obama's Job Performance, Party Identification, and Incumbency, 2012

Party identification	Evaluation of Obama's job performance							
	Incumbent is Republican				Incumbent is Democrat			
	Approve		Disapprove		Approve		Disapprove	
	%	(N)	%	(N)	%	(N)	%	(N)
Democrat	78	(79)	35	(8)	100	(152)	69	(14)
Independent	46	(48)	3	(71)	84	(84)	26	(57)
Republican	7	(14)	0	(141)	70	(14)	8	(56)

Source: Authors' analysis of the 2012 ANES survey.

Note: The numbers in parentheses are the totals on which the percentages are based. Numbers are weighted.

That is, does a voter's decision to support a presidential candidate make him or her more likely to support a congressional candidate of the same party, so that the congressional candidate, as the saying goes, rides into office on the president's coattails?

Expectations about presidential coattails have been shaped in substantial measure by the period of the New Deal realignment. Franklin D. Roosevelt won by landslide margins in 1932 and 1936 and swept enormous congressional majorities into office with him. Research has indicated, however, that such strong pulling power by presidential candidates may have been a historical aberration and, in any event, that presidential candidates' pulling power has declined in recent decades.[16] In an analysis of the coattail effect since 1868, John A. Ferejohn and Randall L. Calvert pointed out that the effect is a combination of two factors: how many voters a presidential candidate can pull to congressional candidates of his party and how many congressional seats can be shifted between the parties by the addition of that number of voters.[17] (The second aspect is called the seats/votes relationship, or the swing ratio.)

Ferejohn and Calvert discovered that the relationship between presidential and congressional voting from 1932 through 1948 was virtually the same as it was from 1896 through 1928 and that the impact of coattails was strengthened by an increase in the swing ratio. In other words, the same proportion of votes pulled in by a presidential candidate produced more congressional seats in the New Deal era than in the past. After 1948, they argued, the coattail effect declined because the relationship between presidential and congressional voting decreased. Analyzing data from presidential elections from 1956 through 1980, Calvert and Ferejohn reached similar conclusions about the length of presidential coattails.[18] They found that although every election during the period exhibited significant coattail voting, over time the extent of such voting probably declined. More recently, James E. Campbell and Joe A. Sumners concluded from an analysis of Senate elections that presidential coattails exert a modest but significant influence on the Senate vote.[19] And Franco Mattei and Joshua Glasgow showed that coattails exerted a systematic effect in open districts, an effect that persisted into the twenty-first century.[20]

Data on the percentage of respondents who voted Democratic for the House and Senate in 2012, controlling for their presidential vote and their party identification, are presented in Table 10-6. For both houses, the expected relationship is apparent. Within each party identification category, the proportion of Obama voters who supported Democratic congressional candidates is significantly higher than the proportion of Romney voters who supported Democratic candidates.

Because we know that this apparent relationship could be just an accidental consequence of the distribution of different types of voters among Democratic and Republican districts, in Table 10-7 we present the same data on House voting in 2012, but this time controlling for the party of the House incumbent. When we made this comparison in 1996, we found that despite this additional control, the relationship held up very well. Within every category for which comparisons were possible, Dole voters supported Democratic candidates at substantially lower rates than did Clinton voters. In 2012 (as well as in 2000–2008), however, there are so few defectors within the two major parties that the comparisons are largely limited to independents, where the effect remains substantial. These limited data are consistent with the interpretation that the presidential vote exerted some small influence on the congressional vote, although not as strong an influence as partisanship and congressional incumbency.

TABLE 10-6   Percentage Who Voted Democratic for the House and Senate, by Party Identification and Presidential Vote, 2012

| | Party identification | | | | | |
| | Democrat | | Independent | | Republican | |
Presidential vote	%	(N)	%	(N)	%	(N)
House						
Romney	51	(20)	10	(162)	4	(253)
Obama	92	(288)	75	(158)	50	(23)
Senate						
Romney	56	(17)	19	(157)	8	(222)
Obama	97	(251)	87	(143)	74	(20)

Source: Authors' analysis of the 2012 ANES survey.

Note: The numbers in parentheses are the totals on which the percentages are based. Numbers are weighted.

TABLE 10-7   Percentage Who Voted Democratic for the House, by Presidential Vote, Party Identification, and Incumbency, 2012

Party identification	Voted for Romney		Voted for Obama	
	%	(N)	%	(N)
	Incumbent is Democrat			
Democrat	68	(14)	100	(153)
Independent	19	(54)	90	(88)
Republican	8	(57)	84	(12)
	Incumbent is Republican			
Democrat	[0]	(5)	77	(88)
Independent	5	(75)	53	(51)
Republican	0	(139)	12	(8)

Source: Authors' analysis of the 2012 ANES survey.

Note: The numbers in parentheses are the totals on which the percentages are based. Numbers are weighted. The number in brackets is the total number voting for either Romney or Obama when there are fewer than ten total voters.

CONCLUSION

In this chapter we have considered a variety of possible influences on voters' decisions in congressional elections. We found that social forces have some impact on that choice. There is evidence from the work of other researchers that issues also have an effect. Incumbency has a major and consistent impact on voters' choices. It solidifies the support of the incumbent's partisans, attracts independents, and leads to defections by voters who identify with the challenger's party. Incumbent support is linked to a positive evaluation of the representative's job by the voters. The tendency to favor incumbents currently appears to benefit the Republican Party in House races. Within the context of this incumbency effect, voters' choices also seem to be affected by their evaluations of the job the president is doing and by their vote for president. Partisanship has some direct impact on the vote, even after controlling for incumbency. The total effect of partisanship is, however, larger, because most incumbents represent districts that have more partisans of their party than of the opposition. Thus, the long-term advantage of Democrats in congressional elections was built on a three-part base: there were more Democrats than Republicans in the electorate; most incumbents of both parties achieved high levels of approval in their constituencies; and the incumbents had resources that made it possible for them to create direct contacts with voters. With the GOP now in the majority in Congress, their members may continue to benefit from the last two factors while they try to reduce their disadvantage on the first.

Chapter 11

The 2012 Elections and the
Future of American Politics

While the Change and Continuity series has considered the entirety of American national elections (see especially Chapters 3, 4, and 5), it has been primarily focused on elections since the advent of high-quality polling, especially the American National Election Studies, which had its first full national survey of public opinion and voting behavior in 1952. In that sense, we are examining elections that extend over a period that is now entering its seventh decade. And we are studying national elections in their entirety—presidential nomination campaigns, presidential general election campaigns, and congressional general election campaigns in particular. That means our analyses make it possible to speak of long-term changes and continuities in the politics of American national elections.

THE GREAT CONTINUITIES:
THE ELECTORAL SYSTEM AND THE PARTY SYSTEM

Continuity of the Electoral System

While much has changed in the nature of political campaigns and in the way citizens relate to issues, candidates, and the political parties since 1952, there are two great continuities. First, the electoral system—that is, the means of access to winning the three sets of national offices—is governed, for all intents and purposes, by the same constitutional design: members of the House are elected for two-year terms in single-member districts by plurality rule,[1] Senators are elected for terms of six years, rotating so that one-third are up for election every two years,[2] and the president is elected for up to two four-year terms every four years through public votes that determine who will be the members of the Electoral College.[3] In practice, it is the state parties that determine slates of candidates for electors. The winners of these various contests have successfully cast a majority of their votes for one candidate for president and for one candidate for vice president throughout this period and, thus, have been the voting body that elected the president and vice president every four years.[4]

The only major change in this fundamental design of the electoral system in this post–World War II era has been in the presidential nominating process, which changed most dramatically in the 1970s, as described in Chapter 1. That process is not a constitutional issue and so can be changed simply because the various state and national party organizations have chosen to do so, perhaps in concert with the state legislatures (which set the legal terms for presidential primary elections). Of course, in another sense, presidential nominations are still done exactly the same way as always, or at least since 1832. The nomination is determined by vote of the delegates to the parties' national conventions (and since 1936, decided by the vote of a simple majority of delegates). What has changed is the way in which the two parties select and perhaps instruct their delegates. With this one exception, what is known as the electoral system has been broadly continuous since 1936.

Changes in Systems Supporting the Electoral System

To be sure, two additional systems that are related to the electoral system, albeit not a part of that system, have changed dramatically since 1952: the media of mass communications and campaign finance. In 1952, television was just beginning its massive growth, and its potential effects on campaigns and elections became apparent in 1960. By that point, a majority of American households had a television. John Kennedy and Richard Nixon were of the new generation that would understand the power of television, although it was Kennedy who was truly comfortable with—indeed would be considered a master of—that medium. The first televised debates were held that year and demonstrated just how powerful the medium was.

Cable television further transformed how campaigns are conducted and how the public views them. By 1970, television was universal, and 80 percent of viewing was of one of the three broadcast networks, while only 6 percent of viewers subscribed to cable television. But by 2005, seven in eight homes received cable or satellite television, coming with over one hundred channels on average, and including an increasing variety of twenty-four-hour news stations. More viewing was done that year on cable channels than on broadcast networks. And the Internet, even more recently, is again altering patterns of news gathering and political engagement.[5] We know that it is now possible for a large number of people to select news attuned to their political opinions, which not only reinforces and extend those views in a liberal or conservative, Democratic or Republican direction, but also reduces the set of agreed-upon political facts that heretofore provided a shared basis for tempering the intensity of political disagreements.

The Internet has had (and is still having) great consequences for newspapers, news magazines, television, and even cable television. The rise of social media, captured most publicly in Barack Obama's 2008 and 2012 campaigns, is still transforming the way campaigns are conducted.

The second system to change radically and repeatedly has been that of campaign finance. This, too, is transformative in ways yet to be fully revealed. In Chapter 1 we discussed briefly the system of campaign finance based on the Federal Election Campaign Act of 1972, its amendments in 1974 and 1976, and its modification in the wake of the Supreme Court case *Buckley v. Valeo* from later that year. That regulatory system evolved over the years, in both presidential and congressional campaigns, particularly noted by the growth of political action committees (PACs) in the 1970s; the spreading use of "soft money" by the political parties as a way to acquire and spend money on campaign-related projects (e.g., turnout drives) that did not have federal limits; and the spread of issue advocacy ads, independent of the parties and candidates, that dramatically increased political campaign expenditures during election campaigns. In 2002, the Bipartisan Campaign Reform Act (BCRA) was passed to regulate some of these changes (sparking yet other changes), especially changing the latter two features described above. The Supreme Court issued a series of rulings about BCRA, but the major decision is the 2009 case (with the ruling issued in 2010) *Citizens United v. Federal Election Commission* (commonly called *Citizens United*), which invalidated many of the central features of BCRA. As we write this, the Supreme Court is considering a new challenge that would end limiting the number of candidates to which individuals can give. If so, there would be essentially one significant remnant of the reforms of the 1970s, a limit on how much can be given to any one candidate or party, and it is reasonable to speculate that that remaining regulation would be vulnerable to challenge. The decision in *Citizens United*, which ruled that "money is speech" and thus under the protection of the First Amendment—even when contributed by corporations or unions—has opened financial avenues in ways barely imaginable only a decade or so ago. How changes in the media and campaign finance will affect public opinion and voting behavior is a work very much still in progress.

Continuity in the Party System

The second great continuity is that the United States has one of the most nearly pure two-party systems in the world. The simple fact that the Democratic and Republican Parties form this two-party system and that the constitutional design of American elections has been largely constant provide the basis of this continuity in national elections since 1952. Indeed, that these two have continued as America's two major parties since about 1860 means not only that there is a two-party system but also that it is the same two parties that have dominated the American electoral system for a time longer than virtually any other nation can claim even to have been a democracy at all.

The ambition of candidates to seek election and reelection, as discussed in Chapters 1 and 9, means that the overwhelming majority of state and national candidates and officeholders for elections to those offices are affiliates of one or the other of these two parties. As we noted earlier, there actually are often a great many more candidates for major office, including the presidency, but the role of these third-party candidates is ordinarily tangential or simply trivial. To be sure, third-party presidential candidates have won considerable numbers of votes in the last seventy years, peaking at the quite remarkable 19 percent of votes cast for H. Ross Perot in 1992 (albeit zero electoral votes), and the 13.5 percent cast for George Wallace in 1968 (and forty-six electoral votes; Wallace being the only presidential candidate since 1952 to win electoral votes as a third-party candidate), but even they did not prevent a major-party candidate (Bill Clinton and Richard Nixon, respectively) from winning an outright majority of the electoral votes and thus the presidency. And in the Congress, the percentage of third-party candidates elected to either the House or the Senate has not risen above a paltry 2 percent in this period, and these few winners almost always caucused with one of the two political parties, acting, that is, as at least a pseudo-partisan.

As a result, the typical general election campaign is effectively, and often exclusively, a contest between a Republican and a Democrat. This structures how they act as candidates and officeholders. This structures how campaigns are run through and observed by the media. And this structures how citizens observe the candidates and campaigns, how they evaluate the alternatives, and how they vote. In other words, the two-party system permeates the full range of electoral behavior, in all its manifestations.

The electoral and the party systems interact and reinforce one another. That all national and most state and local races are conducted under a plurality-winner-take-all, or a near equivalent, system means that all offices are subject to what Maurice Duverger referred to as the mechanical effect from counting votes and the psychological effect among voters that generate a two-party system.[6] Added to this are, of course, the candidates. They have incentives to cement that two-party system into place, largely as they enter elective politics as a career choice. Doing so gives them every incentive to seek to climb the informal hierarchy of offices that Joseph Schlesinger called the "opportunity structure." Because that is headed by the presidency, the general idea is that looking forward to a long successful career in politics, hopefully climbing to the top of the ladder, all but requires entering politics as a Democrat or as a Republican and staying that way for most people, most of the time.[7]

THE GREAT CHANGE: DEPOLARIZATION AND THE RETURN OF PARTISAN POLARIZATION

In 1952, the two political parties were structured primarily along the lines set during the Great Depression and the creation of the New Deal party system during Franklin Roosevelt's presidency, which in turn formed in light of the decline of a Republican majority coalition. The Republican Party achieved majority status at the turn of the twentieth century and held power in the national government for most of the first third of the century. A durable Democratic Party majority emerged by 1932 in a replacement (or as it was known then, a "partisan realignment") sparked by the Great Depression. Roosevelt created a majority party that drew its support most heavily from the cities and from working-class voters, especially those in blue-collar jobs belonging to the industrial and trade unions, and thus largely in the Northeast, Mid-Atlantic, and those Midwest states that border the Great Lakes. These tended to include Catholics and Jews and others who were often the children and grandchildren of the great migration at the end of the nineteenth century and thus of the Eastern and Southern European immigrants, particularly those organized in Democratic machines. In the middle to late 1930s, Roosevelt added the African American population that had recently migrated from the South to the North to this set of groups that made up the New Deal coalition.

This collective grouping was added to the core of the Democratic Party: the solid, one-party South. The great majority of the white South had been overwhelmingly Democratic since the 1860s. It became the only competitive party in the South at the turn of the twentieth century, when it defeated a burgeoning threat from the Populist Party, which was the only serious threat to Democratic hegemony in that region. At the same time, it also reinforced itself as a "lily-white" party in that region, through passage of Jim Crow laws (and other aspects, including the systematic use of violence, that created the Jim Crow system of segregation) to disenfranchise African Americans, along with a good number of poor whites. As the 1950s opened, then, the South made up a very large portion of the Democratic Party, both in terms of electoral votes Democratic presidential candidates could win and in terms of seats controlled in both houses of Congress (see Chapter 9). The Republicans held a majority in the House after World War II for two congresses, in 1947–1948 and 1953–1954. In 1947–1948, the South made up a majority of Democratic representatives. While they were not a majority of all Democrats in other years, they came very close. The result is that, even then, they held a very large minority, so large that the Democratic Party could rarely act in the House or Senate without southern support.

The Republican Party could, in some sense, be defined as the rest of the country, but should largely be understood as a mixture of two groups. These groupings were sometimes called the Main Street and Wall Street wings of the party, and sometimes referred to by the peak leader of each of the two groups, the Taft Republicans (after Ohio Senator Robert Taft), typically economically conservative, Middle America, and isolationist, and the Rockefeller Republicans (after New York Governor and U.S. Vice President Nelson Rockefeller), typically highly educated, residing in or near cities of the coasts, socially liberal and internationalist in outlook.

Both parties thus had internal divisions in this period—indeed, it is hard to imagine a party seeking to win electoral majorities that does not have a diversity of views within it. But by the 1950s, both were stretched particularly broadly and thus were unusually vulnerable to internal divisions. The Democratic Party had been reasonably united early in the New Deal, in large part because southern Democrats were supportive of the first wave of New Deal legislation. The party began to split regionally during the second wave of New Deal legislation after the 1936 elections, and over social issues, particularly those related to race. Thus as the 1950s opened, the party had a semblance of remaining unity, and it could still be well described by the coalition that FDR had put together, even though it was under strain.

But the 1950s was the time of the civil rights movement, and this drove a first wedge deeply into the party that culminated with the passage of the Civil Rights and Voting Rights Acts along with other legislation making up Lyndon Johnson's Great Society programs in the mid-1960s.[8] This led directly to a dramatic and nearly instantaneous increase of African Americans in the Democratic Party, going from a small to an overwhelming majority who identified themselves as Democrats, and they voted accordingly. It was accompanied by the slow exit of white southerners from the party. In addition, time and prosperity weakened the ties of Catholics along with them and others who made up the former working class, but who were now moving up to the middle class. Manufacturing jobs also waned and associated unions lost their political vitality. Thus, their ties to the party weakened.

Thus, the Democratic Party was internally polarized in the 1950s and 1960s, as it consisted of elected officials and other party leaders moving toward both ideological poles. The Republican Party was, as noted above, split in two groups also, although less fully divided than the Democrats. Nonetheless, from 1952 well into the 1970s, the spread of opinion among elected officials (and among the public) in both parties was sufficiently great as to call this an era of depolarization of the two parties. The movement of conservative southerners from Democratic to Republican loyalties and the associated chain of events affecting the two parties reversed, first slowly and then dramatically, the depolarization, leading to the current partisan polarization.

The Republican Party changed, in large measure as the mirror image of changes in the Democratic Party. Thus, Republicans picked up much of what the Democrats lost in the South, such that, by 1995 when it finally reemerged with a majority, the Republican Party in the Congress was led almost in its entirety by southern Republicans. Conversely, the loss of social liberalism in the party effectively cost it any serious chance of majority support in the Northeast and especially New England, where the GOP's huge advantage in 1952 became a dramatic Democratic advantage by 2012.

The great change described thus far was that the Democrats lost their most conservative elements and the Republicans their most liberal wing. The members of the two parties, that is, *sorted* themselves out on ideology, so that the parties hold much less diversity within their ranks; virtually all Democrats are toward the left half of the ideological spectrum, and virtually all Republicans are toward the right half. What Ronald Regan referred to as the "big tent" of a party became a much smaller and more cohesive tent on each side.

This sorting was true at all levels, from the top level of the political elites to the base of political publics. It happened first at the elite level, appearing quite clearly in the Congress, for example, beginning in the 1980s and proceeding through to today. The sorting is also true in the public, albeit moving into place more slowly but nonetheless decisively. The major difference is that the elected officials and the rest of the party elites have become more *polarized*—that is, the two parties in Congress not only vote differently from one another, they appear to be taking ever-more extreme positions, moving farther and farther apart. The result is that few moderates are elected to national office (and likely to state legislatures either).[9] The public has not polarized to anywhere near the same degree, if they have polarized at all—on this later issue political scientists disagree.[10] No one disagrees that the public is much more sorted, however, and to that extent, the public is a reasonably close approximation to the elites in terms of sorting.[11]

This section has reviewed the kinds of changes discussed in Chapters 1, 3, and 5, and parts of 9 and 10. The rest of this chapter lays out additional features we have studied that reflect these continuities and changes. We first consider turnout, as in Chapter 4, which has some remaining features of institutional development, along with a considerable degree of continuity with some relevant changes along the lines of the "great sort." We then turn to the public opinion and voting behavior considered in Chapters 6 through 8 and then remaining features of congressional campaigns and elections in Chapter 9 and 10.

CHANGE AND CONTINUITY IN TURNOUT

Here, we highlight three basic aspects of our analysis in turnout from Chapter 4. The first is that, over the course of American political history, the dominant flow has been toward expansion of suffrage, albeit with several notable exceptions, with a major political question of this sort looming today. The second is that, in many ways, turnout since the 1950s has had a great deal of continuity, in no small measure due to the continuity in the party system. However, and thirdly, there are some signs that even turnout is being affected by the great sort.

One of the central questions for understanding turnout at any time is who is eligible to vote—asking both who is eligible for citizenship and which citizens are eligible to vote. The primary thrust of American democracy has been expansion of both. Thus, for example, in the eighteenth and early nineteenth centuries, the United States may have been the first democratic republic in the modern era, but slaves were excluded from citizenship and suffrage was limited to males (and in many places to white males), often requiring them to hold property and/or have paid taxes. By the middle of the nineteenth century, property-holding requirements were gone and we had essentially achieved one version of universal suffrage—all white male citizens were eligible to vote. The Civil War Amendments (especially the Fifteenth) extended that right to all males, the Nineteenth Amendment (ratified in 1920) extended suffrage to women, and the one amendment within our primary time frame, the Twenty-sixth (1972), provided suffrage for eighteen-, nineteen-, and twenty-year-olds.

This general expansion of the suffrage is counterbalanced in part by two major kinds of legislation that have reduced turnout from what it otherwise might have been. The most direct were the Jim Crow laws that were intended (successfully) to all but eliminate freed slaves and their offspring from the franchise, sweeping up poor whites and others along the way, and undermining the effect of the Civil War Amendments. The second form has been one kind or another of registration laws. These laws were the centerpiece of the third party known as the American (or "Know-nothing") Party in the 1850s, which contested the newly formed Republican Party to replace the Whigs as America's second major party. Their proposals were to reduce or eliminate opportunities for the then-recent wave of immigration (largely of Irish and Germans, but also other Central and Eastern Europeans) to become voters. While immigrant movement to citizenship and voting was slowed in this period, the American Party failed, and the Republicans adopted only parts of the American Party's proposed restrictions as they moved to defeat that party at the polls.

Registration latched more firmly into the American voting regime in the early part of the twentieth century, as part of the Progressive and other parties' "good government" reforms. It was during this time that voting registration became commonplace throughout the nation, and the design of these registration laws was to make it the responsibility of the individuals who wanted to vote to ensure their registration, rather than it being the responsibility of the government to ensure registration of all eligible voters, as in most of the rest of the advanced democracies. These registration laws had the intended effect of reducing turnout among the poorer and the immigrant populations, especially in the North. In that way, they were similar to the Jim Crow laws in the South, which were directed at a somewhat different population, but designed to give an edge to upper- and middle-class voters over working- and lower-class voters. This opt-in system of registration to vote was justified as good government on the grounds that it would reduce fraudulent voting.

The post-1952 period has been typified by attempts to increase turnout through easing of registration requirements and other aspects that increase the cost and complication of turnout. Most notable is the so-called motor-voter bill (1993), which got its nickname because the law's provisions allowed voter registration at various places, including where one gets a driver's license. Current legislative initiatives, however, are moving mostly in the opposite direction, particularly voter identification laws that, in the name of avoiding fraudulent voting, require voters to present a state-issued voter identification card in order to vote. Such laws are likely to have their greatest effects on both immigrants and on minority and poor voters (and also on the youngest voters), thus blending both targets from prior eras and also hitting disproportionately those more likely to vote Democratic than others.

Actual turnout rates thereby fluctuate in part as a function of who are eligible voters. As we have seen, since 1952 the turnout for presidential elections has hewed to a fairly restricted range of the mostly mid-50s to the lower to mid-60s in terms of percentage of the politically eligible and voting-eligible population (see Figure 4-2). Congressional elections are typically in the low to mid-40 percentile ranges.

This limited variation is nonetheless important, as 10 percent of our population represents tens of millions of people. The major explanations for the over-time changes (amid over-time continuity) relate to political parties and to how the public views the government, as well as the large-scale changes in population reviewed elsewhere. Two general trends are the decline in such measures as trust and sense of external efficacy of the government, notable from the mid-1960s on, and the decline and regathering of strength of partisanship from the early 1970s to the most recent decades. The two together suggest a decline and the resurgence of turnout, as partisanship declined and then resurged, but to a somewhat lower peak, due to the declining views of government overall. We will see again this idea that partisanship declined in relevance and importance to the public, just as the divisions within the parties grew most pronounced, and the parties became more important once again, as the great sort and polarization of partisan elites gathered strength. So let us turn to those continuities and changes now.

CONTINUITIES IN ELECTORAL PARTISANSHIP

Perhaps the single most important fact for understanding American electoral behavior is the continuing relevance of partisan attachments. As we discussed in Chapter 8, the way we as election observers understand partisanship has undergone several important changes over the last few decades. But the three major continuities stand out.

The first is that substantial majorities have found, and continue to find, the two political parties and their own partisanship of central importance for their relationship to the political system and especially to electoral politics. The proportion of "pure" independents as we head toward 2016 is essentially identical to what it was in 1956, having changed only from 9 percent in 1956 to 10 percent in 2012. There was considerable interest in and concern about the growth of independence and hence the decline of partisanship, especially in the 1970s, as we discussed in Chapter 8. The proportion of pure independents did increase by roughly 50 percent, but of course that is a growth from near 10 percent to a peak of just 15 percent in 1972 and 1976, a growth that has now settled back to the levels of the 1950s and 1960s. The proportions of independents that lean toward one party or the other also increased and still show some signs of volatility. But in the scheme of things, these are modulated variations over time. The dominant thrust is of no more than moderate change about a rather constant level.

The second and related continuity is that the balance of partisanship between the two parties has fluctuated about an overall continuously modest but real advantage for Democrats. That is, as we noted in Chapter 8, since 1952 the balance of Democrats to Republicans has been in the range of 55–45 to 60–40 or even more. It is very important to note that there has been a long-term move toward parity between the two parties. Thus, the balance was typically closer to 60–40 earlier and is now more regularly at the bottom end of that range. Indeed, if we take the proportion of those who said first that they were Democrats to Republicans (i.e., exclude "leaners") in 2012, that proportion is but 53 percent, just below the historical range. More important, if we look at the three partisan groupings—adding "leaners" back in—the two parties are essentially tied in support (and actually were numerically so in 2012). Thus, there is a long-term secular movement of the balance between the two parties in loyalties in the electorate toward parity, but a parity that still, as it were, "leans" toward the Democrats.

The third major continuity is that partisanship is closely related to the choices voters make. Being a partisan is just as strongly related to turnout as ever. Claiming to be a Democrat is just as closely related to how one evaluates candidates and issues and as closely related to the vote—for president and for Congress—as ever. Indeed, this is another set of cases in which these relationships were strong in the 1950s and 1960s and began to sag in strength into the 1970s and 1980s, but have reasserted themselves to approximately their earlier levels. This broad but not unvarying stability is sort of the fly wheel that keeps a balance both in the public and in office. But there are some very important changes in the electorate, too.

CHANGES IN THE PARTISAN ELECTORATE

We have already discussed some important changes in the makeup of the electorate, those that underlie the analyses in Chapter 5 in particular. One aspect of some of these changes that has become apparent only recently is that people are sorting themselves by their decisions as to where to live in ways that reinforce partisan sorting in the public. Thus, the regeneration of cities is due in significant degree to the attraction urban areas have for the young, the professionals, and others who are likely to be Democrats. Smaller towns and rural areas are either attracting more conservative (often older) voters who are likely to identify as Republican or disproportionately losing potential Democratic votes. In either event, geographic mobility has played a major role in public sorting and in creating more solid one-party areas. This sort of micro-change goes along with the changes in overall configuration of the population already noted, particularly the coming of the baby boomers to voting age in the 1960s and 1970s, and then the increasing aging of that population as baby boomers near retirement. This generational shift accompanies other changes, such as huge new immigration, and thus the coming of not only Latinos as a growing electoral force, but also the apparently soon-to-come era in which whites no longer are a majority of the voting-age population. Each of these is directly or indirectly related to the partisan nature of the electorate and ultimately to its vote.

If these changes help us understand the dynamics of party identification in post-war America, the great sort they helped induce in the public's partisanship has had effects on other variables, often those directly related to the vote. It appears, for example, that elite polarization has led to a truly substantial increase in the proportion of the public who see the parties and their candidates taking different positions (and seeing those positions "correctly") and thus being able to cast a vote based on one or more prospective issues. It is simply much easier to know or correctly guess where a Republican and where a Democrat stand on issue after issue, and thus incorporate prospective issues into their decision calculus. Or while retrospective voting has been continuously important, partisan sorting has increased its distribution, with incumbent-party partisans likely to want to reward their party more strongly and out-party partisans opposing more strongly, thus strengthening the potency of retrospective voting as well. Finally, the great sort and increased partisan polarization of elites has appeared to make all kinds of political judgments easier. Examples we illustrated include evaluations of the president's performance overall and in particular areas, such as the economy or war-making, and judgments about which party will best handle highly important problems or put the country on the right track. In short, elite partisan polarization and public sorting have permeated throughout the electoral arena. We suggest that this means the political parties are seen sending signals to the electorate with greater relevance and meaning and the public is conditioning their beliefs and choices on partisanship in ways quite different from the 1970s. We conclude this section, however, by noting that all this is a question of relative balance, that partisanship has always been important, waxing and waning within relatively confined ranges.

CHANGE AND CONTINUITY IN THE U.S. CONGRESS

It is not surprising that the significant changes we have outlined, particularly the polarization of elites and the shifts in the partisan electorate, have had substantial impacts on the institutional operation of the Congress and on congressional elections. Indeed, these institutional and electoral forces have interacted to amplify the effects, feeding back on one another over time. However, it is also true that many of the most significant patterns of the past have persisted into this new polarized era.

Despite the fact that three of the last four congressional election years (2006, 2008, and 2010) have resulted in "wave elections" in which one party was hit with the loss of a large number of House seats, the advantages of incumbency we discussed in Chapter 9 still persist. It is still true that most elections involve incumbents and that the great majority of incumbents win, in both the House and the Senate. This fact affects the governing choices of the incumbents, the decisions of potential candidates about whether to run, and the choices of individuals who control campaign-relevant resources about whom to support.

Still, the great changes have had profound consequences and have produced a new equilibrium in governing and elections. The realignment of the South from a Democratic bastion to a Republican one, coupled with its echo in parts of the North leading to increased Democratic support there, created the much more ideologically homogeneous legislative party coalitions we have today, with little or no overlap between those coalitions. This development, in turn, led to the transformation of legislative governance in both chambers. The weak party organizations and the dominant role of committees in the period from World War II through the early 1970s gradually gave way to a pattern of majority-party dominance in which committee contingents were responsive to their respective party caucuses in most matters.

When the party coalitions were very diverse and overlapping, members were reluctant to vest party leaders with significant powers because those members could not confidently predict what ideological orientation future leaders would have. Conservative Democrats might be satisfied with one of their own being a powerful leader, but they could not be sure that a liberal northerner would not be chosen subsequently, and that could lead to policies they would dislike. Republicans were in a parallel situation. When partisan realignment gradually reduced party heterogeneity, however, members' reluctance to delegate power to leaders also declined. This resulted in the reform era of the 1970s, when the House Democrats undermined the protections that the seniority system gave to committee leaders, forcing them to become responsive to party opinion. The reforms also greatly increased the influence of party leaders, particularly by transferring control over the legislative agenda from independent committees to those leaders. The Senate experienced some parallel, but less extensive, reforms at the same time, and the effects of these moves were reinforced when the Republicans took congressional control in the 1994 elections and they moved even further in strengthening the parties than the Democrats had. Since then these patterns (which we have labeled *conditional party government*[12]) have been further reinforced.

In this more partisan governing environment, the policies each party pursued became more divergent. This presented clearer pictures of the orientations of the parties to the electorate, as we discussed above, making it easier for voters to make their vote choice in light of their policy preferences. This enhanced party sorting, making rank-and-file preferences also more homogeneous, although not nearly so much as among elites. This was especially true of the most politically active citizens, the type who were most likely to vote in party primaries. As a result, the more extreme elements of each party's voter base had an increasingly strong influence over candidate selection. And the parties' increasing success at political gerrymandering, creating more districts that were safe for each party, created conditions that put even greater emphasis on the opinions of primary electorates.

Another area in which the enhancement of party government had an electoral impact was in campaign funding. Before the reform era, congressional candidates were largely on their own in fund-raising; the portion of such funds that came from parties and independent spending was miniscule. But as parties became more important (and more dependable) in governing, their role in raising money and channeling it to their candidates expanded as well. The parties also became more active in candidate recruiting, training, and advising, as we discussed in Chapter 9. This trend was paralleled by the rise of campaign spending by independent ideological groups and later the super PACs. Both the party spending and the independent spending enhanced incentives for members to support their parties within the government, or at least to not work independently with members of the other party, furthering the development of polarization.

Thus due to electoral developments we have experienced the rise of stronger, more homogeneous, and more policy-motivated parties in Congress, parties that are more divergent from one another regarding preferred policy outcomes. When unified government occurs, the majority party can often achieve a large part of its legislative program (although even then institutional features like the filibuster can frustrate some initiatives). However, when divided government is in effect, a compromise outcome is often difficult to achieve because a result that is desirable to one side is often anathema to the other, and an outcome in the middle is far from what a large portion of the members on both sides want. These are the conditions that resulted in the government shutdown during the fight over the budget and the debt ceiling in October 2013. Moreover, since the results under unified government are pleasing to the majority party but less so to the middle of the electorate (and are mostly seen as just awful by the minority party), unified government can easily create the electoral conditions that produce divided government, as the first two years of the Obama administration led to the Republican landslide of 2010. This feedback loop between elections and government, and then the subsequent elections, is structured by the changing political conditions we have documented, and it is very difficult to foresee any developments that are likely to break the pattern.

Appendix

TABLE A7-1   Evaluation of Government Performance on Most Important Problem and Major-Party Vote, 1972–2008

A. Evaluation of government performance on most important problem (percent)

Government performance	1972[a]	1976	1980	1984	1988	1992	1996[a]	2000[a]	2004[a]	2008[a]
Good job	12	8	4	16	8	2	7	10	60	26
Only fair job	58	46	35	46	37	28	44	44		43
Poor job	30	46	61	39	56	69	48	47	40	31
Total	100	100	100	101	101	99	99	101	100	100
(N)	(993)	(2,156)[b]	(1,319)	(1,797)	(1,672)	(1,974)[b]	(752)[b]	(856)[b]	(1,024)[b]	(2,083)[b]

B. Percentage of major-party vote for incumbent party's nominee

Government performance	Nixon[a]	Ford	Carter	Reagan	Bush	Bush	Clinton[a]	Gore[a]	Bush	McCain
Good job	85	72	81	89	82	70	93	70	76	74
(N)	(91)	(128)[b]	(43)	(214)	(93)	(27)[b]	(38)[b]	(58)[b]	(460)[b]	(383)[b]
Only fair job	69	53	55	65	61	45	68	60	47	
(N)	(390)	(695)[b]	(289)	(579)	(429)	(352)[b]	(238)[b]	(239)[b]	(658)[b]	
Poor job	46	39	33	37	44	39	44	37	11	21
(N)	(209)	(684)[b]	(505)	(494)	(631)	(841)[b]	(242)[b]	(230)[b]	(305)[b]	(512)[b]

Source: Authors' analysis of ANES surveys.

Note: The numbers in parentheses are the totals on which the percentages are based.

[a] In 1972, 1996, 2000, and 2004, the questions were asked of a randomly selected half-sample. In 1972 respondents were asked whether the government was being (a) very helpful, (b) somewhat helpful, or (c) not helpful at all in solving this most important problem. In 2004 respondents were asked whether the government was doing (a) a very good job, (b) a good job, (c) a bad job, or (d) a very bad job. "Good job" includes both "very good" and "good job"; "poor job" includes both "bad" and "very bad."

[b] Number is weighted.

TABLE A7-2 Evaluation of Party Seen as Better on Most Important Problem and Major-Party Vote, 1972–2000, 2008

Party better	1972[a]	1976	1980	1984	1988	1992	1996[a]	2000[a]	2008
A. Distribution of responses on party better on most important problem (percent)									
Republican	28	14	43	32	22	13	22	23	27
No difference[c]	46	50	46	44	54	48	54	50	18
Democratic	26	37	11	25	24	39	24	27	55
Total	100	101	100	101	100	100	100	100	100
(N)	(931)	(2,054)[b]	(1,251)	(1,785)	(1,655)	(1,954)[b]	(746)[b]	(846)[b]	(1,932)[b]
B. Percentage of major-party voters who voted Democratic for president									
Republican	6	3	12	5	5	4	15	9	6
(N)	(207)	(231)[b]	(391)	(464)	(295)	(185)[b]	(137)[b]	(143)[b]	(429)[b]
No difference[c]	32	35	63	41	46	45	63	52	29
(N)	(275)	(673)[b]	(320)	(493)	(564)	(507)[b]	(250)[b]	(227)[b]	(237)[b]
Democratic	75	89	95	91	92	92	97	94	87
(N)	(180)	(565)[b]	(93)	(331)	(284)	(519)[b]	(133)[b]	(153)[b]	(800)[b]

Source: Authors' analysis of ANES surveys.

Notes: The numbers in parentheses are the totals on which the percentages are based. Question wording, 1972–2000: "Thinking of the most important problem facing the United States, which party do you think is best in dealing with it?" 2008: "Thinking of the most important political problem facing the United States, which party do you think is best in dealing with it?"

[a] In 1972, 1996, and 2000, the questions were asked of a randomly selected half-sample. In 1972 respondents were asked which party would be more likely to get the government to be helpful in solving the most important problem. This question was not asked in 2004.

[b] Number is weighted.

[c] In 2008 the middle response allowed was "other."

TABLE A8-1   Approval of Incumbent's Handling of Job, by Party Identification, 1972–2008 (percent)

Year	Strong Democrat	Weak Democrat	Independent, leans Democrat	Party identification Independent	Independent leans Republican	Weak Republican	Strong Republican
2012	94	79	74	43	18	20	6
2008	3	11	6	26	46	47	74
2004	6	26	23	39	78	89	98
2000	92	88	81	65	49	52	23
1996	98	89	85	66	45	49	18
1992	12	28	20	32	65	71	91
1988	24	43	37	70	82	83	94
1984	22	48	32	76	90	93	96
1980	73	54	44	35	19	19	9
1976	24	55	46	69	87	85	96
1972	38	65	52	73	87	92	94

Source: Authors' analysis of ANES surveys.

Note: To approximate the numbers on which these percentages are based, see Tables 8-2, 8-3, A8-2, and A8-3.

TABLE A8-2   Party Identification in Presidential Years, Pre-election Surveys, 1952–1976 (percent)

Party identification	1952	1956	1960	1964	1968	1972	1976
Strong Democrat	23	22	24	27	20	15	15
Weak Democrat	26	24	25	25	26	25	24
Independent, leans Democratic	10	7	6	9	10	11	12
Independent, no partisan leanings	5	9	9	8	11	15	15
Independent, leans Republican	8	9	7	6	9	10	10
Weak Republican	14	14	14	14	15	13	14
Strong Republican	14	16	15	11	10	10	9
Total	100	101	100	100	101	99	99
(N)	(1,689)	(1,690)	(1,132)	(1,536)	(1,531)	(2,695)	(2,218)

Source: Authors' analysis of ANES surveys.

TABLE A8-3   Party Identification among Whites, 1952–1978 (percent)

Party identification[a]	1952	1954	1956	1958	1960	1962	1964	1966	1968	1970	1972	1974	1976	1978
Strong Democrat	21	22	20	26	20	22	24	17	16	17	12	15	13	12
Weak Democrat	25	25	23	22	25	23	25	27	25	22	25	20	23	24
Independent, leans Democratic	10	9	6	7	6	8	9	9	10	11	12	13	11	14
Independent, no partisan leaning	6	7	9	8	9	8	8	12	11	13	13	15	15	14
Independent, leans Republican	7	6	9	5	7	7	6	8	10	9	11	9	11	11
Weak Republican	14	15	14	17	14	17	14	16	16	16	14	15	16	14
Strong Republican	14	13	16	12	17	13	12	11	11	10	11	9	10	9
Apolitical	2	2	2	3	1	3	1	1	1	1	1	3	1	3
Total	99	99	99	100	99	101	99	101	100	99	99	99	100	101
(N)	(1,615)	(1,015)	(1,610)[b]	(1,638)[b]	(1,739)[b]	(1,168)	(1,394)[b]	(1,131)	(1,387)	(1,395)	(2,397)	(2,246)[b]	(2,490)[b]	(2,006)

Source: Authors' analysis of ANES surveys.

[a] The percentage supporting another party is not presented; it usually totals less than 1 percent and never totals more than 1 percent.

[b] Numbers are weighted.

TABLE A8-4   Party Identification among Blacks, 1952–1978 (percent)

Party Identification[a]	1952	1954	1956	1958	1960	1962	1964	1966	1968	1970	1972	1974	1976	1978
Strong Democrat	30	24	27	32	25	35	52	30	56	41	36	40	34	37
Weak Democrat	22	29	23	19	19	25	22	31	29	34	31	26	36	29
Independent, leans Democratic	10	6	5	7	7	4	8	11	7	7	8	15	14	15
Independent, no partisan leaning	4	5	7	4	16	6	6	14	3	12	12	12	8	9
Independent, leans Republican	4	6	1	4	4	2	1	2	1	1	3	-[b]	1	2
Weak Republican	8	5	12	11	9	7	5	7	1	4	4	-[b]	2	3
Strong Republican	5	11	7	7	7	6	2	2	1	0	4	3	2	3
Apolitical	17	15	18	16	14	15	4	3	3	1	2	4	1	2
Total	100	101	100	100	101	100	100	100	101	100	100	100	99	100
(N)	(171)	(101)	(146)	(161)[c]	(171)[c]	(110)	(156)	(132)	(149)	(157)	(267)	(224)[c]	(290)[c]	(230)

Source: Authors' analysis of ANES surveys.

[a] The percentage supporting another party is not presented; it usually totals less than 1 percent and never totals more than 1 percent.

[b] Less than 1 percent.

[c] Numbers are weighted.

TABLE A8-5   White Major-Party Voters Who Voted Democratic for President, by Party Identification, 1952–1976 (percent)

Party identification	1952	1956	1960	1964	1968	1972	1976
Strong Democrat	82	85	91	94	89	66	88
Weak Democrat	61	63	70	81	66	44	72
Independent, leans Democratic	60	65	89	89	62	58	73
Independent, no partisan leanings	18	15	50	75	28	26	41
Independent, leans Republican	7	6	13	25	5	11	15
Weak Republican	4	7	11	40	10	9	22
Strong Republican	2	a	2	9	3	2	3

Source: Authors' analysis of ANES surveys.

Note: To approximate the numbers on which these percentages are based, see Table 8-2. Actual *N*s will be smaller than those that can be derived from these tables because respondents who did not vote (or voted for a non-major-party candidate) have been excluded from the calculations. Numbers also will be lower because the voting report is provided in the postelection interviews, which usually contain about 10 percent fewer respondents than the pre-election interviews in which party identification is measured.

a Less than 1 percent.

TABLE A8-6   Approval of Incumbent's Handling of the Economy among Partisan Groups, 1984–1996 (percent)

Year	Attitudes toward handling of the economy	Party Identification							
		Strong Democrat	Weak Democrat	Independent, leans Democrat	Independent	Independent, leans Republican	Weak Republican	Strong Republican	Total
1984	Approve	17	41	32	68	84	86	95	58
	Disapprove	83	59	68	32	16	14	5	42
	Total	100	100	100	100	100	100	100	100
	(N)	(309)	(367)	(207)	(179)	(245)	(277)	(249)	(1,833)
1988	Approve	19	35	32	57	76	79	92	54
	Disapprove	81	65	68	43	24	21	8	46
	Total	100	100	100	100	100	100	100	100
	(N)	(337)	(332)	(229)	(185)	(262)	(262)	(269)	(1,876)
1992[a]	Approve	3	9	6	9	31	34	66	20
	Disapprove	97	91	94	91	69	66	34	80
	Total	100	100	100	100	100	100	100	100
	(N)	(425)	(445)	(340)	(267)	(310)	(347)	(266)	(2,401)
1996[a]	Approve	96	82	76	58	46	49	30	66
	Disapprove	4	18	24	42	54	50	70	34
	Total	100	100	100	100	100	100	100	100
	(N)	(310)	(325)	(228)	(131)	(188)	(263)	(209)	(1,655)

Source: Authors' analysis of ANES surveys.

[a] Numbers are weighted.

TABLE A8-7   Balance-of-Issues Positions among Partisan Groups, 1976–1996 (percent)

Issue positions closer to[a]	Strong Democrat	Weak Democrat	Independent, leans Democrat	Independent	Independent, leans Republican	Weak Republican	Strong Republican	Total
1976								
Democratic candidate	28	27	22	15	12	9	3	18
Neutral[b]	32	26	37	29	27	23	27	29
Republican candidate	39	47	40	55	61	67	69	53
Total	99	100	99	99	100	99	99	100
(N)	(422)	(655)	(336)	(416)	(277)	(408)	(254)	(2,778)
1980								
Democratic candidate	26	23	27	20	12	10	9	19
Neutral	34	37	33	43	40	43	31	37
Republican candidate	40	40	40	37	48	48	60	43
Total	100	100	100	100	100	101	100	99
(N)	(245)	(317)	(161)	(176)	(150)	(202)	(127)	(1,378)
1984								
Democratic candidate	57	49	59	35	23	29	14	39
Neutral	32	37	28	48	46	40	39	38
Republican candidate	11	14	13	17	32	32	47	23
Total	100	100	100	100	101	101	100	100
(N)	(331)	(390)	(215)	(213)	(248)	(295)	(256)	(1,948)
1988								
Democratic candidate	49	36	50	33	21	21	11	32
Neutral	34	40	38	48	46	43	35	40
Republican candidate	17	24	12	19	33	36	53	29
Total	100	100	100	100	100	100	99	101

TABLE A8-7 (Continued)

Issue positions closer to[a]		Party Identification							
	Strong Democrat	Weak Democrat	Independent, leans Democrat	Independent	Independent, leans Republican	Weak Republican	Strong Republican	Total
(N)	(355)	(359)	(240)	(215)	(270)	(281)	(279)	(1,999)
1992[b]								
Democratic candidate	40	36	30	26	13	13	9	25
Neutral	55	57	65	70	74	77	74	67
Republican candidate	5	7	4	5	13	11	17	9
Total	100	100	99	101	100	101	100	101
(N)	(380)	(389)	(313)	(235)	(283)	(335)	(238)	(2,192)
1996[b]								
Democratic candidate	44	27	35	17	13	9	1	22
Neutral	27	36	34	43	27	23	14	29
Republican candidate	30	37	31	40	60	68	85	49
Total	101	100	100	100	100	100	100	100
(N)	(313)	(333)	(229)	(140)	(195)	(268)	(217)	(1,696)

Source: Authors' analysis of ANES surveys.

[a] The Democratic category on the condensed balance-of-issues measure includes any respondent who is at least slightly Democratic; the Republican category includes any respondent who is at least slightly Republican. The neutral category is the same as the neutral category on the seven-point issue scale (see Table 6-5).

[b] Numbers are weighted.

Notes

INTRODUCTION

1. For an analysis of the strategies in this election, see John H. Kessel, *The Goldwater Coalition: Republican Strategies in 1964* (Indianapolis: Bobbs-Merrill, 1968).

2. See, for example, Benjamin Ginsberg and Martin Shefter, *Politics by Other Means: The Importance of Elections in America* (New York: Basic Books, 1990); and Matthew A. Crenson and Benjamin Ginsberg, *Downsizing Democracy: How America Sidelined Its Citizens and Privatized Its Public* (Baltimore: Johns Hopkins University Press, 2002).

3. See Sheryl Gay Stolberg and Bill Vlasic, "U.S. Moving to Overhaul Ailing Auto Industry," *New York Times*, March 30, 2009, A1; and Jeffrey McCracken and John D. Stoll, "GM Blitzes Washington in Attempt to Win Aid," *Wall Street Journal*, November 15, 2008, http://online.wsj.com/news/articles/SB122670818143330019.

4. For a record of the public's opinion of the Affordable Care Act ("Obamacare") see Real Clear Politics, "Public Approval of Health Care Law," http://www.realclearpolitics.com/epolls/other/obama_and_democrats_health_care_plan-1130.html.

5. See, for example, Pete Kasperowicz, "House Votes 232-185 to Block the IRS from Enforcing Obamacare," *The Hill*, August 2, 2013, http://thehill.com/blogs/floor-action/house/315267-house-votes-to-block-irs-enforcement-of-obamacare.

6. See Gerald F. Seib, "Was the Point Republicans Made in the Shutdown Worth the Price?" *Wall Street Journal*, October 16, 2013, http://online.wsj.com/news/articles/SB10001424052702304384104579139961910774786; and Jonathan Weisman and Ashley Parker, "Shutdown Is Over," *New York Times*, October 17, 2013, A1.

7. See Nicole Mellow, "Voting Behavior: How the Democrats Rejuvenated Their Coalition," in *The Elections of 2012*, ed. Michael Nelson (Thousand Oaks, Calif.: CQ Press, 2014); and for the argument underlying these claims, see John B. Judis and Ruy Teixeira, *The Emerging Democratic Majority* (New York: A Lisa Drew Book/Scribner, 2002).

8. Lanny J. Davis, "The Obama Realignment," *Wall Street Journal*, November 6, 2008, A19.

9. Paul R. Abramson, John H. Aldrich, and David W. Rohde, *Change and Continuity in the 2008 and 2010 Elections* (Washington, D.C.: CQ Press, 2012), 284.

10. Kevin P. Phillips, *The Emerging Republican Majority* (New Rochelle, N.Y.: Arlington House, 1969).

11. Phil Gailey, "Republicans Start to Worry about Signs of Slippage," *New York Times*, August 25, 1988, E5.

12. For a discussion of the history of this concept, see Theodore Rosenof, *Realignment: The Theory That Changed the Way We Think about American Politics* (Lanham, Md.: Rowman and Littlefield, 2003).

13. V. O. Key Jr., "A Theory of Critical Elections," *Journal of Politics* 17 (February 1955): 4.

14. V. O. Key Jr., "Secular Realignment and the Party System," *Journal of Politics* 21 (May 1959): 198.

15. These states were, and still are, the most heavily Democratic states. Both voted Republican in seventeen of the eighteen presidential elections between 1856 and 1924, voting Democratic only when the Republican Party was split in 1912 by Theodore Roosevelt's Progressive Party candidacy. For a discussion of partisan change in the New England states, see Chapter 3.

16. V. O. Key Jr., *Parties, Politics, and Pressure Groups*, 5th ed. (New York: Thomas Y. Crowell, 1964), 186.

17. In addition to the eleven states that formed the Confederacy (Alabama, Arkansas, Florida, Georgia, Louisiana, Mississippi, North Carolina, South Carolina, Tennessee, Texas, and Virginia), Delaware, Kentucky, Maryland, and Missouri were slave states. The fifteen free states in 1848 were Connecticut, Illinois, Indiana, Iowa, Maine, Massachusetts, Michigan, New Hampshire, New Jersey, New York, Ohio, Pennsylvania, Rhode Island, Vermont, and Wisconsin. By 1860 three additional free states—California, Minnesota, and Oregon—had been admitted to the Union.

18. John H. Aldrich, *Why Parties? A Second Look* (Chicago: University of Chicago Press, 2011), 282–287.

19. Thomas G. Hansford and Brad T. Gomez, "Estimating the Electoral Effects of Voter Turnout," *American Political Science Review* 104 (May, 2010): 268–288.

20. Byron E. Shafer, ed., *The End of Realignment? Interpreting American Electoral Eras* (Madison: University of Wisconsin Press, 1991). See, for example, Joel H. Silbey, "Beyond Realignment and Realignment Theory," 3–23; Everett Carll Ladd, "Like Waiting for Godot: The Uselessness of 'Realignment' for Studying Change in Contemporary American Politics," 24–36; and Byron E. Shafer, "The Notion of an Electoral Order: The Structure of Electoral Politics at the Accession of George Bush," 37–84. Shafer's book also contains an excellent bibliographical essay: Harry F. Bass, "Background to Debate: Reader's Guide and Bibliography," 141–178.

21. David R. Mayhew, *Electoral Realignments: A Critique of an American Genre* (New Haven, Conn.: Yale University Press, 2002).

22. Edward G. Carmines and James A. Stimson, *Issue Evolution: Race and the Transformation of American Politics* (Princeton, N.J.: Princeton University Press, 1989), 12–13.

23. Carmines and Stimson, *Issue Evolution*, 13.

24. Key, "Secular Realignment and the Party System," 198–199.

25. The theory of punctuated equilibrium was first developed by the evolutionary biologists and paleontologists Niles Eldredge and Stephen Jay Gould. See Niles Eldredge and Stephen Jay Gould, "Punctuated Equilibria: An Alternative to Phyletic Gradualism" in Thomas J. M. Schropf, ed. *Models of Paleobiology* (San Francisco: Freeman, Cooper and Company, 1972).

26. Carmines and Stimson, *Issue Evolution*, 13.

27. John H. Aldrich argues that the decline of local party machines, technological innovations—particularly the advent of television—and the rise of a policy-motivated activist class allowed ambitious politicians to bypass the party organization and create "candidate-centered" campaigns. The result was the demise of the traditional "mass political party" (i.e., the party as organization), and in its place followed a new type of party, one that provides services (e.g., expertise, financial and in-kind resources) to its candidates. The emergent activist class also pressured the parties to democratize their presidential nomination systems. Reforms, such as the Democratic Party's McGovern-Fraser Commission, resulted in the proliferation of primaries as the main vehicle by which party nominees are chosen. See Aldrich, *Why Parties: A Second Look*, 255–292.

28. Aldrich, *Why Parties: A Second Look*, 263.

29. See Russell J. Dalton, Paul Allen Beck, and Scott C. Flanagan, "Electoral Change in Advanced Industrial Democracies," in *Electoral Change in Advanced Industrial Democracies: Realignment or Dealignment?* eds. Russell J. Dalton, Scott C. Flanagan, and Paul Allen Beck (Princeton, NJ: Princeton University Press, 1984), 14.

30. Ronald Inglehart and Avram Hochstein, "Alignment and Dealignment of the Electorate in France and the United States," *Comparative Political Studies* 5 (October 1972): 343–372.

31. Mark Hugo Lopez, Ana Gonzalez-Barrerra, and Seth Motel, "As Deportations Rise to Record Levels, Most Latinos Oppose Obama's Policy: President's Approval Rating Drops, but Obama Has a Big Lead over 2012 GOP Rivals," *Pew Hispanic Center*, December 28, 2011, http://www.pewhispanic.org/files/2011/12/Deportations-and-Latinos.pdf.

32. According to Michael P. McDonald, 221,925,820 Americans were eligible to vote. See McDonald, "2012 General Election Turnout Rates," http://elections.gmu.edu/Turnout_2012G.html. We say "on or before" November 6 because in 2012 about one-third of voters voted before Election Day.

33. Voters may also be influence by random factors as well, but by their very nature, these random factors cannot be systematically explained.

34. For two excellent summaries of research on voting behavior, see Russell J. Dalton and Martin P. Wattenberg, "The Not So Simple Act of Voting," in *Political Science: The State of the Discipline II*, ed. Ada W. Finifter (Washington, D.C.: American Political Science Association, 1993), 193–218; and Morris P. Fiorina, "Parties, Participation, and Representation in America: Old Theories Face New Realities," in *Political Science: The State of the Discipline*, eds. Ira Katznelson and Helen V. Milner (New York: Norton, 2002), 511–541.

35. For a more extensive discussion of our arguments, see Paul R. Abramson, John H. Aldrich, and David W. Rohde, "Studying American Elections," in *The Oxford Handbook of American Elections and Political Behavior*, ed. Jan E. Leighley (New York: Oxford University Press, 2010), 700–715.

36. Paul F. Lazarsfeld, Bernard R. Berelson, and Hazel Gaudet, *The People's Choice: How the Voter Makes Up His Mind in a Presidential Campaign* (New York: Duell, Sloan, and Pearce, 1944), 27. See also Bernard R. Berelson, Paul F. Lazarsfeld, and William McPhee, *Voting: A Study of Opinion Formation in a Presidential Campaign* (Chicago: University of Chicago Press, 1954).

37. See Robert R. Alford, *Party and Society: The Anglo-American Democracies* (Chicago: Rand McNally, 1963); Richard F. Hamilton, *Class and Politics in the United States* (New York: Wiley, 1972); and Seymour Martin Lipset, *Political Man: The Social Bases of Politics*, exp. ed. (Baltimore: Johns Hopkins University Press, 1981). For a more recent book using the perspective, see Jeff Manza and Clem Brooks, *Social Cleavages and Political Change: Voter Alignments in U.S. Party Coalitions* (New York: Oxford University Press, 1999).

38. Angus Campbell et al., *The American Voter* (New York: Wiley, 1960). For a recent assessment of the contribution of *The American Voter*, see William G. Jacoby, "The American Voter," in Leighley, *Oxford Handbook of American Elections and Political Behavior*, 262–277.

39. The Michigan model conceptualizes party identification as the individual's enduring attachment to a political party. The theory contends that party identification is socialized early in life and remains stable throughout adulthood. Dissatisfied with this static view of party loyalties, Morris P. Fiorina reconceptualized party identification as "a running tally of retrospective evaluations of party promises and performance." Fiorina, *Retrospective Voting in American National Elections* (New Haven, Conn.: Yale University Press, 1981), 84. For a counterargument to Fiorina, see Larry M. Bartels, "Beyond the Running Tally: Partisan Bias in Political Perceptions," *Political Behavior* 24 (June 2002): 117–150.

40. Anthony Downs, *An Economic Theory of Democracy* (New York: Harper and Row, 1957); William H. Riker, *A Theory of Political Coalitions* (New Haven, Conn.: Yale University Press, 1962).

41. See, for example, William H. Riker and Peter C. Ordeshook, "A Theory of the Calculus of Voting," *American Political Science Review* 62 (March 1968): 25–32; John A. Ferejohn and Morris P. Fiorina, "The Paradox of Not Voting: A Decision Theocratic Analysis," *American Political Science Review* 68 (June 1974): 525–536; and Fiorina, *Retrospective Voting in American National Elections*. For an

excellent introduction to American voting behavior that relies on a rational choice perspective, see Rebecca B. Morton, *Analyzing Elections* (New York: Norton, 2006).

42. For a more extensive discussion of the merits and limitations of these approaches, see Paul R. Abramson, John H. Aldrich, and David W. Rohde, "Studying American Elections," in Leighley, *Oxford Handbook of American Elections and Political Behavior*, 700–715.

43. Most of the respondents were interviewed before and after the election. Many of the questions we are interested in, such as whether people voted, how they voted for president, and how they voted for Congress, were asked in the survey conducted after the election. The postelection survey included 1,929 respondents.

44. The 2002 midterm survey was conducted by telephone. The ANES did not conduct a midterm survey in 2006 or 2010.

45. For the first time in the history of the ANES Time Series, face-to-face interviews were supplemented with data collected from an Internet survey using a panel of regular survey participants administered by GfK (formerly Knowledge Networks). The Internet survey includes 3,860 respondents, but in order to ensure a consistent presentation with our previous books, we have elected to restrict our analyses to those data collected via the face-to-face sample.

46. For an overview of how the ANES is currently constructed and its recent innovations in measurement, see the collection of essays found in John H. Aldrich and Kathleen M. McGraw, eds., *Improving Public Opinion Surveys: Interdisciplinary Innovation and the American National Election Studies* (Princeton, N.J.: Princeton University Press, 2012).

47. For a brief nontechnical introduction to polling, see Herbert Asher, *Polling and the Public: What Every Citizen Should Know*, 7th ed. (Washington, D.C.: CQ Press, 2007). For a more advanced discussion, see Herbert F. Weisberg, *The Total Survey Error Approach: A Guide to the New Science of Survey Research* (Chicago: University of Chicago Press, 2005).

48. For a brief discussion of the procedures used by the Survey Research Center to carry out its sampling for in-person interviews, see Paul R. Abramson, *Political Attitudes in America: Formation and Change* (San Francisco: W. H. Freeman, 1983), 18–23. For a more detailed description, see Survey Research Center, *Interviewer's Manual*, rev. ed. (Ann Arbor, MI: Institute for Social Research, 1976).

49. The magnitude of the sampling error is greatest for proportions near 50 percent and diminished somewhat for proportions above 70 percent or below 30 percent. The magnitude of the error diminishes markedly for proportions above 90 percent or below 10 percent.

50. For an excellent table that allows us to evaluate differences between two groups, see Leslie Kish, *Survey Sampling* (New York: Wiley, 1965), 580. Kish defines differences between two groups to be significant if the results are more than two standard errors apart.

51. For 2012—as well as for 1958, 1960, 1974, 1976, 1992, 1994, 1996, 1998, 2000, 2002, 2004, and 2008—a weighting procedure is necessary to obtain a representative result, and so we report the weighted number of cases.

52. Actually, the 2012 ANES survey includes a black oversample and a Latino oversample. The weighting factors we employ reduce the numbers of blacks and Latinos so that they approximate the actual proportion of blacks and Latinos in the electorate. In the weighted pre-election survey, there are 1,451 whites, 244 blacks, and 223 Latinos. In the unweighted survey, which presents the actual numbers interviewed, there are 918 whites, 511 blacks, and 472 Latinos.

53. There also were numerous state-level ballot measures—initiatives, referenda, and state constitutional amendments—for which to vote. Three states, Maine, Maryland, and Washington, voted to allow same-sex marriage. And voters in Colorado and Washington voted to legalize marijuana, though voters in Oregon voted down a similar measure.

1. THE NOMINATION STRUGGLE

1. Between 1832 and 2012 no successful major-party nominee ever won the presidency without winning the nomination of his party at a national party convention.

2. Or, in the case of Gerald R. Ford in 1976, he secured his first nomination. Ford had been appointed vice president in the wake of incumbent vice president Spiro Agnew's resignation, and then he rose to the presidency upon the resignation of Richard M. Nixon in 1974, in the wake of the Watergate scandals.

3. See Paul R. Abramson, John H. Aldrich, and David W. Rohde, *Change and Continuity in the 1980 Elections* Washington, D.C.: CQ Press, 1981).

4. See Joseph A. Schlesinger, *Ambition and Politics: Political Careers in the United States* (Chicago: Rand McNally, 1966); and Schlesinger, *Political Parties and the Winning of Office* (Ann Arbor: University of Michigan Press, 1991).

5. We count Huntsman in the "other" category, as his most recent office was ambassador to China. In many respects, his candidacy was based more on his service as governor than as ambassador.

6. In addition to the fifty states, also included are events for the District of Columbia, various territories, and, for the Democrats, even Americans Living Abroad.

7. As well as procedures used for the remaining units.

8. Kevin J. Coleman, "The Presidential Nominating Process and the National Party Conventions, 2012: Frequently Asked Questions," Congressional Research Service, May 14, 2012, http://www.crs.gov, R42533.

9. Theodore H. White, *The Making of the President, 1968* (New York: Pocket Books, 1970).

10. Ibid., 153.

11. He was helped in this effort by the fact that one-third of the delegates had been chosen in 1967, before Johnson's renomination faced serious opposition.

12. The Republican Party does not require that its delegates be bound. Many states (especially those that hold primaries and follow Democratic Party rules) do bind Republican delegates.

13. To be sure, there were calls from supporters of Clinton for her to maintain her candidacy, especially in light of the still unresolved situation about the delegates from Florida and Michigan. The Clinton campaign, however, chose to slowly wind down the level of competition and effectively accept defeat, without actually withdrawing formally until the convention itself. For a discussion of the importance of superdelegates in 1984, see Paul R. Abramson, John H. Aldrich, and David W. Rohde, *Change and Continuity in the 1984 Elections*, rev. ed. (Washington, D.C.: CQ Press, 1987), 25. For the best journalistic account of the 2008 nomination contest, including a discussion of the role played by superdelegates, see Dan Balz and Haynes Johnson, *The Battle for America 2008: The Story of an Extraordinary Election* (New York: Viking, 2009).

14. This account of the importance of pre-primary campaigning is developed in Phil Paolino, "Candidate Name Recognition and the Dynamics of the Pre-primary Period of the Presidential Nomination Process" (PhD diss., Duke University, 1995).

15. See John Aldrich, "The Invisible Primary and Its Effects on Democratic Choice," *PS: Political Science & Politics* 42 (2009): 33–38.

16. See Paul R. Abramson, John H. Aldrich, and David W. Rohde, *Change and Continuity in the 2000 and 2002 Elections* (Washington, D.C.: CQ Press, 2003), chap. 1, for more details on the nomination campaigns in 2000.

17. *Citizens United v. Federal Election Commission*, 558 U.S. 310.

18. EMILY's List, a group that supports female candidates, draws its name from an acronym of this line.

19. See, for example, Thomas E. Mann, "Money in the 2008 Elections: Bad News or Good?" http://www.brookings.edu/opinions/2008/0701_publicfinance_mann.aspx.

20. See, for example, Michael Muskal and Dan Morain, "Obama Raises $55 Million in February; Clinton Reports Surge in Funds," *Los Angeles Times*, March 7, 2008.

21. U.S. Court of Appeals for the District of Columbia Circuit, *Speechnow.org v. Federal Election Commission*, March 26, 2010.

22. "Restore Our Future: Independent Expenditures, Communication Costs and Coordinated Expenditures as of April 11, 2013," Center for Responsive Politics, http://www.opensecrets.org/pacs/indexpend.php?strID=C00490045 &cycle=2012

23. See, for example, William Oremus, "The Biggest Political Donations of All Time," *Slate*, January 27, 2012, http://www.slate.com/articles/news_and_politics/politics/2012/01/sheldon_adelson_newt_gingrich_and_the_largest_campaign_donations_in_u_s_history_.html.

24. These are based on their reports to the FEC through the end of 2011 and through the end of May 2012.

25. See John H. Aldrich, *Before the Convention: Strategies and Choices in Presidential Nomination Campaigns* (Chicago: University of Chicago Press, 1980). Larry M. Bartels, in *Presidential Primaries and the Dynamics of Public Choice* (Princeton, N.J.: Princeton University Press, 1988), examines the electoral process underlying these dynamics.

26. Actually, there was a potentially serious third candidate in 1980, California governor Jerry Brown. In this contest, he acquired the nickname "Governor Moonbeam" and so received very little support. Thus this case was reduced almost immediately to two major or serious candidates.

27. We use New Hampshire rather than Iowa because Iowa has varied from being less than a week before New Hampshire to being several weeks before and because the window of time available to other states opens only after the New Hampshire primary. The campaign is considered to have ended when a candidate has secured the commitment of a majority of delegates or when his or her last opponent or opponents announce their concession.

28. See Paul R. Abramson, John H. Aldrich, and David W. Rohde, *Change and Continuity in the 2008 and 2010 Elections* (Washington, D.C.: CQ Press, 2012).

29. Candidates typically suspend their campaigns rather than withdraw their candidacies completely. Ordinarily this has to do with financial regulations that favor keeping their candidacies alive for legal purposes, but for Paul this decision also included the ability to run and campaign on issues and principles he cared about.

30. Only Jon Huntsman sought to build a campaign on their support, and he never had a chance. Why support him, as a more moderate Mormon former governor (who had recently been ambassador to China in the Obama administration), when there was a stronger one already in the race?

2. THE GENERAL ELECTION CAMPAIGN

1. Until 2008 neither Maine nor Nebraska had divided its electoral vote under these systems, but in that year Obama succeeded in carrying one of Nebraska's congressional districts, thus gaining one of the state's votes.

2. The 12 states were Colorado, Florida, Iowa, Michigan, Nevada, New Hampshire, New Mexico, North Carolina, Ohio, Pennsylvania, Virginia, and Wisconsin. See Susan Page, "Obama Has Tough Road in Key States," *USA Today*, November 4–6, 2011, 1A. Many other lists included Minnesota in the battleground category.

3. For a discussion of electoral-vote strategies in 1988–1996, see Daron R. Shaw, "The Methods Behind the Madness: Presidential Electoral-College Strategies, 1988–1996," *Journal of Politics* 61 (November 1999), 893–913.

4. The five successful incumbents (and their average approval in Gallup surveys conducted in March, April, and May) were Eisenhower 1956 (70), Johnson 1964 (76), Nixon 1972 (56), Reagan 1984 (54), and Clinton 1996 (54). The unsuccessful candidates were Johnson 1968 (36), Ford 1976 (48), Carter 1980 (40), and Bush 1992 (40). (Johnson's approval is only for March, because he withdrew from consideration at the end of that month.) The approval data are from Gallup polls, and for presidents through Reagan they were obtained from George Edwards, ed., with Alec M. Gallup, *Presidential Approval: A Source Book* (Baltimore: Johns Hopkins University Press, 1996). For George H. W. Bush and Clinton, the data were taken respectively from the August 1992 and May 1996 issues of *Gallup Poll Monthly.*

5. Data reported at http://www.pollingreport.com.

6. The organizations (and number of polls) were ABC-*Washington Post* (5), CNN (4), CBS-*New York Times* (3), Pew Research (5), and NBC-*Wall Street Journal* (4). The data were obtained from http://www.realclear politics.com.

7. It is worth noting that Obama was a "first party-term" incumbent. That is, he succeeded a president of the opposite party. James E. Campbell points out that twelve first party-term incumbents have sought reelection since 1900, and eleven were successful. See "The Miserable Presidential Election of 2012: A First Party-Term Incumbent Survives," *Forum* 10 (2012), 20–28.

8. Patick O'Connor, Carol E. Lee, and Sara Murray, "Big Bet Six Months Ago Paved Way for President," *Wall Street Journal*, November 7, 2012, http://online .wsj.com/news/articles/SB10001424127887324894104578103751218075988.

9. Ibid.

10. Ibid.

11. Michael D. Shear, "Romney Confronts Power of the Presidency," *New York Times*, May2, 2012, http://thecaucus.blogs.nytimes.com/2012/05/02/ romney-confronts-power-of-the-presidency/?_r=0.

12. These scenarios are drawn from Marc Ambinder, "Chicago Hope," *National Journal*, January 7, 2012, 20.

13. See Michael Cooper, "Platform's Sharp Turn to the Right Has Conservatives Cheering," *New York Times*, August 29, 2012, A11.

14. Ibid.

15. Quoted in Jeff Zelany, "Romney Vows to Deliver Country from Economic Travails," *New York Times*, August 31, 2012, A1.

16. See Michael Cooper, "2 Platforms, Poles Apart, in Their View of the Nation," *New York Times*, September 5, 2102, A1.

17. Quoted in Jeff Zelany and Mark Landler, "Clinton Urges Second Term to Let Obama Finish Job," *New York Times*, September 6, 2012, A1.

18. "Bill Clinton's Speech at the Democratic National Convention (Full Transcript)," *Washington Post*, September 5, 2012, http://articles.washington post.com/2012-09-05/politics/35497433_1_applause-transcript-laughter.

19. David Bauder, "Democratic Convention Beats Football in Ratings," *Yahoo! News,* September 7, 2012, http://news.yahoo.com/democratic-convention-beats-football-ratings-234533124.html.

20. These quotations were taken from Helene Cooper and Peter Baker, "Obama Makes Case for 2nd Term: 'Harder' Path to 'Better Place,'" *New York Times,* September 6, 2012, http://www.nytimes.com/2012/09/07/us/politics/obama-in-democratic-convention-speech-asks-for-more-time.html?_r=0.

21. See http://pollingreport.com.

22. "Full Transcript of the Mitt Romney Secret Video," *Mother Jones,* September 19, 2012, http://www.motherjones.com/politics/2012/09/full-transcript-mitt-romney-secret-video.

23. Ibid.

24. Adam Nagourney, Ashley Parker, Jim Rutenberg, and Jeff Zeleny, "How a Race in the Balance Went to Obama," *New York Times,* November 8, 2012, P14.

25. Quoted in Jonathan Easley, "GOP Takes Aim at 'Skewed' Polls," *The Hill,* September 25, 2012, 1.

26. Ibid. As it turned out, the national poll results indicate that in 2012 the proportion of Democrats in the set of voters was six percentage points larger than the proportion of Republicans (38 percent versus 32). "The polls were conducted by Edison Research of Somerville, N.J., for the National Election Pool, a consortium of ABC News, Associated Press, CBS News, CNN, Fox News and NBC News. The national results are based on voters in 350 randomly chosen precincts across the United States, and include absentee voters and early voters interviewed by telephone." "President Exit Polls," *New York Times,* http://elections.nytimes.com/2012/results/president/exit-polls. The results cited in this chapter were taken from the "2012 Fox News Exit Polls," http://www.foxnews.com/politics/elections/2012-exit-poll.

27. Nagourney et al., "How a Race in the Balance," P14.

28. Ibid.

29. Ibid.

30. Quoted in Michael Cooper, David Kocieniewski, and Jackie Calmes, "Entering Stage Right, Romney Moved to the Center," *New York Times,* October 5, 2012, A12.

31. Ibid.

32. Brian Selter, "Presidential Debate Draws over 70 Million Viewers, *New York Times,* October 5, 2012, A12.

33. Nia-Malika Henderson, "Presidentail Race Reset, Romney Backers Say," *Washington Post,* October 4, 2012, http://articles.washingtonpost.com/2012-10-04/politics/35502407_1_romney-backers-obama-and-romney-mitt-romney.

34. Alessandra Stanley, "Night of Withering Ripostes, Mostly Delivered by Biden," *New York Times,* October 12, 2012, http://www.nytimes.com/2012/10/12/us/politics/biden-takes-off-gloves-in-vice-presidential-debate.html.

35. Quoted in Jim Ruttenberg and Jeff Zeleny, "Rivals Bring Bare Fisits to Rematch," *New York Times*, October 16, 2012, http://www.nytimes.com/2012/10/17/us/politics/obama-and-romney-turn-up-the-temperature-at-their-second-debate.html.

36. Shirin Ghermezian, "Obama/Romney Presidential Debate Poll Results," *Enstarz*, October 16, 2012, http://www.enstarz.com/articles/8168/20121017/obama-romney-presidential-debate-poll-results-list.htm.

37. Quoted in Dan Balz and David Nakamura, "Obama Keeps Romney on His Heels in Last Debate," *Washington Post*, October 22, 2012, http://articles.washingtonpost.com/2012-10-22/politics/35501075_1_obama-and-mitt-romney-foreign-policy-first-debate.

38. Ibid.

39. See "Presidential Debate Polls Show Win for Obama," *Huffington Post*, October 23, 2012, http://www.huffingtonpost.com/2012/10/23/presidential-debate-polls_n_2004065.html

40. See Robert S. Erikson and Christopher Wlezien, *The Timeline of Presidential Elections* (Chicago: University of Chicago Press, 2012), 79–81, and the references cited therein. Also see John Sides, "Do Presidential Debates Really Matter?" *Washington Monthly*, September/October 2012, 19–21.

41. Ibid.

42. See http://realclearpolitics.com.

43. Helene Cooper, "Obama Begins Swing-State Blitz, Pushing Through 8 States in Two Days," *New York Times*, October 25, 2012, A13.

44. Jim Rutenberg and Jeremy W. Peters, "G.O.P. Turns Fire on Obama Pillar, the Auto Bailout," *New York Times*, October 30, 2012, A1.

45. Ibid.

46. Quoted in Maureen Dowd, "The 'I' of the Storm," *New York Times*, October 31, 2012, A23.

47. Quoted in Martha T. Moore, "As New Jersey Struggles, Christie Puts Politics Aside," *USA Today*, November 1, 2012, 8A.

48. Ibid.

49. Quoted in Mark Landler, "Embracing Role as Surrogate, Clinton Hits Campaign Trail," *New York Times*, September 12, 2012, A12.

50. O'Connor et al., "Big Bet Six Months Ago."

51. Josh Mitcheell and Sara Murray, "Labor Market Inches Forward," *Wall Street Journal*, November 3-4, 2012, 1.

52. See Paul R. Abramson, John H. Aldrich, and David W. Rohde, *Change and Continuity in the 2008 and 2010 Elections* (Washington, D.C.: CQ Press, 2011), chap. 2.

53. Quoted in Michael Scherer, "Inside the Secret World of Quants and Data Crunchers Who Helped Obama Win," *Time*, November 19, 2012, 58. Most of the details in this section are drawn from this article.

54. Ibid.

55. Ibid.

56. Ibid, 60.

57. See Campaign Finance Institute, "Money vs. Money-Plus: Post-Election Reports Reveal Two Different Campaign Strategies," January 11, 2013, http://cfinst.org/Press/PReleases/13-01-11/Money_vs_Money-Plus_Post-Election_Reports_Reveal_Two_Different_Campaign_Strategies.aspx. The other figures and the quotations cited below on this topic are also from that source.

58. Scherer, "Inside the Secret World," 60.

59. Ibid.

60. These data and quotations were taken from David M. Drucker, "Romney Looks to Close Ground-Game Gap." *Roll Call*, October 11, 2012, 5.

61. Brody Mullins, "Activists Pour Cash into Voter Turnout," *Wall Street Journal*, October 30, 2012, http://online.wsj.com/news/articles/SB100014240529 702047893045780850327781105620.

62. Neil King, Jr., "Obama Gains among Latinos," *Wall Street Journal*, June 27, 2012, http://online.wsj.com/news/articles/SB1000142405270230356150457749 2642990259950.

63. See Ethan Bronner, "Voter ID Rules Fail Court Tests across Country," *New York Times*, October 3, 2012, A1.

64. Quoted in Felicia Sonmez, David Nakamura, and David A. Farenthold, "Obama and Romney Begin Final Push with Only Hours until Election Day," *Washington Post*, November 4, 2013, http://articles.washingtonpost.com/2012-11-04/politics/35504799_1_obama-and-romney-mitt-romney-poll.

65. See Felicia Sonmez, "Romney to Close 17-Month Campaign with Election Day Stops in Ohio, Pennsylvania," *Washington Post*, November 5, 2013, http://articles.washingtonpost.com/2012-11-05/politics/35506491_1_ann-romney-mitt-romney-supporters.

66. Sonmez et al., "Obama and Romney Begin Final Push."

67. See Mark Landler and Michael D. Shear, "Candidates Make Last Pleas as Legal Skirmishes Begin," *New York Times*, November 5, 2012, A1.

68. Peter Baker, "His Last Race, Win or Lose," *New York Times*, November 5, 2012, A10.

69. Landler and Shear, "Candidates Make Last Pleas."

70. Quoted in David Nakamura, "A Nostalgic Obama Reurns to Iowa for the End of His Last Campaign," *Washington Post*, November 5, 2013, http://articles.washingtonpost.com/2012-11-05/politics/35505454_1_david-plouffe-president-obama-first-lady-michelle-obama.

71. There has been a lot of interesting research in recent years on the impact of presidential campaigns on outcomes. In adddition to the Erikson and Wlezien volume already cited, see Lynn Vavreck, *The Message Matters* (Princeton, N.J.: Princeton University Press, 2009); Thomas H. Holbrook, *Do Campaigns Matter?* (Thousand Oaks, Calif.: Sage, 1996); James E. Campbell, *The American Campaign* (College Station: Texas A&M University Press, 2000); and Darron R. Shaw, "A Study of Presidential Campaign Effects from 1956 to 1992," *Journal of Politics* 61 (May 1999): 387–422.

72. See Jeremy W. Peters, "Rove's On-Air Rebuttal of Fox's Ohio Vote Call Raises Questions about His Role," *New York Times*, November 8, 2012, A8.

73. Sarah Wheaton, "For First Time on Record, Black Voting Rate Outpaced Rate for Whites in 2012," *New York Times*, May 8, 2013, http://www.nytimes.com/2013/05/09/us/politics/rate-of-black-voters-surpassed-that-for-whites-in-2012.html.

74. The data used here are the Voting Eligible Population Highest Office Turnout Rate. The 2012 data are available at http://elections.gmu.edu/Turnout_2012G.html, and the 2008 data are at http://elections.gmu.edu/Turnout_2008G.html.

75. See, for example, Michael Hirsch, "He Blew It," *National Journal*, November 10, 2012, 37–39.

76. Ibid.

3. THE ELECTION RESULTS

1. Real Clear Politics, "General Election: Romney vs. Obama," http://www.realclearpolitics.com/epolls/2012/president/us/general_election_romney_vs_obama-1171.html

2. For an approach that combines information from statistical forecasting models and weights their past performance in order to make future predictions, we recommend Jacob M. Montgomery, Florian M. Hollenbach, and Michael D. Ward, "Improving Predictions Using Ensemble Bayesian Model Averaging," *Political Analysis* 20 (Summer 2012): 271–291.

3. James E. Campbell, "Editor's Introduction—Forecasting the 2012 American National Elections," *PS: Political Science and Politics* 45 (October 2012): 610–612. The forecasts begin on p. 614. Opinion polls offer a snapshot of the electorate at the time of the survey and thus vary with the ebbs and flows of the campaign. Statistical forecast models are based on "fundamentals," factors that have been shown to be predictive across many elections. Most of these fundamentals, such as leading economic indicators, war fatalities during past presidential term, and presidential approval, to name a few, are often known and measured before the general election campaign even begins.

4. Felicia Sonmez and Josh Hicks, "Mitt Romney Casts Ballot in Massachusetts," *Washington Post*, November 6, 2012, http://www.washingtonpost.com/blogs/post-politics/wp/2012/11/06/15369; Dan Amira, "Mitt Romney Cleaned Out His Refrigerator on the Morning of the Election," *New York*, July 31, 2013, http://nymag.com/daily/intelligencer/2013/07/romney-trash-day-refrigerator.html.

5. United States Election Project, "2012 Early Voting Statistics," http://elections.gmu.edu/early_vote_2012.html.

6. Kathleen Hennessey, "President Obama Flies to Chicago to Vote Early in Person," *Los Angeles Times*, October 25, 2012, http://articles.latimes.com/2012/oct/25/news/la-pn-president-obama-votes-early-in-chicago-20121025.

7. Chris Chase, "Barack Obama Played Election Day Basketball Game with Scottie Pippen," *USA Today*, November 6, 2012, http://www.usatoday.com/story/gameon/2012/11/06/barack-obama-scottie-pippen-election-day-pickup/1686751/.

8. Ashley Parker and Michael Barbaro, "Long Quest for Presidency Concludes with a Concession Speech," *New York Times*, November 7, 2012, A7. For a Romney campaign postmortem, see Ashley Parker, "Romney's Chief Strategist Dissects Campaign," *New York Times*, December 6, 2012, http://thecaucus.blogs.nytimes.com/2012/12/06/romneys-chief-strategist-dissects-campaign/?_r=0.

9. Parker and Barbaro, "Long Quest for Presidency."

10. Jeff Zeleny and Jim Rutenberg, "Obama's Night: Tops Romney for 2nd Term in Bruising Run; Democrats Turn Back G.O.P. for Senate," *New York Times*, November 7, 2012, A1.

11. Obama's victory also marks only the second time in U.S. history that three consecutive incumbent presidents have been reelected. One has to go back to the rise of Jefferson's Democratic-Republican Party to find the first instance of three straight incumbents being reelected: Jefferson in 1804, James Madison in 1812, and James Monroe in 1820.

12. George W. Bush's popular-vote margin in 2004 was 2.4 percentage points, and Woodrow Wilson's margin in 1916 was 3.1 points.

13. As noted in Chapter 2, since 1972 Maine has used a system in which the statewide plurality-vote winner receives two electoral votes and the plurality winner in each of the state's congressional districts receives that district's single electoral vote. Nebraska has used a similar system to allocate its Electoral College votes since the 1992 election. In our previous books, we have not always reported these district-level results, but we do so here because in the 2008 election Obama narrowly won one Electoral College vote from Nebraska's 2nd Congressional District.

14. Electors from the Electoral College officially gathered in their respective state capitals to cast ballots for president and vice president on December 17, 2012. For more on the workings of the Electoral College, visit the Office of the Federal Registrar, http://www.archives.gov/federal-register/electoral-college/index.html.

15. The last presidential nominee to lose his home state was Al Gore in 2000. In that extraordinarily close and contested election, had Gore won Tennessee, he would have been elected president.

16. Tom Cohen, "Obama Takes Key Battlegrounds to Win Re-election," *CNN*, November, 7, 2012, http://www.cnn.com/2012/11/06/politics/election-2012. This differs from our list of battleground states in Chapter 2 because the number of states seen as competitive at the end of the election season was smaller.

17. For a cross-national comparison of U.S. presidential selection rules, see Matthew Søberg Shugart, "The American Process of Selecting a President: A Comparative Perspective," *Presidential Studies Quarterly* 34 (September 2004): 632–655.

18. Constitutional provisions detailing the workings of the Electoral College are found in Article II, Section I, with some sections being superseded by the Twelfth, Twentieth, and Twenty-fifth Amendments. For a history of the Constitutional Convention debate about president selection, see Shlomo Slonim, "The Electoral College at Philadelphia: The Evolution of an ad hoc Congress for the Selection of the President," *Journal of American History* 73 (June 1986): 35–58.

19. The respective plurality winners of the popular vote were Andrew Jackson in 1824, Samuel J. Tilden in 1876, incumbent President Grover Cleveland in 1888, and Al Gore in 2000. In 1824, no candidate won a majority of the electoral vote, so the election was thrown to the House of Representatives, where Adams was elected. In 1824, over a fourth of the electoral votes were chosen by state legislatures.

20. From 1828 to 2012, there were fourteen elections in which a candidate won a plurality—not a majority—of the national vote and won a majority of the electoral vote. These fourteen winners were James K. Polk (Democrat) in 1844, with 49.5 percent of the popular vote; Zachary Taylor (Whig) in 1848, with 47.3 percent; James Buchanan (Democrat) in 1856, with 45.3 percent; Abraham Lincoln (Republican) in 1860, with 39.9 percent; James A. Garfield (Republican) in 1880, with 48.3 percent; Grover Cleveland (Democrat) in 1884, with 48.9 percent; Cleveland in 1892, with 46.0 percent; Woodrow Wilson (Democrat) in 1912, with 41.8 percent; Wilson in 1916, with 49.2 percent; Harry S. Truman (Democrat) in 1948, with 49.5 percent; John F. Kennedy (Democrat) in 1960, with 49.7 percent; Richard M. Nixon (Republican) in 1968, with 43.4 percent; Bill Clinton (Democrat) in 1992, with 43.0 percent; and Clinton in 1996, with 49.2 percent. The results for Kennedy can be questioned, however, mainly because voters in Alabama voted for individual electors, and one can argue that Nixon won more popular votes than Kennedy.

21. Maurice Duverger, *Political Parties: Their Organization and Activity in the Modern State,* trans. Barbara North and Robert North (New York: Wiley, 1963), 217. In the original, Duverger's proposition is "le scrutin majoritaire à un seul tour tend au dualisme des partis." Duverger, *Les Partis Politiques* (Paris: Armand Colin, 1958), 247. For a discussion, see William H. Riker, "The Two-Party System and Duverger's Law: An Essay on the History of Political Science," *American Political Science Review* 76 (December 1982): 753–766. For a more recent statement by Duverger, see "Duverger's Law Forty Years Later," in *Electoral Laws and Their Political Consequences,* eds. Bernard Grofman and Arend Lijphart (New York: Agathan Press, 1986), 69–84. For more general discussions of the effects of electoral laws, see Rein Taagepera and Matthew Shugart, *Seats and Votes: The Effects and Determinants of Electoral Systems* (New Haven, Conn.: Yale University Press, 1989); and Gary W. Cox, *Making Votes Count: Strategic Coordination of the World's Electoral Systems* (Cambridge, UK: Cambridge University Press, 1997).

22. Duverger's inclusion of "a single ballot" in his formulation is redundant because in a plurality vote win system, there would be no need for second ballots or runoffs unless needed to break ties. With a large electorate, ties will be extremely rare.

23. Duverger, *Political Parties*, 218.

24. William H. Riker, *The Art of Political Manipulation* (New Haven, Conn.: Yale University Press, 1986), 79.

25. For the most extensive evidence for the 1968, 1980, and 1992 elections, see Paul R. Abramson et al., "Third-Party and Independent Candidates in American Politics: Wallace, Anderson, and Perot," *Political Science Quarterly* 110 (Fall 1997): 349–367. For the 1996 and 2000 elections, see Paul R. Abramson, John H. Aldrich, and David W. Rohde, *Change and Continuity in the 1996 and 1998 Elections* (Washington, D.C.: CQ Press, 1999), 118–120; and Paul R. Abramson, John H. Aldrich, and David W. Rohde, *Change and Continuity in the 2000 and 2002 Elections* (Washington, D.C.: CQ Press, 2003), 124–126.

26. Paul R. Abramson, John H. Aldrich, and David W. Rohde, *Change and Continuity in the 2004 and 2006 Elections* (Washington, D.C.: CQ Press, 2007), 55.

27. Strategic voting can occur under other voting systems as well, including runoff elections and proportional representation. For evidence about Israel and the Netherlands, see Paul R. Abramson et al., "Strategic Abandonment or Sincerely Second Best? The 1999 Israeli Prime Ministerial Election," *Journal of Politics* 66 (August 2004): 706–728; and Abramson et al., "Comparing Strategic Voting under FPTP and PR," *Comparative Political Studies* 43 (January 2010): 61–90.

28. Britain provides an excellent example of the effects of plurality vote win systems on third parties. In Britain, as in the United States, candidates for the national legislature run in single-member districts, and in all British parliamentary districts the plurality vote winner is elected. In all seventeen general elections since World War II ended in Europe, the Liberal Party (and more recently the Alliance and the Liberal Democratic Parties) has received a smaller percentage of seats in the House of Commons than its percentage of the popular vote. For example, in the May 2010 election the Liberal Democrats won 23.0 percent of the popular vote, but won only 8.8 percent of the seats in the House of Commons.

29. The New England states are Connecticut, Maine, Massachusetts, New Hampshire, Rhode Island, and Vermont. Although the U.S. Census Bureau labels several border states and the District of Columbia as southern, we use an explicitly political definition—the eleven states that made up the old Confederacy, which are Alabama, Arkansas, Florida, Georgia, Louisiana, Mississippi, North Carolina, South Carolina, Tennessee, Texas, and Virginia.

30. These states are Arizona, Colorado, Idaho, Montana, Nevada, New Mexico, Utah, and Wyoming.

31. For a comparison of Wallace's regional strength in 1968, Anderson's regional strength in 1980, and Perot's regional strength in 1992, see Paul R. Abramson, John H. Aldrich, and David W. Rohde, *Change and Continuity in the 1992 Elections,* rev. ed. (Washington, D.C.: CQ Press, 1995), 73–76.

32. Although there are rare exceptions, presidential electors are pledged to support a presidential and a vice presidential candidate. Over 8,000 pledged electors have been selected since 1944, and only 8 have failed to vote for the presidential candidate they were pledged to support. The most recent example of a faithless elector occurred in the 2004 presidential election, when an unknown Minnesota elector, pledged to Democratic presidential nominee John Kerry and vice presidential nominee John Edwards, cast his or her presidential ballot for Edwards.

33. Third-party candidates are not always underrepresented in the Electoral College. In 1948, J. Strom Thurmond, the States' Rights Democrat, won only 2.4 percent of the popular vote but won 7.3 percent of the electoral vote. Thurmond won 55 percent of the popular votes in the four states he carried (Alabama, Louisiana, Mississippi, and South Carolina), all of which had low turnout. He received no popular vote at all in thirty-one of the forty-eight states.

34. See George C. Edwards III, *Why the Electoral College Is Bad for America,* 2nd ed. (New Haven, Conn.: Yale University Press, 2011).

35. Edwards argues that a "constitutional amendment is not a pipe dream," noting that a constitutional amendment to establish direct election of the president passed the House on a bipartisan vote in 1969. The amendment, which was publicly endorsed by President Nixon, was filibustered in the Senate, however, by southern senators. See Edwards, *Why the Electoral College Is Bad for America,* 203.

36. For the most extensive argument in favor of this reform, see John R. Koza et al., *Every Vote Equal: A State-Based Plan for Electing the President by National Popular Vote,* 4th ed. (Los Altos, Calif.: National Popular Vote Press, 2013).

37. In 2012, the Pennsylvania legislature defeated a bill that would have allocated two electors to the statewide winner and the remaining electors in proportion to the candidates' shares of the popular vote in the state. Obama defeated Romney in Pennsylvania and collected the state's twenty electoral votes. Had the proportional allocation system been adopted (and voting remained the same), the president would have received twelve electoral votes and Romney eight, not enough to change the Electoral College outcome.

38. Adoption of the district system would likely increase the incentive for state legislatures to gerrymander given that presidential electors would now be at stake.

39. Clark Benson of POLIDATA conducted the analysis, titled "2012 Presidential Results by Congressional District," on behalf of *The Cook Political Report,* http://cookpolitical.com/story/5606. One should always be cautious when constructing counterfactuals such as this. Had the election taken place under these rules, the candidates most certainly would have campaigned using

different strategies, and in all likelihood voter participation would have changed in response to varying levels of electoral competition across districts.

40. A.C. Thomas and colleagues offer a systematic study of alternative elector apportionment proposals using data from 1956 to 2004. They conclude that both the current Electoral College and the direct popular vote are substantially less biased than the district method. See A. C. Thomas, Andrew Gelman, Gary King, and Jonathan N. Katz, "Estimating Partisan Bias of the Electoral College under Proposed Changes in Elector Apportionment," *Statistics, Politics, and Policy* 4 (Issue 1, 2013): 1–13.

41. Daniel Gans views much of presidential election history as what statisticians call a "random walk," meaning that party success from one election to the next is essentially random. See Daniel J. Gans, "Persistence of Party Success in American Presidential Elections," *Journal of Interdisciplinary History* 2 (Winter 1986): 221–237.

42. Walter Dean Burnham, *Critical Elections and the Mainsprings of American Politics* (New York: Norton, 1970).

43. Stanley Kelley Jr. uses three criteria to classify an election as a landslide: if the winning candidate wins fifty-three percent of the popular vote *or* wins eighty percent of the electoral vote *or* wins eighty percent of the states. This definition may be too generous, but Reagan's 1984 victory, which met all three of Kelley's criteria, was most certainly a landslide. See Stanley Kelley Jr., *Interpreting Elections* (Princeton, N.J.: Princeton University Press, 1983); and for a discussion of Reagan's landslide specifically, see Paul R. Abramson, John H. Aldrich, and David W. Rohde, *Change and Continuity in the 1984 Elections* (Washington, D.C., CQ Press, 1986) 70–73.

44. Two other incumbents during this period had lower popular vote totals when they stood for reelection (Jimmy Carter in 1980 and George H. W. Bush in 1992); both lost.

45. For two studies of the Whig Party, see Michael F. Holt, *The Rise and Fall of the Whig Party: Jacksonian Politics and the Onset of the Civil War* (New York: Oxford University Press, 1999); and Daniel Walker Howe, *The Political Culture of the American Whigs* (Chicago: University of Chicago Press, 1979).

46. Former Whigs founded the Constitutional Union Party in 1860. Its candidate, John Bell, won 12.6 percent of the popular vote and 39 of the 303 electoral votes.

47. For a discussion of agenda-setting during this period, see William H. Riker, *Liberalism against Populism: A Confrontation between the Theory of Democracy and the Theory of Social Choice* (San Francisco: W. H. Freeman, 1982), 213–232; and John H. Aldrich, *Why Parties? A Second Look* (Chicago: University of Chicago Press, 2011), 130–162.

48. Not all scholars agree with this assessment. The most important dissent is found in David R. Mayhew, *Electoral Realignments: A Critique of an American Genre* (New Haven, Conn.: Yale University Press, 2002), 43–69.

49. The election of 1912 is the last in which a party other than the Democrats and Republicans finished among the top two vote getters. Former Republican president Theodore Roosevelt, running as the nominee of the Progressive Party (the "Bull Moose Party"), finished second in both the popular and Electoral College votes.

50. After the 2000 election, the Republicans and Democrats each had fifty senators, and the Republicans held control of the Senate by virtue of Vice President Dick Cheney's tie-breaking vote. When Sen. James M. Jeffords of Vermont left the Republican Party to become an independent and to vote with the Democrats on the organization of the Senate, the Democrats took control of the Senate from June 2001 until January 2003.

51. See David R. Mayhew, "Incumbency Advantage in U.S. Presidential Elections: The Historical Record," *Political Science Quarterly* 123 (Summer 2008): 201–228. An individual-level study of survey responses from the 1952 through 2000 American National Election Studies suggests that incumbent presidential candidates—controlling for a variety of other factors—enjoy an advantage of six percentage points over their challengers in the popular vote; see Herbert F. Weisberg, "Partisanship and Incumbency in Presidential Elections," *Political Behavior* 24 (December 2002): 339–360.

52. Jodi Enda, "When Republicans Were Blue and Democrats Were Red," *Smithsonian*, November 1, 2012, http://www.smithsonianmag.com/history-archaeology/When-Republicans-Were-Blue-and-Democrats-Were-Red-176776491.html. The association of Republicans with the color red is actually a bit curious, given the color's historical association with revolution and socialism. For example, the song "The Red Flag," composed by James Connell in 1889, became the official song of the British Labour Party. As for flags specifically, the flag of the Soviet Union featured a solid red field with a gold hammer and sickle. Fear of the Soviet Union and the spread of communism in America, particularly during the 1950s, was called the "Red Scare."

53. Since ratification of the Twenty-third Amendment in 1961, the District of Columbia has had three electoral votes, which it first cast in the 1964 election.

54. Romney visited Los Angeles on September 17, 2012, to speak to the U.S. Hispanic Chamber of Commerce Annual National Convention and Business Expo.

55. We tabulated these counts based on data reported in "Presidential Campaign Stops: Who's Going Where," *Washington Post*, September 12, 2012, http://www.washingtonpost.com/wp-srv/special/politics/2012-presidential-campaign-visits. We only count candidates' public appearances held after the party conventions. Thus, the data do not reflect the fact that Romney attended the Republican National Convention, which was held in Tampa, Florida. Private fund-raisers were excluded from our tally.

56. This is not to say that campaigns view only larger states as important to their electoral strategy. New Hampshire, for example, has only four electoral votes, but it was a battleground state in 2012. Obama made seven general

election campaign visits to New Hampshire, and Romney made six. Obama won the Granite State by 5.6 percentage points.

57. U.S. Department of Commerce, *Statistical Abstract of the United States,* 101st ed. (Washington, D.C.: Government Printing Office, 1980), 514.

58. See Dennis Cauchon, "In Ohio: Voters Choose Obama as Auto Bailout Resonates," *USA Today,* November 7, 2012, http://www.usatoday.com/story/news/politics/2012/11/06/ohio-election-results/1658389; and Joe Hallett, "Auto Bailout, High Turnout Helped Obama Win Ohio," *Columbus Dispatch* (OH), November 8, 2012, 1A. Romney's opposition to the auto bailout was declared in an op-ed piece published in *The New York Times,* titled "Let Detroit Go Bankrupt," November 18, 2008, A35.

59. Similarly constructed inferences often lead to hyperbolic comparisons of "red states" versus "blue states," creating an illusion of a deeply divided electorate, but see Morris P. Fiorina, with Samuel J. Abrams and Jeremy C. Pope, *Culture War? The Myth of a Polarized America,* 3rd ed. (New York: Pearson/Longman, 2010); and Andrew Gelman et al., *Red State, Blue State, Rich State, Poor State: Why Americans Vote the Way They Do* (Princeton, N.J.: Princeton University Press, 2008).

60. We use the Census Bureau's definition of the Northeast, which includes Connecticut, Maine, Massachusetts, New Hampshire, New Jersey, New York, Pennsylvania, Rhode Island, and Vermont.

61. In the three elections preceding Clinton's victory in 1992, the Republicans fared quite well in the Northeast. The region was solidly pro-Reagan in 1980 (losing only Rhode Island) and 1984, and George H. W. Bush won six of the region's nine states in 1988.

62. Edward M. Burmila, "The Electoral College after Census 2010 and 2020: The Political Impact of Population Growth and Redistricting," *Perspectives on Politics* 7 (December 2009): 837–847.

63. Florida induced a mild case of déjà vu in the days following the 2012 election. A record number of voters cast ballots in Florida in 2012, totaling over 8.4 million votes. Roughly 4.5 million people voted early or used absentee ballots. Tallying those ballots took an additional two days, meaning that the election results in Florida did not become official until the Thursday after election day. In the interim, some grew concerned that the closeness of the race would trigger an automatic recount under Florida law, bringing back memories of Florida's recount debacle during the 2000 presidential election. Those fears were abated when Obama was declared the winner by 0.9 percent (roughly 74,000 votes)—Florida law requires a recount if the margin is less than 0.5 percent. See Lizette Alvarez, "Vote Count Confirms Obama Win in Florida," *New York Times,* November 10, 2012, http://www.nytimes.com/2012/11/11/us/politics/florida-to-address-delays-as-it-confirms-obama-victory.html.

64. Mark Baldassare, *A California State of Mind: The Conflicted Voter in a Changing World* (Berkeley: University of California Press, 2002), 159.

65. *CNN*, 2012 Election Center, http://www.cnn.com/election/2012/results/state/CA/president.

66. Joseph A. Schlesinger, *Political Parties and the Winning of Office* (Ann Arbor: University of Michigan Press, 1991).

67. See Schlesinger, *Political Parties and the Winning of Office*, figure 5-1, 112. Schlesinger does not report the exact values, but he provided them to us in a personal communication. Including the District of Columbia, which has voted for president since 1964, increases the standard deviation because the District always votes more Democratic than the most Democratic state. We report Schlesinger's results for states, not for his alternative results that include D.C. Likewise, our updated results are for the fifty states.

68. Since 1988, the last election reported by Schlesinger, state-by-state variation in party competition has increased slightly: 1988 (5.60), 1992 (5.96), 1996 (6.70), 2000 (8.51), 2004 (8.39), 2008 (9.54), and 2012 (10.29), standard deviations in parentheses.

69. See Aldrich, *Why Parties? A Second Look*, Part 3.

70. Burmila, "The Electoral College after Census 2010 and 2020," 843.

71. V. O. Key Jr., *Southern Politics in State and Nation* (New York: Knopf, 1949), 5.

72. There have been many excellent studies of the postwar South. For one that presents state-by-state results, see Alexander P. Lamis, *The Two-Party South,* 2nd exp. ed. (New York: Oxford University Press, 1990). For three other studies, see Earl Black and Merle Black, *Politics and Society in the Postwar South* (Cambridge, Mass.: Harvard University Press, 1987); Black and Black, *The Rise of Southern Republicans* (Cambridge, Mass.: Harvard University Press, 2002); and David Lublin, *The Republican South: Democratization and Partisan Change* (Princeton, N.J.: Princeton University Press, 2004).

73. South Carolina was the most solidly Democratic, with an average Democratic vote share of 91.4 percent; Tennessee had the lowest, with 56.7 percent of the vote going to the Democrats. Estimates calculated by the authors.

74. See Nancy J. Weiss, *Farewell to the Party of Lincoln: Black Politics in the Age of FDR* (Princeton, N.J.: Princeton University Press, 1983).

75. Earlier that month, southern Democrats suffered a defeat at the Democratic presidential nominating convention. Their attempts to weaken the national party's civil rights platform were defeated. At the same time, Hubert Humphrey, then mayor of Minneapolis, argued that the platform was too weak and offered an amendment for a stronger statement. Humphrey's amendment passed by a vote of 651½–582½.

76. Kennedy made a symbolic gesture that may have helped him with African Americans. Three weeks before the election, Martin Luther King Jr. was arrested in Atlanta for taking part in a sit-in demonstration. Although all the other demonstrators were released, King was held on a technicality and sent to the Georgia State Penitentiary. Kennedy telephoned King's wife to express his concern, and his brother Robert F. Kennedy Jr., acting as a private citizen, made

a direct appeal to a Georgia judge that led to King's release on bail. This incident received little notice in the press, but it had a great effect on the African American community. See Theodore H. White, *The Making of the President, 1960* (New York: Atheneum, 1961), 321–323.

77. Alabama, Georgia, Louisiana, Mississippi, and South Carolina are considered the five Deep South states. They are also the five of the six states with the highest percentage of African Americans.

78. John B. Judis and Ruy Teixeira, *The Emerging Democratic Majority* (New York:/Scribner, 2002). See also Ruy Teixeira, "The Emerging Democratic Majority Turns 10," *Atlantic*, November 9, 2012, http://www.the atlantic.com/politics/archive/2012/11/the-emerging-democratic-majority-turns-10/265005/.

79. Pew Hispanic Center, "An Awakened Giant: The Hispanic Electorate Is Likely to Double by 2030," November 14, 2012, http://www.pewhispanic .org/2012/11/14/an-awakened-giant-the-hispanic-electorate-is-likely-to-double-by-2030.

80. U.S. Census Bureau, "American Community Survey," http://www.census. gov/acs/www.

81. Scholars have already noted the electoral consequences of Hispanic population growth. Alan Abramowitz argues that, since 2000, increases in the Hispanic vote have transitioned New Mexico from a swing state to a safe-Democratic state and caused the formerly Republican-leaning states of Colorado and Nevada to become Democratic-leaning. See Abramowitz, "The Emerging Democratic Presidential Majority: Lessons of Obama's Victory" (paper presented at the Annual Meeting of the American Political Science Association, Chicago, August, 2013); see also Charles S. Bullock III and M. V. Hood III, "A Mile-Wide Gap: The Evolution of Hispanic Political Emergence in the Deep South," *Social Science Quarterly* 87 (December 2006): 1117–1135, which shows the growing electoral strength of Hispanics in three southern states: Georgia, North Carolina, and South Carolina.

82. See, for instance, Paul R. Abramson, John H. Aldrich, and David W. Rohde, *Change and Continuity in the 1984 Elections*, rev. ed. (Washington, D.C.: CQ Press, 1987), 70–75.

83. According to Marjorie Randon Hershey, the Republicans had a "clear and continuing advantage" in presidential elections. See Marjorie Randon Hershey, "The Campaign and the Media," in *The Election of 1988: Reports and Interpretations*, eds. Gerald M. Pomper et al. (Chatham, N.J.: Chatham House, 1989), 74.

84. Pew Hispanic Center, "An Awakened Giant," 5.

85. Estimates for the size of the Latino electorate in Florida are taken from exit polls. Estimates for Texas, where exit polls were not conducted, were calculated by the authors from the U.S. Census, Current Population Survey, 2012, November Supplement.

86. Arian Campo-Flores, "Cuban-Americans Move Left," *Wall Street Journal*, November 8, 2012, http://online.wsj.com/news/articles/SB100014241278873240 73504578107412795405272.

87. Peter Nicholas, "Republicans Reconsider Immigration Laws," *Wall Street Journal*, November 9, 2012, http://online.wsj.com/news/articles/SB20001424127 88732407350457810744020069 39484.

88. Andrew Gelman, Jonathan N. Katz, and Gary King, "Empirically Evaluating the Electoral College," in *Rethinking the Vote: The Politics and Prospects of Electoral Reform*, eds. Ann N. Crigler, Marion R. Just, and Edward J. McCaffrey (New York: Oxford University Press, 2004), 75–88.

89. For a figure demonstrating the Republican dominance between 1972 and 1988, see Abramson et al., *Change and Continuity in the 1992 Elections*, rev. ed., 47.

90. See Daron R. Shaw, *The Race to 270: The Electoral College and the Campaign Strategies of 2000* (Chicago: University of Chicago Press, 2006).

91. We elected to start to measure in 1988, which reports the electoral balance following the 1972, 1976, 1980, 1984, and 1988 elections, so as to eliminate observations that would have to use the 1968 presidential election in which electoral votes were cast for a third-party candidate.

92. An admitted weakness of this measure is that it does not account for the average vote share within a state over time. Thus, a state that consistently sided with the same party by narrow margins is equivalent to a state that consistently sided with the same party by large margins—both are categorized as "uncompetitive."

4. WHO VOTED?

1. Michael McDonald reports that the voting-eligible population in 2012 was 221,925,820. This number is calculated by subtracting from the voting-age population those who are ineligible to vote, such as noncitizens, citizens living abroad, and, when state law applies, felons and those judged mentally incompetent. McDonald estimates that close to nineteen million voting-age people living in the United States are ineligible to vote. McDonald, "2012 General Election Turnout Rates," United States Election Project, http://elections.gmu.edu/early_vote_2012.html.

2. The turnout measure for the United States divides the number of voters by the voting-age population. The International Voter Turnout Database measures turnout for the other countries by the dividing the number of voters by the number of people registered. In most democracies, voter registration is the responsibility of government, which maintains the voter rolls and automatically registers all eligible citizens for voting. Registration in the United States, however, is an individual responsibility. The U.S. Census estimates that 65.1 percent of Americans adults are registered to vote. See U.S. Census Bureau, "Voting and Registration," http://www.census.gov/hhes/www/socdemo/voting.

3. For a comprehensive discussion of turnout change in comparative perspective, see Mark N. Franklin, *Voter Turnout and the Dynamics of Electoral Competition in Established Democracies since 1945* (New York: Cambridge University Press, 2004).

4. In Australia, nonvoters may be subject to a small fine. In Belgium, which first adopted compulsory voting in 1892, nonvoters may suffer from future disenfranchisement and may find it difficult to obtain a public sector job. For more on the effect of compulsory voting on voter turnout, see Pippa Norris, *Election Engineering: Voting Rules and Political Behavior* (New York: Cambridge University Press, 2002); and Carolina Fornos, Timothy Power, and James C. Garand, "Explaining Voter Turnout in Latin America, 1980–2000," *Comparative Political Studies* 37 (October 2004): 909–940.

5. For a review, see André Blais and Kees Aarts, "Electoral Systems and Turnout," *Acta Politica* 41 (2006): 180–196.

6. Several democracies have experienced substantial declines in turnout in recent elections. Great Britain, for instance, has seen turnout declines as large as twelve percentage points in recent elections. In our sample of democracies, average parliamentary turnout during the 1990s was 77.6 percent ($N = 71$); average turnout since then has dropped roughly five percentage points to 72.8 percent ($N = 94$). This average remains substantially higher than turnout in U.S. national elections.

7. This chapter focuses on one form of political participation: voting. For an excellent study of other forms of political participation, see M. Margaret Conway, *Political Participation in the United States,* 3rd ed. (Washington, D.C.: CQ Press, 2000). For a major study of other forms of political participation, see Sidney Verba, Kay Lehman Schlozman, and Henry E. Brady, *Voice and Equality: Civic Voluntarism in American Politics* (Cambridge, Mass.: Harvard University Press, 1995). For a collection of essays on voting as well as other forms of political participation, see Russell J. Dalton and Hans-Dieter Klingemann, eds., *The Oxford Handbook of Political Behavior* (New York: Oxford University Press, 2007).

8. Alexander Keyssar, *The Right to Vote: The Contested History of Democracy in the United States,* rev. ed. (New York: Basic Books, 2000), 2. Keyssar's book is arguably the definitive account of the legal and political history of suffrage in the United States.

9. The Seventeenth Amendment to the United States Constitution, ratified in 1913, established direct election of U.S. senators by popular vote.

10. In 1790, ten of the thirteen states had property requirements for voting, and three of the thirteen limited suffrage to white males only. By 1820, property requirements were in effect in nine of the twenty-three states, and fourteen of the twenty-three states had race exclusions. See Keyssar, *The Right to Vote,* table A.3 and table A.5.

11. For a useful summary of the history of turnout in the United States, see Michael P. McDonald, "American Voter Turnout in Historical Perspective," in *The Oxford Handbook of American Elections and Political Behavior,* ed. Jan E. Leighley (New York: Oxford University Press, 2010), 125–143.

12. It is difficult to calculate the exact number of voters who turn out for an election. It is common to use the total number of ballots cast for the presidency as a substitute for the number of voters, since in most elections more people vote for president than for any other office.

13. Women's suffrage was adopted in many of the western territories of the United States as a way of attracting female settlers. Wyoming, Utah, Washington, and Montana enfranchised women decades before they joined the union. Wyoming officially became the first state to give women the right to vote in 1890 when it obtained statehood.

14. At the outset of the Civil War, only five states—all in New England—granted blacks the right to vote. A sixth state, New York, allowed blacks who met a property requirement to vote. The Fifteenth Amendment was ratified in 1870. See Keyssar, *The Right to Vote*, 69–83.

15. See Martin J. Kousser, *The Shaping of Southern Politics: Suffrage Restrictions and the Establishment of the One-Party South, 1880-1910* (New Haven, Conn.: Yale University Press, 1974). For a more general discussion, see Paul Kleppner, *Who Voted? The Dynamics of Electoral Turnout, 1870-1980* (New York: Praeger, 1982), 55–82.

16. There has been a great deal of disagreement about the reasons for and the consequences of registration requirements. For some of the more interesting arguments, see Walter Dean Burnham, "The Changing Shape of the American Political Universe," *American Political Science Review* 59 (March 1965): 7–28; Philip E. Converse, "Change in the American Electorate," in *The Human Meaning of Social Change*, eds. Angus Campbell and Philip E. Converse (New York: Russell Sage, 1972), 266–301; Walter Dean Burnham, "Theory and Voting Research: Some Reflections on Converse's 'Change in the American Electorate,'" *American Political Science Review* 68 (September 1974): 1002–1023. For two other perspectives, see Frances Fox Piven and Richard A. Cloward, *Why Americans Still Don't Vote and Why Politicians Want It That Way* (Boston: Beacon Press, 2000); and Matthew A. Crenson and Benjamin Ginsberg, *Downsizing America: How America Sidelined Its Citizens and Privatized Its Public* (Baltimore: Johns Hopkins University Press, 2002).

17. This term originates from the fact that, in 1856, two Australian colonies (now states) adopted a secret ballot to be printed and administered by the government.

18. For a rich source of information on the introduction of the Australian ballot and its effects, see Jerrold G. Rusk, "The Effect of the Australian Ballot on Split-Ticket Voting, 1876–1908," *American Political Science Review* 64 (December 1970): 1220–1238.

19. The secret ballot, like a few of the other "good government" electoral reforms of the Progressive Era, such as literacy tests, often had unintended consequences or were used in the South to disenfranchise African Americans. An analysis by Jac C. Heckelman estimates that the introduction of the secret ballot lowered voter turnout in U.S. gubernatorial elections by seven percentage points. See Heckelman, "The Effect of the Secret Ballot on Voter Turnout Rates," *Public Choice* 82 (No. 1/2, 1995): 107–124.

20. Keyssar, *The Right to Vote*, 115.

21. Burnham presents estimates of turnout among the "politically-eligible population" between 1789 and 1984 in "The Turnout Problem," in *Elections American Style*, ed. James A. Reichley (Washington, D.C.: Brookings Institution, 1987), 113–114. In a series of personal communications, Burnham provided us with estimates of turnout among the "voting-eligible population" between 1988 and 2004: 52.7 percent in 1988, 56.9 percent in 1992, 50.8 percent in 1996, 54.9 percent in 2000, and 60.7 percent in 2004. McDonald and Popkin's estimates of turnout between 1948 and 2000 are available in Michael P. McDonald and Samuel L. Popkin, "The Myth of the Vanishing Voter," *American Political Science Review* 95 (December 2001): 996. McDonald's estimates for the 2004, 2008, and 2012 elections are available on his United States Elections Project website, http://elections.gmu.edu/voter_turnout.htm.

22. Only Maine and Vermont allow prisoners to vote, and in ten states felons are permanently disfranchised.

23. McDonald's estimates of the eligible population do not account for the number of permanently disfranchised felons "since statistics on recidivism, deaths and migration of felons are largely unknown." See McDonald, "Voter Turnout Frequently Asked Questions," http://elections.gmu.edu/FAQ.html#felons.

24. McDonald, "2012 General Election Turnout Rates," http://elections.gmu/edu/Turnout_2012G.html.

25. Thomas E. Patterson, *The Vanishing Voter: Public Involvement in an Age of Uncertainty* (New York: Knopf, 2002). See also Pippa Norris, *Democratic Participation Worldwide* (Cambridge, UK: Cambridge University Press, 2002).

26. See note 19.

27. Burnham estimated turnout in 1960 at 65.4 percent, and McDonald and Popkin estimated it at 63.8 percent. See Burnham, "Turnout Problem," 114; and McDonald and Popkin, "Myth of the Vanishing Voter," 966.

28. See Glenn Firebaugh and Kevin Chen, "Vote Turnout among Nineteenth Amendment Women: The Enduring Effects of Disfranchisement," *American Journal of Sociology* 100 (January 1995): 972–996.

29. For estimates of this reform on turnout, see Raymond E. Wolfinger and Jonathan Hoffman, "Registering and Voting with Motor Voter," *PS: Political Science and Politics* 34 (March 2001): 86–92. David Hill argues that while motor voter legislation has made the election rolls more representative, it has had little effect on turnout. See David Hill, *American Voter Turnout: An Institutional Perspective* (Boulder, Colo.: Westview Press, 2006), 49–52, 55.

30. We follow Paul Gronke's usage of *early voting* as "a blanket term used to describe any system where voters can cast their ballots before the official election day . . . [including] in-person early voting, no-excuse absentee balloting, and vote-by-mail." See Paul Gronke, "Early Voting Reforms and American Elections," *William and Mary Bill of Rights Journal* 17 (Issue 2, 2008): 423–451.

31. Theory suggests that easing the "cost" of voting by making it more convenient should increase voting turnout. Yet scholarly research on the effect of

early voting on turnout is mixed, with some showing the effect to be quite small and others showing the increase to be as large as 10 percent. For a review, see Paul Gronke, Eva Galanes-Rosenbaum, and Peter A. Miller, "Early Voting and Turnout," *PS: Political Science & Politics* 40 (October 2007): 639–645.

32. In 2011, Florida's Republican-controlled legislature and Republican governor, Rick Scott, changed the state's election laws and reduced the number of early voting days from fourteen to eight, while also limiting the number of hours early-voting polling places could be open. The law also ended early voting on the Sunday before the election. Critics argued that the law was aimed at limiting voter turnout among blacks and other groups that support the Democratic Party. In 2008, blacks in Florida were twice as likely as whites to vote early, and black churches used the Sunday before the 2008 election to mobilize voters. Opponents filed suit, but the federal court allowed Florida's restricted early-voting schedule to go forward. See Lizette Alvarez, "Court Approves Schedule for Florida Early Voting," *New York Times*, September 14, 2012, A16.

33. National Conference of State Legislatures, "Absentee and Early Voting," http://www.ncsl.org/legislatures-elections/elections/absentee-and-early-voting.aspx.

34. The 2012 CPS is based on over 133,000 respondent households nationally with sizeable (and representative) samples drawn for each state. The CPS is commonly used in studies of turnout, though the U.S. Census Bureau measures only voting behavior along with demographic variables (i.e., federal law does not allow the Bureau to measure individual's political attitudes). The most important study to use the CPS remains Raymond E. Wolfinger and Steven J. Rosenstone, *Who Votes?* (New Haven, Conn.: Yale University Press, 1980).

35. As Wolfinger and Rosenstone demonstrate, about one-fifth of this decline resulted from the enfranchisement of eighteen-, nineteen-, and twenty-year-olds. Their nationwide enfranchisement stemmed from the 1971 ratification of the Twenty-sixth Amendment, which made it possible for more people to vote, but because these youth have low levels of voting, overall levels of turnout declined. See Wolfinger and Rosenstone, *Who Votes?* 58.

36. For our analysis of the reasons for the increase in turnout in 1992, see Paul R. Abramson, John H. Aldrich, and David W. Rohde, *Change and Continuity in the 1992 Elections*, rev. ed. (Washington, D.C.: CQ Press, 1995), 120–123. As we point out, it is difficult to demonstrate empirically that Perot's candidacy made an important contribution to the increase in turnout. For additional analyses, see Stephen M. Nichols and Paul Allen Beck, "Reversing the Decline: Voter Turnout in 1992," in *Democracy's Feast: Elections in America*, ed. Herbert F. Weisberg (Chatham, N.J.: Chatham House, 1995), 62–65.

37. When appropriate, we also rely on estimates from the 2012 CPS and exit poll data. The Census Bureau published a detailed report of its 2012 survey in May 2013. See U.S. Census Bureau, "The Diversifying Electorate—Voting Rates by Race and Hispanic Origin in 2012 (and Other Recent Elections)," http://www.census.gov/prod/2013pubs/p20-568.pdf. Interested readers can access data

from the 2012 CPS, November Supplement (as well as other Census studies), using the Census Bureau's DataFerrett website, http://dataferrett.census.gov.

Exit polls were conducted by Edison Research of Somerville, New Jersey, for the "National Election Pool," a consortium of ABC News, Associated Press, CBS News, CNN, Fox News, and NBC News. The exit polls are not a representative sample of the nation. Instead, polls were conducted in thirty-one states. Precincts in each state were selected by a stratified-probability sample, and every *n*th voter in the precinct was given a questionnaire to complete. In states with significant early and/or absentee voting, a supplemental telephone survey was conducted.

38. Respondents to the postelection survey of the ANES are asked:

In talking to people about elections, we often find that a lot of people were not able to vote because they weren't registered, they were sick, or they just didn't have time. Which of the following statements best describes you?

One, I did not vote (in the election this November);

Two, I thought about voting this time—but didn't;

Three, I usually vote, but didn't this time;

Four, I am sure I voted.

39. We classified respondents as voters if they were sure that they voted.

40. These studies suggest, however, that African Americans are more likely to falsely claim to have voted than whites. As a result, racial differences are always greater when turnout is measured by the vote validation studies. Unfortunately, we have no way of knowing whether this difference between the races has changed as African American turnout has increased with time. For results for the 1964, 1976, 1978, 1980, 1984, 1986, and 1988 elections, see Paul R. Abramson and William Claggett, "Racial Differences in Self-Reported and Validated Voting in the 1988 Presidential Election," *Journal of Politics* 53 (February 1991): 186–187. For a discussion of the factors that contribute to false reports of voting, see Brian D. Silver, Barbara A. Anderson, and Paul R. Abramson, "Who Overreports Voting?" *American Political Science Review* 80 (June 1986): 613–624. For a more recent study that argues that biases in reported turnout are more severe than Silver, Anderson, and Abramson claim, see Robert Bernstein, Anita Chadha, and Robert Montjoy, "Overreporting Voting: Why It Happens and Why It Matters," *Public Opinion Quarterly* 65 (Spring 2001): 22–44.

41. Barry Burden reports that the overreporting of voter turnout in the ANES increased with time. He attributes this to declining response rates for the ANES rather than question wording changes or other problems with the survey. See Burden, "Voter Turnout and the National Election Studies," *Political Analysis* 8 (July 2000): 389–398. For counterarguments to Burden, see Michael P. McDonald, "On the Overreport Bias of the National Election Study Turnout Rate," *Political Analysis* (May 2003): 180–186; and Michael D. Martinez, "Comment on 'Voter Turnout and the National Election Studies,'" *Political Analysis* (May 2003): 187–192.

42. Sidney Verba and Norman H. Nie, *Participation in America: Political Democracy and Social Equality* (New York: Cambridge University Press, 1972).

43. See Henry E. Brady, Sidney Verba, and Kay Lehman Schlozman, "Beyond SES: A Resource Model of Political Participation," *American Political Science Review* 89 (June, 1995): 271–294; Verba, Lehman Schlozman, and Brady, *Voice and Equality*.

44. Respondents were classified by the interviewer into one of the following categories: white; black/African American; white and black; other race; white and another race; black and another race; white, black, and another race. We classified only respondents who were white as whites; except for Asians, respondents in the other categories were classified as blacks.

45. For 1964, see U.S. Census Bureau, "Voting Participation in the National Election: November 1964," table 1, http://www.census.gov/hhes/www/socdemo/voting/publications/p20/1964/tab01.pdf. For 2004, see U.S. Census Bureau, "Voting and Registration in the Election of November 2004," table B, http://www.census.gov/prod/2006pubs/p20-556.pdf.

46. Paul R. Abramson, John H. Aldrich, and David W. Rohde, *Change and Continuity in the 2008 Elections* (Washington, D.C.: CQ Press, 2009).

47. See Frederick C. Harris, *Something Within: Religion in African-American Political Activism* (New York: Oxford University, 1999).

48. Benjamin Highton and Arthur L. Burris, "New Perspectives on Latino Voter Turnout in the United States," *American Politics Research* 30 (May 2002): 285–306, utilize CPS data to investigate socioeconomic, ethnic, and place-of-birth differences among Latinos. These authors find that native-born Latinos are more likely to turn out. Matt Barreto, however, using data from California, finds that Latino immigrants were more likely to vote than were native-born Latinos. Clearly, this warrants further investigation. See Barreto, "Latino Immigrants at the Polls: Foreign-born Voter Turnout in the 2002 Election," *Political Research Quarterly* 58 (March 2005): 79–86.

49. Abramson et al., *Change and Continuity in the 2008 Elections*, 98.

50. For an early example of this work, see M. Kent Jennings, "Another Look at the Life Cycle and Political Participation," *American Journal of Political Science* 23 (November 1979): 755–771. For a review, see M. Margaret Conway, *Political Participation in the United States*.

51. See Benjamin Highton and Raymond E. Wolfinger, "The First Seven Years of the Political Life Cycle," *American Journal of Political Science* 45 (January 2001): 202–209.

52. Jan E. Leighley and Jonathan Nagler, "Socioeconomic Class Bias in Turnout, 1972–1988: The Voters Remain the Same," *American Political Science Review* 86 (September 1992): 725–736.

53. See Warren E. Miller, Arthur H. Miller, and Edward J. Schneider, *American National Studies Data Sourcebook, 1952–1978* (Cambridge, Mass.: Harvard University Press, 1980), table 5.23, 317.

54. For example, Robert D. Putnam and David E. Campbell, *American Grace: How Religion Divides and Unites Us* (New York: Simon and Schuster, 2012).

55. See the Pew Religion and Public Life Project, Religious Landscape Survey, http://religions.pewforum.org/comparisons#. When asked "How important is religion in your life?" 56 percent of Americans say "very important," 26 percent say "somewhat important," while 16 percent say religion is "not at all important" in their life. Fifteen percent report attending religious services "more than once a week," 24 percent "once a week," and 15 "once or twice a month." Only 11 percent of Americans say they "never" attend religious services.

56. See Dietram A. Scheufele, Matthew C. Nisbet, Dominque Brossard, and Erik C. Nisbet, "Social Structure and Citizenship: Examining the Impacts of Social Setting, Network Heterogeneity, and Informational Variables on Political Participation," *Political Communication* 21 (No. 3, 2004): 315–338.

57. For general treatments, see Clyde Wilcox and Lee Sigelman, "Political Mobilization in the Pews: Religious Contacting and Electoral Turnout," *Social Science Quarterly* 82 (September, 2001): 524–535; and David E. Campbell, "Acts of Faith: Churches and Political Engagement," *Political Behavior* 26 (June 2004): 155–180. For an examination of the mobilizing role of churches in the African American community, see Fredrick C. Harris, "Something Within: Religion as a Mobilizer of African-American Political Activism, *Journal of Politics* 56 (February 1994): 42–68.

58. Federal law prohibits the Census Bureau from measuring religious preferences on the Current Population Study.

59. Miller, Miller, and Schneider, *American National Studies Data Sourcebook,* table 5.23, 317. Between 1952 and 1976, Catholics were on average 8.0 percentage points more likely to vote in presidential elections, and between 1958 and 1988 they were 10.8 percentage points more likely to vote in midterm elections.

60. Exit poll questions regarding religion were not asked in all states, and thus the number of respondents to the religion questions ($n = 9,731$ for denomination questions; $n = 5,131$ for religiosity questions) is substantially lower than the number of respondents in exit polls generally ($N = 26,565$). Nationally aggregated responses to the exit poll are also unweighted, so the exit poll results for religion may differ from those produced by a nationally representative probability sample, such as that used by the ANES.

61. The Pew Religion and Public Life Project, Religious Landscape Survey provides estimates of the size of religious groups in the population. Protestant denominations were approximately 45 percent of the U.S. population and Catholics were 24 percent.

62. For a study of Conservative Christian mobilization in a recent U.S. election, see J. Quin Monson and J. Baxter Oliphant, "Microtargeting and the Instrumental Mobilization of Religious Conservatives," in *A Matter of Faith: Religion in the 2004 Presidential Election,* ed. David E. Campbell (Washington, D.C.: Brookings Institution, 2007).

63. Respondents were asked, "Would you call yourself a born-again Christian, that is, have you personally had a conversion experience related to Jesus Christ?"

64. Lyman A. Kellstedt, "An Agenda for Future Research," in *Rediscovering the Religious Factor in American Politics,* eds. David C. Leege and Lyman A. Kellstedt (Armonk, N.Y.: M. E. Sharpe, 1993), 293–299.

65. For details regarding the construction of the religious commitment measure, see Abramson, Aldrich, and Rohde, *Change and Continuity in the 2008 Elections,* chap. 4, note 51.

66. Kenneth D. Wald, *Religion and Politics in the United States,* 4th ed. (Lanham, Md.: Rowman and Littlefield, 2003), 161.

67. R. Stephen Warner, *New Wine in Old Wineskins: Evangelicals and Liberals in a Small-Town Church* (Berkeley: University of California Press, 1977), 173.

68. The branching questions used to classify respondents into specific denominational categories were changed in 2008, and therefore it is not possible to replicate our analyses of the 1992, 1996, 2000, and 2004 categories. In creating these new classifications, we relied largely on the Pew Forum on Religion and Public Life, *U.S. Religious Landscape Survey: Religious Affiliation, Diverse and Dynamic* (Washington, D.C.: Pew Forum on Religion and Public Life, 2008), 12. In addition, we were assisted by Corwin D. Smidt. Our classification for 2008 used the following procedures. We used the variable v083185x in the 2008 ANES survey to determine the respondent's denomination. Codes 110, 150, 200, 229, 230, and 270 for this variable were classified as mainline; codes 120–149, 165–200, 221, 223, and 250–269 were classified as evangelical.

69. Wolfinger and Rosenstone, *Who Votes?* 102.

70. For the effect of education on political knowledge and political awareness, see Michael X. Delli Carpini and Scott Keeter, *What Americans Know about Politics and Why It Matters* (New Haven, Conn.: Yale University Press, 1996); and John R. Zaller, *The Nature and Origins of Mass Opinion* (New York: Cambridge University Press, 1992), respectively. In "Beyond SES: A Resource Model of Political Participation," Brady, Verba, and Lehman Schlozman discuss how education enhances both political engagement and civic skills.

71. Richard A. Brody, "The Puzzle of Political Participation in America," in *The New American Political System,* ed. Anthony King (Washington, D.C.: American Enterprise Institute, 1978), 287–324.

72. U.S. Census Bureau, *Statistical Abstract of the United States, 1962* (Washington, D.C.: Government Printing Office, 1962), tables 1 and 129; and U.S. Census Bureau, 2011 American Community Survey, http://factfinder2.census.gov.

73. Ruy A. Teixeira, *The Disappearing American Voter* (Washington, D.C.: American Enterprise Institute, 1992).

74. The Gallup poll provides the best evidence regarding church attendance over the past six decades. While church attendance has declined on average, Catholics appear to be driving the decline. Since 1955, weekly church attendance among Catholics has dropped by nearly 30 percent. Weekly church attendance among Protestants has been stable throughout the period. Interestingly, the percentage of Catholics attending church weekly is now roughly equal to the rate

among Protestants. See Lydia Saad, "Churchgoing among U.S. Catholics Slides to Tie Protestants," Gallup, April 9, 2009, http://www.gallup.com/poll/117382/church-going-among-catholics-slides-tie-protestants.aspx.

75. Robert D. Putnam makes a similar argument, claiming that political disengagement was largely the result of the baby boom generation and that generational succession reduced other forms of civic activity as well: "The declines in church attendance, voting, political interest, campaign activities, associational membership and social trusts are attributable almost entirely to generational succession." See Putnam, *Bowling Alone: The Collapse and Revival of American Community* (New York: Simon and Schuster, 2000), 265.

76. George I. Balch, "Multiple Indicators in Survey Research: The Concept 'Sense of Political Efficacy,'" *Political Methodology* 1 (Spring 1974): 1–43. For an extensive discussion of feelings of political efficacy, see Paul R. Abramson, *Political Attitudes in America: Formation and Change* (San Francisco: W. H. Freeman, 1983): 135–189.

77. Steven J. Rosenstone and John Mark Hansen, *Mobilization, Participation, and Democracy in America* (New York: Macmillan, 1993), 214–215.

78. Ruy A. Teixeira, *Why Americans Don't Vote: Turnout Decline in the United States, 1960–1964* (New York: Greenwood Press, 1987). In his more recent study, *The Disappearing American Voter,* Teixeira develops a measure of party-related characteristics that includes strength of party identification, concern about the electoral outcome, perceived difference between the parties, and knowledge about the parties and the candidates. See also Rosenstone and Hansen, *Mobilization, Participation, and Democracy.*

79. Our first analysis studied the decline of turnout between 1960 and 1980. See Paul R. Abramson, John H. Aldrich, and David W. Rohde, *Change and Continuity in the 1980 Elections,* rev. ed. (Washington, D.C.: CQ Press, 1983), 85–87. For a more detailed analysis using probability procedures, see Paul R. Abramson and John H. Aldrich, "The Decline of Electoral Participation in America," *American Political Science Review* 76 (September 1982): 502–521. For our analyses from 1984 through 2008, see Abramson, Aldrich, and Rohde, *Change and Continuity in the 2008 Elections,* 105–108, and Chapter 4, note 73.

80. ANES respondents are asked, "Generally speaking, do you usually think of yourself as a Republican, a Democrat, an Independent, or what?" Persons who call themselves Republicans are asked, "Would you call yourself a strong Republican or a not very strong Republican?" Those who call themselves Democrats are asked, "Would you call yourself a strong Democrat or a not very strong Democrat?" Those who called themselves independents, named another party, or who had no preference were asked, "Do you think of yourself as closer to the Republican party or to the Democratic party?"

81. The seminal work on party identification is Angus Campbell, Philip E. Converse, Warren E. Miller, and Donald E. Stokes, *The American Voter* (New York: Wiley, 1960), 120–167.

82. See Morris P. Fiorina, "The Voting Decision: Instrumental and Expressive Aspects," *Journal of Politics* 38 (May 1976): 390–413; and John H. Aldrich, "Rational Choice and Turnout," *American Journal of Political Science* 37 (February 1993): 246–278.

For a detailed discussion of party identification from 1952 to 2012, along with tables showing the distribution of party identification among whites and blacks during these years, see Chapter 8 in this volume, as well as the Appendix.

83. As Steven E. Finkel notes, the relationship between political efficacy and political participation is likely reciprocal. Not only do feelings of efficacy increase the likelihood of participation, but participation increases individuals' feelings of efficacy. See Steven E. Finkel, "Reciprocal Effects of Participation and Political Efficacy: A Panel Analysis," *American Journal of Political Science* 29 (November 1985): 891–913.

84. Our measure of external efficacy is based on the responses to two statements: "Public officials don't care much what people like me think" and "People like me don't have any say about what the government does." Respondents who disagreed with both of these statements were scored as high in feelings of effectiveness; those who agreed with one statement and disagreed with the other were scored as medium, and those who agreed with both statements were scored as low. Respondents who scored "don't know" or "not ascertained" to one statement were scored high or low according to their answer on the other statement. Those with "don't know" or "not ascertained" responses to both statements were excluded from the analysis. Since 1988, ANES respondents have been asked whether they "strongly agreed," "agreed," "disagreed," or "strongly disagreed" with the statements. We classified respondents who "neither agreed nor disagreed" with both statements as medium on our measure. This decision has little effect on the results since few respondents "neither agree nor disagree" with both statements, typically less than 5 percent. In 2008 and 2012, this standard measure of feelings of "external" political efficacy was asked of only half of the sample.

85. See Abramson and Aldrich, "The Decline of Electoral Participation in America," 515.

86. The procedure uses the 1960 distribution of partisans by levels of efficacy as our base, thus assuming that levels of turnout for each subgroup (e.g., strong partisan/high efficacy, strong partisan/medium efficacy) would have remained the same if partisanship and efficacy had not declined. We multiply the size of each subgroup (set at 1960 levels) by the proportion of the whites who reported voting in each subgroups in the 2012 election. We then sum the products and divide by the sum of the subgroup sizes. The procedure is detailed in Abramson, *Political Attitudes in America: Formation and Change*, 296.

87. For a discussion of political trust, see Abramson, *Political Attitudes in America*, 193–238. For a more recent discussion, see Marc J. Hetherington, *Why Trust Matters: Declining Political Trust and the Demise of American Liberalism* (Princeton, N.J.: Princeton University Press, 2005). Russell J. Dalton reports a decline in confidence in politicians and government in fifteen of sixteen democracies. Although many of the trends are not statistically significant, the

overall decline is impressive. Dalton's report includes results from the ANES, where the trend toward declining confidence is unlikely to occur by chance on two of the three questions. See Dalton, *Democratic Challenges, Democratic Choices: The Erosion of Political Support in Advanced Industrial Democracies* (Oxford, UK: Oxford University Press, 2004), 28–32.

88. Respondents were asked, "How much of the time do you think you can trust the government in Washington to do what is right—just about always, most of the time, or only some of the time?"

89. This question was asked of a randomly selected half-sample in 2008.

90. See Brad T. Gomez, Thomas G. Hansford, and George A. Krause, "The Republicans Should Pray for Rain: Weather, Turnout, and Voting in U.S. Presidential Elections," *Journal of Politics* 69 (August 2007): 649–663.

91. The recent proliferation in electoral laws allowing early voting is likely to diminish the chances that bad weather on election day will reduce voter turnout. Laws that allow citizens to vote by mail, such as those found in Oregon and Washington, make election day weather inconsequential.

92. In the past half century, a handful of elections could be classified—based on pre-election polling—as "dead heats" going into election day. Recall from Chapter 3, for example, that the average of nine pre-election polls in 2012 showed a virtual tie between Obama and Romney. By contrast, in 1964, the final Gallup poll before the election predicted a twenty-eight point victory in the popular vote for Lyndon Johnson over Barry Goldwater.

93. See Anthony Downs, *An Economic Theory of Democracy* (New York: Harper and Row, 1957); and William H. Riker and Peter C. Ordeshook, "A Theory of the Calculus of Voting," *American Political Science Review* 72 (March 1968): 25–42.

94. These are Colorado, Florida, Iowa, Michigan, Minnesota, Nevada, New Hampshire, New Mexico, North Carolina, Ohio, Pennsylvania, Virginia, and Wisconsin.

95. Rosenstone and Hansen, *Mobilization, Participation, and Democracy in America*, 181–182.

96. The use of randomized field experiments in political science predates the work of Gerber and Green, though these authors are certainly responsible for the revived interest in the research design in the discipline. In the 1920s, Harold Gosnell sent postcards to randomly assigned nonvoters emphasizing the importance of voter registration before the 1924 presidential election. Gosnell found a significant increase in voter registration among those who received the postcard treatment compared to those in his control group who received nothing. In the 1950s, Samuel Eldersveld used random assignment to test the effectiveness of mail, phone, and in-person canvassing in a local mayoral race. It would be decades before another field experiment design was published in the academic journals of political science. See Harold F. Gosnell, *Getting Out the Vote* (Chicago: University of Chicago Press, 1927); and Samuel J. Eldersveld, "Experimental Propaganda Techniques and Voting Behavior," *American Political Science Review* 50 (March 1956): 154–165.

97. For an introduction to field experimentation in the social sciences, see Alan S. Gerber and Donald P. Green, *Field Experiments: Design, Analysis, and Interpretation* (New York: Norton, 2012).

98. For a summary of findings in this research program, see Donald P. Green and Alan S. Gerber, *Get Out the Vote: How to Increase Voter Turnout*, 2nd ed. (Washington, D.C.: Brookings Institution, 2008).

99. This is not to say that it is impossible to make causal inferences from survey data. Panel designs, where survey respondents are interviewed repeatedly at multiple time periods, can establish causal (temporal) order. Paul R. Abramson and William Claggett, for instance, use ANES panel data from 1990 and 1992 to show the effects of party contact on voter turnout persists even after one takes into account that the political elites are more likely to contact people who have participated in the past. See Abramson and Claggett, "Recruitment and Political Participation," *Political Research Quarterly* 54 (December 2001): 905–916.

100. Respondents were asked, "The political parties try to talk to as many people as they can to get them to vote for their candidate. Did anyone from the political parties call or come around to talk with you about the campaign this year?"

101. Seymour Martin Lipset, *Political Man: The Social Bases of Politics*, expanded ed. (Baltimore: Johns Hopkins University Press, 1981), 226–229.

102. See James DeNardo, "Turnout and the Vote: The Joke's on the Democrats," *American Political Science Review* 74 (December 1980): 406–420; and Thomas G. Hansford and Brad T. Gomez, "Estimating the Electoral Effects of Voter Turnout," *American Political Science Review* 104 (May 2010): 268–288.

103. In addition to the partisan effect of high turnout, Hansford and Gomez argue that incumbents from both parties lose vote share as turnout becomes higher, suggesting that marginal voters are less supportive of incumbents than dedicated voters.

104. As reported by the National Conference of State Legislatures, "Voter Identification Requirements," http://www.ncsl.org/legislatures-elections/elections/voter-id.aspx. Since the 2012 election, North Carolina, which has a Republican legislature and governor, has also passed a strict voter identification requirement, bringing the total to thirty-four states.

105. Abramson, Aldrich, and Rohde, *Change and Continuity in the 1980 Elections*, 88–92; *Change and Continuity in the 1984 Elections*, 119–124; *Change and Continuity in the 1988 Elections*, 108–112.

106. Abramson, Aldrich, and Rohde, *Change and Continuity in the 1992 Elections*, 124–128.

107. Abramson, Aldrich, and Rohde, *Change and Continuity in the 1996 and 1998 Elections*, 86–89.

108. Paul R. Abramson, John H. Aldrich, and David W. Rohde, "The 2004 Presidential Election: The Emergence of a Permanent Majority," *Political Science Quarterly* 120 (Spring 2005): 43.

109. Abramson, Aldrich, and Rohde, *Change and Continuity in the 1992 Elections*, 110–112.

110. See Campbell et al., *The American Voter*, 96–115.

111. It is common in our earlier analyses to find Republicans turning out at a higher rate than Democrats. In 2008, we found that if Democrats had voted at the same rate as Republicans, Obama's vote share would have increased about 3.5 percentage points. In the 2004 election, we estimate that Kerry would have gained 3.4 percentage points in the vote if Democrats had been as likely to vote as Republicans. Depending on the states in which these votes were cast, Kerry could have won the election.

112. The kind and number of issues used varied from election to election. We used only issues on which respondents were asked to state their own positions and where they thought the major-party candidates were located. See Table 6-4 for the number of issues used in each election between 1980 and 2008.

113. Our issue scale differs slightly from the one used in our 2008 analysis, which included seven items. The 2012 ANES no longer asks respondents' opinions regarding the role of women in society. Consequently, this item has been removed from our scale.

114. In their county-level analysis of the electoral effect of voter turnout in the 1944 through 2000 presidential elections, Hansford and Gomez use simulations from their statistical model to demonstrate that a four percentage-point swing in turnout (from two percentage points below to two points above actual turnout) leads to an average change in Democratic vote share at the national level of just under one percentage point. However, small changes are not necessarily trivial. The authors go on to show that varying turnout from two points above and below observed values causes an average change of approximately twenty Electoral College votes per presidential election in non-southern states. See Hansford and Gomez, "Estimating the Electoral Effects of Voter Turnout," 284.

115. For the most influential statement of this argument, see Wolfinger and Rosenstone, *Who Votes?* 108–114.

116. Frances Fox Piven and Richard A. Cloward, *Why Americans Don't Vote* (New York: Pantheon Books, 1988), 21. See also Piven and Cloward, *Why Americans Still Don't Vote*.

5. SOCIAL FORCES AND THE VOTE

1. For a classic treatment of the subject, see M. Kent Jennings and Richard G. Niemi, *Generations and Politics: A Panel Study of Young Adults and Their Parents* (Princeton, N.J.: Princeton University Press, 1981).

2. See Larry M. Bartels, "What's the Matter with *What's the Matter with Kansas?*" *Quarterly Journal of Political Science* 1 (Issue 2, 2006): 201–226.

3. See Paul R. Abramson, John H. Aldrich, and David W. Rohde, *Change and Continuity in the 2008 and 2010 Elections* (Washington, D.C.: CQ Press, 2012), 116–141.

4. The social characteristics used in this chapter are the same as those used in Chapter 4. The variables are described in the notes to that chapter.

5. In 2012, the National Election Pool consortium was composed of ABC News, Associated Press, CBS News, CNN, Fox News, and NBC News.

6. As noted in Chapter 4, footnote 37, the exit polls are not a representative sample of the nation. The exit polls were conducted separately in thirty-one states. Precincts in each state were selected by a stratified-probability sample, and every *n*th voter in the precinct was offered a questionnaire to complete. In states with significant early and/or absentee voting, the sample was supplemented with a telephone survey.

We draw on 2012 exit poll reports from Fox News (http://www.foxnews.com/politics/elections/2012-exit-poll), *The New York Times* (http://elections.nytimes.com/2012/results/president/exit-polls), CNN (http://www.cnn.com/election/2012/results/race/president), and *The Washington Post* (http://www.washingtonpost.com/wp-srv/special/politics/2012-exit-polls). For a discussion of the 2008 exit polls, see Abramson, Aldrich, and Rohde, *Change and Continuity in the 2008 and 2010 Elections,* 117–139.

Exit polls have three main advantages: (1) they are less expensive to conduct than the multistage probability samples conducted by the American National Election Studies; (2) because of their lower cost, a large number of people can be sampled; and (3) because people are selected to be interviewed as they leave the polling stations, the vast majority of respondents have actually voted. But these surveys also have four disadvantages: (1) organizations that conduct exit polls must now take into account the growing number of voters who vote early—about a third of all voters in 2012; (2) the self-administered polls used for respondents leaving the polls must be relatively brief; (3) it is difficult to supervise the field work to ensure that interviewers are using the proper procedures to select respondents; and (4) these studies are of relatively little use in studying turnout because people who do not vote are not sampled. For a discussion of the procedures used to conduct exit polls and their limitations, see Albert H. Cantril, *The Opinion Connection: Polling, Politics, and the Press* (Washington, D.C.: CQ Press, 1991), 142–144, 216–218.

7. This brief discussion cannot do justice to the complexities of black electoral participation. For an important study based on the 1984 ANES survey of blacks, see Patricia Gurin, Shirley Hatchett, and James S. Jackson, *Hope and Independence: Blacks' Response to Electoral and Party Politics* (New York: Russell Sage Foundation, 1989). For two important studies that use this survey, see Michael C. Dawson, *Behind the Mule: Race and Class in African American Politics* (Princeton, N.J.: Princeton University Press, 1994); and Katherine Tate, *From Politics to Protest: The New Black Voter in American Elections* (Cambridge, Mass.: Harvard University Press, 1994). For a summary of recent research on

race and politics, see Michael C. Dawson and Cathy Cohen, "Problems in the Politics of Race," in *Political Science: The State of the Discipline,* eds. Ira Katznelson and Helen V. Milner (New York: Norton, 2002), 488–510.

8. Even with an oversample of black respondents, the weighted ANES data show only three black respondents who voted for Romney. The pool poll, which has a substantially larger number of respondents than the ANES, shows no significant age differences among blacks in their support for Obama. Gender differences among blacks are evident, however. Only 3 percent of black women voted for Romney; 11 percent of black men did.

9. For a review of research on Latinos as well as African Americans, see Paula McClain and John D. Garcia, "Expanding Disciplinary Boundaries: Black, Latino, and Racial Minority Groups in Political Science," in *Political Science: The State of the Discipline II,* ed. Ada W. Finifter (Washington, D.C.: American Political Science Association, 1993), 247–279. For analyses of Latino voting in the 1996 elections, see Rudolfo O. de la Garza and Louis DeSipio, eds., *Awash in the Mainstream: Latino Politics in the 1976 Election* (Boulder, Colo.: Westview Press, 1999). For a review, see John D. Garcia, "Latinos and Political Behavior: Defining Community to Examine Critical Complexities," in *The Oxford Handbook of American Elections and Political Behavior,* ed. Jan E. Leighley (New York: Oxford University Press, 2010), 397–414.

10. The accuracy of the pool poll results, which are based on 255 interviews with Cuban Americans in Florida, has been questioned. Another exit poll of 3,800 Florida Hispanic voters and conducted by Democratic pollsters suggests that Obama beat Romney 51-49 percent among Cuban Americans. Despite the larger number of survey respondents, we are unfamiliar with the sampling methods employed by these researchers and cannot endorse their finding. A third study uses ecological regression techniques to analyze aggregate vote returns from select precincts in Miami-Dade County, Florida, and suggests that Romney won 59 percent of the Cuban American vote. We cannot endorse the use of aggregate data when evidence from a high-quality random sample of individual voters who self-identify as Cuban Americans is available. For a report of these various results, see Juan O. Tamayo, "Did Obama or Romney Win the Cuban-American Vote?" *Miami Herald,* November 12, 2012, http://www.miamiherald .com/2012/11/12/3094299/winner-of-cuban-american-vote.html.

11. For three reviews of research on women in politics, see Susan J. Carroll and Linda M. Zerelli, "Feminist Challenges to Political Science," in Finifter, *Political Science: The State of the Discipline II,* 55–76; Nancy Burns, "Gender: Public Opinion and Political Action," in Katznelson and Milner, *Political Science: The State of the Discipline,* 462–487; and Kira Sanbonmastu, "Organizing American Politics, Organizing Gender," in Leighley, *Oxford Handbook of American Elections and Political Behavior,* 415–432.

12. The gender gap in 1980, coupled with Ronald Reagan's opposition to abortion rights and the Equal Rights Amendment, led the former president of the National Organization for Women, Eleanor Smeal, to write a report for the

Democratic National Committee detailing how Democrats could take back the White House if the party placed a woman on the ticket in the next election. In 1984, Democratic Congresswoman Geraldine Ferraro became the first female vice presidential nominee in U.S. history. Reagan won reelection in a landslide.

13. See Paul R. Abramson, John H. Aldrich, and David W. Rohde, *Change and Continuity in the 1980 and 1982 Elections* (Washington, D.C.: CQ Press, 1983), 290.

14. The ANES survey reports six types of marital status: married, divorced, separated, widowed, never married, and partners who are not married.

15. See Sheryl Gay Stolberg, "Obama Signs Away 'Don't Ask, Don't Tell,'" *New York Times*, December 22, 2010, http://www.nytimes.com/2010/12/23/us/politics/23military.html; and Jackie Calmes and Peter Baker, "Obama Says Same-Sex Marriage Should be Legal," *New York Times*, May 10, 2012, A1.

16. Exit polls ask voters to cast a "secret ballot" after they have left the polling station. They are handed a short form that records the respondent's behavior, political views, and demographic information. Use of this procedure reduces the pressure for the respondent to answer in a socially "acceptable" way. Five percent of respondents to the 2012 pool poll acknowledged being gay, lesbian, or bisexual.

17. Respondents were asked, "Do you consider yourself to be heterosexual or straight, homosexual or gay (lesbian), or bisexual?" This question was asked during a computer-assisted self-interview (CASI) portion of the face-to-face interview in which the respondent enters his or her response into a tablet computer.

18. Paul R. Abramson, John H. Aldrich, and David W. Rohde, *Change and Continuity in the 2004 and 2006 Elections* (Washington, D.C.: CQ Press, 2007), 124–127. For cross-national evidence, see Ronald Inglehart, *Modernization and Postmodernization: Cultural, Economic, and Political Change in 43 Societies* (Princeton, N.J.: Princeton University Press, 1997), 255; and Russell J. Dalton, *Citizen Politics: Public Opinion and Political Parties in Advanced Industrial Democracies,* 6th ed. (Washington, D.C.: CQ Press, 2014), 157–165.

19. Jeffrey M. Stonecash, *Class and Party in American Politics* (Boulder, Colo.: Westview Press, 2000), 87–121; Larry M. Bartels, *Unequal Democracy: The Political Economy of the New Gilded Age* (New York: Russell Sage Foundation, 2008), 64–126.

20. For the single best summary, see Kenneth D. Wald and Allison Calhoun-Brown, *Religion and Politics in the United States,* 6th ed. (Lanham, Md.: Rowman and Littlefield, 2011). For a discussion of religion and politics in a comparative context, see Pippa Norris and Ronald Inglehart, *Sacred and Secular: Religion and Politics Worldwide* (Cambridge, UK: Cambridge University Press, 2004).

21. David E. Campbell, ed. *A Matter of Faith: Religion in the 2004 Presidential Election* (Washington, D.C.: Brookings Institution), 1.

22. The exception to this generalization is religious devotion among African Americans, who overwhelmingly support the Democratic Party. Among non-Christian denominations, Jewish voters remain decidedly loyal to the Democrats.

23. See Robert D. Putnam and David E. Campbell, *American Grace: How Religion Divides and Unites Us* (New York: Simon and Schuster, 2010).

24. The Catholic Church had an uneasy relationship with the Obama administration during the president's first term. During the debate over health care reform in 2009, for instance, the U.S. Conference of Catholic Bishops supported the president's efforts to reform the health care system, but threatened to oppose any bill that provided public funding for abortion or contraception. The Catholic Church has actually lobbied for decades for the adoption of a universal health care system, a more "liberal" system than what was eventually adopted under the Affordable Care Act. See David D. Kirkpatrick, "Some Catholic Bishops Assail Health Plan," *New York Times*, August 28, 2009, A1. During the early stages of the implementation of "Obamacare," several Catholic organizations sued the Obama administration, challenging its rule that employers, including religious institutions, offer contraceptive coverage in their employee's health insurance policies. See Louise Radnofsky, "Catholics Sue over Health Mandate," *Wall Street Journal*, May 23, 2012, http://online.wsj.com/news/articles/SB100014240527023 04019404577418291623540400.

25. The Pew Research: Religion & Public Life Project, estimates that only 2 percent of American Catholics are African American. Thus, Latinos are the main contributor to Obama's nonwhite support. See Pew Research, "A Portrait of American Catholics on the Eve of Pope Benedict's Visit to the U.S.," http://www .pewforum.org/2008/03/27/a-portrait-of-american-catholics-on-the-eve-of-pope-benedicts-visit-to-the-us.

26. Pew Research, Religion & Public Life Project, "The Catholic 'Swing' Vote," http://www.pewforum.org/2012/10/11/the-catholic-swing-vote.

27. The question, which was asked to all Christians, was "Would you call yourself a born-again Christian, that is, have you personally had a conversion experience related to Jesus Christ?" This question was not asked in the 2004 ANES survey.

28. Lyman A. Kellstedt, "An Agenda for Future Research," in *Rediscovering the Religious Factor in American Politics,* eds. David C. Leege and Lyman A. Kellstedt (Armonk, N.Y.: M. E. Sharpe, 1993), 293–299.

29. Abramson, Aldrich, and Rohde, *Change and Continuity in the 2008 and the 2010 Elections,* 124–125.

30. Morris P. Fiorina and his colleagues have pointed out that ANES surveys suggest that the relationship between church attendance and the tendency to vote Republican was substantially higher in 1992 than in 1972, although the relationship leveled off or declined slightly between 1992 and 2004. See Morris P. Fiorina, with Samuel J. Abrams and Jeremy C. Pope, *Culture War? The Myth of a Polarized America,* 2nd ed. (New York: Pearson/ Longman, 2006), 134.

31. Robert Axelrod, "Where the Votes Come From: An Analysis of Electoral Coalitions," *American Political Science Review* 66 (March 1972): 11–20. Axelrod updates his results through the 1984 elections. For his most recent estimate, including results from 1952 to 1980, see Axelrod, "Presidential Coalitions in

1984," *American Political Science Review* 80 (March 1986): 281–284. Using Axelrod's categories, Nelson W. Polsby estimates the social composition of the Democratic and Republican presidential coalitions between 1952 and 2000. See Nelson W. Polsby and Aaron Wildavsky, *Presidential Elections: Strategies and Structures of American Politics,* 11th ed. (Lanham, Md.: Rowman and Littlefield, 2004), 32. For an update through 2004, see Nelson W. Polsby and Aaron Wildavsky, with David A. Hopkins, *Presidential Elections: Strategies and Structures in American Politics,* 12th ed. (Lanham, Md.: Rowman and Littlefield, 2008), 28.

32. John R. Petrocik, *Party Coalitions: Realignment and the Decline of the New Deal Party System* (Chicago: University of Chicago Press, 1981).

33. Harold W. Stanley, William T. Bianco, and Richard G. Niemi, "Partisanship and Group Support over Time: A Multivariate Analysis," *American Political Science Review* 80 (September 1986): 969–976. Stanley and his colleagues assess the independent contribution that group membership makes toward Democratic loyalties after controls are introduced for membership in other pro-Democratic groups. For an update and an extension through 2004, see Harold W. Stanley and Richard G. Niemi, "Partisanship, Party Coalitions, and Group Support, 1952–2004," *Presidential Studies Quarterly* 36 (June 2006): 172–188. For an alternative approach, see Robert S. Erikson, Thomas D. Lancaster, and David W. Romero, "Group Components of the Presidential Vote, 1952–1984," *Journal of Politics* 51 (May 1989): 337–346.

34. For a discussion of the contribution of the working class to the Democratic presidential coalition, see Paul R. Abramson, *Generational Change in American Politics* (Lexington, Mass.: D. C. Heath, 1975).

35. See Axelrod, "Where the Votes Come From."

36. The NORC survey, based on 2,564 civilians, used a quota sample that does not follow the probability procedures used by the University of Michigan Survey Research Center. Following the procedures used at the time, southern blacks were not sampled. Because the NORC survey overrepresented upper-income groups and the middle and upper-middle classes, it cannot be used to estimate the contribution of social groups to the Democratic and Republican presidential coalitions.

37. Abramson, *Generational Change in American Politics,* 65–68.

38. As Figure 5-1 shows, Clinton did win a majority of the white major-party vote in 1992 and 1996.

39. Racial voting, as well as our other measures of social cleavage, is affected by including Wallace voters with Nixon voters in 1968, Anderson voters with Reagan voters in 1980, Perot voters with Bush voters in 1992, and Perot voters with Dole voters in 1996. For the effects of including these independent or third-party candidates, see Paul R. Abramson, John H. Aldrich, and David W. Rohde, *Change and Continuity in the 1996 and 1998 Elections* (Washington, D.C.: CQ Press, 1999), 102, 104–106, 108, and 111.

40. The statements about low turnout in 1996 are true regardless of whether one measures turnout based on the voting-age population or the voting-eligible

population. Turnout among the voting-eligible population fell about nine percentage points between 1960 and 1996. And even though black turnout fell in 1996, it was still well above its levels before the Voting Rights Act of 1965.

41. As we explain in Chapter 3, we consider the South to include the eleven states of the old Confederacy. Because the 1944 NORC survey and the 1948 University of Michigan Survey Research Center survey did not record the respondents' states of residence, we cannot included these years in our analysis of regional differences among the white electorate.

42. George H. W. Bush was born in Massachusetts and raised in Connecticut. As an adult he moved to Texas, thus making him a resident of the south.

43. Cheney had served as the U.S. representative from Wyoming from 1979 to 1989. When he became the chief executive officer of an oilfield services corporation in 1995, he established his residence in Texas. Being a resident of Texas would have complicated running on the same ticket as Bush because the Twelfth Amendment specifies that electors "vote by ballot for President and Vice-President, one of whom, at least, shall not be an inhabitant of the same state with themselves."

44. See, for example, Chapter 3, where we compare Kennedy's black support in the South in 1960 with Carter's in 1976.

45. Officially known as the Labor-Management Relations Act, this legislation, passed in 1947, qualified or amended much of the National Labor Relations Act of 1935 (known as the Wagner Act). Union leaders argued that the Taft-Hartley Act placed unwarranted restrictions on organized labor. This act was passed by the Republican-controlled Eightieth Congress, vetoed by Truman, and passed over his veto.

46. This is a four-percentage-point increase over the 2008 ANES estimate. The Bureau of Labor Statistics estimates that 11.3 percent of wage and salary workers are members of a union. African American workers have a higher rate of union membership (13.4 percent) than white workers (11.1 percent). See Bureau of Labor Statistics, "Economic News Release: Union Members Summary," January 23, 2013, http://www.bls.gov/news.release/union2.nr0.htm.

47. This percentage may well be too low. According to the 2008 pool poll, Obama received 53 percent of the vote. Members of union households made up 21 percent of the electorate, and 50 percent voted for Obama. These numbers thus suggest that 23 percent of Obama's vote in 2008 came from members of union households. Even if one takes into account that not all these union voters were white, these numbers suggest that about one in five of Obama's votes came from union households.

48. Peyton M. Craighill and Scott Clement, "Can Unions Save the White Working-Class Vote for Democrats?" *Washington Post*, November 20, 2012, http://www.washingtonpost.com/blogs/the-fix/wp/2012/11/20/can-unions-save-the-white-working-class-vote-for-democrats.

49. See Robert R. Alford, *Party and Society: The Anglo-American Democracies* (Chicago: Rand McNally, 1963); Seymour Martin Lipset, *Political Man: The Social*

Bases of Politics, exp. ed. (Baltimore: Johns Hopkins University Press, 1981); and Inglehart, *Modernization and Postmodernization.*

50. The variation in class voting is smaller if one focuses on class differences in the congressional vote, but the data clearly show a decline in class voting between 1952 and 2008. See Dalton, *Citizen Politics,* 6th ed., 161.

51. Readers should bear in mind that in 2000, 2004, and 2008, there was no measure of the head of household's occupation or of the spouse's occupation, but our analysis of the 1996 data suggests that this limitation probably does not account for the negative level of class voting in the 2000 contest. Bartels discusses our attempts to maintain comparability in measuring social class in the face of changing survey measurement in *Unequal Democracy,* 70–71.

52. As we point out in *Change and Continuity in the 2000 and 2002 Elections,* when we define social class according to the respondent's own occupation, the overall size of the working class falls and the overall size of the middle class grows. Because the relatively small size of the working class in 2000, 2004, and 2008 results mainly from a redefinition of the way our measure of social class is constructed, we assumed that the sizes of the working and middle classes in 2000, 2004, and 2008 were the same as they were in the 1996 ANES. See Abramson, Aldrich, and Rohde, *Change and Continuity in the 2000 and 2002 Elections,* chap. 4, 313, n26.

53. See Anat Shenker-Osorio, "Why Americans All Believe They Are 'Middle Class,'" *Atlantic,* August 1, 2013, http://www.theatlantic.com/politics/archive/2013/08/why-americans-all-believe-they-are-middle-class/278240.

54. See Mark N. Franklin, "The Decline of Cleavage Politics," in *Electoral Change: Responses to Evolving Social and Attitudinal Structures in Western Countries,* eds. Mark N. Franklin, Thomas T. Mackie, and Henry Valen, with others (Cambridge, UK: Cambridge University Press, 1992), 383–405. See also Inglehart, *Modernization and Postmodernization,* 237–266.

55. Jeff Manza and Clem Brooks, *Social Cleavages and Political Change: Voter Alignments and U.S. Party Coalitions* (New York: Oxford University Press, 1999).

56. Exit polls conducted between 1972 and 2012 show the same pattern. In all eleven elections, Jews have been more likely to vote Democratic than white Catholics, and white Catholics have been more likely to vote Democratic than white Protestants. For a breakdown of religious voting in the 2012 election, see Fox News, "2012 Fox News Exit Polls," http://www.foxnews.com/politics/elections/2012-exit-poll.

57. For a discussion of the impact of religion on the 1960 election, see Philip E. Converse, "Religion and Politics: The 1960 Election," in *Elections and the Political Order,* ed. Angus Campbell et al. (New York: Wiley, 1967), 96–124.

58. According to the 2012 *Statistical Abstract of the United States,* as of 2010, 2.1 percent of the U.S. population was Jewish, and according to the Pew Forum on Religion and Public Life, only 1.7 percent was. The *Statistical Abstract* results are based mainly on information provided by Jewish organizations, whereas the Pew results are based on a representative survey of 35,000 Americans. The Pew

survey is presented in Pew Forum on Religion and Public Life, *U.S. Religious Landscape Survey: Religious Affiliation, Diverse and Dynamic* (Washington, D.C.: Pew Forum on Religion and Public Life, 2008), 12. For the *Statistical Abstract,* see U.S. Census Bureau, *The 2012 Statistical Abstract of the United States: The National Data Book,* table 76, http://www.census.gov/compendia/statab/2012/tables/12s0077.pdf.

59. States are listed in descending order according to their estimated number of Jews.

60. Since 1860, the Democrats have won the presidency only twice without winning New York: 1916, when Woodrow Wilson narrowly defeated Charles Evans Hughes by a margin of twenty-three electoral votes, and 1948, when Harry Truman defeated Thomas Dewey. Dewey, the governor of New York, won 46.0 percent of the popular vote in his home state, and Truman won 45.0 percent. Henry A. Wallace, the Progressive candidate in 1948, won 8.2 percent of the New York vote, substantially better than his share in any other state.

61. For an expanded treatment of the Catholic vote in 1960 and 2004, see J. Matthew Wilson, "The Changing Catholic Voter: Comparing Responses to John Kennedy in 1960 and John Kerry in 2004" in Campbell, *A Matter of Faith.*

62. Robert Huckfeldt and Carol Weitzel Kohfeld provide strong evidence that Democratic appeals to blacks weakened the party's support among working-class whites. See Huckfeldt and Kohfeld, *Race and the Decline of Class in American Politics* (Urbana: University of Illinois Press, 1989).

63. For evidence on this point, see Paul R. Abramson, *Political Attitudes in America: Formation and Change* (San Francisco: W. H. Freeman, 1983), 65–68.

64. Edward G. Carmines and James A. Stimson, *Issue Evolution: Race and the Transformation of American Politics* (Princeton, N.J.: Princeton University Press, 1999). For a critique of their thesis, see Alan I. Abramowitz, "Issue Evolution Reconsidered: Racial Attitudes and Partisanship among the American Electorate," *American Journal of Political Science* 38 (February 1994): 1–24.

65. James W. Ceaser and Andrew E. Busch, *Upside Down and Inside Out: The 1992 Elections and American Politics* (Lanham, Md.: Rowman and Littlefield, 1993), 168–171.

6. CANDIDATES, ISSUES, AND THE VOTE

1. This set of attitudes was first formulated and tested extensively in Angus Campbell, Philip E. Converse, Warren E. Miller, and Donald E. Stokes, *The American Voter* (New York: Wiley, 1960), using data from what are now called the American National Election Studies surveys. The authors based their conclusions primarily on data from a survey of the 1956 presidential election, a rematch between the Democrat Adlai Stevenson and Republican (and this time the incumbent) Dwight Eisenhower. Recently, Michael S. Lewis-Beck, William G. Jacoby, Helmut Norpoth, and Herbert F. Weisberg applied similar methods to

data from 2000 and 2004. See their *The American Voter Revisited* (Ann Arbor: University of Michigan Press, 2008).

2. See, for example, Wendy M. Rahn et al., "A Social-Cognitive Model of Candidate Appraisal," in *Information and Democratic Processes*, eds. John A. Ferejohn and James H. Kuklinski (Urbana: University of Illinois Press, 1990), 136–159, and sources cited therein.

3. For the most extensive explication of the theory and tests in various electoral settings, see Gary W. Cox, *Making Votes Count: Strategic Coordination in the World's Electoral Systems* (New York: Cambridge University Press, 1997). For an examination in the American context, see Paul R. Abramson et al., "Third-Party and Independent Candidates in American Politics: Wallace, Anderson, and Perot," *Political Science Quarterly* 110 (Fall 1995): 349–367.

4. These elections are discussed in Paul R. Abramson, John H. Aldrich, and David W. Rohde, *Change and Continuity in the 1980 Elections*, rev. ed. (Washington, D.C.: CQ Press, 1983); Abramson, Aldrich, and Rohde, *Change and Continuity in the 1992 Elections*, rev. ed. (Washington, D.C.: CQ Press, 1995); Abramson, Aldrich, and Rohde, *Change and Continuity in the 1996 and 1998 Elections* (Washington, D.C.: CQ Press, 1999); and Abramson, Aldrich, and Rohde, *Change and Continuity in the 2000 and 2002 Elections* (Washington, D.C.: CQ Press, 2003).

5. We reproduced the feeling thermometer most recently in Abramson, Aldrich, and Rohde, *Change and Continuity in the 2000 and 2002 Elections,* 123.

6. See the references cited in note 4.

7. The questions in 2008 offered different response options, so we cannot easily compare the two elections. However, it appears that the difference in evaluating Obama and McCain in 2008 was much smaller, with the exception of the intelligence questions. See Abramson et al., *Change and Continuity in the 2008 and 2010 Elections*, 146, table 62-A.

8. See Abramson et al., *Change and Continuity in the 2008 and 2010 Elections,* for data and discussions about the 2008 data.

9. The only consistent exception since 1972 has been a women's rights scale, for which public opinion had become so favorable to the liberal end of the issue scale that it was dropped from the survey in 2012, due to lack of variation in opinion.

10. To maintain comparability with previous election surveys, for surveys from 1996 through 2012 we have excluded respondents who did not place themselves on an issue scale from columns II, III, and IV of Table 6-4. Because we do not know the preferences of these respondents on the issue, we have no way to measure the ways in which their issue preferences may have affected their votes.

11. For details, see Abramson, Aldrich, and Rohde, *Change and Continuity in the 1980 Elections*, 130, table 6-3; Abramson et al., *Change and Continuity in the 1984 Elections*, rev. ed. (Washington, D.C.: CQ Press, 1987), 174, table 6-2; and Abramson et al., *Change and Continuity in the 1988 Elections*, rev. ed. (Washington, D.C.: CQ Press, 1991), 165, table 6-2; Abramson et al., *Change and*

Continuity in the 1992 Elections, 186, table 6-6; Abramson et al., *Change and Continuity in the 1996 and 1998 Elections*, 135, table 6-6; Abramson et al., *Change and Continuity in the 2000 and 2002 Elections*, 137, table 6-4; Abramson et al., *Change and Continuity in the 2004 and 2006 Elections*, 152, table 6-4; and Abramson et al., *Change and Continuity in the 2008 and 2010 Elections*, 158, table 6-4.

12. Although this is evidence that most people claim to have issue preferences, it does not demonstrate that they do. For example, evidence indicates that some use the midpoint of the scale (point 4) as a means of answering the question even if they have ill-formed preferences. See John H. Aldrich et al., "The Measurement of Public Opinion about Public Policy: A Report on Some New Issue Question Formats," *American Journal of Political Science* 26 (May 1982): 391–414.

13. We use *apparent issue voting* to emphasize several points. First, voting involves too many factors to infer that closeness to a candidate on any one issue was the cause of the voter's choice. The issue similarity may have been purely coincidental, or it may have been only one of many reasons the voter supported that candidate. Second, we use the median perception of the candidates' positions rather than the voter's own perception. Third, the relationship between issues and the vote may be caused by rationalization. Voters may have decided to support a candidate for other reasons and also may have altered their own issue preferences or misperceived the positions of the candidates to align themselves more closely with their already favored candidate. See Richard A. Brody and Benjamin I. Page, "Comment: The Assessment of Policy Voting," *American Political Science Review* 66 (June 1972): 450–458.

14. Many individuals, of course, placed the candidates at different positions than did the public on average. Using average perceptions, however, reduces the effect of individuals rationalizing their perceptions of candidates to be consistent with their own vote rather than voting for the candidate whose views are actually closer to their own.

15. See Abramson et al., *Change and Continuity in the 1980 Elections*.

7. PRESIDENTIAL PERFORMANCE AND CANDIDATE CHOICE

1. See Paul R. Abramson, John H. Aldrich, and David W. Rohde, *Change and Continuity in the 2000 and 2002 Elections* (Washington, D.C.: CQ Press, 2003), chap. 7.

2. Bush became the first sitting vice president to be elected president since Democratic vice president Martin Van Buren was elected in 1836. As Nelson W. Polsby et al point out, a sitting vice president may have many of the disadvantages of being an incumbent without the advantages of actually being president. See Polsby et al, *Presidential Elections: Strategies and Structures of American Politics*, 13th ed. (Lanham, Md.: Rowman and Littlefield, 2002), 86–92.

3. See Paul R. Abramson, John H. Aldrich, and David W. Rohde, *Change and Continuity in the 1992 Elections*, rev. ed. (Washington, D.C.: CQ Press, 1995), 203–208.

4. V. O. Key Jr., *Politics, Parties, and Pressure Groups*, 5th ed. (New York: Crowell, 1964), 568. Key's theory of retrospective voting is most fully developed in *The Responsible Electorate: Rationality in Presidential Voting, 1936–1960* (Cambridge, Mass.: Harvard University Press, 1966).

5. Anthony Downs, *An Economic Theory of Democracy* (New York: Harper and Row, 1957).

6. Morris P. Fiorina, *Retrospective Voting in American National Elections* (New Haven, Conn.: Yale University Press, 1981), 83.

7. See Benjamin I. Page, *Choices and Echoes in Presidential Elections: Rational Man and Electoral Democracy* (Chicago: University of Chicago Press, 1978). Page argues that "party cleavages" distinguish the party at the candidate and mass levels.

8. Arthur H. Miller and Martin P. Wattenberg, "Throwing the Rascals Out: Policy and Performance Evaluations of Presidential Candidates, 1952–1980," *American Political Science Review* 79 (June 1985): 359–372.

9. Note that this question is quite different from the questions we analyzed in early election studies. These were questions asking the respondent about the government's handling of the most important problems facing the country. This question does not specifically ask about the government, nor does it ask about the most important problem, per se. It is more general in its coverage, and only by inference is attributable to the government.

10. Each respondent assesses government performance on the problem he or she considers the most important. In the seven surveys from 1976 to 2000, respondents were asked, "How good a job is the government doing in dealing with this problem—a good job, only fair, or a poor job?" In 1972 respondents were asked a different but related question (see the note to Table A7-1 in the Appendix). In 2004 respondents were asked another question (see Abramson et al., *Change and Continuity in the 2008 and 2010 Elections*, chap. 6, note 10) and were given four options for assessing the government's performance: "very good job," "good job," "bad job," and "very bad job."

11. See, for example, RealClearPolitics, "Direction of Country," http://www.realclearpolitics.com/epolls/other/direction_of_country-902.html.

12. See Gerald H. Kramer, "Short-Term Fluctuations in U.S. Voting Behavior, 1896–1964," *American Political Science Review* 65 (March 1971): 131–143; Fiorina, *Retrospective Voting*; M. Stephen Weatherford, "Economic Conditions and Electoral Outcomes: Class Differences in the Political Response to Recession," *American Journal of Political Science* 22 (November 1978): 917–938; D. Roderick Kiewiet and Douglas Rivers, "A Retrospective on Retrospective Voting," *Political Behavior* 6 (1984): 369–393; D. Roderick Kiewiet, *Macroeconomics and Micropolitics: The Electoral Effects of Economic Issues* (Chicago: University of Chicago Press, 1983); Michael S. Lewis-Beck, *Economics and Elections: The Major*

Western Democracies (Ann Arbor: University of Michigan Press, 1988); Alberto Alesina, John Londregan, and Howard Rosenthal, *A Model of the Political Economy of the United States* (Cambridge, Mass.: National Bureau of Economic Research, 1991); Michael B. MacKuen, Robert S. Erikson, and James A. Stimson, "Peasants or Bankers? The American Electorate and the U.S. Economy," *American Political Science Review* 86 (September 1992): 597–611; and Robert S. Erikson, Michael B. MacKuen, and James A. Stimson, *The Macro Polity* (Cambridge, UK: Cambridge University Press, 2002).

13. John Mueller, *War, Presidents and Public Opinion* (New York: Wiley, 1973).

14. See Abramson et al., *Change and Continuity in the 2004 and 2006 Elections*, chap. 7, 172–176, esp. table 7-6, 174; and Abramson et al., *Change and Continuity in the 2008 and 2010 Elections*, chap. 7, 183–184, esp. table 7-6, 184.

15. Fiorina, *Retrospective Voting*.

16. In the 1984 and 1988 surveys, this question was asked in both the pre-election and the postelection waves of the survey. Because attitudes held by the public before the election are what count in influencing its choices, we use the first question. In both surveys, approval of Reagan's performance was more positive in the postelection interview: 66 percent approved of his performance in 1984, and 68 percent approved in 1988.

17. Gary C. Jacobson demonstrates that evaluations of presidential performance have become much more sharply related to party identification in recent years compared to the earlier years of the ANES studies. See Jacobson, "Party Polarization in National Politics: The Electoral Connection," in *Polarized Politics: Congress and the President in a Partisan Era*, vol. 5 (Washington, D.C.: CQ Press, 2000) 17–18..

18. A summary measure of retrospective evaluations could not be constructed using either the 1972 or the 2004 ANES data. We were able to construct an alternative measure for 2004. See Abramson et al., *Change and Continuity in the 2004 and 2006 Elections*, chap. 7, tables 7-9 and 7-10, 178–180, and 371, n18. For procedures we used to construct this measure between 1976 and 2000, see Abramson et al., *Change and Continuity in the 2000 and 2002 Elections*, chap. 7, 328, n13. A combined index of retrospective evaluations was created to allow an overall assessment of retrospective voting in 2008 and 2012. To construct the summary measure of retrospective evaluations, we used the following procedures. First, we awarded respondents four points if they approved of the president's performance, two if they had no opinion, and zero if they disapproved. Second, respondents received four points if they thought the government had done a very good job in the last four years, three if they thought the government had done a good job, one if they thought the government had done a bad job, and two if they had no opinion. Finally, respondents received four points if they thought the incumbent president's party would do a better job handling the most important problem, zero points if they thought the challenger's party would do a better job, and two points if they thought there was no difference between the parties, neither party would do well, both parties would do the same, another

party would do the better job, or they had no opinion. For all three questions, "don't know" and "not ascertained" responses were scored as two, but respondents with more than one such response were excluded from the analysis. Scores on our measure were the sum of the individual values for the three questions and thus ranged from a low of zero (strongly against the incumbent's party) to twelve (strongly for the incumbent's party). These values were then grouped to create a seven-point scale corresponding to the seven categories in Table 7-9.

19. This measure was different in 2012 than in prior elections. This is the first time we have employed the "right track/wrong track" question. Other election years are also not always comparable, although they are more similar to each than to 2012. See Paul R. Abramson, John H. Aldrich, and David W. Rohde, *Change and Continuity in the 1996 and 1998 Elections* (Washington, D.C.: CQ Press, 1999), 158–159, for data on our (different) summary measure from 1972 to 1996; and Abramson et al., *Change and Continuity in the 2000 and 2002 Elections*, 164–165; Abramson et al., *Change and Continuity in the 2004 and 2006 Elections*, 178–180; Abramson et al., *Change and Continuity in the 2008 and 2010 Elections*, 187–191, for analyses of those elections, respectively, in these terms.

20. The characterization of earlier elections is taken from Abramson et al., *Change and Continuity in the 2000 and 2002 Elections*, 164.

21. For data from the 1976 and 1980 elections, see Paul R. Abramson, John H. Aldrich, and David W. Rohde, *Change and Continuity in the 1980 Elections*, rev. ed. (Washington, D.C.: CQ Press, 1983), table 7-8, 155–157; from the 1984 election, see Abramson et al., *Change and Continuity in the 1984 Elections*, rev. ed. (Washington, D.C.: CQ Press, 1987), table 7-8, 203–204; from the 1988 election, see Abramson et al., *Change and Continuity in the 1988 Elections*, rev. ed. (Washington, D.C.: CQ Press, 1991), table 7-7, 195–198; from the 1996 election, see Abramson et al., *Change and Continuity in the 1996 and 1998 Elections*, 159–161; from the 2000 election, see Abramson et al., *Change and Continuity in the 2000 and 2002 Elections*, 165–166; and from the 2004 election, see Abramson et al., *Change and Continuity in the 2004 and 2006 Elections*, 178–180. The small number of seven-point issue scales included in the ANES survey precluded performing this analysis with 1992 data.

8. PARTY LOYALTIES, POLICY PREFERENCES, AND THE VOTE

1. Angus Campbell et al., *The American Voter* (New York: Wiley, 1960). For more recent statements of the "standard" view of party identification, see Warren E. Miller and J. Merrill Shanks, *The New American Voter* (Cambridge, Mass.: Harvard University Press, 1996), 117–183; and Michael S. Lewis-Beck, William G. Jacoby, Helmut Norpoth, and Herbert F. Weisberg, *The American Voter Revisited* (Ann Arbor: University of Michigan Press, 2008), 161–301.

2. Campbell, *American Voter*, 121. See also Morris P. Fiorina, *Retrospective Voting in American National Elections* (New Haven, Conn.: Yale University Press, 1981), 85–86.

3. For the full wording of the party identification questions, see Chapter 4, note 80.

4. Most "apoliticals" in this period were African Americans living in the South. Because they were disenfranchised, questions about their party loyalties were essentially meaningless to them. For the most detailed discussion of how the American National Election Studies creates its summary measure of party identification, see Arthur H. Miller and Martin P. Wattenberg, "Measuring Party Identification: Independent or No Partisan Preference?" *American Journal of Political Science* 27 (February 1983): 106–121. Note that, in 2012, the ANES did not include the category "apolitical."

5. Some also consider it to be a part of the individual's social identity. See, for example, Donald P. Green, Bradley Palmquist, and Eric Schickler, *Partisan Hearts and Minds: Political Parties and the Social Identities of Voters* (New Haven, Conn.: Yale University Press, 2002).

6. For evidence of the relatively high level of partisan stability among individuals from 1965 to 1982, see M. Kent Jennings and Gregory B. Markus, "Partisan Orientations over the Long Haul: Results from the Three-Wave Political Socialization Panel Study," *American Political Science Review* 78 (December 1984): 1000–1018. For analyses from 1965 to 1997, see Laura Stoker and M. Kent Jennings, "Of Time and the Development of Partisan Polarization," *American Journal of Political Science* 52 (July 2008): 619–635.

7. V. O. Key Jr., *The Responsible Electorate: Rationality in Presidential Voting, 1936-1960* (Cambridge, Mass.: Harvard University Press, 1966).

8. Morris P. Fiorina, "An Outline for a Model of Party Choice," *American Journal of Political Science* 21 (August 1977): 601–625; Fiorina, *Retrospective Voting*, 65–83.

9. Benjamin I. Page provides evidence of this. See Page, *Choices and Echoes in Presidential Elections: Rational Man and Electoral Democracy* (Chicago: University of Chicago Press, 1978). Anthony Downs, in *An Economic Theory of Democracy* (New York: Harper and Row, 1957), develops a theoretical logic for such consistency in party stances on issues and ideology over time. For more recent theoretical and empirical development, see John H. Aldrich, *Why Parties? A Second Look* (Chicago: University of Chicago Press, 2011).

10. Robert S. Erikson, Michael B. MacKuen, and James A. Stimson, *The Macro Polity* (Cambridge, UK: Cambridge University Press, 2002).

11. Green et al., *Partisan Hearts and Minds*.

12. See, for example, Donald Green, Bradley Palmquist, and Eric Schickler, "Macropartisanship: A Replication and Critique," *American Political Science Review* 92 (December 1998): 883–899; and Robert S. Erikson, Michael B. MacKuen, and James A. Stimson, "What Moves Macropartisanship: A Reply to Green, Palmquist, and Schickler," *American Political Science Review* 92 (December 1998): 901–912.

13. There is some controversy about how to classify these independent leaners. Some argue that they are mainly "hidden" partisans who should be considered identifiers. For the strongest statement of this position, see Bruce E. Keith et al.,

The Myth of the Independent Voter (Berkeley: University of California Press, 1992). In our view, however, the evidence on the proper classification of independent leaners is mixed. On balance, the evidence suggests that they are more partisan than independents with no partisan leanings, but less partisan than weak partisans. See Paul R. Abramson, *Political Attitudes in America: Formation and Change* (San Francisco: W. H. Freeman, 1983), 80–81, 95–96. For an excellent discussion of this question, see Herbert B. Asher, "Voting Behavior Research in the 1980s: An Examination of Some Old and New Problem Areas," in *Political Science: The State of the Discipline*, ed. Ada W. Finifter (Washington, D.C.: American Political Science Association, 1983), 357–360.

14. See, for example, Martin P. Wattenberg, *The Decline of American Political Parties, 1952–1996* (Cambridge, Mass.: Harvard University Press, 1998).

15. Gary C. Jacobson, "The 2008 Presidential and Congressional Elections: Anti-Bush Referendum and Prospects for a Democratic Majority," *Political Science Quarterly* 124 (Spring 2009): 1–20; and Jacobson, "The Effects of the George W. Bush Presidency on Partisan Attitudes," *Presidential Studies Quarterly* 39 (June 2009): 172–209.

16. See Paul R. Abramson and Charles W. Ostrom Jr., "Macropartisanship: An Empirical Reassessment," *American Political Science Review* 86 (March 1991): 181–192; and Paul R. Abramson and Charles W. Ostrom, "Question Wording and Partisanship: Change and Continuity in Party Loyalties during the 1992 Election Campaign," *Public Opinion Quarterly* 58 (Spring 1994): 21–48.

17. These surveys were conducted annually between 1972 and 1978, in 1980, annually between 1982 and 1991, in 1993, and in every even-numbered year between 1994 and 2008. The surveys conducted between 1972 and 2002 were conducted in February, March, and April. The 2004 survey was conducted from September through December, the 2006 survey from March through August, and the 2008 survey from April through November.

18. See Gallup, "Party Affiliation," http://www.gallup.com/poll/15370/party-affiliation.aspx, which includes polling results on these questions from 2004 to date. Note that the Gallup wording does differ from that of the ANES. Gallup asks partisanship "as of today," while the ANES asks "generally speaking."

19. See Paul R. Abramson, John H. Aldrich, and David W. Rohde, *Change and Continuity in the 2004 and 2006 Elections* (Washington, D.C.: CQ Press, 2007), 186–192.

20. The ANES did not conduct a congressional election survey in 2006.

21. The November 1–4 2012 Gallup poll, by contrast, reports 12 percent independent leaners for Republicans and 15 percent for Democrats. See http://www.gallup.com/poll/15370/party-affiliation.aspx.

22. For evidence on the decline of Republican Party loyalties among older blacks between 1962 and 1964, see Paul R. Abramson, *Generational Change in American Politics* (Lexington, Mass.: D. C. Heath, 1975), 65–69.

23. For the results of the white vote by party identification for the three leading candidates in 1968, 1980, 1992, and 1996, see Paul R. Abramson, John H. Aldrich, and David W. Rohde, *Change and Continuity in the 1996 and 1998 Elections* (Washington, D.C.: CQ Press, 1999), 186–187. Among blacks there is virtually no relationship between party identification and the vote. Even the small number of blacks who identify as Republicans usually either do not vote or vote for the Democratic presidential candidate.

24. In fact, among the 125 white pure independents who voted in 1992, 37 percent voted for Clinton, 41 percent for Ross Perot, and 22 percent for Bob Dole.

25. See also Larry M. Bartels, "Partisanship and Voting Behavior, 1952–1996," *American Journal of Political Science* 44 (January 2000): 35–50.

26. Bernard R. Berelson, Paul F. Lazarsfeld, and William N. McPhee, *Voting: A Study of Opinion Formation in a Presidential Campaign* (Chicago: University of Chicago Press, 1954), 215–233. The extent to which voters' perceptions were affected, however, varied from issue to issue.

27. See Richard A. Brody and Benjamin I. Page, "Comment: The Assessment of Policy Voting," *American Political Science Review* 66 (June 1972): 450–458; Page and Brody, "Policy Voting and the Electoral Process: The Vietnam War Issue," *American Political Science Review* 66 (September 1972): 979–995; and Fiorina, "Outline for a Model of Party Choice."

28. As we point out in Chapter 7, the ANES has asked the standard presidential approval question since 1970.

29. The question measuring approval of the president's handling of economic policy was not asked in ANES surveys before 1984. In our study of these earlier elections, an alternative measure of economic retrospective evaluations was created and shown to be almost as strongly related to party identification. See Paul R. Abramson, John H. Aldrich, and David W. Rohde, *Change and Continuity in the 1984 Elections*, rev. ed. (Washington, D.C.: CQ Press, 1987), table 8-6, 221. We also found nearly as strong a relationship between partisanship and perceptions of which party would better handle the economy in the data from 1972, 1976, and 1980 as from later surveys reported here. See Abramson, Aldrich, and Rohde, *Change and Continuity in the 1980 Elections*, rev. ed. (Washington, D.C.: CQ Press, 1983), 170, table 8-6, 173.

30. Table 8-6 includes elections from 2000 on, while earlier elections can be found in Table A8-7 in the Appendix. For a description of this measure, see Chapter 6. Because this measure uses the median placement of the candidates on the issue scales in the full sample, much of the projection effect is eliminated. For the relationship between party identification and the balance of issues measure in 1972, see Abramson, Aldrich, and Rohde, *Change and Continuity in the 1980 Elections*, table 8-5, 171.

31. This earlier measure and its relationship with partisan identification are reported in Paul R. Abramson, John H. Aldrich, and David W. Rohde, *Change and Continuity in the 2000 and 2002 Elections* (Washington, D.C.: CQ Press, 2003),

table 8-7, 185–186, discussed on 184–189; and in Abramson et al., *Change and Continuity in the 2004 and 2006 Elections*, table 8-7, 202, discussed on 201–203.

32. As we saw in Chapter 7, that conclusion applies to those individual components of the measure that are the same as in earlier surveys.

33. As in Chapter 7, we cannot directly compare the results for 2012 with those for earlier elections, except in very general terms. For an interpretation and the data over the previous seven elections, see Abramson et al., *Change and Continuity in the 2000 and 2002 Elections*, table 8-8, 187–188, discussed on 189; and Abramson et al., *Change and Continuity in the 2004 and 2006 Elections*, table 8-8, 203, discussed on 203–204.

34. See, for example, Aldrich, *Why Parties?*

35. Two important articles assess some of these relationships: Gregory B. Markus and Philip E. Converse, "A Dynamic Simultaneous Equation Model of Electoral Choice," *American Political Science Review* 73 (December 1979): 1055–1070; and Benjamin I. Page and Calvin C. Jones, "Reciprocal Effects of Policy Preferences, Party Loyalties and the Vote," *American Political Science Review* 73 (December 1979): 1071–1089. For a brief discussion of these articles, see Richard G. Niemi and Herbert F. Weisberg, *Controversies in Voting Behavior*, 2nd ed. (Washington, D.C.: CQ Press, 1984), 89–95. For an excellent discussion of complex models of voting behavior and the role of party identification in these models, see Asher, "Voting Behavior Research in the 1980s," 341–354. For another excellent introduction to some of these issues, see Richard G. Niemi and Herbert F. Weisberg, "Is Party Identification Stable?" in *Controversies in Voting Behavior*, 3rd ed., eds. Richard G. Niemi and Herbert F. Weisberg (Washington, D.C.: CQ Press, 1993), 268–283.

9. CANDIDATES AND OUTCOMES IN 2012

1. One independent was Bernard Sanders of Vermont, who was elected as an independent to the House from 1990 through 2004. Sanders had previously been elected mayor of Burlington, Vermont, running as a socialist. However, throughout his House service he caucused with the Democrats, and he continued that course after his initial election to the Senate in 2006. The second independent is Angus King of Maine. King had served as governor of Maine from 1995 to 2003, also as an independent, before being elected senator for the first time in 2012. We will count both of these senators as Democrats in all of the analysis in this chapter.

2. *Incumbents* here is used only to indicate elected incumbents. This includes all members of the House because the only way to become a representative is by election. In the case of the Senate, however, vacancies may be filled by appointment. We do not count appointed senators as incumbents. In 2012 the only appointed senator who ran for election was Dean Heller of Nevada, who had been appointed in May of 2011.

3. The classification of primary versus general-election defeats is complicated by the atypical processes used in California and Louisiana. In both states, all candidates run together in a single primary. If no candidate wins a majority at that point, the top two (regardless of party) compete in the general election. Thus the general may include two Democrats or two Republicans. This type of situation seems more akin to a primary runoff than the usual idea of a general election, so we classify results that way. If two candidates of the same party face each other in the general election, we count that as a primary, with the winner unopposed in the general election. If both are incumbents, the defeat is treated as a primary loss.

4. The Republicans had won control of the House in eight consecutive elections from 1894 through 1908, far short of the Democratic series of successes.

5. The regional breakdowns used in this chapter are as follows: *East*: Connecticut, Delaware, Maine, Massachusetts, New Hampshire, New Jersey, New York, Pennsylvania, Rhode Island, and Vermont; *Midwest*: Illinois, Indiana, Iowa, Kansas, Michigan, Minnesota, Nebraska, North Dakota, Ohio, South Dakota, and Wisconsin; *West*: Alaska, Arizona, California, Colorado, Hawaii, Idaho, Montana, Nevada, New Mexico, Oregon, Utah, Washington, and Wyoming; *South*: Alabama, Arkansas, Florida, Georgia, Louisiana, Mississippi, North Carolina, South Carolina, Tennessee, Texas, and Virginia; *Border*: Kentucky, Maryland, Missouri, Oklahoma, and West Virginia. This classification differs somewhat from the one used in earlier chapters (and in Chapter 10), but it is commonly used for congressional analysis.

6. Over the years changes in the southern electorate have also made southern Democratic constituencies more like northern Democratic constituencies, and less like Republican constituencies, North or South. These changes also appear to have enhanced the homogeneity of preferences within the partisan delegations in Congress. This partisan congressional polarization has been the subject of a great deal of research over the last three decades. Two good overviews are offered by John H. Aldrich, *Why Parties? A Second Look* (Chicago: University of Chicago Press, 2011); and Sean M. Theriault, *Party Polarization in Congress* (New York: Cambridge University Press, 2008).

7. The ratings were taken from various issues of *The Cook Political Report*. Competitive races are those Cook classified as only leaning to the incumbent party, toss-ups, or those tilted toward the other party.

8. See Paul R. Abramson, John H. Aldrich, and David W. Rohde, *Change and Continuity in the 1996 and 1998 Elections* (Washington, D.C.: CQ Press, 1999), 207–212.

9. These polling data were taken from http://pollingreport.com, retrieved June 13, 2013.

10. For a discussion of the increased role of national party organizations in congressional elections over the last three decades, see Paul S. Herrnson, *Congressional Elections*, 5th ed. (Washington, D.C.: CQ Press, 2008), chap. 4.

11. See Shira Toeplitz, "NRCC's Recruiting Aim: Stay on Offense," *Roll Call*, January 19, 2011, 8.

12. See Shira Toeplitz and Joshua Miller, "DCCC Casts Large Net This Cycle," *Roll Call*, July 28, 2013, 8.

13. See Susan David, "Dems Recruit Candidates outside the Political Arena," *USA Today*, April 17, 2012, 6A.

14. See Shira Toeplitz, "Lesson Learned: NRSC Welcoming Everyone," *Roll Call*, April 13, 2011, 4.

15. Joshua Miller and Kyle Trygstad, "McConnell Picks Top Races in Majority Quest," *Roll Call*, May 31, 2012, 11.

16. See Josh Lederman, "Bivens Drops out; Carmona Locks up Ariz. Nomination," *The Hill*, March 29 2012, 19.

17. See Jonathan Weisman, "Ignoring Deadline to Quit, G.O.P. Senate Candidate Defies His Party Leaders," *New York Times,* August 21, 2012, http://www.nytimes.com/2012/08/22/us/politics/ignoring-calls-to-quit-akin-appeals-to-voters-in-ad.html?_r=0.

18. See Russell Berman, "Boehner Tops Pelosi with $70M," *The Hill*, May 23, 2012, 1.

19. Jared Allen, "House Chairmen Respond to Speaker Pelosi's Call for Cash," *The Hill*, Oct. 22, 2008, 3.

20. Josh Lederman, "DCCC Has No Room for Deadbeats," *The Hill*, March 22, 2012, 1.

21. Super PACs are a new kind of PAC (political action committee) that "may raise unlimited sums of money from corporations, unions, associations and individuals, then spend unlimited sums to overtly advocate for or against political candidates. . . . Unlike traditional PACs, Super PACs are prohibited from donating money directly to political candidates." See http://www.opensecrets.org/pacs/superpacs.php

22. Fredreka Schouten, "Outside Groups Target Senate," *USA Today*, October 1, 2012, 1A.

23. *The Rhodes Cook Letter*, February, 2013, 14.

24. Ibid., 10.

25. Richard F. Fenno Jr., *Home Style: House Members in Their Districts* (Boston: Little, Brown, 1978). For a discussion of how relationships between representatives and constituents have changed over time, see Fenno, *Congress at the Grassroots* (Chapel Hill: University of North Carolina Press, 2000).

26. For example, analysis of Senate races in 1988 indicated that both the political quality of the previous office held and the challenger's political skills had an independent effect on the outcome of the race. See Peverill Squire, "Challenger Quality and Voting Behavior in U.S. Senate Elections," *Legislative Studies Quarterly* 17 (May 1992): 247–263. For systematic evidence on the impact of candidate quality in House races, see Gary C. Jacobson, *The Electoral Origins of Divided Government: Competition in U.S. House Elections, 1946–1988* (Boulder, Colo.: Westview Press, 1990), chap. 4.

27. A recent analysis uses expert survey responses instead of office experience to measure candidate quality. It concludes that quality candidates do better, and that the effect increases as ideological differences decline. See Matthew K. Buttice and Walter J. Stone, "Candidates Matter: Policy and Quality Differences in Congressional Elections," *Journal of Politics* 74 (July, 2012): 870–887.

28. Data on office backgrounds were taken from issues of *The Cook Political Report*, supplemented by other sources.

29. Data on earlier years are taken from our studies of previous national elections.

30. Note that the figures in this paragraph include races in which only one of the parties fielded a candidate, as well as contests in which both did.

31. See Jacobson, *The Electoral Origins of Divided Government;* Jon R. Bond, Cary Covington, and Richard Fleischer, "Explaining Challenger Quality in Congressional Elections," *Journal of Politics* 47 (May 1985): 510–529; and David W. Rohde, "Risk-Bearing and Progressive Ambition: The Case of Members of the U.S. House of Representatives," *American Journal of Political Science* 23 (February 1979): 1–26.

32. L. Sandy Maisel and Walter J. Stone, "Determinants of Candidate Emergence in U.S. House Elections: An Exploratory Study," *Legislative Studies Quarterly* 22 (February 1997): 79–96.

33. See Peverill Squire, "Preemptive Fund-raising and Challenger Profile in Senate Elections," *Journal of Politics* 53 (November 1991): 1150–1164; and Jay Goodliffe, "The Effect of War Chests on Challenger Entry in U.S. House Elections," *American Journal of Political Science* 45 (October 2001): 1087–1108.

34. Jeffrey S. Banks and D. Roderick Kiewiet, "Explaining Patterns of Candidate Competition in Congressional Elections," *American Journal of Political Science* 33 (November 1989): 997–1015.

35. David Canon, *Actors, Athletes, and Astronauts* (Chicago, University of Chicago Press, 1990).

36. See Kenneth J. Cooper, "Riding High Name Recognition to Hill," *Washington Post*, December 24, 1992, A4.

37. See Thomas E. Mann and Raymond E. Wolfinger, "Candidates and Parties in Congressional Elections," *American Political Science Review* 74 (September 1980): 617–632.

38. See David R. Mayhew, "Congressional Elections: The Case of the Vanishing Marginals," *Polity* 6 (Spring 1974): 295–317; Robert S. Erikson, "Malapportionment, Gerrymandering, and Party Fortunes in Congressional Elections," *American Political Science Review* 66 (December 1972): 1234–1245; Warren Lee Kostroski, "Party and Incumbency in Postwar Senate Elections: Trends, Patterns, and Models," *American Political Science Review* 67 (December 1973): 1213–1234.

39. Edward R. Tufte, "Communication," *American Political Science Review* 68 (March 1974): 211–213. The communication involved a discussion of Tufte's earlier article, "The Relationship between Seats and Votes in Two-Party Systems," *American Political Science Review* 67 (June 1973): 540–554.

40. See John A. Ferejohn, "On the Decline of Competition in Congressional Elections," *American Political Science Review* 71 (March 1977): 166–176; Albert D. Cover, "One Good Term Deserves Another: The Advantage of Incumbency in Congressional Elections," *American Journal of Political Science* 21 (August 1977): 523–541; and Albert D. Cover and David R. Mayhew, "Congressional Dynamics and the Decline of Competition in Congressional Elections," in *Congress Reconsidered*, 2d ed., eds. Lawrence C. Dodd and Bruce I. Oppenheimer (Washington, D.C.: CQ Press, 1981), 62–82.

41. Morris P. Fiorina, *Congress: Keystone of the Washington Establishment*, 2nd ed. (New Haven, Conn.: Yale University Press, 1989), esp. chaps. 4–6.

42. See several conflicting arguments and conclusions in the following articles published in the *American Journal of Political Science* 25 (August 1981): John R. Johannes and John C. McAdams, "The Congressional Incumbency Effect: Is It Casework, Policy Compatibility, or Something Else? An Examination of the 1978 Election" (512–542); Morris P. Fiorina, "Some Problems in Studying the Effects of Resource Allocation in Congressional Elections" (543–567); Diana Evans Yiannakis, "The Grateful Electorate: Casework and Congressional Elections" (568–580); and McAdams and Johannes, "Does Casework Matter? A Reply to Professor Fiorina" (581–604). See also Johannes, *To Serve the People: Congress and Constituency Service* (Lincoln: University of Nebraska Press, 1984), esp. chap. 8; and Albert D. Cover and Bruce S. Brumberg, "Baby Books and Ballots: The Impact of Congressional Mail on Constituent Opinion," *American Political Science Review* 76 (June 1982): 347–359. The evidence in Cover and Brumberg for a positive electoral effect is quite strong, but the result may be applicable only to limited circumstances.

43. Ferejohn, "On the Decline of Competition," 174.

44. Cover, "One Good Term," 535.

45. More recent research shows that the link between party identification and voting has strengthened again. See Larry M. Bartels, "Partisanship and Voting Behavior, 1952–1996," *American Journal of Political Science* 44 (January 2000): 35–50.

46. For an excellent analysis of the growth of, and reasons for, anti-Congress sentiment, see John R. Hibbing and Elizabeth Theiss-Morse, *Congress as Public Enemy* (New York: Cambridge University Press, 1995).

47. For an analysis that contends that the variations in incumbents' vote percentages have little implication for incumbent safety, see Jeffrey M. Stonecash, *Reassessing the Incumbency Effect* (Cambridge, UK: Cambridge University Press, 2008).

48. The body of literature on this subject has grown to be quite large. Some salient early examples, in addition to those cited later, are Gary C. Jacobson, *Money in Congressional Elections* (New Haven, Conn.: Yale University Press, 1980); Jacobson, "Parties and PACs in Congressional Elections," in *Congress Reconsidered*, 4th ed., eds. Lawrence C. Dodd and Bruce I. Oppenheimer (Washington, D.C.: CQ Press, 1989), 117–152; Jacobson and Samuel Kernell, *Strategy and Choice in Congressional Elections*, 2d ed. (New Haven, Conn.: Yale

University Press, 1983); John A. Ferejohn and Morris P. Fiorina, "Incumbency and Realignment in Congressional Elections," in *The New Direction in American Politics*, eds. John E. Chubb and Paul E. Peterson (Washington, D.C.: Brookings Institution, 1985), 91–115.

49. See Jacobson, *The Electoral Origins of Divided Government*, 63–65.

50. See Jacobson and Kernell, *Strategy and Choice in Congressional Elections*, 2d ed.

51. Evidence indicates that challenger spending strongly influences public visibility and that substantial amounts of spending can significantly reduce the recognition gap between the challenger and the incumbent. See Jacobson, *The Politics of Congressional Elections*, 7th ed., 134.

52. The 2012 spending data were obtained from the website of the Federal Election Commission, http://www.fec.gov.

53. See Paul R. Abramson, John H. Aldrich, and David W. Rohde, *Change and Continuity in the 2008 and 2010 Elections* (Washington, D.C.: CQ Press, 2011), 248–252, and the earlier work cited there.

54. See Jacobson, *The Electoral Origins of Divided Government*, 54–55; and the work cited in note 47 above.

55. Donald Philip Green and Jonathan S. Krasno, "Salvation for the Spendthrift Incumbent: Reestimating the Effects of Campaign Spending in House Elections," *American Journal of Political Science* 32 (November 1988): 884–907.

56. Gary C. Jacobson, "The Effects of Campaign Spending in House Elections: New Evidence for Old Arguments," *American Journal of Political Science* 34 (May 1990): 334–362. Green and Krasno's response can be found in the same issue on pages 363–372.

57. Gary C. Jacobson, *The Politics of Congressional Elections*, 8th ed. (Boston: Pearson, 2013), 156.

58. Alan I. Abramowitz, "Explaining Senate Election Outcomes," *American Political Science Review* 82 (June 1988): 385–403; Alan Gerber, "Estimating the Effect of Campaign Spending on Senate Election Outcomes Using Instrumental Variables," *American Political Science Review* 92 (June 1998): 401–411.

59. Gary C. Jacobson, "Campaign Spending and Voter Awareness of Congressional Candidates" (paper presented at the Annual Meeting of the Public Choice Society, New Orleans, May 11–13, 1977), 16.

60. Indeed an incumbent in a district that is tilted toward the opposite party may need to spend more to be able to distinguish himself or herself from his or her party's unattractive but (in recent decades) precise party reputation. See Henry A. Kim and Brad l. Leveck, "Money, Reputation, and Incumbency in U.S. House Elections, or Why Marginals Have Become More Expensive," *American Political Science Review* 107 (August, 2013): 492–504.

61. Spending data are taken from http://www.fec.gov.

62. Challengers were categorized as having strong experience if they had been elected U.S. representative, to statewide office, to the state legislature, or to countywide or citywide office (e.g., prosecutor, mayor).

63. Paul R. Abramson, John H. Aldrich, and David W. Rohde, *Change and Continuity in the 1980 Elections*, rev. ed. (Washington, D.C.: CQ Press, 1983), 202–203. See also Paul Gronke, *The Electorate, the Campaign, and the Office: A Unified Approach to Senate and House Elections* (Ann Arbor: University of Michigan Press, 2001).

64. Other Democratic Senate winners in 2000 who spent millions of their own money included Maria Cantwell of Washington and Mark Dayton of Minnesota.

65. Quoted in Angela Herrin, "Big Outside Money Backfired in GOP Loss of Senate to Dems," *Washington Post*, November 6, 1986, A46.

66. See David W. Rohde, *Parties and Leaders in the Postreform House* (Chicago: University of Chicago Press, 1991), esp. chap. 3; and Rohde, "Electoral Forces, Political Agendas, and Partisanship in the House and Senate," in *The Postreform Congress*, ed. Rodger H. Davidson (New York: St. Martin's Press, 1992), 27–47.

67. For discussions of the ideological changes in the House and Senate over the last four decades, see John H. Aldrich and David W. Rohde, "The Logic of Conditional Party Government: Revisiting the Electoral Connection," in *Congress Reconsidered*, 7th ed., eds. Lawrence Dodd and Bruce Oppenheimer (CQ Press, 2001), 269–292; Gary C. Jacobson, "The Congress: The Structural Basis of Republican Success," in *The Elections of 2004*, ed. Michael Nelson (Washington, D.C.: CQ Press, 2005), 163–186; and Sean Theriault, *Party Polarization in Congress* (New York: Cambridge University Press, 2008).

68. See Paul R. Abramson, John H. Aldrich, and David W. Rohde, *Change and Continuity in the 1992 Elections*, rev. ed. (Washington, D.C.: CQ Press, 1995), 339–342; and John H. Aldrich and David W. Rohde, "The Transition to Republican Rule in the House: Implications for Theories of Congressional Politics," *Political Science Quarterly* 112 (Winter 1997–1998): 541–567.

69. For an interesting journalistic account of the Tea Party group in the House, see Robert Draper, *When the Tea Party Came to Town* (New York: Simon and Schuster, 2012).

70. See Molly K. Hoper, "Boehner Tightens Grip on GOP Rank and File," *The Hill*, November 20, 2012, 1.

71. Jonathan Strong, "Dissidents Pushed Off Prominent Committees," *Roll Call*, December 4, 2012, 1.

72. See *CQ Weekly*, November 19, 2012, 2337.

73. *CQ Weekly*, January 7, 2013, 7.

74. *CQ Weekly*, March 4, 2013, 390.

75. See Jonathan Strong, "Boehner Pledges to Stick to the 'Hastert Rule,'" *Roll Call*, March 6, 2013, 1.

76. An early discussion of the importance of party reputations is contained in Gary W. Cox and Mathew D. McCubbins, *Legislative Leviathan* (Berkeley: University of California Press, 1993). A more recent and extensive consideration is Jeffrey D. Grynaviski, *Partisan Bonds: Political Representation and Democratic Accountability* (New York: Cambridge University Press, 2010).

77. The literature on the filibuster is substantial. A good entry point is Gregory Koger, *Filibustering: A Political History of Obstruction in the House and Senate* (Chicago: University of Chicago Press, 2010).

78. The data cited were taken from "Senate Action on Cloture Motions," http://www.senate.gov/pagelayout/reference/cloture_motions/clotureCounts.htm.

79. See Barbara Sinclair, "The New World of U.S. Senators," in *Congress Reconsidered*, 7th ed., eds. Lawrence Dodd and Bruce Oppenheimer (Washington, D.C.: CQ Press, 2003), 1–26.

80. See Ramsey Cox, "Reid: Senate Dems Will Vote to Limit GOP Use of Filibuster," *The Hill*, November 27, 2012, 3.

81. Quoted in Humberto Sanchez, "Reid Tangles with GOP over Possibility of Using Nuclear Option for Nominees," *Roll Call*, May 24, 2013, 3.

82. The most recent line of research on these questions was launched by the publication of David R. Mayhew's *Divided We Govern* (New Haven, Conn.: Yale University Press, 1991). Mayhew contended that divided government was not less likely to produce major legislation. For a discussion of research following on Mayhew's analysis, see David W. Rohde and Meredith Barthelemy, "The President and Congressional Parties in an Era of Polarization," in *Oxford Handbook of the American Presidency*, eds. George C. Edwards III and William G. Howell (New York: Oxford University Press, 2009).

83. These data on public laws were taken from Ezra Klein, "Goodbye and Good Riddance, 112th Congress," *Washington Post*, January 4, 2013, http://www.washingtonpost.com/blogs/wonkblog/wp/2013/01/04/goodbye-and-good-riddance-112th-congress; and *CQ Weekly*, January 28, 2013, 222..

84. Quoted in Richard Wolf, "Partisan Pledges Sour Conciliatory Remarks," *USA Today*, November 8, 2012, 1A.

85. Quoted in Nia-Malika Henderson, "McConnell to Obama: Move to Center," *Washington Post*, November 7, 2012, http://www.washingtonpost.com/blogs/post-politics/wp/2012/11/07/mcconnell-to-obama-move-to-center/.

86. Norman Ornstein, "Optimism about the 113th Congress," *Roll Call*, November 15, 2012, 28.

87. Quoted in *CQ Weekly*, January 7, 2013, 31.

88. Quoted in Niels Lesniewski, "No, Ted Cruz Doesn't Trust Paul Ryan," *Roll Call*, May 23, 2013, 3.

89. See Jonathan Weisman, "In Congress, Gridlock and Harsh Consequences," *New York Times*, July 7, 2013, http://www.nytimes.com/2013/07/08/us/politics/in-congress-gridlock-and-harsh-consequences.html.

90. Earlier research indicated that for these purposes voters may tend to regard a president whose predecessor either died or resigned from office as a continuation of the first president's administration. Therefore, these data are organized by term of administration, rather than term of president. See Abramson et al., *Change and Continuity in the 1980 Elections*, rev. ed., 252–253.

91. Edward R. Tufte, "Determinants of the Outcomes of Midterm Congressional Elections," *American Political Science Review* 69 (September 1975):

812–826; Tufte, *Political Control of the Economy* (Princeton, N.J.: Princeton University Press, 1978); and Jacobson and Kernell, *Strategy and Choice in Congressional Elections*, 2nd ed.

92. The Jacobson-Kernell hypothesis was challenged by Richard Born in "Strategic Politicians and Unresponsive Voters," *American Political Science Review* 80 (June 1986): 599–612. Born argued that economic and approval data at the time of the election were more closely related to outcomes than were parallel data from earlier in the year. Jacobson, however, offered renewed support for the hypothesis in an analysis of both district-level and aggregate data. See Gary C. Jacobson, "Strategic Politicians and the Dynamics of House Elections, 1946–86," *American Political Science Review* 83 (September 1989): 773–793.

93. Alan I. Abramowitz, Albert D. Cover, and Helmut Norpoth, "The President's Party in Midterm Elections: Going from Bad to Worse," *American Journal of Political Science* 30 (August 1986): 562–576.

94. Bruce I. Oppenheimer, James A. Stimson, and Richard W. Waterman, "Interpreting U.S. Congressional Elections: The Exposure Thesis," *Legislative Studies Quarterly* 11 (May 1986): 228.

95. Robin F. Marra and Charles W. Ostrom Jr., "Explaining Seat Change in the U.S. House of Representatives 1950–86," *American Journal of Political Science* 33 (August 1989): 541–569.

96. Brian Newman and Charles W. Ostrom Jr., "Explaining Seat Changes in the U.S. House of Representatives, 1950–1998," *Legislative Studies Quarterly* 28 (2002): 383–405.

97. In addition, evidence indicates that divided government may also reduce the vulnerability of the president's party in midterms. See Stephen P. Nicholson and Gary M. Segura, "Midterm Elections and Divided Government: An Information-driven Theory of Electoral Volatility," *Political Research Quarterly* 52 (September 1999), 609–629.

98. These data were taken from http://realclearpolitics.com, accessed June 26, 2013.

99. Stuart Rothenberg, "Ranking Potential Flips for 2014 House Rematches," *Roll Call*, May 7, 2013, 6.

100. *Roll Call*, April 28, 2009, 11.

101. Nathan Gonzalez, "Utah 4: Matheson v. Love, Round Two," *Rothenberg Political Report*, April 5, 2013, 1.

102. See Kyle Trygstad, "Many Democrats Size Up Increasingly Tempting House Seats in California," *Roll Call*, March 13, 2013, 6.

103. *CQ Weekly*, June 10, 2013, 1002.

104. See Adam Litpak, "Justices Void Oversight of States, Issue at Heart of Voting Rights Act," *New York Times*, June 26, 2013, A1.

105. See Jess Bravin and Tamara Audi, "Top Court Quashes Arizona Voter Law," *Wall Street Journal*, June 17, 2013, http://online.wsj.com/news/articles/SB1 0001424127887324520904578551302940183818.

106. Andrew Kohut, "The Numbers Prove It: The GOP Is Estranged from America," *Washington Post*, March 22, 2013, http://articles.washingtonpost .com/2013-03-22/opinions/37923872_1_democratic-party-republican-party-polls.

107. Janet Hook, "Tough Place to Fill Job Openings: U.S. Senate," *Wall Street Journal*, June 17, 2013, http://online.wsj.com/news/articles/SB100014241278873 24423904578521120682205816.

108. Jeremy Peters, "As Senators Head for Exit, Few Step Up to Run for Seats," *New York Times*, May 3, 2013, http://www.nytimes.com/2013/05/04/us/ politics/as-senators-head-for-the-exit-few-step-up-to-run.html. For an argument about the dysfunctionality of Congress, see Thomas E. Mann and Norman J. Ornstein, *It's Even Worse than It Looks: How the American Constitutional System Collided with the New Politics of Extremism* (New York: Basic Books, 2012).

109. Quoted in Jeff Zeleny, "Top Donors to Republicans Seek More Say in Senate Races," *New York Times*, February 2, 2013, http://www.nytimes.com/ 2013/02/03/us/politics/top-gop-donors-seek-greater-say-in-senate-races.html.

110. Quoted in Martha T. Moore and Fredreka Schouten, "The Architect's Designs Incur the Wrath of GOP's Grass Roots," *USA Today*, February 15, 2013, 5A.

111. Quoted in Alexandra Jaffe, "Akin Says Republican Bigwigs 'Kill Grassroots Heart' of GOP," *The Hill*, February 13, 2013, 19.

112. Alexandra Jaffe, "Capito Takes Friendly Fire on Day One," *The Hill*, November 27, 2012, 1.

113. See John Eligon, "In Supporting Candidates, Democrats Weigh Electability," *New York Times*, May 29, 2013, A12.

114. Quoted in Neil King, Jr., "GOP Issues Scathing Self-Analysis," *Wall Street Journal*, March 18, 2013, http://online.wsj.com/news/articles/SB1000142412788 73234153045783673119333111522.

115. Quoted in Sarah Wheaton and Michael D. Shear, "Blunt Report Says G.O.P. Needs to Regroup for '16," *New York Times*, March 19, 2013, A13.

116. Ibid.

117. Quoted in Neil King Jr., "Some on Right See Red Flags in GOP Report," *Wall Street Journal*, March 23, 2013, http://online.wsj.com/news/articles/SB1000 14241278873243732045783760080110567510.

10. THE CONGRESSIONAL ELECTORATE IN 2012

1. As we saw in Chapter 5, the 2012 NES survey results slightly overreported the Democratic share of the presidential vote. In contrast, there is a somewhat larger bias in the House vote in favor of the GOP. According to the 2012 NES survey, the Democrats received 47 percent of the major-party party vote, while official results show that the Democrats received 50.6 percent of the actual national vote. To simplify the presentation of the data, we have eliminated from

consideration votes for minor-party candidates in all the tables in this chapter. Furthermore, to ensure that our study of choice is meaningful, in all tables except Tables 10-1 and 10-2 we include only voters who lived in congressional districts in which both major parties ran candidates.

2. We will confine our attention in this section to voting for the House because this group of voters is more directly comparable to the presidential electorate. We employ the same definitions for social and demographic categories as used in Chapters 4 and 5.

3. See Larry M. Bartels, "Partisanship and Voting Behavior, 1952–1996," *American Journal of Political Science* 44 (January 2000): 35–50.

4. Recall that in Chapter 5 we noted that the data on religion of respondents in the ANES were not available at the time we did our analysis. In that chapter we employed exit poll data to fill in the gap. In this chapter we do not present the parallel exit poll data on House voting and religion because the numbers are almost identical to those in Table 5-1, deviating by only a percentage point or two in almost every instance.

5. Paul R. Abramson, John H. Aldrich, and David W. Rohde, *Change and Continuity in the 1980 Elections*, rev. ed. (Washington, D.C.: CQ Press, 1983), 213–216.

6. Alan I. Abramowitz, "Choices and Echoes in the 1978 U.S. Senate Elections: A Research Note," *American Journal of Political Science* 25 (February 1981): 112–118; and Abramowitz, "National Issues, Strategic Politicians, and Voting Behavior in the 1980 and 1982 Congressional Elections," *American Journal of Political Science* 28 (November 1984): 710–721.

7. See Michael Ensley, "Candidate Divergence, Ideology, and Vote Choice in U.S. Senate Elections," *American Politics Research* 35 (2007): 103–122.

8. Robert S. Erikson and Gerald C. Wright, "Voters, Candidates, and Issues in Congressional Elections," in *Congress Reconsidered*, 3rd ed., eds. Lawrence C. Dodd and Bruce I. Oppenheimer (Washington, D.C.: CQ Press, 1985), 91–116.

9. Robert S. Erikson and Gerald C. Wright, "Voters, Candidates and Issues in Congressional Elections," in *Congress Reconsidered*, 6th ed., eds. Lawrence C. Dodd and Bruce I. Oppenheimer (Washington, D.C.: CQ Press, 1993), 148–150.

10. Robert S. Erikson and Gerald C. Wright, "Voters, Candidates and Issues in Congressional Elections," in *Congress Reconsidered*, 8th ed., ed. Lawrence C. Dodd and Bruce I. Oppenheimer (Washington, D.C.: CQ Press, 2005), 93–95. See also Stephen Ansolabehere, James M. Snyder Jr., and Charles Stewart III, "Candidate Positioning in U.S. House Elections," *American Journal of Political Science* 45 (January 2001): 136–159.

11. For the wording the NES party identification questions, see Chapter 4, note 74.

12. Albert D. Cover, "One Good Term Deserves Another: The Advantage of Incumbency in Congressional Elections," *American Journal of Political Science* 21 (August 1977): 523–541. Cover includes in his analysis not only strong and weak partisans, but also independents with partisan leanings.

13. It should be noted that the 2012 NES survey may contain biases that inflate the percentage who report voting for House incumbents. For a discussion of this problem in earlier years, see Robert B. Eubank and David John Gow, "The Pro-incumbent Bias in the 1978 and 1980 Election Studies," *American Journal of Political Science* 27 (February 1983): 122–139; and David John Gow and Robert B. Eubank, " The Pro-Incumbent Bias in the 1982 Election Study," *American Journal of Political Science* 28 (February 1984): 224–230.

14. Richard F. Fenno Jr., "If, as Ralph Nader Says, Congress Is 'The Broken Branch,' How Come We Love Our Congressmen So Much?" in *Congress in Change: Evolution and Reform*, ed. Norman J. Ornstein (New York: Praeger, 1975), 277–287. This theme is expanded and analyzed in Fenno, *Home Style: House Members in Their Districts* (Boston: Little, Brown, 1978).

15. Abramson et al., *Change and Continuity in the 1980 Elections*, 220–221.

16. Opinion on this last point is not unanimous, however. See Richard Born, "Reassessing the Decline of Presidential Coattails: U.S. House Elections from 1952–80," *Journal of Politics* 46 (February 1984): 60–79.

17. John A. Ferejohn and Randall L. Calvert, "Presidential Coattails in Historical Perspective," *American Journal of Political Science* 28 (February 1984): 127–146.

18. Calvert and Ferejohn, "Coattail Voting in Recent Presidential Elections," *American Political Science Review* 77 (June 1983): 407–419.

19. James E. Campbell and Joe A. Sumners, "Presidential Coattails in Senate Elections," *American Political Science Review* 84 (June 1990): 513–524.

20. Franco Mattei and Joshua Glasgow, "Presidential Coattails, Incumbency Advantage, and Open Seats," *Electoral Studies* 24 (2005): 619–641.

11. THE 2012 ELECTIONS AND THE FUTURE OF AMERICAN POLITICS

1. Perhaps the biggest "constitutional" change was the substantial redistricting that ensued in the wake of *Baker v. Carr* and other Supreme Court cases that defined "one person, one vote" more clearly. Note also that the fact of single-member districts is not constitutional, but was created by an act of Congress in 1842.

2. Senators were chosen by state legislatures until ratification of the Seventeenth Amendment to the Constitution in 1913 (although some states had held a state primary election, called the "Oregon system," to instruct state legislators in who to choose for the Senate).

3. The Twenty-second Amendment to the Constitution was ratified in 1951, which limited the president to two terms in office. As Franklin Roosevelt was the only president to serve for more than two terms, and as his opponent in 1944, Thomas Dewey, called for this amendment during the campaign, it is ironic that the first president to be limited by the Constitution to two terms was Republican Dwight Eisenhower, the successor to Dewey in his party.

4. The Electoral College failed to select a president in 1800 (when Thomas Jefferson and his running mate Aaron Burr tied in the Electoral College) and in 1824 (when the House selected John Quincy Adams over Andrew Jackson and Henry Clay in what Jackson supporters called [likely incorrectly] a "corrupt bargain"). In 1876, several slates of electors were disputed and the resolution was decided through actions in both houses of Congress, effectively selecting Rutherford B. Hayes as president over Samuel Tilden. The Electoral College vote was determinative in all other cases.

5. The information in this paragraph comes from Markus Prior, *Post-Broadcast Democracy: How Media Choice Increases Inequality in Political Involvement and Polarizes Elections* (New York: Cambridge University Press, 2007).

6. As discussed in Chapter 3, the *mechanical* effect is the way that single-member districts lead to the exaggeration of plurality votes and often translate them into majorities, and that exaggeration of the vote for the leading party comes most heavily at the expense of any third parties. The *psychological* effect is the voter reaction to the mechanical effect, such that people are not willing to "waste" their vote on a sure loser and so are likely to choose between only the two leading parties (see Chapter 6). Maurice Duverger, *Political Parties: Their Organization and Activity in the Modern State* (New York: Wiley 1954) (originally published in French in 1951).

7. Joseph A. Schlesinger, *Ambition and Politics: Political Careers in the United States* (Chicago: Rand McNally, 1966).

8. The Vietnam War drove a second wedge in the Democratic Party in the middle to late 1960s.

9. Boris Shor, and Nolan McCarty, "The Ideological Mapping of American Legislatures," *American Political Science Review* 105 (2011): 530–551.

10. See, for example, Alan I. Abramowitz, *The Disappearing Center: Engaged Citizens, Polarization, and American Democracy* (New Haven, Conn.: Yale University Press, 2010), in which he argues for public polarization; and Morris P. Fiorina, Samuel J. Abrams, and Jeremy Pope, *Culture War? The Myth of a Polarized America* (New York: Pearson Longman, 2010), who argue the opposite.

11. See Matthew Levendusky, *The Partisan Sort: How Liberals Became Democrats and Conservatives Became Republicans* (Chicago: University of Chicago Press, 2009).

12. For a recent summary, see John H. Aldrich and David W. Rohde, "Consequences of Electoral and Institutional Change: The Evolution of Conditional Party Government in the U.S. House of Representatives," in *New Directions in American Political Parties*, ed., Jeffrey M. Stonecash (New York: Routledge, 2010), 234–250.

Suggested Readings

(Readings preceded by an asterisk include materials on the 2012 elections.)

Chapter 1: The Nomination Process

Abramson, Paul R., John H. Aldrich, Phil Paolino, and David W. Rohde. "'Sophisticated' Voting in the 1988 Presidential Primaries." *American Political Science Review* 86 (March 1992): 55–69.

Abramson, Paul R., John H. Aldrich, and David W. Rohde. "Progressive Ambition among United States Senators: 1972–1988." *Journal of Politics* 49 (February 1987): 3–35.

Aldrich, John H. *Before the Convention: Strategies and Choices in Presidential Nomination Campaigns.* Chicago: University of Chicago Press, 1980.

_____. "The Invisible Primary and Its Effects on Democratic Choice." *PS: Political Science and Politics* 42 (January 2009): 33–38.

*Balz, Dan. *Collision 2012: Obama vs. Romney and the Future of Elections in America.* New York: Viking, 2013, 87–235.

Bartels, Larry M. *Presidential Primaries and the Dynamics of Public Choice.* Princeton, N.J.: Princeton University Press, 1988.

Brams, Steven J. *The Presidential Election Game.* New Haven, Conn.: Yale University Press, 1978, 1–79.

*Burden, Barry C. "The Nominations: Ideology, Timing, and Organization." In *The Election of 2012*, edited by Michael Nelson, 21–46. Washington, D.C.: CQ Press, 2014.

Busch, Andrew E. "Assumptions and Realities of Presidential Primary Frontloading." In *Nominating the President: Revolution and Evolution in 2008 and*

Beyond, edited by Jack Citrin and David Karol, 77–93. Lanham, Md.: Rowman and Littlefield, 2009.

*Ceaser, James W., Andrew E. Busch, and John J. Pitney Jr. *After Hope and Change: The 2012 Election and American Politics*. Lanham, Md.: Rowman and Littlefield , 2013, 51–90.

Citrin, Jack, and David Karol. "Introduction." In *Nominating the President: Evolution and Revolution in 2008 and Beyond*, edited by Jack Citrin and David Karol, 1–25. Lanham, Md.: Rowman and Littlefield, 2009.

*Cook, Rhodes. "Un-conventional Wisdom: The 2012 Conventions and the Nominating Process." In *Barack Obama and the New America: The 2012 Election and the Changing Face of Politics*, edited by Larry J. Sabato, 75–84. Lanham, Md.: Rowman and Littlefield, 2013.

Hasen, Richard L. "The Changing Nature of Campaign Financing for Presidential Primary Candidates." In *Nominating the President: Evolution and Revolution in 2008 and Beyond*, edited by Jack Citrin and David Karol, 27–45. Lanham, Md.: Rowman and Littlefield, 2009.

Polsby, Nelson W., Aaron Wildavsky, Steven E. Schier, and David A. Hopkins. *Presidential Elections: Strategies and Structures of American Politics*. 13th ed. Lanham, Md.: Rowman and Littlefield, 2012, 93–146.

Thompson, Dennis F. "The Primary Purpose of Presidential Primaries." *Political Science Quarterly* 125 (Summer 2010): 205–232.

Chapter 2: The General Election Campaign

*Alter, Jonathan. *The Center Holds: Obama and His Enemies*. New York: Simon and Schuster, 2013.

*Balz, Dan. *Collision 2012: Obama vs. Romney and the Future of Elections in America*. New York: Viking, 2013, 239–354.

Brams, Steven J. *The Presidential Election Game*. New Haven, Conn.: Yale University Press, 1978, 80–133.

Burmila, Edward M. "The Electoral College after Census 2010 and 2020: The Political Impact of Population Growth." *Perspectives on Politics* 7 (December 2009): 837–847.

*Ceaser, James W., Andrew E. Busch, and John J. Pitney Jr. *After Hope and Change: The 2012 Elections and American Politics*. Lanham, Md.: Rowman and Littlefield, 2013, 91–130.

Geer, John G. *In Defense of Negativity: Attack Ads in Presidential Campaigns.* Chicago: University of Chicago Press, 2006.

*Heatherington, Marc J. "The Election: How the Campaign Mattered." In *The Election of 2012*, edited by Michael Nelson, 47–72. Washington, D.C.: CQ Press, 2014.

Iyengar, Shanto, and Donald Kinder. *News That Matters: Television and American Opinion.* Chicago: University of Chicago Press, 1987.

Johnston, Richard, Michael G. Hagen, and Kathleen Hall Jamieson. *The 2000 Presidential Election and the Foundations of Party Politics.* Cambridge, NY: Cambridge University Press, 2004.

Polsby, Nelson W., Aaron Wildavsky, Steven E. Schier, and David A. Hopkins. *Presidential Elections: Strategies and Structures of American Politics.* 13th ed. Lanham, Md.: Rowman, 2012, 147–207.

*Popkin, Samuel L. *The Candidate: What It Takes to Win and Hold the White House.* New York: Oxford University Press, 2012.

*Rutenberg, Jim. "Data You Can Believe In." *New York Times Magazine,* June 23, 2013, 22–29, 36.

Shaw, Daron R. *The Race to 270: The Electoral College and the Campaign Strategies of 2000 and 2004.* Chicago: University of Chicago Press, 2006.

*Wolffe, Richard L. *The Message: The Reselling of President Obama.* New York: Grand Central Publishing, 2013.

Chapter 3: The Election Results

Abramson, Paul R., John H. Aldrich, Phil Paolino, and David W. Rohde. "Third-Party and Independent Candidates in American Politics: Wallace, Anderson, and Perot." *Political Science Quarterly* 110 (Fall 1995): 349–367.

Black, Earl, and Merle Black. *The Vital South: How Presidents Are Elected.* Cambridge, Mass.: Harvard University Press, 1992.

Burnham, Walter Dean. *Critical Elections and the Mainsprings of American Politics.* New York: Norton, 1970.

Katznelson, Ira, and Quinn Mulroy. "Was the South Pivotal? Situated Partisanship and Policy Coalitions during the New Deal and Fair Deal." *Journal of Politics* 74 (April 2012): 604–620.

Kelley, Stanley, Jr. *Interpreting Elections.* Princeton, N.J.: Princeton University Press, 1983.

Lamis, Alexander P. *The Two-Party South*. Exp. ed. New York: Oxford University Press, 1990.

Levendusky, Matthew S., and Jeremy C. Pope. "Red States vs. Blue States: Going Beyond the Mean." *Public Opinion Quarterly* 75 (Summer 2011): 227–248.

Mayhew, David R. *Electoral Realignments: A Critique of an American Genre*. New Haven, Conn.: Yale University Press, 2002.

_____. "Incumbency Advantage in U.S. Presidential Elections: The Historical Record." *Political Science Quarterly* 123 (Summer 2008): 201–228.

Miller, Gary, and Norman Schofield. "Activists and Partisan Realignment in the United States." *American Political Science Review* 97 (May 2003): 245–260.

Nardulli, Peter F. *Popular Efficacy in the Democratic Era: A Reexamination of Electoral Accountability in the United States, 1828–2000*. Princeton N.J.: Princeton University Press, 2005.

Schlesinger, Joseph A. *Political Parties and the Winning of Office*. Ann Arbor: University of Michigan Press, 1991.

Sundquist, James L. *Dynamics of the Party System: Alignment and Realignment of Political Parties in the United States*. Rev. ed. Washington, D.C.: Brookings Institution, 1983.

Chapter 4: Who Voted?

Aldrich, John H. "Rational Choice and Turnout." *American Journal of Political Science* 37 (February 1993): 246–278.

Ansolabehere, Stephen, and Shanto Iyengar. *Going Negative: How Political Advertisements Shrink and Polarize the Electorate*. New York: Free Press, 1995.

Burnham, Walter Dean. "The Turnout Problem." In *Elections American Style*, edited by A. James Reichley, 97–133. Washington, D.C.: Brookings Institution, 1987.

Conway, M. Margaret. "The Scope of Participation in the 2008 Presidential Race: Voter Mobilization and Electoral Success." In *Winning the Presidency: 2008*, edited by William J. Crotty, 110–122. Boulder, Colo.: Paradigm, 2009.

Crenson, Matthew A., and Benjamin Ginsberg. *Downsizing Democracy: How America Sidelined Its Citizens and Privatized Its Public*. Baltimore: Johns Hopkins University Press, 2002.

Deufel, Benjamin J., and Orit Kedar. "Race and Turnout in U.S. Elections: Exposing Hidden Effects." *Public Opinion Quarterly* 74 (Summer 2010): 286–318.

Hansford, Thomas G., and Brad T. Gomez. "Estimating the Electoral Effects of Voter Turnout." *American Political Science Review* 104 (May 2010): 268–288.

Highton, Benjamin. "Voter Registration and Turnout in the United States." *Perspectives on Politics* 3 (September 2004): 507–515.

Holbrook, Thomas M., and Scott D. McClurg. "The Mobilization of Core Supporters: Campaigns, Turnout, and Electoral Composition in United States Presidential Elections." *American Journal of Political Science* 49 (October 2005): 689–703.

Manza, Jeff, and Christopher Uggen. *Locked Out: Felon Disfranchisement and American Democracy.* New York: Oxford University Press, 2006.

Martinez, Michael D., and Jeff Gill. "The Effects of Turnout on Partisan Outcomes in U.S. Presidential Elections 1960–2000." *Journal of Politics* 67 (November 2005): 1248–1274.

McDonald, Michael P., and Samuel L. Popkin. "The Myth of the Vanishing Voter." *American Political Science Review* 95 (December 2001): 963–974.

Miller, Warren E., and J. Merrill Shanks. *The New American Voter.* Cambridge, Mass.: Harvard University Press, 1996, 95–114.

Patterson, Thomas E. *The Vanishing Voter: Public Involvement in an Age of Uncertainty.* New York: Knopf, 2002.

Piven, Frances Fox, and Richard A. Cloward. *Why Americans Still Don't Vote: And Why Politicians Want It That Way.* Boston: Beacon Press, 2000.

Putnam, Robert. *Bowling Alone: The Collapse and Revival of American Community.* New York: Simon and Schuster, 2000.

Rosenstone, Steven J., and John Mark Hansen. *Mobilization, Participation, and Democracy in America.* New York: Macmillan, 1993.

Teixeira, Ruy A. *The Disappearing American Voter.* Washington, D.C.: Brookings Institution, 1992.

Wolfinger, Raymond E., and Steven J. Rosenstone. *Who Votes?* New Haven, Conn.: Yale University Press, 1980.

Chapter 5: Social Forces and the Vote

Alford, Robert R. *Party and Society: The Anglo-American Democracies.* Chicago: Rand McNally, 1963.

Axelrod, Robert. "Where the Votes Come from: An Analysis of Electoral Coalitions, 1952–1968." *American Political Science Review* 66 (March 1972): 11–20.

Bartels, Larry M. *Unequal Democracy: The Political Economy of the New Gilded Age.* Princeton, N.J.: Princeton University Press, 2008.

Brewer, Mark D., and Jeffrey M. Stonecash. *Split: Class and Cultural Divides in American Politics.* Washington, D.C.: CQ Press, 2007.

Campbell, David E., John C. Green, and Geoffrey C. Layman. "The Party Faithful: Partisan Images, Candidate Religion, and the Impact of Party Identification." *American Journal of Political Science* 55 (January 2011): 42–58.

Gelman, Andrew. *Red States, Blue States, Rich States, Poor States: Why Americans Vote the Way They Do.* Princeton, NJ: Princeton University Press, 2008.

Hamilton, Richard R. *Class and Politics in the United States.* New York: Wiley, 1972.

Huckfeldt, Robert, and Carol Weitzel Kohfeld. *Race and the Decline of Class in American Politics.* Urbana: University of Illinois Press, 1989.

Lipset, Seymour Martin. *Political Man: The Social Bases of Politics.* Exp. ed. Baltimore: Johns Hopkins University Press, 1981.

Manza, Jeff, and Clem Brooks. *Social Cleavages and Political Change: Voter Alignments and U.S. Party Coalitions.* New York: Oxford University Press, 1999.

Miller, Warren E., and J. Merrill Shanks. *The New American Voter.* Cambridge, Mass.: Harvard University Press, 1996, 212–282.

Stanley, Harold W., and Richard G. Niemi. "Partisanship, Party Coalitions, and Group Support, 1952–2004." *Presidential Studies Quarterly* 36 (June 2006): 172–188.

Tate, Katherine. *From Protest to Politics: The New Black Voters in American Elections.* Enl. ed. Cambridge, Mass.: Harvard University Press, 1994.

Chapter 6: Candidates, Issues, and the Vote

*Abramowitz, Alan I. *The Polarized Public: Why American Government Is So Dysfunctional.* Boston: Pearson, 2013.

*_____. "Voting in a Time of Polarization: Why Obama Won and What It Means." In *Barack Obama and the New America: The 2012 Election and the*

Changing Face of Politics, edited by Larry J. Sabato, 45–58. Lanham, Md: Rowman and Littlefield, 2013.

Campbell, Angus, Philip E. Converse, Warren E. Miller, and Donald E. Stokes. *The American Voter*. New York: Wiley, 1960, 168–265.

Carmines, Edward G., and James A. Stimson. *Issue Evolution: Race and the Transformation of American Politics*. Princeton, NJ: Princeton University Press, 1989.

Claggett, William J. M., and Byron E. Shafer. *The American Public Mind: The Issues Structure of Mass Politics in the Postwar United States*. New York: Cambridge University Press, 2010.

Fiorina, Morris P., with Samuel J. Abrams and Jeremy C. Pope. *Culture War? The Myth of a Polarized America*. 3rd ed. New York: Pearson Longman, 2010.

Gerber, Elisabeth R., and John E. Jackson. "Endogenous Preferences and the Study of Institutions." *American Political Science Review* 87 (September 1993): 639–656.

Hillygus, D. Sunshine, and Todd G. Shields. *The Persuadable Voter: Wedge Issues in Presidential Campaigns*. Princeton, NJ: Princeton University Press, 2008.

Lau, Richard R., David J. Andersen, and David P. Redlawsk. "An Exploration of Correct Voting in Recent U.S. Presidential Elections." *American Journal of Political Science* 52 (April 2008): 395–411.

Lau, Richard R., and David P. Redlawsk. *How Voters Decide: Information Processing in Election Campaigns*. Cambridge, UK, and New York: Cambridge University Press, 2006.

Lewis-Beck, Michael S., William G. Jacoby, Helmut Norpoth, and Herbert F. Weisberg. *The American Voter Revisited*. Ann Arbor: University of Michigan Press, 2008, 161–301.

Popkin, Samuel L. *The Reasoning Voter: Communication and Persuasion in Presidential Campaigns*. Chicago: University of Chicago Press, 1991.

Shafer, Byron E., and William J. M. Claggett. *The Two Majorities: The Issue Context of Modern American Politics*. Baltimore: Johns Hopkins University Press, 1995.

Chapter 7: Presidential
Performance and Candidate Choice

Dalton, Russell J. *Democratic Challenges, Democratic Choices: The Erosion of Political Support in Advanced Industrial Democracies*. Oxford, UK, and New York: Oxford University Press, 2004.

Downs, Anthony. *An Economic Theory of Democracy.* New York: Harper and Row, 1957.

Fiorina, Morris P. *Retrospective Voting in American National Elections.* New Haven, Conn.: Yale University Press, 1981.

Jacobson, Gary C. *A Divider, Not a Uniter: George W. Bush and the American People.* New York: Pearson Longman, 2008.

Key, V. O., Jr. *The Responsible Electorate: Rationality in Presidential Voting, 1936–1960.* Cambridge, Mass.: Harvard University Press, 1966.

Kiewiet, D. Roderick. *Macroeconomics and Micropolitics: The Electoral Effects of Economic Issues.* Chicago: University of Chicago Press, 1983.

Lewis-Beck, Michael S. *Economics and Elections: The Major Western Democracies.* Ann Arbor: University of Michigan Press, 1988.

Riker, William H. *Liberalism against Populism: A Confrontation between the Theory of Democracy and the Theory of Social Choice.* San Francisco: W. H. Freeman, 1982.

Tufte, Edward R. *Political Control of the Economy.* Princeton, NJ: Princeton University, 1978.

Chapter 8: Party Loyalties, Policy Preferences, and the Vote

Abramson, Paul R. *Political Attitudes in America: Formation and Change.* San Francisco: W. H. Freeman, 1983.

Aldrich, John H. *Why Parties? The Origin and Transformation of Political Parties in America.* Chicago: University of Chicago Press, 1995.

_____. *Why Parties? A Second Look.* Chicago: University of Chicago Press, 2011.

Bartels, Larry M. "Partisanship and Voting Behavior, 1952–1996." *American Journal of Political Science* 44 (January 2000): 35–50.

Campbell, Angus, Philip E. Converse, Warren E. Miller, and Donald E. Stokes. *The American Voter.* New York: Wiley, 1960, 120–167.

Dalton, Russell J. *The Apartisan American: Dealignment and Changing Electoral Politics.* Washington, D.C.: CQ Press, 2013.

Fiorina, Morris P. "Parties, Participation, and Representation in America: Old Theories Face New Realities." In *Political Science: The State of the Discipline,* edited by Ira Katznelson and Helen V. Milner, 511–541. New York: Norton, 2002.

Green, Donald, Bradley Palmquist, and Eric Schickler. *Partisan Hearts and Minds: Political Parties and the Social Identities of Voters*. New Haven, Conn.: Yale University Press, 2002.

Hershey, Marjorie Randon. *Party Politics in America*. 15th ed. Boston: Pearson, 2013.

*Jacobson, Gary C. "How the Economy and Partisanship Shaped the 2012 Presidential and Congressional Elections." *Political Science Quarterly* 128 (Spring 2013), 1–38.

Keith, Bruce E., David B. Magleby, Candice J. Nelson, Elizabeth Orr, Mark C. Westlye, and Raymond E. Wolfinger. *The Myth of the Independent Voter*. Berkeley: University of California Press, 1992.

Lewis-Beck, Michael S., William G. Jacoby, Helmut Norpoth, and Herbert F. Weisberg. *The American Voter Revisited*. Ann Arbor: University of Michigan Press, 2008, 111–160.

Milkis, Sidney M., Jesse H. Rhodes, and Emily J. Charnock. "What Happened to Post-partisanship? Barack Obama and the New American Party System." *Perspectives on Politics* 10 (March 2012), 57–76.

Miller, Warren E., and J. Merrill Shanks. *The New American Voter*. Cambridge, Mass.: Harvard University Press, 1996, 117–185.

Wattenberg, Martin P. *The Decline of American Political Parties, 1952–1996*. Cambridge, Mass.: Harvard University Press, 1998.

Williamson, Vanessa, Theda Skocpol, and John Coggin. "The Tea Party and the Remaking of Republican Conservatism." *Perspectives on Politics* 9 (March 2011): 25–43.

Chapter 9: Candidates and Outcomes in 2012

Abramowitz, Alan I. *The Disappearing Center: Engaged Citizens, Polarization, and American Democracy*. New Haven, Conn.: Yale University Press, 2010.

Abramowitz, Alan I., Brad Alexander, and Matthew Gunning. "Incumbency, Redistricting, and the Decline of Competition in U.S. House Elections." *Journal of Politics* 68 (February 2006): 75–88.

Aldrich, John H., Michael Brady, Scott de Marchi, Ian McDonald, Brendan Nyhan, David W. Rohde, and Michael Tofias. "Party and Constituency in the U.S. Senate, 1933–2004." In *Why Not Parties? Party Effects in the United States Senate*, edited by Nathan W. Monroe, Jason M. Roberts, and David W. Rohde, 39–51. Chicago: University of Chicago Press, 2008.

Brunell, Thomas L., and Bernard Grofman. "Explaining Divided U.S. Senate Delegations, 1788–1996: A Realignment Approach." *American Political Science Review* 92 (June 1998): 391–399.

Carson, Jamie, Erik J. Engstrom, and Jason M. Roberts. "Candidate Quality, the Personal Vote, and the Incumbency Advantage in Congress." *American Political Science Review* 101 (May 2007): 289–301.

Druckman, James N., Martin J. Kifer, and Michael Parkin. "Campaign Communications in U.S. Congressional Elections." *American Political Science Review* 103 (August 2009): 343–366.

Fenno, Richard F., Jr. *Home Style: House Members in Their Districts.* Boston: Little, Brown, 1978.

Grynaviski, Jeffrey D. *Partisan Bonds: Political Reputations and Legislative Accountability.* New York: Cambridge University Press, 2010.

Jacobson, Gary C. "Congress: Partisanship and Polarization." In *The Elections of 2012*, edited by Michael Nelson, 145–171. Washington, D.C.: CQ Press, 2014.

————. *The Politics of Congressional Elections.* 8th ed. Boston: Pearson, 2013, 5–115, 161–286.

Lau, Richard R., and Gerald M. Pomper. "Effectiveness of Negative Campaigning in U.S. Senate Elections." *American Journal of Political Science* 46 (January 2002): 47–66.

Rohde, David W. *Parties and Leaders in the Postreform House.* Chicago: University of Chicago Press, 1991.

Schlesinger, Joseph A. *Ambition and Politics: Political Careers in the United States.* Chicago: Rand McNally, 1966.

Stone, Walter J., and L. Sandy Maisel. "The Not-so-Simple Calculus of Winning: Potential U.S. House Candidates' Nomination and General Election Prospects." *Journal of Politics* 65 (November 2003): 951–977.

Stonecash, Jeffrey M. *Reassessing the Incumbency Effect.* Cambridge, UK and New York: Cambridge University Press, 2008.

Chapter 10: The Congressional Electorate in 2012

Abramowitz, Alan I., and Jeffrey A. Segal. *Senate Elections.* Ann Arbor: University of Michigan Press, 1992.

Beck, Paul Allen, Lawrence Baum, Aage R. Clausen, and Charles E. Smith Jr. "Patterns and Sources of Ticket Splitting in Subpresidential Voting." *American Political Science Review* 86 (December 1992): 916–928.

Burden, Barry C., and David C. Kimball. *Why Americans Split Their Tickets: Campaigns, Competition, and Divided Government.* Ann Arbor: University of Michigan Press, 2002.

Buttice, Matthew K., and Walter J. Stone. "Candidates Matter: Policy and Quality Differences in Congressional Elections." *Journal of Politics* 74 (July 2012): 870–887.

Dalager, Jon K. "Voters, Issues, and Elections: Are the Candidates' Messages Getting Through?" *Journal of Politics* 58 (May 1996): 486–515.

Fenno, Richard F., Jr. "If, as Ralph Nader Says, Congress Is 'The Broken Branch,' Why Do We Love Our Congressmen so Much?" In *Congress in Change: Elections and Reform*, edited by Norman J. Ornstein, 277–287. New York: Praeger, 1975.

Jacobson, Gary C. *The Electoral Origins of Divided Government: Competition in U.S. House Elections, 1946–1988.* Boulder, Colo.: Westview Press. 1990.

_____. *The Politics of Congressional Elections.* 8th ed. Boston: Pearson, 2013, 120–160.

Mann, Thomas E., and Norman J. Ornstein. *It's Even Worse than It Looks: How the American Constitutional System Collided With the New Politics of Extremism.* New York: Basic Books, 2012.

Sigelman, Lee, Paul J. Wahlbeck, and Emmett H. Buell Jr. "Vote Choice and the Preference for Divided Government: Lessons of 1992." *American Journal of Political Science* 41 (July 1997): 879–894.

Chapter 11: The 2012 Elections and the Future of American Politics

*Ceaser, James W., Andrew E. Busch, and John J. Pitney Jr. *After Hope and Change: The 2012 Elections and American Politics.* Lanham, Md.: Rowman and Littlefield, 2013, 157–181.

*MacManus, Susan. "From 2012 to 2016: Further Thoughts on the Permanent Campaign." In *Barack Obama and the New America: The 2012 Election and the Changing Face of Politics.* edited by Larry J. Sabato, 195–225. Lanham, Md.: Rowman and Littlefield, 2013.

*Mayhew, David R. "The Meaning of the 2012 Election." In *The Elections of 2012*, edited by Michael Nelson, 203–222. Washington, D.C.: CQ Press, 2014.

Index